Multicultural Education

Multicultural Education
Issues and Perspectives

SECOND EDITION

Edited by

JAMES A. BANKS
University of Washington, Seattle

CHERRY A. McGEE BANKS
University of Washington, Bothell

ALLYN AND BACON
Boston   London   Toronto   Sydney   Tokyo   Singapore

Series Editor: *Virginia C. Lanigan*
Production Administrator: *Annette Joseph*
Production Coordinator: *Susan Freese*
Editorial-Production Service: *Grace Sheldrick, Wordsworth Associates*
Composition Buyer: *Linda Cox*
Manufacturing Buyer: *Megan Cochran*
Cover Administrator: *Linda K. Dickinson*
Cover Designer: *Studio 9*

Copyright © 1993, 1989 by Allyn and Bacon
A Division of Simon & Schuster, Inc.
160 Gould Street
Needham Heights, Massachusetts 02194

This book is printed on
recycled, acid-free paper.

Library of Congress Cataloging-in-Publication Data
Multicultural education : issues and perspectives / edited by James A.
  Banks, Cherry A. McGee Banks.—2nd ed.
     p.   cm.
  Includes bibliographical references (p.) and index.
  ISBN 0–205–14044–0
    1. Intercultural education—United States.   2. Minorities—
Education—United States.   3. Educational anthropology—United
States.   4. Educational equalization—United States.   I. Banks,
James A.   II. Banks, Cherry A. McGee.
LC1099.3.M85   1993
370.19′341—dc20   9–17709
                                                          CIP

Printed in the United States of America

10 9 8 7 6 5 4   97 96 95 94

BRIEF CONTENTS

CONTENTS

PREFACE

Several important developments in U.S. society today make multicultural education an imperative. They include the work-force demands of the twenty-first century, the demographic changes in the nation's population, the widening gap between the rich and the poor, and the global challenges the nation faces. As we enter the twenty-first century, students must be able to compete in a global economy that is primarily service and knowledge oriented. However, if significant educational reforms are not successfully implemented, there will be a mismatch between the knowledge and skills demands of the work force and the knowledge and skills of a large proportion of U.S. workers. Many of these workers will be women, people of color, or immigrants. Between now and the turn of the century, about 83 percent of the new entrants to the U.S. work force will be members of these groups.

Approaches to school reform that do not include important aspects of multicultural education will not be successful because the learning and motivational characteristics of students from diverse cultural groups often differ in significant ways from those institutionalized within the school. Demographers predict that students of color will make up about 46 percent of the nation's school-age population by the year 2020. These students are already majorities in the nation's twenty-five largest school districts as well as in California, our most populous state.

Not only will tomorrow's students become increasingly diverse, but they will also become increasingly poor. The gap between the relatively affluent 85 percent of U.S. society and the desperately poor 15 percent of the population continues to widen. Women and children are highly concentrated among the low-income population. About one out of five children in the United States is poor. Fifteen million children in the nation live in female-headed households.

As important as it is for multicultural education to help students from diverse cultural groups attain the academic skills needed to function in a knowledge society, a pluralistic education is an imperative for *all* students. A multicultural education is an education for life in a free and democratic society. It helps students transcend their cultural boundaries and acquire the knowledge, attitudes, and skills needed to engage in public discourse with people who differ from themselves. Multicultural education also helps students acquire the skills needed to participate in civic action, which is an integral part of a democratic nation. Multicultural education is not only grounded in the nation's democratic traditions, but it also is essential for the survival of a democratic, pluralistic nation in the next century.

Multicultural Education: Issues and Perspectives, Second Edition, is designed to help present and future educators acquire the concepts, paradigms, and explanations needed to become effective practitioners in a culturally diverse society. This second edition has been revised to reflect current and emerging research, concepts, and debates about the education of students from both genders and from different cultural, racial, and ethnic groups. Exceptionality is a part of our concept of diversity because there are exceptional students in each group discussed in this book.

Five new authors and several new topics are a part of this second edition. New topics included are the effective schools movement (Chapter 15) and cultural influences on learning (Chapter 16). Each chapter in *Multicultural Education, Second Edition,* contains new data, interpretations, and developments. The Multicultural Resources in the Appendix have been substantially revised. New entries as well as new census data have been added to the Glossary.

This book consists of six parts. The chapters in Part One discuss how race, gender, class, and exceptionality interact to influence student behavior. Social class and religion and their effects on education are discussed in Part Two. Part Three describes how educational opportunity differs for female and male students and how schools can foster gender equity. The issues, problems, and opportunities for educating students of color and students with language differences are discussed in Part Four. Part Five focuses on exceptionality, describing the issues involved in creating equal educational opportunity for students who have disabilities and who are gifted. The final part of *Multicultural Education,* Second Edition, Part Six, discusses multicultural education as a process of school reform.

The Appendix consists of a list of books for further reading. The Glossary defines many of the key concepts and terms used in the book.

Lanaguage and Multicultural Education

To implement multicultural education, educators must transform the way they think about the nation's past, present, and future. To change our thinking, it is necessary to change our language. Language and thinking are related in an interactive way. Our language influences how we think; the way we think influences our language. Concepts and phrases such as *The New World, The Discovery of America,* and *The Westward Movement* reveal a set of covert and implicit beliefs and assumptions about the Americas before the Europeans arrived. They do not recognize the peoples and cultures that existed in the Americas before the fifteenth century. The implementation of multicultural education requires that we create and use concepts and terms that recognize and give voice to the many cultures, peoples, and groups that make up the United States.

In preparing this Second Edition of *Multicultural Education,* the authors have tried to use language that empowers and gives voice to various groups, rather than terms that stigmatize them. In most cases, the authors use *African American* rather than *Black* to clearly link African Americans with their homeland. *Native American* and *Indian* are used synonymously to reflect current practice. *Hispanic* and *Latino* are used to refer to ethnic groups with roots in Spain. The usage of *Hispanic* and *Latino* varies by regions in the United States. Authors use those terms interchangeably. To reflect the way that most ethnic groups define themselves, the names of ethnic groups are not hyphenated. In addition, the phrase *students with disabilities* is used rather than *handicapped students.*

Until there is full equality within our society, concepts and terms for groups will continue to change. Changing language reflects, in part, efforts by groups on the margins of society to become a part of a transformed center. As educators, we must remain knowledgeable about and sensitive to language changes and usage if we are to be positive factors in school reform.

Acknowledgments

We are grateful to the authors who revised their chapters for this second edition of *Multicultural Education* and to the new authors for writing their chapters and then revising them in response to our comments and suggestions. We would like to thank Professors William Martin, University of West Florida; Rodolfo Martinez, Wayne State University; and Frank Stone, University of Connecticut, for reviewing the first edition of this book and making helpful suggestions for this second edition.

A group of our colleagues graciously responded to a user survey that we designed to solicit feedback on the first edition. We wish to thank the following people for taking time from their busy schedules to provide us with helpful feedback: Dr. Jean T. Adenika, University of California, Irvine; Dr. Robert S. Austin, Seton Hall University, Sea Girt, New Jersey; Dr. Rosa Briceno, San Jose State University, San Jose, California; Dr. David Julian Hodges, Hunter College, New York, New York; Dr. Edith W. King, University of Denver, Denver, Colorado; Dr. S. Timothy Reagan, Central Connecticut State University, New Britain; Dr. Mary Rusittee, South Dakota University, Brookings; Sister Marie Shaun, College of Saint Catherine, St. Paul, Minnesota; and Dr. Jose E. Vega, University of Wisconsin, River Falls.

We are also grateful to Grace Sheldrick, Wordsworth Associates, for her editorial wisdom and sage advice.

Our daughters, Angela, a college freshman, and Patricia, a sophomore in high school, have had to endure many long conversations between us about multicultural education. We hope the price they paid for listening will result in their having a better world than ours.

J. A. B.
C. A. McG. B.

Multicultural education helps students from diverse cultural, racial, and ethnic groups to attain knowledge, attitudes, and skills needed to function in a rapidly changing nation and world.

PART ONE

Issues and Concepts

The chapters in this first part of the book define the major concepts and issues in multicultural education, discuss the meaning of culture, and describe the ways in which variables such as race, class, gender, and exceptionality influence student behavior. A *group* is defined as a collectivity of human beings living together and interacting with their physical, social, and metaphysical environments. *Culture* is a group's program for survival and adaptation to these environments.

Multicultural education is an idea, an educational reform movement, and a process whose major goal is to change the structure of educational institutions so that male and female students, exceptional students, and students who are members of diverse racial, ethnic, and cultural groups will have an equal chance to achieve academically in school. It is necessary to conceptualize the school as a social system to implement multicultural education successfully. Each major variable in the school, such as its culture, power relationships, the curriculum and materials, and the attitudes and beliefs of the staff, must be changed in ways that will allow the school to promote educational equality for students from diverse groups.

To transform the schools, educators must be knowledgeable about the influence of particular groups on student behavior, and they must also be able to understand how influences from several groups interact and intersect to affect student behavior. The chapters in this part of the book describe the nature of culture and groups in the United States as well as the ways in which they interact to influence student behavior.

CHAPTER 1

Multicultural Education: Characteristics and Goals

■ JAMES A. BANKS

THE NATURE OF MULTICULTURAL EDUCATION

Multicultural education is at least three things: an idea or concept, an educational reform movement, and a process. Multicultural education incorporates the idea that all students—regardless of their gender and social class and their ethnic, racial, or cultural characteristics—should have an equal opportunity to learn in school. Another important idea in multicultural education is that some students, because of these characteristics, have a better chance to learn in schools as they are currently structured than do students who belong to other groups or have different cultural characteristics.

Some institutional characteristics of schools systematically deny some groups of students equal educational opportunities. For example, in the early grades, girls and boys achieve equally in mathematics and science. However, the achievement test scores of girls fall considerably behind those of boys as children progress through the grades.[1] Girls are less likely than boys to participate in class discussions and to be encouraged by teachers to participate. Girls are more likely than boys to be silent in the classroom. However, not all school practices favor males. As Sadker, Sadker, and Long point out in Chapter 6, boys are more likely to be disciplined than are girls, even when their behavior does not differ from the girls'. They are also more likely than girls to be classified as learning disabled. Males of color, especially African American males, experience a highly disproportionate rate of disciplinary actions and suspensions in school. Some writers have described the situation of African American males as a "crisis" and have called them "endangered" in U.S. society.[2]

In the early grades, the academic achievement of students of color such as African Americans, Hispanics, and American Indians is close to parity with the achievement of White mainstream students. However, the longer these students of color remain in school, the more their achievement lags behind that of White mainstream students. Social-class status is also strongly related to academic achievement. Persell, in Chapter 4, describes how students from the middle and upper classes are treated more positively in schools than are lower-class students and are given a better chance to learn. Exceptional students, whether they are physically or mentally disabled or gifted and talented, often find that they do not

3

experience equal educational opportunities in the schools. The chapters in Part V of this book describe the problems that such exceptional students experience in schools and suggest ways that teachers and other educators can increase their chances for educational success.

Multicultural education is also a reform movement that is trying to change the schools and other educational institutions so that students from all social-class, gender, racial, and cultural groups will have an equal opportunity to learn. Multicultural education involves changes in the total school or educational environment; it is not limited to curricular changes. The variables in the school environment that multicultural education tries to transform are identified and discussed later in this chapter (see Figure 1.5).

Multicultural education is also a process whose goals will never be fully realized. Educational equality, like liberty and justice, are ideals toward which human beings work but never fully attain. Racism, sexism, and discrimination against people with disabilities will exist to some extent no matter how hard we work to eliminate these problems. When prejudice and discrimination are reduced toward one group, they are usually directed toward another group or they take new forms. Because the goals of multicultural education can never be fully attained, we should work continually to increase educational equality for all students.

Multicultural education must be viewed as an ongoing process, and not as something that we "do" and thereby solve the problems that are the targets of multicultural educational reform. When I asked one school administrator what efforts were being taken to implement multicultural education in his school district, he told me that the district had "done" multicultural education last year and that it was now initiating other reforms, such as improving the students' reading scores. This administrator not only misunderstood the nature and scope of multicultural education, but he also did not understand that it could help raise the students' reading scores. A major goal of multicultural education is to improve academic achievement.

MULTICULTURAL EDUCATION: AN INTERNATIONAL REFORM MOVEMENT

Since World War II, many immigrant groups have settled in the United Kingdom and in nations on the European continent such as France, the Netherlands, Germany, Sweden, and Switzerland. Some of these immigrants, such as the Asians and West Indians in England and the North Africans and Indochinese in France, have come from former colonies. Many Southern and Eastern European immigrants have settled in Western and Northern European nations in search of upward social mobility and other opportunities. Groups such as Italians, Greeks, and Turks have migrated to Northern and Western European nations in large numbers. Ethnic and immigrant populations have also increased significantly in Australia and Canada since World War II.

Most of the immigrant and ethnic groups in Europe, Australia, and Canada face problems similar to those experienced by ethnic groups in the United States. Groups such as the Jamaicans in England, the Algerians in France, and the Aborigines in Australia experience achievement problems in the schools and prejudice and discrimination in both the schools and society at large. The problems that Greeks and Italians experience in Australia indicate that race is not always a factor when ethnic conflict and tension develop.

The United Kingdom, various nations on the European continent, and Australia and Canada have implemented a variety of programs to increase the achievement of ethnic and immigrant students and to help students and teachers develop more positive attitudes toward racial, cultural, ethnic, and language diversity.[3]

THE HISTORICAL DEVELOPMENT OF MULTICULTURAL EDUCATION

Multicultural education grew out of the ferment of the civil rights movement of the 1960s. During this decade, African Americans started a quest for their rights that was unprecedented in the United States. A major goal of the civil rights movement of the 1960s was to eliminate discrimination in public accommodations, housing, employment, and education. The consequences of the civil rights movement had a significant influence on educational institutions as ethnic groups—first African Americans and then other groups—demanded that the schools and other educational institutions reform their curricula so that they would reflect their experiences, histories, cultures, and perspectives. Ethnic groups also demanded that the schools hire more Black and Brown teachers and administrators so that their children would have more successful role models. Ethnic groups pushed for community control of schools in their neighborhoods and for the revision of textbooks to make them reflect the diversity of peoples in the United States.

The first responses of schools and educators to the ethnic movements of the 1960s were hurried. Courses and programs were developed without the thought and careful planning needed to make them educationally sound or to institutionalize them within the educational system. Holidays and other special days, ethnic celebrations, and courses that focused on one ethnic group were the dominant characteristics of school reforms related to ethnic and cultural diversity during the 1960s and early 1970s. Grant and Sleeter, in Chapter 3, call this approach *single group studies*. The ethnic studies courses developed and implemented during this period were usually electives and were taken primarily by students who were members of the group that was the subject of the course.

The apparent success of the civil rights movement, plus growing rage and a liberal national atmosphere, stimulated other victimized groups to take actions to eliminate discrimination against them and to demand that the educational system respond to their needs, aspirations, cultures, and histories. The women's rights movement emerged as one of the most significant social reform movements of the late twentieth century. During the 1960s and 1970s, discrimination against women in employment, income, and education was widespread and often blatant. The women's rights movement articulated and publicized how discrimination and institutionalized sexism limited the opportunities of women and adversely affected the nation. The leaders of this movement, such as Betty Friedan and Gloria Steinem, demanded that political, social, economic, and educational institutions act to eliminate sex discrimination and to provide opportunities for women to actualize their talents and realize their ambitions.[4] Major goals of the women's rights movement included equal pay for equal work, the elimination of laws that discriminated against women and made them second-class citizens, the hiring of more women in leadership positions, and greater participation of men in household work and child rearing.

When *feminists* (people who work for the political, social, and economic equality of the sexes) looked at educational institutions, they noted problems similar to those identified by ethnic groups of color. Textbooks and curricula were dominated by men; women were largely invisible. Feminists pointed out that history textbooks were dominated by political and military history—areas in which men had been the main participants.[5] Social and family history and the history of labor and of ordinary people were largely ignored. Feminists pushed for the revision of textbooks to include more history about the important roles of women in the development of the nation and the world. They also demanded that more women be hired for administrative positions in the schools. Although most teachers in the elementary schools were women, most administrators were men.

Other victimized groups, stimulated by the social ferment and the quest for human rights during the 1970s, articulated their grievances and demanded that institutions be reformed so they would face less discrimination and acquire more human rights. People with disabilities, senior citizens, and gay rights advocates were among the groups that organized politically during this period and made significant inroads in changing institutions and laws. Advocates for citizens with disabilities attained significant legal victories during the 1970s. The Education for All Handicapped Children Act of 1975 (P.L. 94-142), which required that students with disabilities be educated in the least restricted environment and institutionalized the word *mainstreaming* in education, was perhaps the most significant legal victory of the movement for the rights of students with disabilities in education (see Chapters 12 and 13).

HOW MULTICULTURAL EDUCATION DEVELOPED

Multicultural education emerged from the diverse courses, programs, and practices that educational institutions devised to respond to the demands, needs, and aspirations of the various groups. Consequently, as Grant and Sleeter point out in Chapter 3, multicultural education is not in actual practice one identifiable course or educational program. Rather, practicing educators use the term *multicultural education* to describe a wide variety of programs and practices related to educational equity, women, ethnic groups, language minorities, low-income groups, and people with disabilities. In one school district, multicultural education may mean a curriculum that incorporates the experiences of ethnic groups of color; in another, a program may include the experiences of both ethnic groups and women. In a third school district, this term may be used the way it is by me and by other authors, such as Grant and Sleeter and Baptiste,[6] that is, to mean a ***total school reform*** *effort designed to increase educational equity for a range of cultural, ethnic, and economic groups.* This broader and more comprehensive notion of multicultural education is discussed in the last part of this chapter. It differs from the limited concept of multicultural education, in which it is viewed as curriculum reform.

MULTICULTURAL EDUCATION AND TENSION AMONG DIVERSE GROUPS

The challenge to multicultural educators, in both theory and practice, is how to increase equity for a particular victimized group without further limiting the opportunities of another. Even though the various groups that are targeted for empowerment and equity in multicultural education share many needs and goals, sometimes they perceive their needs as divergent, conflicting, and inconsistent, as some feminist and ethnic group advocates have in the past.[7] Butler describes this phenomenon in Chapter 8. A major cause of the tension among various victimized groups may be institutionalized practices within society that promote tension, conflict, and divisiveness among them. If this is the case, as some radical scholars suggest,[8] perhaps an important goal of multicultural education should be to help students who are members of particular victimized groups better understand how their fates are tied to those of other powerless groups and the significant benefits that can result from multicultural political coalitions. These coalitions could be cogent vehicles for social change and reform. Jesse Jackson's attempt to form what he called a Rainbow Coalition at the national level in the 1980s had as one of its major goals the formulation of an effective political coalition made up of people from both gender groups and from different racial, ethnic, cultural, and social-class groups.

THE NATURE OF CULTURE IN THE UNITED STATES

The United States, like other Western nation-states such as the United Kingdom, Australia, and Canada, is a multicultural society. The United States consists of a shared core culture as well as many subcultures. In this book, we call the larger shared core culture the *macroculture;* the smaller cultures, which are a part of the core culture, are called *microcultures.* It is important to distinguish the macroculture from the various microcultures because the values, norms, and characteristics of the mainstream (macroculture) are frequently mediated by, as well as interpreted and expressed differently within, various microcultures. These differences often lead to cultural misunderstandings, conflicts, and institutionalized discrimination.

Students who are members of certain cultural, religious, and ethnic groups are sometimes socialized to act and think in certain ways at home but differently at school. One example of this behavior is children who are taught the creation story in the book of Genesis at home but are expected to accept in school the evolutionary explanation of the development and emergence of human beings. A challenge that multicultural education faces is how to help students from diverse groups mediate between their home and community cultures and the school culture. Students should acquire the knowledge, attitudes, and skills needed to function effectively in each cultural setting. They should also be competent to function within and across other microcultures in their society, within the national macroculture, and within the world community.

The Meaning of Culture

In Chapter 2, Bullivant defines *culture* as a group's program for survival in and adaptation to its environment. The cultural program consists of knowledge, concepts, and values shared by group members through systems of communication. Culture also consists of the shared beliefs, symbols, and interpretations within a human group. Most social scientists today view culture as consisting primarily of the symbolic, ideational, and intangible aspects of human societies. The essence of a culture is not its artifacts, tools, or other tangible cultural elements but how the members of the group interpret, use, and perceive them. It is the values, symbols, interpretations, and perspectives that distinguish one people from another in modernized societies; it is not material objects and other tangible aspects of human societies.[9] People within a culture usually interpret the meanings of symbols, artifacts, and behaviors in the same or in similar ways.

Identifying and Describing the U.S. Core Culture

The United States, like other nation-states, has a shared set of values, ideations, and symbols that constitute the core or overarching culture. This culture is shared to some extent by all the diverse cultural and ethnic groups that make up the nation-state. It is difficult to identify and describe the overarching culture in the United States because it is such a diverse and complex nation. It is easier to identify the core culture within an isolated premodern society, such as the Maoris before the Europeans came to New Zealand, than within highly pluralistic, modernized societies such as the United States, Canada, and Australia.[10]

When trying to identify the distinguishing characteristics of U.S. culture, one should realize that the political institutions within the United States, which reflect some of the nation's core values, were heavily influenced by the British. U.S. political ideals and institutions were also influenced by Native American political institutions and practices, especially those related to making group decisions, such as in the League of the Iroquois.[11]

Equality

A key component in the U.S. core culture is the idea, expressed in the Declaration of Independence in 1776, that "all men are created equal, that they are endowed by their Creator with certain unalienable rights, that among these are life, liberty, and the pursuit of happiness."[12] When this idea was expressed by the nation's founding fathers in 1776, it was considered radical. A common belief in the eighteenth century was that human beings were not born with equal rights; that some had few rights and others, such as kings, had divine rights given by God. When considering the idea that "all men are created equal" is a key component of U.S. culture, one should remember to distinguish between a nation's ideals and its actual practices, as well as between the meaning of the idea when it was expressed in 1776 and its meaning today. When the nation's founding fathers expressed this idea in 1776, their conception of men was limited to White males who owned property.[13] White men without property, White women, and all African Americans and Indians were not included in their notion of people who were equal or who had "certain unalienable rights."

Although the idea of equality expressed by the founding fathers in 1776 had a very limited meaning at that time, it has proven to be a powerful and important idea in the quest for human rights in the United States. Throughout the nation's history since 1776, victimized and excluded groups such as women, African Americans, Indians, and other cultural and ethnic groups have used this cogent idea to justify and defend the extension of human rights to them and to end institutional discrimination, such as sexism, racism, and discrimination against people with disabilities. As a result, human rights have gradually been extended to various groups throughout U.S. history. The extension of these rights has been neither constant nor linear. Rather, periods of extension of rights have often been followed by periods of retrenchment and conservatism. Schlesinger calls these patterns "cycles of American history."[14] The United States is still a long way from realizing the ideals expressed in the Declaration of Independence in 1776. However, these ideals remain an important part of U.S. culture and are still used by victimized groups to justify their struggles for human rights and equality.

Individualism and Individual Opportunity

Two other important ideas in the common overarching U.S. culture are individualism and individual social mobility.[15] Individualism as an ideal is extreme in the U.S. core culture. Individual success is more important than commitment to family, community, and nation-state. An individual is expected to experience success by his or her sole efforts. Many Americans believe that a person can go from rags to riches within a generation and that every American boy can, but not necessarily will, become president.

Individuals are expected to experience success by hard work and to pull themselves up by their bootstraps. This idea was epitomized by fictional characters such as Ragged Dick, one of the heroes created by the popular writer Horatio Alger. Ragged Dick attained success by valiantly overcoming poverty and adversity. A related belief is that if you do not succeed, it is because of your own shortcomings, such as being lazy or unambitious; failure is consequently your own fault. These beliefs are taught in the schools with success stories and myths about such U.S. heroes as George Washington, Thomas Jefferson, and Abraham Lincoln. The beliefs about individualism in American culture are related to the Protestant work ethic. This is the belief that hard work by the individual is morally good and that laziness is sinful. This belief is a legacy of the British Puritan settlers in colonial New England. It has had a powerful and significant influence on U.S. culture.

Groups and Individual Opportunity

The belief in individual opportunity has proven tenacious in U.S. society. It remains strong in American culture despite the fact that individuals' chances for upward social, economic, and educational mobility in the United States are highly related to the social-class, ethnic, gender, and other ascribed groups to which they belong. Social scientists have amply documented the extent of social-class stratification in the United States and the ways in which people's chances in life are affected by the groups to which they belong.[16] Jencks and his associates have documented thoroughly the extent to which educational opportunity and life chances are related to social class.[17] The chapters in this book on social class, gender, and ethnicity belie the notion that individual opportunity is a dominant characteristic of U.S. society. Yet the belief in individual opportunity remains strong in the United States.

Individualism and Groupism

Although the groups to which people belong have a cogent influence on their life chances in the United States, Americans—particularly those in the mainstream—are highly individualistic in their value orientations and behavior. The strength of the nuclear family reinforces individualism in U.S. culture. One result of the strong individualism is that married children usually expect their older parents to live independently or in homes for senior citizens rather than with them.

The strong individualism in U.S. culture contrasts sharply with the groupism and group commitment found in Asian nations, such as China and Japan.[18] Individualism is viewed rather negatively in these societies. One is expected to be committed first to the family and group and then to oneself. Some U.S. social scientists, such as Lash and Bellah and Bellah's associates, lament the extent of individualism in U.S. society.[19] They believe it is harmful to the common national culture. Some observers believe that groupism is too strong in China and Japan and that individualism should be more valued in those nations. Perhaps modernized, pluralistic nation-states can best benefit from a balance between individualism and groupism, with neither characteristic dominating.

Expansionism and Manifest Destiny

Other overarching U.S. values that social scientists have identified include the desire to conquer or exploit the natural environment, materialism and consumption, and the belief in the nation's inherent superiority. These beliefs justified Manifest Destiny and U.S. expansion to the West and into other nations and the annexation of one-third of Mexico's territory in 1848. These observations, which reveal the less positive side of U.S. national values, have been developed by social scientists interested in understanding the complex nature of American society.[20]

Greenbaum believes that *distance* is also a key value in U.S. society. He uses this word to describe the formal nature of bureaucratic institutions, as well as unfriendliness and detachment in social relationships.[21] Greenbaum argues that the Anglo-Saxon Protestants, the dominant cultural group in U.S. society, have often used distance in its relationships with other ethnic and cultural groups to keep them confined to their social-class status and group.

In his discussion of the nature of values in U.S. society, Myrdal contends that a major ethical inconsistency exists in U.S. society. He calls this inconsistency "the American dilemma."[22] He states that American Creed values,such as equality and human dignity, exist in U.S. society as ideals. However, they exist alongside the institutionalized discriminatory treatment of African Americans and other ethnic and cultural groups in U.S. society. This variance creates a dilemma in the American mind because Americans try to reconcile their democratic ideals with their treatment of victimized groups. Myrdal states that this dilemma has been an important factor that has enabled ethnic groups to fight discrimination effectively. In their efforts to resolve their dilemma when the inconsistencies between their ideals and actions are pointed out to them by human-rights advocates, Americans, according to Myrdal, often support the elimination of practices that are inconsistent with their democratic ideals or the American Creed. Some writers have refuted Myrdal's hypothesis and contend that most Americans do not experience such a dilemma.[23]

Microcultures in the United States

A nation as culturally diverse as the United States consists of a common overarching culture, as well as of a series of microcultures (see Figure 1.1). These

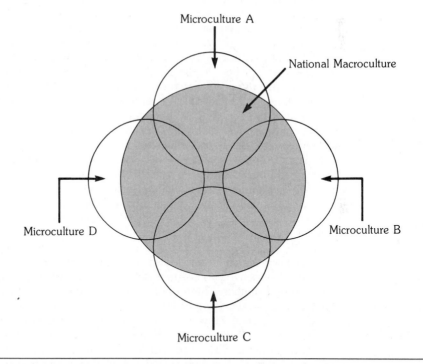

FIGURE 1.1
Microcultures and the National Macroculture   The shaded area represents the national macroculture. A, B, C, and D represent microcultures that consist of unique institutions, values, and cultural elements that are nonuniversalized and are shared primarily by members of specific cultural groups. A major goal of the school should be to help students acquire the knowledge, skills, and attitudes needed to function effectively within the national macroculture, their own microcultures, and within and across other microcultures.

microcultures share most of the core values of the nation-state, but these values are often mediated by the various microcultures and are interpreted differently within them. Microcultures sometimes have values that are somewhat alien to the national core culture. Also, some of the core national values and behaviors may seem somewhat alien in certain microcultures or may take on different forms.

The strong belief in individuality and individualism that exists within the national macroculture is often much less endorsed by some ethnic communities and is somewhat alien within them. African Americans and Hispanic Americans who have not experienced high levels of cultural assimilation into the mainstream culture are much more group oriented than are mainstream Americans. Schools in the United States are highly individualistic in their learning and teaching styles, evaluation procedures, and norms. Many students, particularly African Americans, Hispanics, and American Indians, are group oriented.[24] These students experience problems in the highly individualistic learning environment of the school, as Shade and New point out in Chapter 16. Teachers can enhance the learning opportunities of these students, who are also called field dependent or field sensitive, by using cooperative teaching strategies that have been developed and field-tested by researchers such as Slavin and Cohen.[25]

Some emerging theories indicate that female students may have preferred ways of knowing, thinking, and learning that differ to some extent from those most often preferred by males.[26] Maher describes the dominant inquiry model used in social science as male constructed and dominated. She contends that it strives for objectivity. "Personal feelings, biases, and prejudices are considered inevitable limitations."[27] Feminist pedagogy is based on different assumptions about the nature of knowledge and results in a different teaching method. According to Maher, feminist pedagogy enhances the learning of females and deepens the insight of males. In Chapter 7, Tetreault describes feminist pedagogy techniques she uses to motivate students and to enhance their understandings.

After completing a major research study on women's ways of knowing, Belenky and her colleagues concluded that conceptions of knowledge and truth in the core culture and in educational institutions "have been shaped throughout history by the male-dominated majority culture. Drawing on their own perspectives and visions, men have constructed the prevailing theories, written history, and set values that have become the guiding principles for men and women alike."[28]

These researchers also found an inconsistency between the kind of knowledge most appealing to women and the kind that was emphasized in most educational institutions. Most of the women interviewed in their study considered personalized knowledge and knowledge that resulted from first-hand observation most appealing. However, most educational institutions emphasize abstract, "out-of-context" knowledge.[29] Ramírez and Castañeda found that Mexican American students who were socialized within traditional cultures also considered personalized and humanized knowledge more appealing than abstract knowledge.[30] They also responded positively to knowledge that was presented in a humanized or story format.

Research by Gilligan provides some clues that help us better understand the findings by Belenky and her colleagues about the kind of knowledge women find most appealing. Gilligan describes caring, interconnection, and sensitivity to the needs of other people as dominant values among women and the female microculture in the United States.[31] By contrast, she found that the values of men were more characterized by separation and individualism.

A major goal of multicultural education is to change teaching and learning approaches so that students of both genders and from diverse cultural and ethnic groups will have equal opportunities to learn in educational institutions. This goal suggests that major changes ought to be made in the ways that educational programs are conceptualized, organized, and taught. Educational approaches need to be transformed.

In her research on identifying and labeling students with mental retardation, Mercer found that a disproportionate number of African American and Hispanic students were labeled *mentally retarded* because the testing procedures used in intelligence tests "reflect the abilities and skills valued by the American core culture,"[32] which Mercer describes as predominantly White, Anglo-Saxon, and middle and upper class. She also points out that measures of general intelligence consist primarily of items related to verbal skills and knowledge. Most African American and Hispanic students are socialized within microcultures that differ in significant ways from the U.S. core culture. These students often have not had an equal opportunity to learn the knowledge and skills that are measured in mental ability tests. Consequently, a disproportionate percentage of African American and Hispanic students are labeled *mentally retarded* and are placed in classes for slow learners. Mental retardation, as Mercer points out, is a *socially determined* status. When students are placed in classes for the mentally retarded, the self-fulfilling prophecy develops. Students begin to act and think as though they are mentally retarded.

Groups and Group Identification

Thus far, I have discussed the various microcultures that make up U.S. society. Individuals learn the values, symbols, and other components of their culture from their social group. The group is the social system that carries a culture. As Bullivant points out in Chapter 2, "people belong to, live in and are members of social groups; they are not members of culture." A group is a collectivity of persons who share an identity, a feeling of unity. A group is also a social system that has a social structure of interrelated roles.[33] The group's program for survival, values, ideations, and shared symbols constitutes its culture.

The study of groups is the major focus in sociology. Sociologists believe that the group has a strong influence on the behavior of individuals, that behavior is shaped by group norms, and that the group equips individuals with the behavior patterns they need to adapt to their physical, social, and metaphysical environments (see Chapter 2). Sociologists also assume that groups have independent characteristics; they are more than aggregates of individuals. Groups possess a continuity that transcends the lives of individuals.

Sociologists also assume that knowledge about groups to which an individual belongs provides important clues to and explanations for the individual's behavior. Goodman and Marx write, "Such factors as shared religion, nationality, age, sex, marital status, and education have proved to be important determinants of what people believe, feel, and do."[34] Although membership in a gender, racial, ethnic, social-class, or religious group can provide us with important clues about individuals' behavior, it cannot enable us to predict behavior. Knowing one's group affiliation can enable us to state that a certain type of behavior is probable. *Membership in a particular group does not determine behavior but makes certain types of behavior more probable.*

There are several important reasons that knowledge of group characteristics and modalities can enable us to predict the probability of an individual's behavior but not the precise behavior. This is, in part, because each individual belongs to several groups at the same time (see Figure 1.2). An individual may be White, Catholic, female, and middle class, all at the same time. She might have a strong identification with one of these groups and a very weak or almost nonexistent identification with another. A person can be a member of a particular group, such as the Catholic church, and have a weak identification with the group and a weak commitment to the tenets of the Catholic faith. Religious identification might be another individual's strongest group identification. Identification and attachments to different groups may also conflict. A woman who has a strong Catholic identification but is also a feminist might find it difficult to reconcile her beliefs about equality for women with some positions of the Catholic church, such as its prohibiting women from becoming ordained priests.

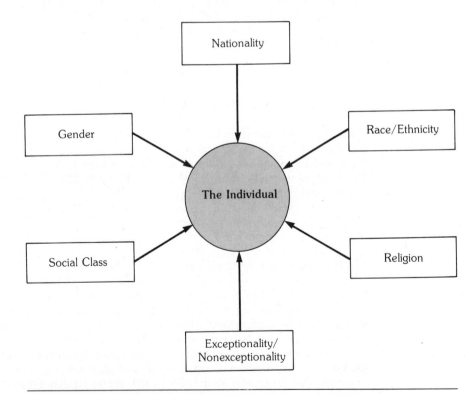

FIGURE 1.2
Multiple Group Memberships An individual belongs to several different groups at the same time. This figure shows the major groups discussed in this book.

The more we know about a student's level of identification with a particular group and the extent to which socialization has taken place within that group, the more accurately we can predict, explain, and understand the student's behavior in the classroom. A knowledge of the importance of a group to a student at a particular time of life and within a particular social context will also help us understand the student's behavior. Ethnic identity may become more important to a person who becomes a part of an ethnic minority when he or she previously belonged to the majority. Many Whites who have moved from the U.S. mainland to Hawaii have commented on how their sense of ethnic identity increased and they began to feel marginalized. Group identity may also increase when the group feels threatened, when a social movement arises to promote its rights, or when the group attempts to revitalize its culture.

The Teaching Implications of Group Identification

What are the implications of group membership and group identity for teaching? As you read the chapters in this book that describe the characteristics of the two gender groups and of social-class, racial, ethnic, religious, and exceptional groups, bear in mind that individuals within these groups manifest these behaviors to various degrees. *Also remember that individual students are members of several of these groups at the same time.* Above I describe the core U.S. culture as having highly individualistic values and beliefs. However, research by Gilligan indicates that the values of women, as compared with those of men, are more often characterized by caring, interconnection, and sensitivity to the needs of others.[35] This observation indicates how core values within the macroculture are often mediated by microcultures within various gender, ethnic, and cultural groups.

As stated above, researchers have found that some students of color such as African Americans and Mexican Americans often have field-sensitive learning styles and therefore prefer more personalized learning approaches.[36] Think about what this means. This research describes a group characteristic of these students and not the behavior of a particular African American or Mexican American student. It suggests that there is a higher probability that these students will have field-sensitive learning styles than will middle-class Anglo-American students. However, students within all ethnic, racial, and social-class groups have different learning styles. Those groups influence students' behavior, such as their learning style, interactively, because they are members of several groups at the same time. *Knowledge of the characteristics of groups to which students belong, about the importance of each of these groups to them, and of the extent to which individuals have been socialized within each group will give the teacher important clues to students' behavior.*

The Interaction of Race, Class, and Gender

When using our knowledge of groups to understand student behavior, we should also consider the ways that such variables as class, race, and gender interact and intersect to influence student behavior. Middle-class and more highly assimilated Mexican American students tend to be more field independent than do lower-class and less assimilated Mexican American students. African American students tend to be more field dependent (group oriented) than are White students;

females tend to be more field dependent than are male students. Therefore, it can be hypothesized that African American females would be the most field dependent when compared to African American and White males and White females. This finding was made by Perney.[37]

Unfortunately, the researcher did not include a social-class measure in the study. After doing a comprehensive review of research on the ways that race, class, and gender influence student behavior in education, Grant and Sleeter concluded that we must look at the ways these variables interact in order to fully understand student behavior.[38]

Figure 1.3 illustrates how the major groups discussed in this book—*gender, race or ethnicity, social class, religion, and exceptionality*—influence student behavior, both singly and interactively. The figure also shows that other variables, such as geographic region and age, also influence an individual's behavior. The ways these variables influence selected student behaviors are described in Table 1.1.

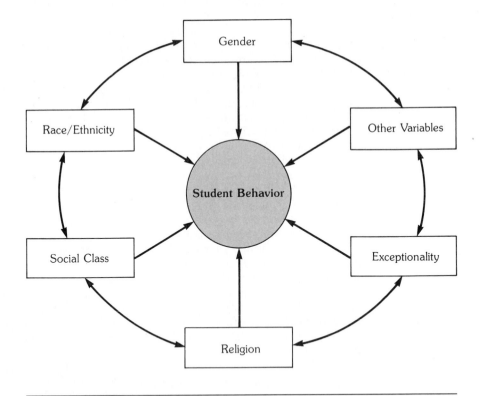

FIGURE 1.3
The Intersection of Variables   The major variables of gender, race or ethnicity, social class, religion, and exceptionality influence student behavior, both singly and interactively. Other variables, such as region and age, also influence student behavior.

TABLE 1.1
Singular and Combined Effects of Variables

Student Behavior	Gender Effects	Race/Ethnicity Effects	Social-Class Effects	Religious Effects	Combined Effects
Learning Styles (Field Independent/Field Dependent)	X[a]	X			X
Internality/Externality			X		
Fear of Success	X	X			?
Self-Esteem	X	X			?
Individual vs. Group Orientation	X	X	X		?

[a]An X indicates that the variable influences the student behavior described in the far-left column. An X in the far-right column means that research indicates that two or more variables combine to influence the described behavior. A question mark indicates that the research is unclear about the combined effects of the variables.

THE SOCIAL CONSTRUCTION OF CATEGORIES

The major variables and categories discussed in this book, such as gender, race, ethnicity, class, and exceptionality, are social categories.[39] The criteria for whether an individual belongs to one of these categories are determined by human beings and consequently are socially constructed. Religion is also a social category. Religious institutions, symbols, and artifacts are created by human beings to satisfy their metaphysical needs.

These categories are usually related to the physical characteristics of individuals. In some cases, as when they have severe or obvious physical disabilities, the relationship between the labels given to individuals and their physical characteristics is direct and would be made in almost any culture or social system. The relationship between categories that are used to classify individuals and their physical characteristics, however, is usually indirect and complex. Even though one's sex is determined primarily by physical characteristics (such as genitalia, chromosome patterns, etc.,), gender is a social construction created and shaped by the society in which individuals and groups function.

Gender

Gender consists of the socially and psychologically appropriate behavior for males and females sanctioned and expected within a society. Gender role expectations vary across cultures and at different times in a society and within microcultures in the same society. Traditionally, normative behavior for males and females has varied among mainstream Americans, African Americans, Native Americans, and Hispanic Americans. Gender role expectations also vary somewhat across social classes within the same society. In the White mainstream society in the 1940s and 1950s, upper-middle-class women often received negative sanctions when they worked outside the home, whereas women in working-class families were frequently expected to become wage earners.

Race

Race is a socially determined category that is related to physical characteristics in a complex way. Two individuals with nearly identical physical characteristics, or phenotypes, can be classified as members of different races in two different societies. In the United States, where racial categories are well defined and highly inflexible, an individual with any acknowledged or publicly known African ancestry is considered Black. One who looks completely Caucasian but who acknowledges some African ancestry is classified as Black. Such an individual would be considered White in Puerto Rico. In Puerto Rico, hair texture, social status, and degree of eminence in the community are often as important as—if not more important than—physical characteristics in determining an individual's racial group or category. There is a saying in Puerto Rico that "money lightens," which means that upward social mobility considerably enhances an individual's opportunity to be classified as White. There is a strong relationship between race and social class in Puerto Rico and in most other Caribbean and Latin American nations.

Our discussion of race as a social category indicates that the criteria for determining the characteristics of a particular race vary across cultures, that an individual considered Black in one society may be considered White in another, and that racial categories reflect the social, economic, and political characteristics of a society.

Social Class

Social scientists find it difficult to agree on criteria for determining social class. The problem is complicated by the fact that societies are constantly in the throes of change. During the 1950s, social scientists often attributed characteristics to the lower class that are found in the middle class today, such as single-parent and female-headed households, high divorce rates, and substance abuse. Today, these characteristics are no longer rare among the middle class, even though their frequency is still higher among lower-class families. Variables such as income, education, occupation, life-style, and values are among the most frequently used indices to determine social-class status in the United States.[40] However, there is considerable disagreement among social scientists about which variables are the most important in determining the social-class status of an individual or family.

Social-class criteria also vary somewhat among various ethnic and racial groups in the United States. Teachers, preachers, and other service professionals were upper class in many rural African American communities in the South in the 1950s and 1960s but were considered middle class by mainstream White society. The systems of social stratification that exist in the mainstream society and in various microcultures are not necessarily identical.

Exceptionality

Exceptionality is also a social category. Whether a person is considered disabled or gifted is determined by criteria developed by society. As Shaver and Curtis point out, disabilities are not necessarily handicaps, and the two should be distinguished. They write, "A disability or combination of disabilities becomes a handicap only when the condition limits or impedes the person's ability to function normally."[41] A person with a particular disability, such as having one arm, might have a successful college career, experience no barriers to his achievements in college, and graduate with honors. However, he may find that when he tries to enter the job market, his opportunities are severely limited because potential employers view him as unable to perform well in some situations in which, in fact, he could perform effectively.[42] This individual has a disability but was viewed as handicapped in one situation—the job market—but not in another—his university.

Mercer has extensively studied the social process by which individuals become labeled as persons with mental retardation. She points out that even though their physical characteristics may increase their chance of being labeled persons with mental retardation, the two are not perfectly correlated. Two people with the same biological characteristics may be considered persons with mental retardation in one social system and not in another social system. An individual may be considered a person with mental retardation at school but not at home. She writes, "Mental retardation is not a characteristic of the individual, nor a meaning inherent in behavior, but a socially determined status, which [people] may occupy in some social systems and not in others."[43] She states that people can change their role by changing their social group.

The highly disproportionate number of African Americans, Hispanics, and particularly males classified as *learning disabled* by the school indicates the extent to which exceptionality is a social category. Mercer found that the school labeled more people *mentally retarded* than did any other institution.[44] Many African American and Hispanic students who are labeled *mentally retarded* function normally and are considered normal in their homes and communities. Boys are more often classified as mentally retarded than are girls. The school, as Mercer and other researchers have pointed out, uses criteria to determine the mental ability of students of color that conflict with their home and community cultures. Some students in all ethnic and cultural groups are mentally retarded and deserve special instruction, programs, and services, as the authors in Part Four of this book suggest. However, the percentage of students of color in these programs is too high. The percentage of students in each ethnic group labeled *mentally retarded* should be about the same as the total percentage of that group in school.

Giftedness is also a social category. Important results of the socially constructed nature of giftedness are the considerable disagreement among experts about how the concept should be defined and the often inconsistent views about how to identify gifted students.[45] The highly disproportionate percentage of middle- and upper-middle-class mainstream students categorized as gifted compared to lower-class students and students of color such as African Americans, Hispanics, and American Indians is also evidence of the social origin of the category. Many students who are classified as gifted do have special talents and abilities, and they do need special instruction to help them actualize them.

In Chapter 14, Clark describes the characteristics of these students and ways in which their needs can be met. However, some students who are classified as gifted by school districts merely have parents with the knowledge, political skills, and power to force the school to classify their children as gifted, which will provide them with special instruction and educational enrichment. In some racially mixed school districts, the gifted programs are made up primarily of middle-class and upper-middle-class mainstream students.

Schools should try to satisfy the needs of students with special gifts; however, they should also make sure that students from all social-class, cultural, and ethnic groups have an equal opportunity to participate in programs for academically and creatively talented students. If schools or districts do not have a population in their gifted programs that represents their various cultural and ethnic groups, steps should be taken to examine the criteria used to identify gifted students and to develop procedures to correct the disproportion. Both excellence and equality should be major goals of education.

THE DIMENSIONS OF MULTICULTURAL EDUCATION

When many teachers think of multicultural education, they think only or primarily of content related to ethnic, racial, and cultural groups. Conceptualizing multicultural education exclusively as content related to various ethnic and cultural groups is problematic for several reasons. Teachers who cannot easily see how their content is related to cultural and normative issues will easily dismiss multicultural education with the argument that it is not relevant to their disciplines. This is done frequently by secondary math and science teachers.

The "irrelevant of content argument" can become a legitimized form of resistance to multicultural education when it is conceptualized primarily or exclusively as content. Math and science teachers often state, "Multicultural education is fine for social studies and literature teachers, but it has nothing to do with me. Math and science are the same, regardless of the culture or the kids." Multicultural education needs to be more broadly defined and understood so that teachers from a wide range of disciplines can respond to it in appropriate ways and resistance to it can be minimized.

Multicultural education is a broad concept with several different and important dimensions. Teachers can examine three dimensions of their instruction when trying to respond to issues in multicultural education. These dimensions are related to (1) content integration, (2) the knowledge construction process, and (3) an equity pedagogy. Each of these aspects of multicultural teaching is defined and illustrated below.

Content Integration

Content integration deals with the extent to which teachers use examples and content from a variety of cultures and groups to illustrate key concepts, principles, generalizations, and theories in their subject area or discipline. The infusion of ethnic and cultural content into the subject area should be logical and not contrived.

More opportunities exist for the integration of ethnic and cultural content in some subject areas than in others. In the social studies, the language arts, and home economics, frequent and ample opportunities exist for teachers to use ethnic and cultural content to illustrate concepts, themes, and principles. There are also opportunities to integrate multicultural content into math and science. However, the opportunities are not as ample as they are in social studies and the language arts.

The Knowledge Construction Process

The knowledge construction process relates to the extent to which teachers help students to understand, investigate, and determine how the implicit cultural assumptions, frames of references, perspectives, and biases within a discipline influence the ways in which knowledge is constructed within it.

Students can analyze the knowledge construction process in science by studying how racism has been perpetuated in science by genetic theories of intelligence, Darwinism, and eugenics. In his important book *The Mismeasure of Man*, Stephen Jay Gould describes how scientific racism developed and was influential in the nineteenth and twentieth centuries.[46] Scientific racism has had a significant influence on the interpretations of mental ability tests in the United States.

Students can examine the knowledge construction process in the social studies when they study such units and topics as the European discovery of America and the westward movement. The teacher can ask the students the latent meanings of concepts such as the European discovery of America and the New World. The students can discuss what these concepts imply or suggest about the Native American cultures that had existed in the Americas for about 40,000 years before the Europeans arrived. When studying the westward movement, the teacher can ask the students, "Whose point of view or perspective does this concept reflect, that of the European Americans or the Lakota Sioux?" "Who was moving west?" "How might a Lakota Sioux historian describe this period in United States history?" "What are other ways of thinking about and describing the westward movement?"

An Equity Pedagogy

Teachers in each discipline can analyze their teaching procedures and styles to determine the extent to which they reflect multicultural issues and concerns. An equity pedagogy exists when teachers modify their teaching in ways that will facilitate the academic achievement of students from diverse racial, cultural, gender, and social-class groups. This includes using a variety of teaching styles and approaches that are consistent with the wide range of learning styles within various cultural and ethnic groups, being demanding but highly personalized when working with groups such as Native American and Alaskan students, and using cooperative learning techniques in math and science instruction in order to enhance the academic achievement of students of color.[47]

Several of the chapters in this book discuss ways in which teachers can modify their instruction in order to increase the academic achievement of students from different cultural groups and from both gender groups, including the chapters that constitute Parts Three and Four and Chapter 16 by Shade and New in Part Six.

An Empowering School Culture

Another important dimension of multicultural education is a school culture and organization that promotes gender, racial, and social-class equity. The culture and organization of the school must be examined by all members of the school staff. They all must also participate in restructuring it. Grouping and labeling practices, sports participation, disproportionality in achievement, disproportionality in enrollment in gifted and special education programs, and the interaction of the staff and the students across ethnic and racial lines are important variables that need to be examined in order to create a school culture that empowers students from diverse racial and ethnic groups and from both gender groups.

Figure 1.4 summarizes the dimensions of multicultural education described above. The next section of this chapter identifies the major variables of the school that must be changed in order to institutionalize a school culture that empowers students from diverse cultural, racial, ethnic, and social-class groups.

The School as a Social System

To implement multicultural education successfully, we must think of the school as a social system in which all of its major variables are closely interrelated. Thinking of the school as a social system suggests that we must formulate and initiate a change strategy that reforms the total school environment to implement multicultural education. The major school variables that must be reformed are presented in Figure 1.5.

Reforming any one of the variables in Figure 1.5, such as the formalized curriculum or curricular materials, is necessary but not sufficient. Multicultural and sensitive teaching materials are ineffective in the hands of teachers who have negative attitudes toward different cultural groups. Such teachers are rarely likely to use multicultural materials or to use them detrimentally. Thus, helping teachers and other members of the school staff gain knowledge about cultural groups and democratic attitudes and values is essential when implementing multicultural programs.

To implement multicultural education in a school, we must reform its power relationships, the verbal interaction between teachers and students, the culture of the school, the curriculum, extracurricular activities, attitudes toward minority languages, the testing program, and grouping practices. The institutional norms, social structures, cause-belief statements, values, and goals of the school must be transformed and reconstructed.

Major attention should be focused on the school's hidden curriculum and its implicit norms and values. A school has both a manifest and a hidden curriculum. The manifest curriculum consists of such factors as guides, textbooks, bulletin boards, and lesson plans. These aspects of the school environment are

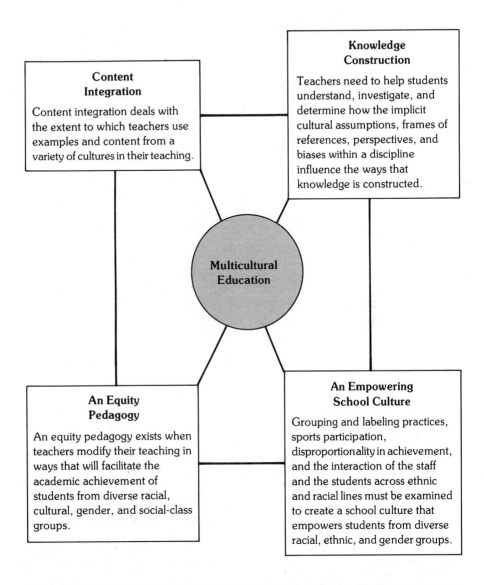

FIGURE 1.4
The Dimensions of Multicultural Education
Reprinted with permission from James A. Banks, "The Dimensions of Multicultural Education," *Multicultural Leader* 1 (Winter/Spring 1991): 4.

important and must be reformed to create a school culture that promotes positive attitudes toward diverse cultural groups and helps students from these groups experience academic success. However, the school's hidden or latent curriculum is often more cogent than its manifest or overt curriculum. The latent curriculum has been defined as the one that no teacher explicitly teaches but that all students

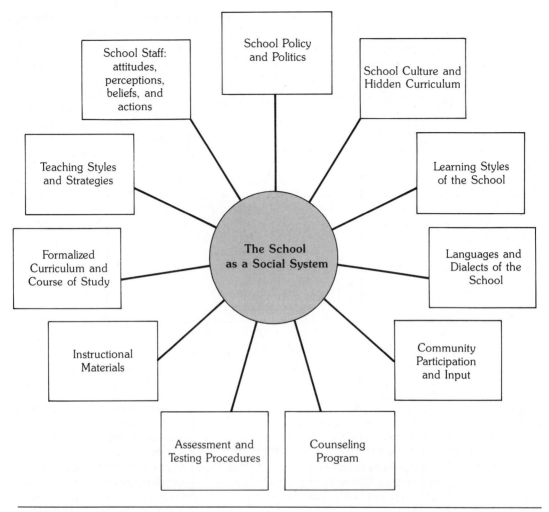

FIGURE 1.5
The School as a Social System   The total school environment is a system consisting of a number of major identifiable variables and factors, such as a school culture, school policy and politics, and the formalized curriculum and course of study. Any of these factors may be the focus of initial school reform, but changes must take place in each of them to create and sustain an effective multicultural school environment.

Adapted with permission from James A. Banks (Ed.), *Education in the 80s: Multiethnic Education* (Washington, D.C.: National Education Association, 1981), Figure 2, p. 22.

learn. It is that powerful part of the school culture that communicates to students the school's attitudes toward a range of issues and problems, including how the school views them as human beings and its attitudes toward males, females, exceptional students, and students from various religious, cultural, racial, and ethnic groups.

When formulating plans for multicultural education, educators should conceptualize the school as a microculture that has norms, values, statuses, and goals like other social systems. The school has a dominant culture and a variety of microcultures. Almost all classrooms in the United States are multicultural because White students, as well as Black and Brown students, are socialized within diverse cultures. Teachers also come from many different groups. Many teachers were socialized in cultures other than the Anglo mainstream, although these may be forgotten and repressed. Teachers can get in touch with their own cultures and use the perspectives and insights they acquired as vehicles for helping them relate to and understand the cultures of their students.

The school should be a cultural environment in which acculturation takes place; teachers and students should assimilate some of the views, perspectives, and ethos of each other as they interact. Teachers and students will be enriched by this process, and the academic achievement of students from diverse groups will be enhanced because their perspectives will be legitimized in the school. Both teachers and students will be enriched by this process of cultural sharing and interaction.

SUMMARY

Multicultural education is an idea stating that all students, regardless of the groups to which they belong, such as those related to gender, ethnicity, race, culture, social class, religion, or exceptionality, should experience educational equality in the schools. Some students, because of their particular characteristics, have a better chance to succeed in school as it is currently structured than have students from other groups. Multicultural education is also a reform movement designed to bring about a transformation of the school so that students from both genders and from diverse cultural and ethnic groups will have an equal chance to experience school success. Multicultural education views the school as a social system that consists of highly interrelated parts and variables. Therefore, in order to transform the school to bring about educational equality, all the major components of the school must be substantially changed. A focus on any one variable in the school, such as the formalized curriculum, will not implement multicultural education.

Multicultural education is a continuing process because the idealized goals it tries to actualize—such as educational equality and the eradication of all forms of discrimination—can never be fully achieved in a human society. Multicultural education, which was born during the social protest of the 1960s and 1970s, is an international movement that exists in various nations on the European continent and in Australia, the United Kingdom, and Canada. A major goal of multicultural education is to help students to develop the knowledge, attitudes, and skills needed to function within their own microcultures, the U.S. macroculture, other microcultures, and within the global community.

QUESTIONS AND ACTIVITIES

1. What are the three components or elements of multicultural education?

2. How does Banks define *multicultural education?*

3. Find other definitions of multicultural education in several books listed under the category "Issues and Concepts" in the Appendix. How are the definitions of multicultural education in these books alike and different from the one presented in this chapter?

4. In what ways did the civil rights and women's rights movements of the 1960s and 1970s influence the development of multicultural education?

5. Ask several teachers and other practicing educators to give you their views and definitions of multicultural education. What generalizations can you make about their responses?

6. Visit a local school and, by observing several classes as well as by interviewing several teachers and the principal, describe what curricular and other practices related to multicultural education have been implemented in the school. Share your report with your classmates or workshop colleagues.

7. What major tensions exist among groups such as various racial and ethnic groups and between feminists and ethnic minorities? Can multicultural education help reduce such tensions? If so, how?

8. What is a macroculture? A microculture?

9. How is *culture* defined? What are the most important components of culture in a modernized society?

10. List and define several core or overarching values and characteristics that make up the macroculture in the United States. To what extent are these values and characteristics consistent with practices in U.S. society? To what extent are they ideals that are inconsistent with realities in U.S. society?

11. What problems result when ideals in U.S. society are taught to students as if they were realities? Give examples of this.

12. How is individualism viewed differently in the United States and in nations such as China and Japan? Why? What are the behavioral consequences of these varying notions of individualism?

13. What is the American dilemma defined by Myrdal? To what extent is this concept an accurate description of values in U.S. society? Explain.

14. How do the preferred ways of learning and knowing among women and students of color often influence their experiences in the schools as they are currently structured? In what ways can school reform help make the school environment more consistent with the learning and cognitive styles of women and students of color?

15. In what ways does the process of identifying and labeling students with mental retardation discriminate against groups such as African Americans and Hispanics?

16. What is a group? What is the relationship between a group and a culture?

17. In what ways can the characteristics of a group help us understand an individual's behavior? In what ways are group characteristics limited in explaining an individual's behavior?

18. How do such variables as race, class, and gender interact to influence the behavior of students? Give examples to support your response.

19. What is meant by the "social construction of categories"? In what ways are concepts such as gender, race, social class, and exceptionality social categories?

20. List and define the four dimensions of multicultural education. How can these dimensions be used to facilitate school reform?

NOTES

1. Myra P. Sadker and David M. Sadker, *Sex Equity Handbook for Schools* (New York: Longman, 1982).

2. Jewelle Taylor Gibbs, ed., *Young, Black, and Male in America: An Endangered Species* (Dover, Mass.: Auburn House Publishing, 1988).

3. James Lynch, *Multicultural Education: Principles and Practice* (Boston: Routledge and Kegan Paul, 1986); James A. Banks and James Lynch, eds., *Multicultural Education in Western Societies* (London: Cassell, 1986).

4. Gloria Steinem, *Outrageous Acts and Everyday Rebellions* (New York: Holt, 1983).

5. Janice Law Trecker, "Teaching the Role of Women in American History," in James A. Banks, ed., *Teaching Ethnic Studies: Concepts and Strategies* (Washington, D.C.: National Council for the Social Studies, 1973), pp. 279–297 (NCSS 43rd Yearbook.)

6. Carl A. Grant and Christine E. Sleeter, *After the School Bell Rings* (Philadelphia: The Falmer Press, 1986); H. Prentice Baptiste, Jr., "Multicultural Education and Urban Schools from a Sociohistorical Perspective: Internalizing Multiculturalism," *Journal of Educational Equity and Leadership* 6 (Winter 1986): 295–312.

7. Lisa Albrecht and Rose M. Brewer, eds., *Bridges of Power: Women's Multicultural Alliances* (Philadelphia: New Society Publishers, 1990).

8. Lee Barton and Stephen Walker, eds., *Race, Class and Education* (London: Croom Helm, 1983).

9. James A. Banks, *Multiethnic Education: Theory and Practice,* 2d ed. (Boston: Allyn and Bacon, 1988), p. 73.

10. Gene Lisitzky, *Four Ways of Being Human: An Introduction to Anthropology* (New York: Viking Press, 1956).

11. Jack Weatherford, *Indian Givers: How the Indians of the Americas Tansformed the World* (New York: Fawcett Columbine, 1988).

12. "Declaration of Independence," in *The Annals of America,* vol. 2 (Chicago: Encyclopaedia Britannica, 1968), pp. 447–449.

13. Thurgood Marshall, "The Meaning of the Constitution Bicentennial," *Ebony* (September 1987): 62, 64, 68.

14. Arthur M. Schlesinger, Jr., *The Cycles of American History* (Boston: Houghton Mifflin, 1986).

15. Lucy R. Garretson, *American Culture: An Anthropological Perspective* (Dubuque, Ia.: Wm. C. Brown Co., 1976).

16. Philip Green, *The Pursuit of Inequality* (New York: Pantheon Books, 1981); G. William Domhoff, *Who Rules America Now?* (New York: Simon and Schuster, 1983).

17. Christopher Jencks et al., *Inequality: A Reassessment of the Effect of Family and Schooling in America* (New York: Basic Books, 1972).

18. Edwin O. Reischauer, *The Japanese* (Cambridge: Harvard University Press, 1981); Fox Butterfield, *China: Alive in the Bitter Sea* (New York: Bantam Books, 1982).

19. Christopher Lasch, *The Culture of Narcissism* (New York: Norton, 1978); Robert N. Bellah et al., *Habits of the Heart: Individualism and Commitment in American Life* (New York: Harper and Row, 1985).

20. William Greenbaum, "America in Search of a New Ideal: An Essay on the Rise of Pluralism,"

Harvard Educational Review 44 (August 1974): 411–440; Aida Negron DeMontilla, *Americanization in Puerto Rico and the Public-School System, 1900–1930* (San Juan: University of Puerto Rico, Editorial Universitaria, 1975).

21. Greenbaum, *America in Search.*

22. Gunnar Myrdal, with the assistance of Richard Sterner and Arnold Rose, *An American Dilemma: The Negro Problem and Modern Democracy* (New York: Harper and Row, 1944, 20th-Anniversary Edition, 1962).

23. Ralph Ellison, "An American Dilemma: A Review," in Joyce A. Ladner, ed., *The Death of White Sociology* (New York: Vintage Books, 1973), pp. 81–95.

24. Manuel Ramírez and Alfredo Castañeda, *Cultural Democracy, Bicognitive Development and Education* (New York: Academic Press, 1974); Janice E. Hale-Benson, *Black Children: Their Roots, Culture, and Learning Styles,* rev. ed. (Baltimore: Johns Hopkins University Press, 1986).

25. Robert E. Slavin, *Cooperative Learning* (New York: Longman, 1983); Elizabeth G. Cohen, *Designing Groupwork: Strategies for Heterogeneous Classrooms* (New York: Teachers College Press, 1986).

26. Carol Gilligan, *In a Different Voice: Psychological Theory and Women's Development* (Cambridge: Harvard University Press, 1982); Mary F. Belenky et al., *Women's Ways of Knowing: The Development of Self, Voice and Mind* (New York: Basic Books, 1986); Diane F. Halpern, *Sex Differences in Cognitive Abilities* (Hillsdale, N.J.: Lawrence Erlbaum Assoc., 1986).

27. Frances A. Maher, "Inquiry Teaching and Feminist Pedagogy," *Social Education* 51 (March 1987): 186.

28. Belenky et al., *Women's Ways,* 5.

29. Ibid., 200.

30. Ramírez and Castañeda, *Cultural Democracy.*

31. Gilligan, *Different Voice.*

32. Jane R. Mercer, *Labeling the Mentally Retarded: Clinical and Social System Perspectives on Mental Retardation* (Berkeley: University of California Press, 1973), p. 32.

33. George A. Theodorson and Achilles G. Theodorson, *A Modern Dictionary of Sociology* (New York: Barnes and Noble, 1969), pp. 176, 395.

34. Norman Goodman and Gary T. Marx, *Society Today,* 4th ed. (New York: Random House, 1982), p. 7.

35. Gilligan, *Different Voice.*

36. Ramírez and Castañeda, *Cultural Democracy.*

37. Violet H. Perney, "Effects of Race and Sex on Field Dependence-Independence in Children," *Perceptual and Motor Skills* 42 (1976): 975–980.

38. Carl A. Grant and Christine E. Sleeter, "Race, Class, and Gender in Education Research: An Argument for Integrative Analysis," *Review of Educational Research* 56 (Summer, 1986): 195–211.

39. These two books have greatly influenced my ideas about the social construction of categories: Peter L. Berger and Thomas Luckman, *The Social Construction of Reality: A Treatise in the Sociology of Knowledge* (New York: Doubleday and Co., 1967); Karl Mannheim, *Ideology and Utopia: An Introduction to the Sociology of Knowledge* (New York: Harcourt Brace, 1936).

40. W. Lloyd Warner with Marchia Meeker and Kenneth Eells, *Social Class in America* (New York: Harper Torchbooks, 1949; reissued 1960).

41. James P. Shaver and Charles K. Curtis, *Handicapism and Equal Opportunity: Teaching about the Disabled in Social Studies* (Reston, Va.: The Foundation for Exceptional Children, 1981), p. 1.

42. I adapted this example from one described by Shaver and Curtis, *Handicapism and Equal Opportunity,* 2.

43. Mercer, *Labeling,* 31.

44. Ibid., 96.

45. Dorothy Sisk, *Creative Teaching of the Gifted* (New York: McGraw-Hill Book Co., 1987).

46. Stephen J. Gould, *The Mismeasurement of Man* (New York: Norton, 1981).

47. Neil Davidson, ed., *Cooperative Learning in Mathematics: A Handbook for Teachers* (Menlo Park, Ca.: Addison-Wesley, 1990).

CHAPTER 2

Culture: Its Nature and Meaning for Educators

■ **BRIAN M. BULLIVANT**

Culture is a term we all use freely in numerous contexts, and for this reason we tend to take the idea of culture for granted. In many Western societies, the word *culture* has assumed importance because it forms part of the terms *multicultural-ism* and *multicultural education*. When used in these two approaches to pluralist education, culture is a defining concept. That is, how we define culture determines the meaning of the term of which it forms a part. Unless we know what culture means, we will find it very difficult to understand the full implications of multiculturalism and multicultural education.

For example, if culture is defined as the heritage and traditions of a social group, then multicultural education means teaching about many (multi-) different heritages and traditions. But if culture is defined as a social group's design for surviving in and adapting to its environment—an approach we favor in this chapter—then one aim of multicultural education is to teach about the many social groups and their different designs for living in our pluralist society.

These are obviously two quite different ways of looking at multicultural education, and they illustrate the necessity to understand the concept of culture. We cannot let the meaning of culture remain vague or take it for granted; thus, this chapter presents a straightforward explanation of this concept and of how it can be used in educational programs.

POPULAR MEANINGS OF CULTURE

The term *culture* is used in several popular but confusing ways. First, it is commonly associated with such aesthetic pursuits as art, drama, ballet, and literature. These make up what is often called a society's *high culture*, as opposed to its *low culture*, that is, more popular art, pop music, and mass-media entertainment. Second, such terms as *hippie culture, adolescent culture*, and *drug culture* imply that distinct groups in society possess these characteristics. Such groups are often termed *subcultures*. A third, scientific use refers to growing material in a chemical laboratory.

The author would like to thank Barry Troyna for his constructive comments on an earlier version of this chapter.

A fourth confusing use of culture is as a term for society. Thus, the term *British culture* is often a loose way of referring to British society *and* its culture. When people use the term in this way, they are referring to the people in Britain as being members of British culture or belonging to British culture. The same loose treatment of the term is frequently used to refer to other countries, but as the discussion of culture in this chapter makes clear, this is an invalid use of the term and should be avoided. We cannot emphasize the correct usage enough: People belong to, live in, or are members of social groups; they are not members of culture. Louis Schneider has stressed, "Putting people into culture is a sad maneuver into which social scientists slip time and time again."[1] We do not want to repeat such a mistake.

ENVIRONMENTS AFFECTING SOCIAL GROUPS

At its most basic, a social group consists of a more or less permanent collectivity of human beings living together and interacting with the varieties of environments that make up its territory. Social groups must survive by adapting to and modifying these environments. The knowledge, ideas, and skills that enable a group to survive can be thought of as its culture or survival program.

The success of a group's survival depends on the kinds of environments the group faces. First, there is the geographical environment, or physical habitat. This provides a variety of natural features that the social group adapts to or modifies through its technology; this constitutes the tools, skills, and knowledge used to achieve practical results. Included in these natural features are soil, minerals, climate, topography, vegetation, and such biotic resources as flora and fauna.

Cultural survival programs vary enormously in their levels of technological development, know-how, and sophistication. How much a social group can modify its living conditions and how much it is forced to adapt thus vary widely. A modern society like the United States, with a sophisticated technology, can modify its geographical environment almost at will. On the other hand, a technologically underdeveloped society is more heavily constrained by the difficulties posed by its geographical environment.

Second, members of a social group have to live together and interact. The social group as a whole has other groups as neighbors who make up a *social environment* with which it also has to interact. Some of these other groups are local and permit face-to-face interaction; others are more distant. On a world scale, major social groups such as nation-states live in regional or global social environments and have to adapt to other nation-states. As we discuss, a major part of culture is made up of all the customs and rules that enable all these different scales of interaction to be carried on smoothly.

Third, there is a kind of environment that we do not usually think about because it cannot be seen or interacted with in this world. Nevertheless it is real for millions of people and strongly influences their lives. Its origin may lie in what is thought to be a basic human drive or universal need to find meaning and explanations in life. One way of satisfying this need for meaning is to develop beliefs that life is governed by a higher order of beings that exist outside humankind, such as a god or gods and other supernatural entities. These are often thought of as living in their own kinds of worlds, such as heaven or paradise. Because they are located outside here-and-now experience or are transcendent, we can refer to these kinds of spiritual worlds as forming a *metaphysical environment.*

Without taking the metaphysical environment into account, it is difficult to understand fully why many social groups live as they do. For example, the lives of traditional Navajo Indians in Arizona would be incomprehensible if one did not know about their beliefs in a dangerous metaphysical environment, populated by sorcerers, witches, and other supernatural beings. The Navajo believe that these beings affect their health and personal well-being; their existence necessitates the adoption of spells to ward off evil influences and the use of ethnomedical practices such as curing ceremonies for people who get sick.

The design of traditional Navajo houses (hogans) and a large body of traditional customs have been developed in response to Navajo views about how to survive in their metaphysical environment. The essential point about these practices and many others in the world is that such metaphysical environments are as real to those who believe in them as the Christian God and heaven are to believing Christians.

Of course, the Navajo interpretations about the causes of illness differ from the ideas of modern Western medicine, and some educational organizations training Navajos to advance in the modern world take account of these differences. For example, the University of Arizona in Tucson offers courses in modern medicine and has also brought in Navajo medicine men to teach students about traditional Indian beliefs. The modern and traditional approaches complement one another.

This sharing of knowledge is an example of one approach adopted to help a group like the Navajo survive in its own environment. It also contains an essential lesson we should learn about living together in a society as pluralistic as the United States. Tolerance and respect for another social group's survival programs are essential ingredients of intercultural understanding.

Institutions and Institutional Agencies

Group life works through social institutions. These are major interrelated systems of social roles and norms (rules) organized to satisfy important social and human needs. Examples of these needs are obtaining food, shelter, and bodily maintenance; child rearing and education of the young; law and order; defense from external threat; and commercial and economic activity. Methods of taking care of these concerns are put into operation by *institutional agencies,* or "action systems" according to Talcott Parsons; these terms are used interchangeably in our discussion below.[2]

Each institutional agency or action system is a permanent organization consisting of a structural arrangement of status positions, plus roles, activities, rules or norms, and all the artifacts necessary for smooth operation. For example, the nuclear family is the major Western action system for taking care of procreation and child rearing. Schools, colleges, and universities are the major kinds of action systems we use to educate the young; the institutional agency of law courts takes care of law and order; the army, navy, and air force are action systems that look after defense.

It is important to remember that some of these institutional agencies control people's access to tangible political and economic power, resources, and social rewards. These kinds of agencies are essential for individual and group survival. The legal, political, commercial, business, and bureaucratic systems are examples of this type of action system. However, other action systems are less essential to promoting people's physical and material well-being. Action systems such as television companies, movie theaters, sports associations, gambling casinos, and many other recreational and social organizations may provide a certain quality and enjoyment to life, but they are not essential in the same way as the former kinds of action systems.

The principles that govern a social group's relations with its natural and social environments also apply to those that concern its relationships with the metaphysical environment. The institution of religion is put into operation through institutional agencies or action systems such as churches and synagogues, with statuses and roles (priests, pastors, rabbis) together with specified activities such as counseling, worship, ministry, and confession.

Operation of Institutional Agencies

The distinctive pattern or style of an institutional agency's operation is determined by its *charter* or ideology. A charter consists of a collection of beliefs, values, and ideas about what the institutional agency aims at (its ends) and how it will arrange its structure and organization (the means) to carry out its aims. These aspects are all contained in a society's cultural program.

Take the example of a school. Its charter contains ideas and beliefs about the ultimate purpose of education, the kinds of pupils it aims to produce (for example, factory workers or democratically conscious citizens), the need for discipline, the content of the curriculum (whether the emphasis is academic or generalist, for example), how the school should be run, the kind of staff most suitable to employ, the types of equipment and technology required, and many other aspects.

How these can vary becomes obvious if one compares two examples: an ethnic day school serving a group of Hasidic Jews in Williamsburg (part of Brooklyn, New York), such as Chaim Potok describes in his book *The Chosen,* and a local high school that most teachers would know. It quickly becomes apparent that both schools are not only very different action systems, organized with different ends in view, but that they also take very different views of the environments to which they are responding. The Jewish school's ideology is influenced much more by the metaphysical environment. Both schools respond to pressures in their social environments, but in different ways.

This short passage from *The Chosen* illustrates part of the Jewish group's concerns:

> *The sidewalks of Williamsburg were cracked squares of cement, the streets paved with asphalt that softened in the stifling summers and broke apart into potholes in the bitter winters. . . . Most of the stores were run by gentiles, but some were owned by Orthodox Jews, members of the Hasidic sects in the area. They could be seen behind their counters, wearing black skullcaps, full beards, and long earlocks, eking out their meager livelihoods and dreaming of Shabbat [Sabbath] and festivals when they could close their stores and turn their attention to their prayers, their rabbi, their God. Every Orthodox Jew sent his male children to a yeshiva, a Jewish*

parochial school, where they studied from eight or nine in the morning to four or five in the evening. On Fridays the students were let out at about one o'clock to prepare for the Shabbat. Jewish education was compulsory for the Orthodox, and because this was [the United States] and not Europe, English education was compulsory as well—so each student carried a double burden: Hebrew studies in the mornings and English studies in the afternoons. The test of intellectual excellence, however, had been reduced by tradition and unvoiced unanimity to a single area of study: Talmud. Virtuosity in Talmud was the achievement most sought after by every student of a yeshiva, for it was the automatic guarantee of a reputation for brilliance.[3]

Contrast this picture with one most teachers in the United States could paint of a typical high school serving a local community. The metaphysical environment of the school would not figure so prominently in the group's thinking, so the religious emphasis would not be apparent. As the social environment might be more important, more time would be given to sports and social activities. One symbol of a student's success and achievement might be whether he or she made one of the many sports teams. Many extracurricular provisions would be made—in the Jewish school there would be little spare time for them—and the timetable would be arranged in a way that would provide opportunities for students to select a wide variety of courses. A high school student's reputation for brilliance in sports might take the place of the reputation for knowledge of the Talmud aimed at by the yeshiva student.

Other organizational differences would be apparent. The yeshiva would be single-sex, for boys only; the high school would be coed. The students of the yeshiva would be obliged to wear some semblance of a uniform, if only a yarmulke or other head covering, at all times. High school students have won the right to wear what they like to school. Discipline would probably not be as strict in the high school as in the yeshiva. All these and many other contrasts you could list emphasize that the two institutional agencies are trying to implement different aims and values contained in two different charters. Knowing something about their respective social groups' cultures enables us to understand the reasons for these obvious differences.

Cultural Program of an Institutional Agency

Much as a computer is programmed by software containing instructions, so an institutional agency's ideology, organization, structure, and operation are programmed by instructions and information that enable it to function properly. They also provide people in the agency with the necessary knowledge and ideas about what behaviors are appropriate and what are not, together with the rules and routines to follow. All these instructions, knowledge, and information are selected from the society's culture.

Culture defines the meanings of all the things with which the group is concerned. It includes some traditional knowledge and ideas about a whole range of issues and survival problems the society has faced in the past and may want to use in the present without modification. Culture also includes the gradually evolving knowledge and ideas that are accumulating as the society faces new problems or as it develops in anticipation of future survival problems.

It is important to recognize that a group's cultural program is never static, but evolves under new adaptation pressures. As some customs and traditions cease to have adaptive value, they are discarded in time and new ones are adopted to suit changing conditions. Change also results when ideas are brought in from contact with other groups, either directly or through the mass media.

One kind of contact that leads to people's acquiring new cultural knowledge and ideas occurs during immigration to another society and consequent exposure to its culture. Immigrants rapidly discover that they have to learn the customary ways of doing things and coping with all sorts of new survival problems and institutional agencies.

This learning is not all one-way, that is, from the receiving society to the immigrants. They bring some new cultural knowledge and ideas into the receiving society because culture is *portable*. That is, once people's behavior and minds are programmed with their culture from birth, it is carried around wherever they go. Some parts of this personal culture are retained for a long time; other parts are changed as a result of exposure to new ideas and knowledge.

MALADAPTIVE CULTURE

This portability of culture has both advantages and disadvantages. When an immigrant group first arrives in a strange receiving society, the traditions and customs in the group's culture provide a source of reassurance and comfort, even though they may not be completely adaptive to its new environments. As time goes on, however, the traditions and customs have increasingly less pragmatic survival value. In other words, they become *maladaptive*. In effect, they are cultural programs that have been frozen as they were when the groups arrived from their countries of origin. Another term for maladaptive cultures is *fossilized cultures*.

Such cultures may provide a source of stability for the original first-generation immigrants, but what of their children, the second generation, who never knew the culture of the old country at first hand? This kind of situation can lead to the children of immigrant parents being caught between two cultures, that of their parents and that of the receiving society into which they have been born. A Greek girl in a high school in Melbourne, Australia, talks about her life and the effect on it of her parents' fossilized culture, which has not been significantly changed during the thirty years since they emigrated from a Greek village:

> **Ellie**
> *My mum [mother] was telling me there are two daughters in her family. Her parents couldn't hack it [cope] because there were two daughters, and they always wanted a son, and it makes you feel unwanted.*
>
> *It's really hard to know if it's because you're Greek or whether it's because they're like that, and they're just being parents. Is it the way they grew up and the way they were brought up is the way you're being brought up? The thing is the Greeks now in Greece are given so much freedom now that we would not think of having [in Melbourne], and just because our parents came here and they brought their customs here, and that's why it's only the Greeks in Australia. . . . They came with traditions that are really old, and they come to a new country where it's really free. They are really vulnerable so they stick to those things. It's only the Greeks in Australia or Melbourne in particular. They're scared to change.*[4]

BASIC IDEAS ABOUT CULTURE

Knowledge and ideas are at the heart of culture, but if this is all culture consists of, then it is very much all in the mind. Social life is more than this, as it consists of behaviors or actions as well as ideas. But when we watch people behaving or carrying out actions in repetitive, patterned ways or customs, we are not seeing bits of a group's culture. Instead, we are seeing the embodiment of a cultural program. In short, behavior is not culture; rather, behavior "contains" it.

Similarly, the thousands of material artifacts a society produces and uses are not strictly culture, even though this is probably one of the commonest ways of thinking about culture. Both behaviors and artifacts contain culture in that ideas and knowledge are embodied or coded in them. They are *cultural forms,* not strictly the program of culture itself. When we want to describe a group's way of life in any detailed way, that is, by giving a "thick description," as anthropologist Clifford Geertz has put it, both the cultural program and cultural forms need to be included.[5]

Culture provides the knowledge and ideas *of* and *for* behavior.[6] That is, people have to know the kinds of knowledge and ideas they must have to carry out a certain kind of behavior properly (*for* behavior) and also to understand what the behavior they see is all about (*of* or *about* behavior).

For example, unless we know the meaning of an action such as using chopsticks, these implements remain just bits of wood, bone, or ivory. We have to acquire the knowledge and ideas about what they mean and what they are used for that are coded into them. If we are members of the social group that uses such implements, we will know the code by virtue of knowing the culture. A stranger in the group would have to watch chopstick-using behavior or ask for instructions in order to learn the code.

Even then, the stranger might not learn all the subtleties of chopstick use immediately but would have to be acquainted with the social group for a long time before finding out that there are rules of politeness and etiquette surrounding the apparently simple process of eating with chopsticks. This tells us that even the instinctive biological need to satisfy hunger has to be carried out in a culturally programmed way.

The chopsticks example also shows that two kinds of behavior can be involved even in such an everyday routine as eating. The first is *instrumental behavior,* which is used to get things done and is programmed by instrumental knowledge from the culture. The second is *expressive behavior.* This overlaps with instrumental behavior but is more concerned with expressing important beliefs, ideas, and values. Politeness and etiquette are not really needed when eating and when using the relevant instrumental behavior, but they are expressions of preferences about the way to eat, the values placed on the food, and the kinds of surroundings in which to eat.

Expressive behavior is an important part of religious rituals. It may not appear to do anything in the instrumental sense, but it expresses important beliefs and ideas to worshipers. However, even rituals that appear to do nothing concrete may have the important function of bringing psychological comfort to the worshipers. Rituals can be important ways of alleviating feelings of frustration or anxiety in times of crises such as floods, tornadoes, and other natural disasters. In this way, even religious rituals can be said to have instrumental functions.

Finally, it is important to keep in mind that persons in a social group need not all follow its cultural program. In most societies, such a program provides a broad range of options, and there will always be people who modify some of the cultural program and behave independently. Each individual can develop a personal culture. Sometimes "doing their own thing" becomes maladaptive for survival, and they can become isolates (remember, culture is primarily a shared program), or even not survive in a very real sense and die. Others who reject the cultural program offend against a society's code of rules and standards and are classed as deviants by the legal institutional agencies and punished.

DISTINGUISHING BETWEEN SUBGROUPS IN SOCIETY

All social groups face different survival problems and have to adapt to many kinds of environments. There is a great variety of cultures and cultural forms around the world. Equally, in most pluralist societies, there are different kinds of subgroups, each of which draws on its own survival programs in adapting to and surviving in its environments.

The subgroups within a pluralist society can be distinguished by outsiders, or they can distinguish themselves because of the characteristics their members share. The most common of these characteristics are social class, ethnicity, racial (phenotypical) differences, and possibly even gender differences. Such subgroups are also likely to have evolved distinctive cultures to program their adaptation to the environments in which they live. Thus, it is possible to refer to social-class cultures, ethnic group cultures, racial group cultures, and even to male and female cultures.

The concept of ethnic group has become prominent in recent literature about pluralism and needs to be clarified. A useful definition of an ethnic group has been provided by Theodorson and Theodorson:

> *A group with a common cultural tradition and a sense of identity which exists as a subgroup of a larger society. The members of an ethnic group differ with regard to certain cultural characteristics from the other members of their society. They may have their own language and religion as well as certain distinctive customs. Probably most important is their feeling of identification as a traditionally distinct group.*[7]

This definition serves for the purposes of this chapter, but it is important to know that some ethnic groups may be *culturally* similar to the wider society yet remain separate and distinct because of their *feelings of identification*. In effect, an ethnic group is not invariably a cultural group. Similarly, racial groups are often thought of as ethnic groups because the shared phenotypical characteristics of their members provide the basis of self-identification and identification by those outside the group.

However, a racial group is different from an ethnic group in one important respect. Members of a racial group cannot easily alter the phenotypical characteristics that distinguish them from members of the wider society; in other words, phenotypical characteristics are immutable. In contrast, members of an ethnic group can shed their cultural customs, abandon their language, and even change religion.

No matter how they are distinguished, subgroups have to take part in activities associated with the wider *public domain* of the pluralist society in which they are situated. For example, in the United States, as in most Western societies, there is one system of law, one currency and medium of exchange, one language of commerce and daily interaction, and one system of government, to mention only a few institutions that all members of a society share. However, in the *private domain* of group life, such as ethnic festivals, religious observances, and recreational and sporting activities, there can be many variations. Members of each subgroup need not share such activities with other groups but can take part in their own.

These differences produce a rich variety of cultural forms in cities inhabited by many ethnic groups. In one part of outer Melbourne, Australia, for example, one can come across Italians playing *bocce* (a kind of lawn bowling) in the park, while down on the seafront a Greek Orthodox priest blesses the fishing fleet and Greek boys dive for the cross he tosses into the water. On a nearby playing field, two ethnic teams, Croatia and Hellas, play soccer and are urged on by supporters in their respective languages. A week earlier there would have been a German Oktoberfest in another outer suburb, with all the dancing, beer drinking, and festivity one associates with this cultural occasion.

VALUES IN THE CULTURAL PROGRAMS

All this variety of cultural forms reflects the respective subgroups' preferences about how to arrange their cultural survival programs. These preferences are termed *values,* and, according to Valentine, "include the ideals, the aims and ends, the ethical and aesthetic standards, and the criteria of knowledge and wisdom embodied within it, taught to and modified by each human genera-tion."[8] A cultural program is a reflection of the values that interpenetrate and lock it together as a unique complex.

Values provide the guidelines that enable individuals and groups to main-tain common goals. For example, such democratic values as free speech, equal-ity before the law, justice, freedom, and national pride provide broad standards from which more precise rules (norms) and sanctions (rewards and punishments) can be derived to guide the behavior of all people who make up the group.

These broad standards are the kinds of values most social groups would want to maintain. However, people can have strong emotional feelings toward the values of the subgroup to which they belong. This is a normal and healthy feature of social life; but when two or more subgroups have strong emotional attachments to extreme kinds of values, tensions can develop. This tension occurs because each subgroup maintains that its values alone are correct and should be adopted by all other subgroups. Such a situation can occur in a culturally pluralist society, and to preserve harmony it may be necessary for the common legal system shared by all groups to impose laws that will ensure that conflict does not occur.

Importance of Value Orientations or World Views

A broader category of value concerns a social group's "world views" or value orientations. These are "broad-gauge propositions concerning what people feel positively about: they influence both the means and ends of striving."[9] The following six value orientations were used to study life in an Orthodox Jewish School in Melbourne, Australia.[10]

1. *Human-supernature orientation*—value judgments and existential propositions about the nature of and human relationships with the metaphysical environment. Examples are beliefs in a God, many gods, or atheism.

2. *Human-nature orientation*—value judgments and existential propositions about human relationships with and use of the natural environment. Examples are the value placed on conserving biotic resources and preserving them from damage, as the underlying philosophy of the Greenpeace organization illustrates, as opposed to the exploitation of natural resources by mining or timber companies.

3. *Human-habitat orientation*—value judgments and existential propositions about the way to design and create a human-made environment. Examples are the concrete jungles in many inner-city areas versus the spacious parks and open spaces preserved as green belts around towns. The highly stylized layout of a Japanese garden is an excellent example of the value placed on arranging the immediate human-made habitat to reflect a sense of harmony and control.

4. *Human-relational orientation*—value judgments and existential propositions about the way to conduct relationships in the social environment. Examples are groups that stress the value of communal living in harmony with one another versus groups that are suspicious of outsiders and live within closed areas to guard their privacy, as occurs in some parts of rural Greece.

5. *Human-activity orientation*—value judgments and existential propositions about the kinds of endeavors carried out individually or as a member of a group in the social environment. Examples are valuing work for its own sake more than getting by with minimal effort.

6. *Human-time orientation*—value judgments and existential propositions about how to use time on a micro-scale and on a macro-scale. Examples are the future-time orientation of many Western societies versus the past-time orientation of some peasant communities; the emphasis put on not wasting time versus being able to do nothing and let time slip by.

Influence of Values and World Views on Adaptation

All social groups are able to exercise choices about how they will adapt to environmental pressures. But the range of choices depends on the level of economic, technical, and social development of the social group in question. Choices of *adaptational styles* also reflect the group's value orientations or world views. The following two descriptions illustrate the contrasts between the ways two societies—British settlers and Australian Aborigines—adapted in colonial times.[11] What kinds of values and value orientations can be detected?

The British Style of Adaptation
Land was an economic resource and the basis of considerable social status and power in Britain. Although it also had some sentimental importance, land could be sold and title to the estate transferred to new owners, because it was a possession like any other good. The British were thus able to move away from a piece of land they sold without a great emotional wrench if it was advantageous to do so. While

occupying land, they were able to farm it and hunt on it without seeing how these two activities might be incompatible.

Possessions and material goods, of which land formed a part, were at the heart of British culture. Early settlers thus followed a similar pattern of establishing private ownership of land in a tangible way by fencing or tilling it, grazing herds of cattle or flocks of sheep on it, building houses and making equipment to further utilize the land. In this they were exploitative, having little regard for the delicate ecological balance in which the land had existed for centuries. They legitimated this activity by their religious, Christian ideology which can be summed up by the term "Protestant ethic."

The Aboriginal Style of Adaptation

The spiritual importance of the land was as compelling as, or even transcended, the economic importance of the land. Its physical features were often of totemic significance, thus embracing both social and cosmological realms. Land could neither be owned, held in title, nor sold or transferred; such concepts being alien to Aboriginal thinking. One could not be separated from nor leave one's land without being emotionally affected to the very core of one's being. Separation from places meant separation from everything that held the key to Aboriginal understanding of life and regeneration of the world, its natural and social resources. Separation from their land for Aborigines meant losing a vital part of their reason for existence in spiritual terms, if not also in purely physical or temporal terms.

For such a view, the British violated sacred sites and desecrated the land by the exploitative use they made of it. Thus the co-existence of farming and hunting techniques were not possible and could not be condoned. They offended the static conservative approach to land that was basic to Aboriginal thinking, and attempted to preserve resources from excessive exploitation, so maintaining the delicate balance of natural species essential to economic survival and the totemic order of religious life.

TRANSMISSION OF A CULTURAL PROGRAM

A culture must be transmitted to each new generation of children if the social group is not to collapse and be absorbed into another society or even become extinct. This follows from the way we have thought of culture as a social group's survival program. Without such a culture and the action systems it programs, a group's survival is threatened, so it is necessary for every person in the group to learn as much of the program as possible.

The ultimate aim of the cultural transmission (enculturation) process is to produce a member of a social group who embodies its culture. The following description of a Japanese man describes such a member:

If you knew of a man named Hashimoto, who spoke only Japanese, ate by preference rice and raw fish, wore a kimono in a home made of bamboo and paper, was enthusiastic about flower arrangements and tea ceremonies, venerated his Emperor as a God, and died by committing suicide because of an insult, you would not only know that he was Japanese, but almost how long ago he lived. . . . You would also know that he had not done all these things out of instinct; that he must have been taught this language, these tastes, these ideas, and for no better reason than that these were the ones the Japanese people happened to have invented, borrowed, and developed before Mr. Hashimoto was born among them.[12]

The key to the cultural transmission process is the language of the social group. This is its system of signs and symbols by which knowledge and meanings are passed on to everyone within the group and particularly to each new generation.

Signs and symbols are not strictly the same but tend to get confused in everyday use. Cultural signs are objects that stand for something else by cultural convention. For example, a red traffic light is a signal for a motor vehicle to stop. Most languages consist of sets of signs. Natural signs or signals need not have a similar arbitrary meaning; for example, smoke is a sign (signal) of fire.[13]

Symbols are somewhat different. They are able to convey abstract meanings and are often used in expressive and ritual behavior to say something important that cannot be said easily in another way. For example, *flag* is the term for a piece of colored and patterned fabric, but the term can express a symbolic message. When people salute the flag, they are reacting to a symbolic message that communicates many things to them about the power and glory of their nation.

Because many religious beliefs cannot be expressed directly, symbols are used extensively in that context to convey important ideas to worshipers. Take the plus sign (+), which in everyday language stands for a cross. In the different language of the Christian religion it becomes the symbol for a crucifix and expresses a whole cluster of beliefs and sentiments about the crucifixion of Jesus Christ. Symbols are thus important ways of communicating ideas about the metaphysical environment.

The problem with signals, signs, and symbols is that their arbitrary meaning can vary from culture to culture. This becomes apparent when one visits another society and gets involved in cross-cultural communication. Take just two simple examples. In traditional Greek culture, the bodily sign or signal for "no" is a *nod* of the head up and down. The sign or signal for "yes" is a *shake* of the head from side to side. Communication between a Greek and someone from another group can be confusing unless both sides know the cultural conventions for "yes" and "no." Even such a simple action as using a *lift* (English term) or *elevator* (American term) can be confusing unless one knows that "G" stands for "Ground Floor" in a lift and for "Floor 1" in an elevator.

SUMMARY: THE MEANING OF CULTURE

We can now bring together all the ideas discussed above in a summary of what culture means:

■ Social groups inherit and further develop cultural programs that are used to organize activities in the institutional agencies or action systems through which the groups survive in and modify their environments. There are broadly three of these: the physical environment, the social environment, and the metaphysical (other worldly) environment.

■ The core of a social group's cultural program consists of knowledge and conceptions that are public, in the sense of being shared by most members of the social group.

■ The knowledge and conceptions are embodied in the behaviors and artifacts of the social group's members; that is, the cultural program provides the knowledge *for* and *of* behavior and artifacts. Behaviors and artifacts are termed *cultural forms.*

■ Another essential component of a cultural program consists of the values a group subscribes to; these values broadly control the group's preferences about how its cultural forms should be organized.

■ Knowledge, conceptions, and values are transmitted among present members of the social group and to those who are born into it through systems of communication, the most important of which are signs and symbols.

■ Part of the cultural program has evolved historically as the social group has adapted to its environments over time. Other parts of the program represent how the social group has modified outdated adaptation strategies to suit its assessment of its present environmental conditions or has added to its own culture by borrowing from other groups and their cultures.

■ More parts of the cultural program consist of the knowledge and conceptions that the group devises to anticipate and cope with its assessment of future problems.

THE MULTICULTURAL SOCIETY

As we saw above, pluralist societies are made up of subgroups that differ from each other on various grounds: social class, ethnicity, race, culture, gender. A number of terms have been used to refer to such societies. The most common description is *multicultural,* which implies the existence of many (multi-) cultures within one society.

As we stress from the outset, people in a multicultural society are not members of these different cultures. They are members of the various subgroups making up the society, each of which is programmed by its own culture. Even this is an oversimplification. Subgroup cultures also overlap and interpenetrate each other, so people do not belong exclusively to one subgroup but have to move in and out of several action systems every day and use the appropriate cultural program belonging to each. Members of subgroups also have to participate in the action systems in the public domain of the wider society.

For example, imagine what life might be like for the following family living in a pluralist Western society. (Our portrayal is a stereotype at some points.) The husband and wife start their day by using the culturally patterned behavior and artifacts appropriate to the institutional agency of the family to prepare breakfast and get the children off to school (another institutional agency) and themselves off to work. The husband's job is in the civil service (another institutional agency); the wife works in a firm of lawyers (another institutional agency). In their respective jobs, husband and wife have to adopt the appropriate cultural forms to function effectively.

In the evening, the whole family goes out to eat in a Chinese restaurant and has to adopt ethnic cultural customs for this kind of action system. On Sunday, the family goes to church because another subgroup to which the family belongs believes in the Christian metaphysical environment. The family uses the religious knowledge, ideas, and beliefs appropriate to that action system.

On paper, this sequence looks very complicated. In fact, it is one with which many people cope every day throughout their lives. As a consequence, in a complex Western society everyone needs a great deal of knowledge about the various subcultures and the institutional agencies they program to enable them to cope successfully with daily living.

Teachers Need Cross-Cultural Sensitivity

This also means that teachers cannot rely on the cultural knowledge appropriate to their own social groups if they want to work effectively in the multicultural classroom, in which children from many ethnic groups may be present. For example, in some inner-city high schools in Melbourne, a class may contain children from as many as twenty different ethnic backgrounds. Teachers need to be sensitive to the possible ways that the cultures of these students may influence their behaviors, perceptions, and attitudes.

Dilemmas for Teachers

Teachers should be aware that sometimes one cultural program interferes with another and poses special problems. For example, girls' gender roles can be influenced by their membership in an ethnic group and by the need to work with boys in class and possibly by boys' and teachers' gender roles. The following conversation about gender relationships took place among a group of year 11 Greek girls in a Melbourne high school in response to the researcher's opening question.

> Q: They had a kind of equal opportunity course here, didn't they?
> A: That was for the teachers so they could become aware of sex discrimination in the form, like letting the boys get away with murder, and not letting the girls because boys are meant to be rowdy and boisterous and the girls are not (first girl).
> Q: Do you think they are?
> A: Yes [emphatically from most girls in the group], Mrs. H. she lets the boys get away with everything. She lets them swear, sometimes she lets the girls get away with things too. . . . When you think about it the girls don't fool around as much . . . in Greek families; it [spoiling boys] exists very much (second girl).
> A: When I say things like why can my brother go out they [my parents] say 'he's a boy . . . and can't get pregnant,' and that's it (third girl).
> Q: Do girls get resigned to this if they're from migrant backgrounds, or do they fight about it? How strong is the feminist movement?
> A: It's quite strong . . . getting stronger. Equal opportunity is quietly strong among Greek women (first girl).
> A: Our modern Greek teacher, he's the biggest chauvinist in the school. Last year A ____ and myself we were so feminist and sticking up for our rights, we got into so much trouble. He thinks that women should stay at home and have kids every couple of years or so, and do the housework and that's it. I bet if he had a daughter he would probably drown the poor baby (second girl).
> A: In Greece, like, they have sons because they don't have to leave them any dowry, and the son can have the second name (fourth girl).[14]

Other kinds of cultural practices can be more extreme. For example, what should a teacher do if he or she comes across a Turkish boy giving his sister a severe beating outside the school gates because he saw her talking to boys during the morning recess? In Turkish culture, a very strong value is placed on a girl's honor, and the boy was putting into effect the norms and sanctions associated with such a value. However, Western societies are not so strict, and this kind of situation can place an Anglo teacher in a dilemma of not knowing whether to intervene and criticize such a traditional practice in the interests of the girl, or to ignore it and allow a harmful situation to continue that might even lead to serious injury.

On the one hand, it would be easy and understandable for the teacher to make an *assumption of normative equivalence*. This extension of Tom Wolfe's idea of "moral equivalence" holds that another cultural group's standards, values, and norms are equivalent to one's own.[15] One can then use this assumption as grounds for criticizing what one finds objectionable in the culture of the other group, even though it may be quite permissible to that group's members. However, when teachers do this, they risk being labeled "culturally insensitive" or even "racist."

On the other hand, teachers can adopt a philosophy of *naive* culture relativism. This philosophy maintains that every cultural program is unique and should not be criticized on the basis of another culture's values. Thus, teachers may overlook and not criticize cultural practices that may be valid in their own cultural context but would not be condoned if they occurred in the teachers' own social group.

The basic right of members of minority groups to have the integrity of their cultures respected is stated in the International Covenant on Civil and Political Rights (Article 27):

> In those States in which ethnic, religious or linguistic minorities exist, persons belonging to such minorities shall not be denied the right, in community with other members of their group, to enjoy their own culture, to profess and practice their own religion, or to use their own language.

The phrase "in community with other members of their group" suggests a way out of the teacher's dilemma. Cultural customs could be immune from criticism provided they occur within the action system of an ethnic community. However, when the same customs occur in another action system, such as a school, which is programmed by the public culture shared by many groups, the rules of the public action system must surely apply. We met this problem on a larger scale earlier in this chapter, and the principle was advocated then that the public good should prevail in situations in which group conflict is generated by competing value systems. It seems appropriate that the same principle should be applied, on a smaller scale, to what occurs in a multicultural school.

Teachers working in multicultural classrooms, however, should try to be sensitive to the many cultural variations they are likely to encounter. In particular, they must be aware that children from different cultural backgrounds have been "programmed" with their group's *subjective culture* during their enculturation. *Subjective culture* is defined by Harry Triandis as the characteristic way in which a cultural group perceives and responds to its social environment.[16]

A conscientious teacher thus might make it his or her business to learn something about the subjective cultures of those children from different ethnic groups in the class. This knowledge will give the teacher a basis from which to make a value judgment about whether an apparently objectionable cultural custom can be condoned.

Recognition of Issues Involving Power

The example of the Turkish boy involved another factor. This is the power he held over his sister because of her gender, and we could have used the perspective of sexism to analyze what occurred. But the incident was still one that was confined mainly to the private culture of a Turkish community. However, teachers need to be aware that there is a wider issue at stake when working in the multicultural classroom. This is the way multicultural education programs can avoid tackling major differences in ethnic communities' access to socioeconomic power and social rewards in the wider world, and its public culture and action systems.

The distinction we made earlier in this chapter between instrumental and expressive aspects of culture provides a basis for our understanding the wider issue of power. Instrumental culture enables a group to achieve *life chances* in the form of economic gains and rewards from its environment. To do this, the group usually has to compete with other groups and use its instrumental culture to best advantage in the competition that occurs in the public spheres of a pluralist society.

On the other hand, the expressive side of culture need not be used to gain the same kinds of rewards; it is concerned mainly with enhancing the group's *life-style.* This is usually confined to the private spheres of a pluralist society in the ethnic communities themselves.

It is necessary to recognize that this distinction between life chances and life-styles risks being an oversimplification of what can actually take place. There is always some overlap between private and public spheres of life, but following Melvin Tumin we are using the distinction to make the point that teachers need to be aware of the two sides of the cultures they will meet in the multicultural classroom.[17]

This necessity applies particularly when teachers use multicultural curriculum materials. These can stress life-styles; for example, the history, heritage, traditions, and customs of cultural groups in the society. Or the materials can stress life chances and deal with problems cultural groups face in gaining equal economic opportunity in the wider society.

The latter approach is not common in many multicultural courses, but it is necessary to ensure that young people leaving the school gain a realistic picture of how a pluralist society operates and have some chance of coping effectively in it. In essence, multicultural education programs should be "politicized" and made more radical so that issues of power and control are tackled and are not covered up by teaching only the often-romanticized aspects of ethnic life-styles.[18]

As we saw when describing institutions, pluralism entails members of various subgroups engaging in the power-controlling institutional agencies, such as political organizations, legal systems, and big businesses. Most of these agencies are controlled by the members of the dominant group in society, and a fairer share of power can be gained only by competing with them, using the knowledge and ideas of their appropriate cultural programs.

Many members of other subgroups, such as recent immigrants, lack such knowledge, so it is difficult for them to compete effectively. Unless they are vigilant, ethnic subgroups may find that multiculturalism can be confined largely to encouraging local, recreational, and other kinds of institutional agencies programmed more by the expressive side of culture than by the instrumental side. Such agencies concentrate on the life-styles of subgroups rather than on their life chances. This one-sided approach gives the impression that the agencies are assisting ethnic groups, but in effect they are doing little to overcome the institutionalized ways by which members of subgroups are denied a fair share of economic power and social rewards.

CONCLUSION

Teachers in multicultural classrooms should be aware of the problems discussed in this chapter. Pluralism is a worldwide phenomenon, and understanding it necessitates the use of appropriate concepts and models. Those of culture, institutional agency or action system, and values provide powerful tools to aid our understanding of the kind of society in which most of us live.

The key concept we discuss in this chapter is culture. We define culture in terms of a group's survival device. This consists of the public knowledge and conceptions embodied in the behavior and artifacts, or cultural forms, that enable the group to adapt to three kinds of environments: the natural, the social, and the metaphysical.

Culture has an expressive side and an instrumental side, and both sides need to be kept in mind when teaching students from diverse cultural backgrounds. The main danger is that a teacher will concentrate only on the expressive side by adopting multicultural programs that stress an ethnic group's customs, heritage, history, and aesthetic aspects. This approach risks ignoring the more sensitive side of ethnic group life, namely, that students must be educated to go out into the pluralist world as adults and make a living in competition with others.

Only by honestly confronting power relationships in a pluralist society will we be able to help students take their places in it. If we can tailor multicultural education programs to this end, perhaps young people will be less inhibited by the frustrations that we ourselves may have experienced in trying to understand why we live as we do. Thus, by being treated honestly in matters of power and control, young people may be encouraged to develop more realistic sets of values rather than suffer the disillusionment and alienation so apparent in many schools.

QUESTIONS AND ACTIVITIES

1. How do the teaching implications of multicultural education differ if culture is defined as (a) the heritage and traditions of a social group or (b) a social group's design for surviving in and adapting to its environment?

2. Which definition of culture above (a or b) does Bullivant prefer? Why?

3. What is the difference between *society* and *culture?* How are these concepts related?

4. Name three kinds of environments to which social groups must adapt. How does knowledge about each environment help us understand a particular group and its culture?

5. Spend several days observing in a local public school and in a parochial school in your community or region. Describe how the ideology, that is, the beliefs, values, and ideas, of the two schools differ. In what ways are the two schools alike? Share your observations with your classmates or fellow workshop participants.

6. Interview several teachers who work in a school that has a population of immigrant students. Ask them about special problems these students experience and what the school is doing to ease their adjustment to U.S. society and culture. Talk to some of the immigrant students about their experiences in the school and in U.S. society. Compare the views of the teachers and students. How are they alike? How are they different? Why?

7. What are values? How do they help a group maintain common goals? What problems develop when the values of groups within a multicultural society conflict? Can the schools help solve these problems? Why or why not? If they can, how?

8. How does cultural knowledge about various groups help teachers work more effectively in multicultural classrooms?

9. Bullivant notes that multicultural materials can focus on *life-styles* or on *life chances*. Which approach to multicultural education does he prefer, and why?

10. Spend several days observing boys and girls in the classroom, on the playground, and in other areas of the school. Pay particular attention to the ways boys and girls interact with teachers, especially in different subjects, such as mathematics and social studies. Based on your observations, write a short paper describing whether there are distinct male and female cultures in that school.

NOTES

1. Louis Schneider and Charles Bonjean, eds., *The Idea of Culture in the Social Sciences* (Cambridge: Cambridge University Press, 1973), p. 119.

2. Talcott Parsons, *Societies: Evolutionary and Comparative Perspectives* (New York: Prentice-Hall, 1966).

3. Chaim Potok, *The Chosen* (London: Heinemann, 1967), pp. 11–12.

4. Brian M. Bullivant, *Getting a Fair Go: Case Studies of Occupational Socialization and Percep-*tions of Discrimination in a Sample of Seven Melbourne High Schools* (Canberra: Australian Government Publishing Service, 1986), p. 224. Also in Brian M. Bullivant, *The Ethnic Encounter in the Secondary School* (Lewes: Falmer Press, 1987).

5. Clifford Geertz, *The Interpretation of Cultures: Selected Essays* (New York: Basic Books, 1973).

6. Alfred L. Kroeber and Clyde Kluckhohn, *Culture: A Critical Review of Concepts and Definitions*

(Cambridge: Harvard University, Peabody Museum of American Archeology and Ethnology Papers) 47, No. 1 (1952): 181.

7. George A. Theodorson and Achilles G. Theodorson, *A Modern Dictionary of Sociology* (London: Methuen, 1970), p. 135.

8. Charles A. Valentine, *Culture and Poverty: Critique and Counter-Proposals* (Chicago: University of Chicago Press, 1968), p. 7.

9. John J. Honigmann, *Personality in Culture* (New York: Harper and Row, 1967), p. 78.

10. Brian M. Bullivant, *The Way of Tradition: Life in an Orthodox Jewish School* (Melbourne: Australian Council for Educational Research, 1978).

11. Brian M. Bullivant, *Pluralism: Cultural Maintenance and Evolution* (Clevedon, England: Multilingual Matters, 1984), pp. 15–17.

12. Gene Lisitzky, *Four Ways of Being Human: An Introduction to Anthropology* (London: Dobson, 1963), pp. 30–31.

13. John Beattie, *Other Cultures* (London: Cohen & West, 1964), pp. 69–73.

14. Bullivant, *Getting a Fair Go,* p. 223.

15. Tom Wolfe, "Are the USA and the USSR Morally Equivalent?" *Quadrant* (October 1985): 10–18.

16. Harry C. Triandis, *The Analysis of Subjective Culture* (New York: John Wiley, 1972).

17. Melvin M. Tumin and W. Plotch, eds., *Pluralism in a Democratic Society* (New York: Praeger, 1977), p. xiv.

18. Brian M. Bullivant, "Towards Radical Multiculturalism: Resolving Tensions in Curriculum and Educational Planning," in Sohan Modgil et al., eds. *Multicultural Education, The Interminable Debate* (Lewes: The Falmer Press, 1986), pp. 33–47.

CHAPTER 3

Race, Class, Gender, and Disability in the Classroom

■ CARL A. GRANT and CHRISTINE E. SLEETER

Schools have always been a focal point of debate. What should be taught? How should students be organized for instruction? How should teachers be prepared? What constitute acceptable standards? As the 1990s began, several changes and tensions in society fueled renewed debate about schooling.

First, during the 1980s, the United States had to come to terms with its loss of undisputed hegemony in the world trade market. For example, as sales of U.S. automobiles plunged, sales of Japanese automobiles soared. While a variety of interpretations can be given for U.S. world economic status, business developments directed considerable attention to schools. Beginning with *A Nation at Risk* in 1983, a spate of reform reports elaborated on the "rising tide of mediocrity" presumed to be spreading from the schools to the rest of society.[1] Most of these reports advocated raising academic requirements for high school graduation; requiring more math and science and computer literacy, teaching higher-order reasoning, lengthening the school day and year, demanding stricter discipline, making it more difficult to be accepted into college, and improving the quality of teachers. Students at-risk of failure were to be identified and remediated.

Second, the United States experienced tremendous growth in ethnic and racial diversity, especially through immigration, and public debate about what that diversity should mean was prolific. For example, a special issue of *Time* magazine placed actor Edward James Olmos's picture on the cover, under the caption "Magnifico! Hispanic culture breaks out of the barrio."[2] Readers of *Time* in April 1990 were told about problems confronting the United States as it moves "Beyond the melting pot"; the main problem would be learning to "maintain a distinct national identity" that builds on commonalities while embracing ethnic diversity.[3] Most talk centered around trying to identify what we have in common in order to promote national unity. While some people argued that new commonalities could be forged from diverse cultural input, others insisted that all immigrants must be turned into "Americans" who embrace traditional definitions of American culture. Discussions of immigration often publicized Asians as the model minority, attributing their presumed success to their embracing of traditional U.S. culture and values. Educators agreed that schools would need to respond to growing racial and ethnic diversity but disagreed about whether schools should promote cultural assimilation or pluralism.

Third, many middle-class and working-class people in the United States experienced an erosion of their life-styles, and the poverty level rose, especially among women and children. Compared to the postwar economic boom, the 1970s and 1980s were decades in which Americans had to learn to settle for less: fewer jobs were available, prices rose, real income of a large proportion of the population fell, and White middle-class families experienced some of the hard times poor families had always lived with.[4] Many people grew skeptical of their ability or that of their children to achieve the American dream. Studs Terkel listened to people describing their concerns and fears:

> The middle class seems to be disappearing here. You have your working poor and your elite. No matter how well you do, you're never quite able to stay ahead. It's harder and harder for the average person to attain the average American dream.[5]

Furthermore, domestic social problems such as drug use and teen pregnancy seemed to be concentrated in a growing underclass dependent on welfare. Middle-class people in the United States, increasingly concerned about their ability to maintain their own standard of living, became less tolerant of those who were poor, whose numbers grew throughout the decade. As schooling was becoming increasingly a prerequisite for employment, its payoff seemed less certain, and competition for the good jobs seemed keener.

Fourth, racial minority groups experienced tension between achieving steady gains in education, as reflected in years of schooling obtained, SAT scores, and other standardized test scores; and simultaneous lack of economic progress and even erosion of gains in life-style, economic status, and rights. For example, between 1970 and 1987 the White–African American education gap closed from 2.3 years to 3 months.[6] At the same time, however, poverty and unemployment hit minority communities harder than White communities, President Bush vetoed the Civil Rights Act of 1990, and the legality of scholarships for minority students was seriously questioned. These occurrences led to growing frustration. For example, Terkel reported the following comment:

> I think Reagan made it very accepted to be a white bigot. It's the most fashionable thing. Now they say: America is white. America isn't single women on welfare. Why should us taxpayers support these people who ride on our backs and bring this country down? I'm afraid of what's gonna happen to blacks in this country. There are a fortunate few who will get over. But for the many, no way. . . . The dividing line is becoming clear and the bitterness is growing. You can't help but wonder why.[7]

Even Asian Americans, held up as the model group who had made it, were not nearly as successful uniformly as the media suggested. It is revealing that some of the most outspoken critics of this stereotype have been Japanese Americans, the group often touted as most successful.[8] But many people in the United States, seeing White women and people of color in professional and administrative positions, believed racism and sexism were no longer problems. Ironically, despite gains in years of schooling and test scores, following the reform reports of the early 1980s, racial and ethnic minority children were described as "at risk of failure" rather than as "promising achievers."[9]

People in the United States with disabilities also experienced both gains and losses. Although special education had expanded services to students with disabilities in schools, they, too, were disproportionately hit by economic losses and threatened by the raising of standards in schools. A triumph was passage of the Americans with Disabilities Act, designed to protect people with disabilities from discrimination; but some observers adopted a wait-and-see attitude because of many loopholes in the act.[10]

Fifth, the 1980s saw increased scholarship in universities by scholars of color, women, and critical theorists, who developed bodies of research and theory about diversity and social inequality. Universities became actively engaged in promoting diversity. The amount of research and curriculum that was multicultural mushroomed, advancing perspectives that differed in some cases sharply from those of most political and economic leaders.

All of this may seem removed from you and your classroom. But students whose parents have been experiencing the tensions discussed here are in your classroom, and local community and business leaders as well as spokespeople for oppressed groups are probably recommending what they believe schools should do to address the current social issues.

A major thread running through the debates about schooling is the relative importance of preparing students for jobs versus preparing them as citizens. Schools have always done both, but recently much of the talk about what schools should do has emphasized job preparation and maintained silence about citizenship. What kind of a nation do we want for ourselves and our children, given the challenges and problems we have been facing? How should limited resources be distributed, given our diversity and virtually everyone's desire for a good life? How should we address the fact that there are not enough good jobs to go around?

Most students we teach usually give one of three reasons for wanting to become teachers: (1) they love kids, (2) they want to help students, (3) they want to make school more exciting than when they were students. If one of these is the reason you chose to enter the teaching profession, then we hope you will see the demographic and social trends described above as being challenging and will realize that your love and help are needed, not just for some students, but for *all* students.

This chapter discusses the importance of race, class, gender, and disability in classroom life and provides alternative approaches to dealing with these issues in the classroom.

RACE, CLASS, GENDER, DISABILITY, AND CLASSROOM LIFE

Ask yourself what you know about race, class, gender, and disability as they apply to classroom life. Could you write one or two good paragraphs about what these words mean? How similar or different would your meanings be from those of your classmates? How much do these ascribed characteristics influence the way you think about teaching? If you and your classmates organize into small discussion groups (try it) and listen closely to each other, you will probably notice some distinct differences in the ways you see the importance of these factors. The point of such an exercise is not to show that you have different ideas and interpretations, but that each of you clearly understands what your ideas and interpretations mean for working with your students: How will you bring excellence and equity to your teaching?

Race, social class, and gender are used to construct major groups of people in society. On your college application form, you were probably asked to indicate your race, gender, and parents' place of employment. Most institutions want to know your color, sex, and social-class background. This information provides the institution with the ability to analyze and report data related to any or all of your ascribed characteristics (and to get into your business). Social scientists studying school practices often report results according to race, class, or gender. As a teacher, it is essential for you to understand the importance of how the ascribed characteristics of race, class, and gender can influence your knowledge and understanding of your students. It is also important for you to consider these ascribed characteristics collectively and not separately. Each of your students is a member of all three status groups, and these simultaneous memberships influence their perceptions and actions.

For example, a child in the classroom is not just Asian American but also male and middle class. Thus, he is linked with an oppressed racial group, but he is also linked with a gender group and a social class that historically have oppressed others. Therefore his view of reality and his actions based on that view will differ from those of a middle-class Asian American girl or a lower-class Asian American boy. A teacher's failure to consider the integration of race, social class, and gender could lead at times to an oversimplified or inaccurate understanding of what occurs in schools, and therefore to an inappropriate or simplistic prescription for educational equity and excellence. You may have noticed, for example, teachers assuming (often mistakenly) that middle- and lower-class Mexican American students identify strongly with each other and that they view issues in much the same way, or that African American male students have the same goals and views as African American female students.

As you are exposed to the media, be alert to how ascribed characteristics are used or not used. Listen to how other teachers talk among themselves about students. Do the teachers refer to the students' race, gender, or socioeconomic class when discussing their educational performance or social life? Do their comments reflect stereotypes or biases? Do they discuss these ascribed characteristics in an integrated or separate manner? Paying attention to these questions will help you develop a keen understanding of the importance of race, class, and gender in classroom life.

We reviewed most of the multicultural education literature written in the English-speaking world—more than 200 journal articles and 68 books—and discovered that educators often work with students of color, students from low-income backgrounds, and White female students according to one of five approaches.[11] As we briefly explain these approaches, ask yourself which one you are most comfortable using in your teaching.

Before we begin this discussion, you should understand two important points. First, space does not allow for a complete discussion of each approach; for a thorough discussion, please refer to *Making Choices for Multicultural Education: Five Approaches to Race, Class and Gender.*[12] Second, if you discover that you are a true eclectic or that none of the approaches satisfies your teaching style, that is fine, as long as you are not straddling the fence. Indecision, dissatisfaction, and frustration in teaching style and technique may confuse your students. Also, to be the dynamic teacher you want to be, you need a teaching philosophy that is well thought out and makes learning exciting for your students. Good teaching requires that you have a complete understanding of what you are doing in the classroom and how you are doing it.

APPROACHES TO MULTICULTURAL EDUCATION

Teaching the Exceptional and Culturally Different

If you believe that a teacher's chief responsibility is to prepare students of color, special-education students, White female students, and low-income students to fit into and achieve well within the existing classroom and later in adult society, this approach may be particularly appealing to you. It may be especially appealing if these students are behind in the main subject areas of the traditional curriculum. The goals of this approach are to equip such students with the cognitive skills, concepts, information, language, and values required by U.S. society and eventually to enable them to hold a job and function within society's institutions and culture. Teachers using this approach often begin by determining the achievement levels of students who are behind, comparing their achievement to White middle-class students, and then working diligently to help them catch up. Starting where the students are and using instructional techniques and content familiar to the students are important. For example, one teacher who used this approach helped two African American students who had moved from a large urban area to a much smaller college town to catch up on their writing skills by having them write letters to the friends they left in the city. A second teacher grouped the girls in her ninth-grade class who were having problems in algebra, allowing the girls to work together, support one another, and not be intimidated by the boys in the class who had received the kind of socialization that produces good math students. A third teacher provided two students with learning disabilities with materials written at their reading level that covered concepts comparable to those the rest of the class was reading about. A fourth teacher placed two Latino students with limited English-speaking abilities into a transitional bilingual program. A teacher may believe that only one or two students in the classroom need this approach or that all the students in the classroom do, especially if the school is located in an inner-city community or barrio.

This approach argues that there is a corpus of knowledge to be learned, and that any deviation from that content should be temporary. A content deviation should provide knowledge that students should have acquired in previous grades. For example, an English as a Second Language (ESL) program is designed to provide language learning and some cultural information so that children with limited English proficiency can learn the curriculum that the typical English-speaking student is learning.

Instructional procedures may be changed more than the curriculum when using this approach. The teacher knows what he or she wants to teach but may be uncertain about how to reach the students successfully. Some teachers try to use the student's preferred learning style. For example, Shade synthesized research on the learning style of African Americans and concluded that "from all

cultural and social reconstructionist that should be a part of the program in the schools in which the approach is being implemented. First, democracy must be actively practiced in the schools. Having students read the Constitution and hear lectures on the three branches of government is a passive way to learn about democracy. For students to understand democracy they must *live* it. They must understand the importance of politics, debate, social action, and the acquisition of power. Commenting on this point, Banks says that oppressed ethnic groups

> *must also develop a sense of political efficacy, and be given practice in social action strategies which teaches them how to get power without violence and further exclusion. . . . Opportunities for social action, in which students have experience in obtaining and exercising power, should be emphasized within a curriculum that is designed to help liberate excluded ethnic groups.*[29]

In the classroom this means that students will be given the opportunity to direct a good deal of their learning and to learn how to be responsible for that direction. This does not mean that teachers abdicate the running of their classroom to the students, but rather that they guide and direct students so they learn how to learn and develop skills for wise decision making. Shor describes this as helping students become subjects rather than objects in the classroom,[30] and Freire says it will produce women and men "who organize themselves reflectively for action rather than men [and women] who are organized for passivity."[31]

A second practice is that students learn how to analyze their own life circumstances. Anyon tells us that we have a practical consciousness that coexists with a theoretical consciousness. Practical consciousness refers to one's commonsense understanding of one's own life, how "the system" works, and "everyday attempts to resolve the class, race, gender and other contradictions one faces."[32] Theoretical consciousness refers to dominant social ideologies. They are explanations one learns for how the world works, that assume conditions and life in the world are fair and just for everyone.

As you know, these two sets of consciousness do not always mesh; most of us learn to live within the boundaries of both of them. For example, students of color are taught that education is the doorway to success and that if they obey the teacher and do their work they will succeed. However, studies indicate that many students of color who comply with school rules and teachers' requests *still* do not receive the career guidance and school work necessary for becoming successful.[33] Furthermore, education pays off better for Whites than for people of color; for example in 1989, the average full-time working White person with four years of high school earned $24,744, whereas the average African American and Latino full-time worker with the same amount of education earned $19,813 and $20,567 respectively.[34] Education that is multicultural and social reconstructionist teaches students to question what they hear about how society works from other sources and to analyze the experiences of people like themselves to understand more fully how society works so that they can make informed choices when pursuing their own life goals.

A third practice is that students learn social action skills to increase their chances for success with the first two recommended practices. Bennett describes social action skills as "the knowledge, attitudes and skills needed to help students bring about political, social and economic changes."[35] In this approach the school is seen as a laboratory or training ground for preparing students to be more socially active. For example, some stories that elementary school children read could deal with issues involving discrimination and oppression and could suggest ways to deal with such problems. Students of all ages should be taught to identify sexist advertising of products sold in their community and how to take action to encourage advertisers to stop these types of practices. Advocates of this approach do not expect children to reconstruct the world, but they do expect the schools to teach students how to do their part in helping the nation achieve excellence and equity in all areas of life.

A fourth practice is coalescing, or getting the poor, people of color, and White women to work together to advance their common interests. The coalescing of groups across the lines of race, class, gender, and disability is important because it can energize and strengthen the fight against oppression. However, getting groups to work together is difficult because they have their own agendas and believe that they would have to place some of their goals second to those of other groups. For example, Davis has examined the struggle for suffrage for people of color and White women, arguing that White middle-class women distanced themselves from African Americans when they feared African American men rather than White women would achieve voting rights.[36] Similarly, African Americans, Latinos, and Asians find themselves divided along gender and class lines to the extent that middle-class males of all colors fail to take seriously the concerns of women and of lower-class members of their racial groups. Albrecht and Brewer's book, *Bridges of Power: Women's Multicultural Alliances,* addresses concerns and issues women face in attempting to coalesce across racial and social class lines.[37]

You now have an idea of the approaches used to teach multicultural education. Which one best suits your teaching philosophy and style? An equally important question is, Which approach will best help to bring excellence and equity to education? We next provide an example of how one teacher brings both excellence and equity to her classroom.

Ms. Julie Wilson and Her Approach to Teaching

The following example describes a few days in the teaching life of Ms. Julie Wilson, a first-year teacher in a medium-large city. Which approach to multicultural education do you think Ms. Wilson is using? Which of her teaching actions do you agree or disagree with? What would you do if assigned to her class?

May 23

Julie Wilson was happy, but also sad that she had just completed her last exam at State U. As she walked back to her apartment, she wondered where she would be this time next year. She had applied for ten teaching positions and had been interviewed three times. As Julie entered her apartment building, she stopped to check the mail. A large fat white envelope addressed to her was stuffed into the small mailbox. She hurriedly tore it open and quickly read the first sentence. "We are pleased to offer you a teaching position. . . . " Julie leaped up the stairs three at a time. She burst into the apartment, waving the letter at her two roommates. "I've got a job! I got the job at Hoover Elementary. My first teaching job, a fifth-grade class!"

Hoover Elementary had been a part of a desegregation plan that brought together students from several different neighborhoods in the city. Hoover was situated in an urban-renewal area to which city officials were giving a lot of time and attention and on which they were spending a considerable amount of money. The city officials wanted to bring the Whites back into the city from suburbs and to encourage the middle-class people of color to remain in the city. They also wanted to improve the life chances for the poor. Julie had been hired because the principal was looking for teachers who had some record of success in working with diverse students. Julie had a 3.5 grade point average and had worked with a diverse student population in her practicum and student teaching experience. She had strong letters of recommendation from her cooperating teacher and university supervisor. Julie also had spent her last two summers working as a counselor in a camp that enrolled a wide diversity of students.

August 25

Julie was very pleased with the way her classroom looked. She had spent the last three days getting it ready for the first day of school. Plants, posters, goldfish, and an old rocking chair added to the warmth of an attractive classroom. There was also a big sign across the room saying "Welcome Fifth-Graders." Tomorrow was the big day.

August 26

Twenty-eight students entered Julie's classroom: fifteen girls and thirteen boys. There were ten White students, three Hmong students, six Latino students, and nine African American students. Three of the students were learning disabled, and two were in wheelchairs. Eleven of the students were from middle-class homes, nine were from working-class homes, and the remaining eight were from very poor homes. Julie greeted each student with a big smile and a friendly hello as they entered the room. She asked their names and told them hers. She then asked them to take the seat with their name on the desk.

After the school bell rang, Julie introduced herself to the whole class. She told them that she had spent most of her summer in England, and that while she was there she had often thought about this day—her first day as a teacher. She talked briefly about some of the places she had visited in England as she pointed to the places on a map. She concluded her introduction by telling them a few things about her family. Her mother and father owned a dairy farm in Wisconsin, and she had one older brother, Wayne, and two younger sisters, Mary and Patricia. Julie asked if there were any students new to the school. Lester, an African American male, raised his hand, along with a female Hmong student, Mai-ka. She asked Mai-ka if she would like to tell the class her complete name, how she had spent her summer, and one favorite thing she liked to do. Then she asked the same of Michael. After Mai-ka and Michael finished introducing themselves, Julie invited the other students to do the same. Julie then asked Marie to tell Mai-ka and Michael about Hoover Elementary.

Once the opening greetings were completed, Julie began a discussion about the importance of the fifth grade and how special this grade was. She explained that this is a grade and class where a lot of learning would take place, along with a lot of fun. As Julie spoke, the students were listening intently. Julie radiated warmth and authority. Some of the students glanced at each other unsmilingly as she spoke of the hard work; however, when she mentioned "a lot of fun," the entire class perked up and looked at each other with big grins on their faces.

Julie had begun working on her educational philosophy in the Introduction to Education course at State U. Although she was continually modifying the way she thought about teaching, her basic philosophical beliefs had remained much the same. One of her major beliefs was that the students should actively participate in planning and shaping their own educational experiences. This, she believed, was as important for fifth-graders as twelfth-graders.

Julie asked the class if they were ready to take care of their classroom governance—deciding on rules, helpers, a discipline code, and time for classroom meetings. The class responded enthusiastically. The first thing the students wanted to do was to decide on the class rules. Several began to volunteer rules:

"No stealing."

"No rock throwing on the playground."

"No sharpening pencils after the bell rings."

"No fighting."

As the students offered suggestions, Julie wrote them on the chalkboard. After giving about sixteen suggestions, the class concluded. Julie commented, "All the rules seem very important"; she then asked the class what they should do with the rules. One student, Richard, suggested that they be written on poster board and placed in the upper corner of the room for all to see. Other class members said, "Yes, this is what we did last year in fourth grade." William, however, said, "Yes, we did do this, but we rarely followed the rules after the first day we made them." Julie assured the class this would not be the case this year, and that they would have a weekly classroom meeting, run by an elected official of the class. She then asked if they thought it would be helpful if they wrote their rules using positive statements, instead of "no" or negative statements. The class said yes and began to change statements such as "no stealing" to "always ask before borrowing," and "no rock throwing" to "rock throwing can severely hurt a friend." Once the rules were completed, the class elected their officers.

After the classroom governance was taken care of, Julie asked the students if they would like her to read them a story. An enthusiastic yes followed her question. Julie glanced at the clock as she picked up *To Break the Silence*[38] from the desk. The book is a varied collection of short stories, especially for young readers, written by authors of different racial backgrounds. It was 11:35. She could hardly believe the morning had gone by so quickly. She read for twenty minutes. All the students seemed to be enjoying the story, except Lester and Ben, two African American male students. Lester and Ben were drawing pictures, communicating nonverbally between themselves, and ignoring the rest of the class members. Julie decided that because they were quiet and not creating a disturbance she would leave them alone.

After lunch, Julie had the class do two activities designed to help her learn about each student both socially and academically. She had the students do a self-concept activity, in which they did sentence completions that asked them to express how they felt about themselves. Then she had them play math and reading games to assess informally their math and reading skills. These activities took the entire afternoon, and Julie was as pleased as the students when the school day came to an end.

When Julie arrived at her apartment, she felt exhausted. She had a quick dinner and shower and then crawled into bed. She set the alarm for 7 P.M., and fell quickly asleep.

By 10:30 that night she had examined the students' self-concept activity and compared the information she had collected from the informal math and reading assessment with the official information from the students' cumulative record cards. She thought about each student's achievement record, social background, race, gender, and exceptionality. She said aloud, "I need to make plans soon to meet every parent. I need to find out about the students' lives at home, the parents' expectations, and if I can get some of them to volunteer."

Julie turned off her desk lamp at 11:45 to retire for the evening. She read a few pages from Richard Wright's *Native Son* and then turned out the light. Tonight she was going to sleep with less tension and nervousness than she had the night before. She felt good about the way things had gone today and was looking forward to tomorrow. As Julie slept, she dreamed of her class. Their faces and most of their names and backgrounds floated through her mind.

Eight of the ten White students were from Briar Creek, a solid middle-class single-unit housing community; these students were performing at grade level or above in all scholastic areas, and each of them was at least a year ahead in some core area subject. Charles, who had used a wheelchair since he was in an automobile accident three years ago, was three years ahead in both reading and math. However, Elaine and Bob had chosen a mixture of positive and negative adjectives when doing the self-concept activity and this concerned Julie. She would keep her eye on them to try to determine the cause of their problems.

Estelle and Todd, the other two White students, were between six months and a year behind in most academic areas. Estelle had been diagnosed as learning disabled, but the information in her personal cumulative file folder seemed ambiguous about the cause of her problem. Julie wondered if Estelle was classified as L.D. based on uncertain reasons. She recalled an article that discussed the learning-disability label as being a social construction rather than a medical condition.

All three of the Hmong students were at grade level or very close in their subjects. However, two of them, Mai-ka and Chee, were having some difficulty speaking English. The Kaying family owned a restaurant in the neighborhood. The rumor mill reported that they were doing very well financially, so well that they had recently opened a restaurant in the downtown area of the city. All of the six Hispanic students were Mexican American, born in the United States. Marie, José, and Lourdes were bilingual, and the other three were monolingual, with English being their primary language. Marie, José, and Lourdes were from working-class homes, and Richard, Jesus, and Carmen were from very poor homes. Lourdes, Carmen, and Richard's achievement scores were at least two years ahead of their grade level. José was working at grade level, and Marie and Jesus were one to two years behind.

Five of the African American students—Lester, Ben, Gloria, Sharon, and Susan—were all performing two years behind grade level in all core area subjects. All five lived in the Wendell Phillips low-rent projects. Two African American students—Shelly and Ernestine—lived in Briar Creek and were performing above grade level in all academic areas. Dolores and Gerard lived in Chatham, a working-class predominantly African American neighborhood; both were performing above grade level in all subjects, except Gerard, who was behind in math. Gerard also had chosen several negative words when doing the self-concept activity.

All students in Julie's class were obedient and came from families that encouraged getting a good education.

May 25, 7:30 A.M.

Julie liked arriving early at school. The engineer, Mike, usually had a pot of coffee perking when she arrived. This was her time to get everything ready for the day. She had been teaching for almost one school year and was proud and pleased with how everything was going. The school principal, Mr. Griffin, had been in her class three times for formal visits and had told others, "Julie is an excellent teacher." He usually offered her one or two minor suggestions, such as "Don't call the roll every day; learn to take your attendance silently," and "The museum has an excellent exhibit on food and the human body your class may enjoy."

Julie had also been surprised by several things. She was surprised at how quickly most of the teachers left school at the end of the day. Out of a staff of twenty classroom teachers, only about five or six came early or stayed late. Even more surprising to her was how she and the other teachers who either came early or stayed late were chided about this behavior. She was surprised at the large number of worksheets and ditto sheets used and at how closely many teachers followed the outline in the books regardless of the needs of students. Also, she noticed, there was a common belief among the staff that her instructional style would not work.

Julie had made several changes in the curriculum. She had adopted a tradebook approach to reading and integrated that with her language arts. She made available to the students a wide assortment of books that featured different races, exceptionalities, and socioeconomic classes. In some stories, both males and females were featured doing traditional as well as nontraditional things. Stories were set in urban and rural settings, and some featured children with disabilities. It had taken Julie several months to get such a diverse collection of books for her students, and she had even spent some of her own money for the books, but the excitement the students had shown about the materials made the expense worthwhile.

She also had several computers in her class. When she discovered that Richard's father owned a computer store, she convinced him to lend the class two computer systems, and she convinced Mr. Griffin to purchase two others at cost. Several of the students from Briar Creek had computers at home. Charles and Elaine, Julie discovered, were wizards at the computer. Julie encouraged them to help the other students (and herself—since she had taken only one computer course at State U). The two students enjoyed this assignment and often had a small group of students remain after school to receive their help. Julie was pleased at how well Charles and Elaine handled this responsibility. Lester and Ben were Charles's favorite students; they liked the computer, but Julie believed they liked Charles and his electric wheelchair even more. Julie had heard them say on several occasions that Charles was "cool." Lester's and Ben's work was showing a steady improvement and Charles enjoyed having two good friends. This friendship, Julie believed, had excellent mutual benefits for all concerned, including herself.

Julie taught most of her math by providing the students with real-life opportunities to see the concept in action. She often took her class to the supermarket, to the bank, and to engineering firms. She made certain that she selected firms that employed men and women of color and White women in positions of leadership. She often requested that a representative from these groups spend a few minutes with the students, explaining their role and duties.

Julie took the students on field trips to supermarkets in different areas of town so the students could compare prices and quality of products (e.g., fruit, meat, and vegetables) between the suburban area and the inner-city area. On two occasions this led to a letter-writing campaign to the owner of the food chain to explain their findings. The students also wondered why the cost of gas was cheaper in the suburban areas than in the inner-city area. This became a math, social studies, and language arts lesson. Letters were written and interviews conducted to ascertain the cost of delivering the gas to the inner city as compared to the suburban area of the city, and to ascertain the rental fee for service station property in the inner city in comparison to the suburban areas. Math skills were used to determine if there needed to be a difference in gas prices between the areas after rental fees and delivery charges were taken into consideration.

Julie used advertisements and editorials from newspapers and magazines to help students see the real-life use of such concepts as sexism, justice, and equity. Julie supplemented her social studies curriculum on a regular basis. She found the text biased in several areas. She would integrate into the assigned curriculum information from the history and culture of different racial and ethnic groups. For example, when teaching about the settling of the local community years ago, she invited a Native American female historian and a White historian to give views on how the settling took place and on problems and issues associated with it. She invited an African American historian and a Latino historian to discuss what was presently happening in the area.

Students were usually encouraged to undertake different projects to provide a comprehensive perspective on the social studies unit under study. Choices were up to the student, but Julie maintained high expectations and insisted that excellence in every phase of the work was always necessary for each student. She made certain that during the semester each student was a project leader. She also made certain that boys and girls worked together. For example, Julie knew that Ben, Lester, and Charles usually stayed close together and did not have a girl as a member of their project team. She also knew that Carmen was assertive and had useful knowledge about the project on which they were working. She put Carmen on the project team.

Julie did have two problems with her class that she could not figure out. Shelly and Ernestine did not get along well with any of the African American students, especially Ben and Lester. George and Hank, two White boys from Briar Creek, had considerable difficulty getting along with José and went out of their way to be mean to Lourdes and Marie. Julie was puzzled by George's and Hank's behavior; she did not think it was racially motivated because both of the boys got along pretty well with Shelly. She labored over this problem and discussed it with the school counselor. She wondered if she didn't have a problem related to a combination of race, class, and gender in George's and Hank's relationship with José, Lourdes, and Marie. She also concluded that she might have a social-class problem among the African American students. Julie decided to discuss her concerns with the students individually. After some discussion, she discovered that Shelly's and Ernestine's problem with Ben and Lester was related to social class and color. Both Shelly and Ernestine had very fair skin color. They had grown up in a predominantly White middle-class community and had spent very little time around other African American students. Ben and Lester were dark-skinned male students who lived in a very poor neighborhood. Julie felt that if her assumptions were true, she would need help with this problem. She was successful in getting an African American child psychiatrist to talk to her class. She did this in relationship to an art unit that examined "color, attitude, and feelings." His discussion enabled Julie to continue her discussion with Shelly and Ernestine and get them to examine their prejudice.

George and Hank admitted to Julie, after several discussions, that they did not care too much for any girls. But Hispanic girls who wore funny clothes and ate non-American foods were a big bore. It took Julie several months of talking with George and Hank, using different reading materials and having them all work on a group project under her direction, to get George and Hank to reduce some of their prejudices. At the end of the semester, Julie still believed this problem had not been completely resolved. Thus, she shared it with the sixth-grade teacher.

At the end of the school year, Julie felt very good about her first year. She knew she had grown as a teacher. She believed her professors at State U, her cooperating teacher, and her university supervisor would give her very high marks. They had encouraged her to become a reflective teacher—committed, responsible, and wholehearted in her teaching effort. Julie believed she was well on her way to becoming a reflective teacher, and she looked forward to her second year with enthusiasm.

She also realized that her sensitivity to things she did not know had grown, and she planned to engage in some learning over the summer. As she had become aware of resentments that students from low-income families felt toward students from upper-income families, she began to wonder what the city was doing to address poverty. She heard that the NAACP (National Association for the Advancement of Colored People), some Latino community leaders, and heads of homeless shelters were trying to work with the city council, and she wanted to find out more about how these groups viewed poverty in the city. She decided to join the NAACP so she could become more familiar with its activities. She also wanted to spend time with some Latino families, because before her teaching experience she had never talked directly with Latino adults; her principal suggested she should meet Luis Reyes, who directed a local community center and could help her do this. In addition, Julie felt somewhat overwhelmed by the amount of background information she had never learned about different groups in America and decided to start reading; because she enjoyed novels, she would start with some by Toni Morrison, Louise Erdrich, James Baldwin, and Maxine Hong Kingston. She would also read the novel written by Sylvia Plath, *The Bell Jar.*

From what you know of Julie, what is her approach to multicultural education? Would you be comfortable doing as Julie did? Discuss Julie's teaching with your classmates. How would you change it?

CONCLUSION

In Julie's classroom, as in yours, race, class, gender, and disability are ascribed characteristics students bring to school that cannot be ignored. To teach with excellence, Julie had to affirm her students' diversity. Why do we say this?

For one thing, Julie needed to pay attention to her students' identities to help them achieve. She needed to acknowledge the importance of African American males to American life to hold the interest of Lester and Ben; she needed to acknowledge Mai-ka's and Chee's prior learning to help them learn English and school material; she needed to become familiar with her students' learning styles so her teaching would be most effective.

For another thing, Julie needed to pay attention to her students' personal and social needs to help them perceive school as a positive experience. Some of her students disliked other students because of prejudices and stereotypes. Some of her students did not know how to relate to people in wheelchairs or to people who looked or talked differently. Some of her students felt negative about their own abilities. These attitudes interfere not only with achievement, but also with one's quality of life, both as students today and later as adults in a pluralistic society.

Julie realized over the year the extent to which schools are connected with their social context. She remembered having to take a course called School and Society and had not understood why it was required. She remembered reading about societal pressures on schools; over the year she had come to see how societal pressures translated into funding, programs, and local debates that directly affected resources and guidelines in her classroom. Further, she realized the extent to which students are connected with their own cultural context. The African American students, for example, emphasized their African American identity and did not want to be regarded as White; teachers who tried to be color blind regarded this as a problem, but teachers who found the community's diversity to be interesting saw it as a strength. On the other hand, immigrant students tried hard to fit in; Julie would not have understood why without considering why their families had immigrated and the pressures the children experienced.

Julie also knew that the future of the United States depends on its diverse children. Her students will all be U.S. adults one day, regardless of the quality of their education. But what kind of adults will they become? Julie wanted them all to be skilled in a variety of areas, to be clear and critical thinkers, and to have a sense of social justice and caring for others. Julie had some personal selfish motives for this: She knew her own well-being in old age would depend directly on the ability of today's children to care for older people when they become adults. She also knew her students of today would be shaping the society in which her own children would one day grow up. She wanted to make sure they were as well prepared as possible to be productive citizens who had a vision of a better society. She drew from all of the approaches, at one time or another, to address specific problems and needs she saw in the classroom. But the approach she emphasized, and the one that guided her planning, was education that is multicultural and social reconstructionist.

How will you approach excellence and equity in your own classroom? We can guarantee that all your students will have their identities shaped partly by their race, social class, and gender; all of them will notice and respond in one way or another to people who differ from themselves; and all of them will grow up in a society that is still in many ways racist, sexist, and classist. You are the only one who can guarantee what you will do about that.

QUESTIONS AND ACTIVITIES

1. Why is it important for teachers to strive to attain both excellence and equity for their students? What can you do to try to acheive both goals in your teaching?

2. What does each of these terms mean to you in relationship to classroom life: *race, class, gender,* and *disability?* How are your notions of these concepts similar to and different from those of your classmates?

3. Give an example of how such variables as race, class, and gender interact to influence the behavior of a particular student.

4. Name the five approaches to multicultural education identified by Grant and Sleeter. What are the assumptions and instructional goals of each approach?

5. In what significant ways does the "education that is multicultural and social reconstructionist" approach differ from the other four approaches? What problems might a teacher experience when trying to implement this approach in the classroom? How might these problems be reduced or solved?

6. Visit a school in your community and interview several teachers and the principal about activities and programs the school has implemented in multicultural education. Using the typology of multicultural education described by the authors, determine what approach or combination of approaches to multicultural education are being used within the school. Share your findings with your classmates or fellow workshop participants.

7. Which approach to multicultural education is Ms. Wilson using? Which aspects of her teaching do you especially like? Which aspects would you change?

8. Which approach to multicultural education described by the authors would you be the most comfortable using? Why?

NOTES

1. National Commission on Excellence in Education, *A Nation at Risk* (Washington, D.C.: U.S. Government Printing Office, 1983).

2. *Time* magazine (July 11, 1988).

3. W. A. Henry III, "Beyond the Melting Pot," *Time* (April 1990): 28–31.

4. This is discussed at length in Ira Shor, *Culture Wars* (Boston: Routledge and Kegan Paul, 1986); and in Michael Omi and Howard Winant, *Racial*

Formation in the United States (New York: Routledge and Kegan Paul, 1986).

5. Studs Terkel, *The Great Divide: Second Thoughts on the American Dream* (New York: Pantheon Books, 1988), p. 69.

6. Bureau of the Census, *Statistical Abstracts of the United States 1989* (Washington, D.C.: U.S. Government Printing Office, 1989), p. 69.

7. Terkel, *The Great Divide,* 67–68.

8. See, for example, Robert Jiobu, *Ethnicity and Assimilation* (Albany, N.Y.: SUNY Press, 1988); Bob Suzuki, "Asian Americans as the 'Model Minority,'" *Change* (November/December 1989): 13–19; and Ronald Takaki, "The Fourth Iron Cage: Race and Political Economy in the 1990's." Unpublished paper presented at the Green Bay Colloquium on Ethnicity and Public Policy, Green Bay, Wisconsin, 1989.

9. Elizabeth Blue Swadener, "Children and Families 'At Risk,'" *Educational Foundations* (Fall 1990):17–39.

10. See "The Americans with Disabilities Act: Where We Are Now?" *The Disability Rag* 12 (1):11–19.

11. Carl Grant, Christine Sleeter, and J. Anderson, "The Literature on Multicultural Education: Review and Analysis," *Educational Studies* 12 (1986): 47–72.

12. Christine E. Sleeter and Carl A. Grant, *Making Choices for Multicultural Education: Five Approaches to Race, Class and Gender* (Columbus, Ohio: Merrill, 1988).

13. Barbara J. Shade, "Afro-American Cognitive Patterns: A Review of the Research," in Barbara J. Shade, ed., *Culture, Style and the Educative Process* (Springfield, Ill.: Charles C Thomas Publisher, 1989), p. 110.

14. Elizabeth Fennema and Penelope L. Peterson, "Effective Teaching for Girls and Boys: The Same or Different?" in David C. Berliner and Barak V. Rosenshine, eds., *Talks to Teachers* (New York: Random House, 1987), pp. 111–125.

15. Jaime Escalante and Jack Dirmann, "The Jaime Escalante Math Program," *Journal of Negro Education* 59 (1990): 407–423.

16. Marcia Westkott, "Women's Studies as a Strategy for Change: Between Criticism and Vision," in Gloria Bowles and Renate D. Klein, eds., *Theories of Women's Studies* (London: Routledge and Kegan Paul, 1983), pp. 210–218.

17. Taly Rutenberg, "Learning Women's Studies," in Gloria Bowles and Renate D. Klein, eds., *Theories of Women's Studies* (London: Routledge and Kegan Paul, 1983), pp. 72–78.

18. Rafael E. Cortada, *Black Studies: An Urban and Comparative Curriculum* (Greenwich, Conn.: Xerox Publishing Group, 1974).

19. Bob H. Suzuki, "An Asian-American Perspective on Multicultural Education: Implications for Practice and Policy." Paper presented at the Second Annual Conference of the National Association for Asian and Pacific American Education, Washington, D.C., 1980.

20. Don T. Nakanishi and Russell Leong, "Toward the Second Decade, a National Survey of Asian American Studies Programs," *Amerasia Journal* 5 (1978):1–2.

21. Paulo Freire, *Pedagogy of the Oppressed* (New York: The Seaburg Press, 1970).

22. Diane Viadero, "Battle over Multicultural Education Rises in Intensity," *Education Week* 10 (1990): 11.

23. John Leo, "A Fringe History of the World," *U.S. News and World Report* (Nov. 12, 1990): 25–26.

24. Jean C. George, *Julie of the Wolves* (New York: Harper and Row, 1972).

25. Scott O'Dell, *Island of the Blue Dolphins* (Boston: Houghton Mifflin, 1960).

26. Jack London, *The Call of the Wild* (New York: Harmony Books, 1977).

27. Carl Grant, "Education That Is Multicultural— Isn't That What We Mean?" *Journal of Teacher Education* 29 (1978):45–49.

28. George B. Shaw, "Back to Methuselah," in John Bartlett, ed., *Familiar Quotations* (Boston: Little, Brown Co., 1980), p. 681.

29. James A. Banks, *Multiethnic Education: Theory and Practice* (Boston: Allyn and Bacon, 1981), p. 149.

30. Ira Shor, *Critical Teaching and Everyday Life* (Boston: South End Press, 1980).

31. Paulo Freire, *The Politics of Education: Culture, Power, and Liberation,* D. Macedo, trans. (Boston: Bergin and Garvey, 1985).

32. Jean Anyon, "Elementary Schooling and Distinctions of Social Class," *Interchange* 12 (1981):118–132.

33. Carl A. Grant and Christine E. Sleeter, *After the School Bell Rings* (Barcombe, England: Falmer Press, 1986).

34. U.S. Department of Commerce, unpublished estimates, *Population Survey* (Table 6, March 1990) (Washington, D.C.: Bureau of the Census, 1990).

35. Christine E. Bennett, *Comprehensive Multicultural Education* (Boston: Allyn and Bacon, 1986), p. 212.

36. Angela Y. Davis, *Women, Race, and Class* (New York: Random House, 1981).

37. Lisa Albrecht and Rose Brewer, *Bridges of Power: Women's Multicultural Alliances* (Santa Cruz, Calif.: New Society Publishers, 1990).

38. Peter A. Barrett, ed., *To Break the Silence* (New York: Dell Publishing Company, 1986).

In classrooms and schools where gender equity exists, both male and female students are able to explore their interests and talents freely and to actualize their potentials.

Social Class and Religion

The two chapters in Part Two of this book discuss the effects of two powerful variables on student behavior, beliefs, and achievement: social class and religion. Social class is a powerful variable in U.S. society despite entrenched beliefs about individual opportunity in the United States. As Persell points out in Chapter 4, three children born at the same time but into different social classes have very unequal educational opportunities. Students from the lower, middle, and upper classes usually attend different kinds of schools and have teachers who have different beliefs and expectations about their academic achievement. The structure of educational institutions also favors middle- and upper-class students. Structures such as tracking, IQ tests, and programs for gifted and mentally retarded students are highly biased in favor of middle- and upper-class students. Persell suggests ways in which teachers and other educators can create equal educational opportunities for students from different social classes.

Students who are socialized within religious families and communities often have beliefs and behaviors that conflict with those of the school. Religious fundamentalists often challenge the scientific theories taught by schools about the origin of human beings. They also attack textbooks and fictional books assigned by teachers that they believe violate or contradict their doctrines. Conflicts about the right to pray in the school sometimes divide communities. The school should help students mediate between their home culture and the school culture. Uphoff, in Chapter 5, describes some promising ways in which this can be done.

CHAPTER 4

Social Class and Educational Equality

■ CAROLINE HODGES PERSELL

Picture three babies born at the same time, but to parents of different social-class backgrounds. The first baby is born into a wealthy, well-educated, business or professional family. The second is born into a middle-class family in which both parents attended college and have middle-level managerial jobs. The third is born into a poor family in which neither parent finished high school or has a steady job. Will these children receive the same education in the United States? Although the United States is based on the promise of equal opportunity for all people, the educational experiences of these three children are likely to be quite different.

Education in the United States is not a single, uniform system that is available to every child in the same way. Children of different social classes are likely to attend different types of schools, to receive different types of instruction, to study different curricula, and to leave school at different rates and times. As a result, when children end their schooling, they are more different from each other than they were when they entered, and these differences may be seen as legitimating the unequal positions people face in their adult lives. If we understand better how schools may contribute to inequalities, we may be in a better position to try to change them.

The nature and meaning of social class are issues often debated by social scientists. Researchers often measure social class by asking survey questions about a person's or a family's educational level, occupation, rank in an organization, and earnings.[1] However social class is measured, it has been found repeatedly to be related to how well students do in school.[2] Although there are a number of exceptions, students from higher social-class backgrounds tend to get better grades and to stay in school longer than do students from lower-class backgrounds. The question is, why does this happen? Is it determined by the individuals, or does something about the educational system contribute to this result? I argue that three things contribute a great deal to the unequal educational results so often documented by social researchers:

1. The structure of schooling in the United States
2. The beliefs held by U.S. educators
3. The curricular and teaching practices in U.S. schools

By *structure of schooling* I mean such features as differences between urban, rural, and suburban schools, and differences between public and private schools. By *educational beliefs* I mean beliefs about IQ (intelligence quotient) and cultural deprivation, two sets of ideas that have been offered to explain why lower-class children often do less well in school. In *curricular and teaching practices* I include tracking of students into certain curricula, teachers' expectations about what different children can learn, and differences in the quantity and quality of what is taught.

This chapter reviews research showing differences in educational structures, beliefs, and practices; examines how these differences are related to the social-class backgrounds of students; considers the consequences they have for student achievement; and analyzes how they affect individuals' adult lives. Lest this be too depressing an account, at the end of the chapter I suggest some ways that teachers and other educators might work to improve education.

EDUCATIONAL STRUCTURES

The three babies described above are not likely to attend the same school, even if they live in the same area. Most students in the United States attend schools that are relatively alike with respect to the social-class backgrounds of the other students. One reason this happens is that people in the United States tend to live in areas that are fairly similar with respect to class and race. If they attend their neighborhood school, they are with students from similar backgrounds. If children grow up in a fairly diverse area such as a large city, mixed suburb, or rural area, they are less likely to attend the same schools. The states with the most private schools, for example, are the states with the largest concentrations of urban areas.[3] If, by chance, students of different backgrounds do attend the same school, they are very likely to experience different programs of study because of tracking and ability grouping.

In older suburbs or cities, children of higher-class families are more likely to attend homogeneous neighborhood schools, selective public schools, or private schools, and to be in higher tracks; lower-class children are also likely to attend school together. Middle-class families try to send their children to special public schools, parochial schools, or private schools if they can afford them.

Private day and boarding schools are also relatively similar with respect to social class, despite the fact that some scholarships are awarded. Researchers who studied elite boarding schools, for example, found that 46 percent of the families had incomes of more than $100,000 per year in the early 1980s.[4]

Let's look more closely at elite private schools and exclusive suburban schools, which are overwhelmingly attended by upper- and upper-middle-class students; at parochial schools, attended by middle-class and working-class students, and at large urban public schools, heavily attended by lower-class pupils. Although these descriptions gloss over many distinctions within each major type of school, they do convey some of the range of differences that exist under the overly broad umbrella we call U.S. education.

Schools of the Upper and Upper-Middle Classes

At most upper- and upper-middle-class high schools, the grounds are spacious and well kept, the computer, laboratory, language, and athletic facilities are extensive, the teachers are well educated and responsive to students and parents, classes are small, nearly every student studies a college preparatory curriculum, and considerable homework is assigned.

At the private schools, these tendencies are often intensified. The schools are quite small, with few having more than 1,200 students. Teachers do not have tenure or belong to unions, so they can be fired by the headmaster or headmistress if they are considered unresponsive to students or parents. Classes are small, often having no more than fifteen students, and sometimes considerably fewer. Numerous advanced placement courses offer the possibility of college credit. Students remark that it is not "cool to be dumb around here."[5] Most students watch very little television during the school week and do a great deal of homework.[6] They have many opportunities for extracurricular activities, such as debate and drama clubs, publications, and music, and the chance to learn sports that colleges value, such as crew, squash, and lacrosse. Students have both academic and personal advisors who monitor their progress, help them solve problems, and try to help them have a successful school experience.

Affluent suburban communities have a robust tax base to support annual costs that in 1990 ran as high as $10,000 per pupil. School board members are elected by members of the community who may know them. Private schools are run by self-perpetuating boards of trustees, many of whom are alumni/ae of the school. The school head is chosen by the board of trustees and may be replaced by them if they are not satisfied.

Private Parochial Schools

Many differences exist among parochial schools, but in general these schools are relatively small. More of these high school students study an academic program and do more homework than do their public-school peers. They also are subjected to somewhat stricter discipline.[7] The classes, however, are often larger than elite private, suburban, or urban school classes, with sometimes as many as forty or fifty pupils per class. Some non-Catholic middle- and working-class parents, especially those in urban areas, send their children to parochial schools.[8]

The costs at parochial schools are relatively low, especially compared to private schools, because these schools are subsidized by religious groups. These schools have relatively low teacher salaries and usually have no teachers' unions. Currently there are more lay teachers and fewer nuns, sisters, priests, and brothers as teachers. The schools are governed by the religious authority that runs them.

Urban Schools

Urban schools are usually quite large, and they are part of an even larger school system that is invariably highly bureaucratic. They usually offer varied courses of study, including academic, vocational, and general curricular tracks. The school systems of large cities and older, larger suburbs tend to lack both political and economic resources. These systems have become highly centralized, with school board members generally elected on a citywide basis.[9] School board members are often concerned members of the community who may send their own children to private schools, and they may have little knowledge about or power over the daily operations of the public system. The authority of professional educators is often buttressed by bureaucratic procedures and by unionization of teachers and administrators. At least one observer[10] has described the system as one of organizational paralysis, rather than governance.

Economically, the large city school systems are also relatively powerless. Their shrinking tax bases make them dependent on nonlocal sources (state and federal monies) to balance their budgets. Moreover, the property tax base of public education in the United States results in vastly unequal resources for urban, suburban, and rural schools, and for major regional variations in educational expenditures.

In general, then, one's social-class background is related to the school one attends, the size of the school, the political and economic resources available to the school, and the curricula offered.

EDUCATIONAL BELIEFS

Two educational concepts have been particularly important in influencing educational practices in the twentieth century. These are *IQ* and *cultural deprivation*. These concepts have also dominated explanations of differences in school achievement among students of different social classes. Considerable attention has been devoted to determining which concept provides the more correct explanation. However, even though they seem to be competing explanations, they actually have many common assumptions and share many significant consequences.

A great deal of educational thought and research have been devoted to the study of intelligence quotient, or IQ. The concept of IQ has been used to explain why some children learn more slowly than others, why African American children do less well in school than White children, and why lower-class children do less well than middle- and upper-middle-class children. IQ tests are often used to justify variations in education, achievement, and rewards. The justification usually is that because some people are more intelligent than others, they are entitled to more of these other things as well. Such justification occurs in curricular tracking and in student exposure to different educational programs and resources.

IQ tests, however, were designed to *differentiate* people. This was done by dropping from the final intelligence test those items that *everyone* answered correctly (about 60 percent of the initial items) and including only those questions that some portion (about 40 to 60 percent) of the respondents answered incorrectly. This was done even when the rejected items represented the best possible measure of achievement or aptitude.

Critics of IQ tests have raised a number of good points about the accuracy of the tests. For example, IQ tests do not measure such important features of intelligence as creative or divergent thinking, logic, and critical reasoning. The idea of multiple intelligences is well developed by Howard Gardner in his book *Frames of Mind.* [11]

IQ tests have good predictive validity for grades in school, which was what Binet designed them for originally. The real question is, how valid are IQ tests or grades for predicting success in life? Many studies find little relationship between educational achievement and performance on the job, in a variety of occupations. [12]

IQ testing, especially at an early age, may be inefficient because it may rule out the late bloomer, the early rebel, or the child whose family does not stress test-taking skills. Yet, those people may have a great deal to contribute to society.

IQ tests are criticized for being culturally biased. To do well on an IQ test, an individual needs to have learned White middle-class, U.S. English. One section of the WPPSI (Wechsler Preschool-Primary Scale of Intelligence) requires children to repeat sentences verbatim to the examiner. Children who know a different dialect may provide a simultaneous translation of the sentence read and say it in their own dialect, but they are penalized for not repeating the sentence exactly. They have shown a much more advanced skill than rote memory, but in the test scoring it is a handicap. Even nonverbal tasks such as stacking blocks can be culturally loaded, because more middle-class homes have blocks than do lower-class homes. The ideological significance of IQ tests becomes most apparent in the explanations that have been offered for different educational results.

There is a big controversy in the behavioral and social sciences over whether differences in IQ test scores among students of different classes are the result of genetic deficits (nature) or of cultural deprivation (nurture). Advocates of each position take for granted the importance of IQ test scores.

Arthur Jensen rekindled the genetic controversy when he asserted in 1969 that 80 percent of the variation in intelligence is determined by heredity. [13] Even though it is clear that some portion of IQ is transmitted genetically from parent to child, no one knows exactly how much. A continuing study of more than 100 identical and fraternal twins, separated in infancy and reared apart, found that about 70 percent of the variation in IQ was associated with genetic variation. [14] The authors of the study note that genetic differences may influence the environments that children and adolescents find congenial. Thus, even though heredity may play an important role, the environment in which an individual is raised is also very important. Thus, their results do not detract from the value or importance of parenting, education, and other shaping influences. We know that traits such as height, which are highly heritable, can vary dramatically in different environments.

Economic and social environments facilitate the development of genetic potential. This fact has led to another explanation for differential school achievement, namely, cultural deprivation.

The cultural deprivation explanation sees low-income or minority children as failing to achieve in school because of their deficient home environments, disorganized family structure, inadequate child-rearing patterns, undeveloped language and values, and low self-esteem.

Let us consider the issue of self-esteem, which is related to a person's social status. If cultural deprivation and family deficiencies were the factors that produced low self-esteem in children, we would expect very young children to show the same low self-esteem that older ones do. But the reverse is the case. The older the children and the more time they spend in school, the more their self-esteem plummets.[15] This result suggests that something happens to the initially high self-esteem of lower-class youngsters as they encounter predominantly middle-class institutions. Hence, it is not the so-called pathology of their homes that seems to affect their self-esteem, but something else.

Much of the social science literature has been filled with debates between the IQ and cultural deprivation positions, in what might be today's version of a nature-nurture controversy. But this controversy directs attention away from the common premises and consequences shared by both explanations of differences in test performance and school achievement. These premises include the following:

1. Both genetic and cultural-deficit theorists assume that IQ is important for success in life and appear to agree with the necessity of early testing and selection in schools. They do not question the need for performance on tests designed to differentiate children.

2. Supporters of both theories place the blame for academic failure on children and their families. Thus, they divert attention from the entire educational system and how it produces certain outcomes, including failure among certain types of children. (Not every upper-class child has a high IQ, but do you think that those with lower IQs are allowed to fail at the same rate as lower-class and minority children?)

3. Accepting these theories is the same as justifying whatever educators do, because the fault presumably lies with the children.

4. These concepts have self-fulfilling potency; that is, if teachers believe that children *cannot* learn because of their genetic or cultural deficits, they will expect less of them and teach them less, and, indeed, it is likely that the children will learn less. Their lower grades tend to confirm the predictions. Hence, the self-fulfilling nature of the prophecy.

5. These theories divert attention from questions about how children learn and what kinds of cognitive skills they have. Such theories make it less likely that effective forms of teaching and learning will happen.

6. Finally, and perhaps most important, the genetic and cultural-deficit theories of differences in school achievement offer compensatory education as the sole solution to poverty, thus diverting attention from structural inequalities of power and wealth. Thus, both views leave existing structures of inequalities unchallenged.

I am not suggesting that intellectual or cultural differences do not exist between individuals. Differences in intelligence or culture may affect the speed at which students can learn certain things, and they also influence the effectiveness of different pedagogical approaches. What is important, however, is how intellectual differences are labeled, regarded, and treated by schools, because those beliefs contribute to the maintenance of educational and social inequalities.

In China, for example, where different concepts of individual intellectual abilities have prevailed, teachers work with slow learners until they learn. As the leaders of a school in Peking said, "Of course people differ in ability. But a student who is weak in one field may be strong in another. And these abilities are not something innate and unchanging. Abilities grow when they are made use of, through practice. . . . As abilities grow by being used they are not constant, and it does not make any sense to say that a given individual has so and so much ability."[16]

The widespread use of IQ testing and the explanations offered for differences in IQ and school achievement are critically important for the curricular and teaching practices in schools.

CURRICULAR AND TEACHING PRACTICES

As noted earlier, schools attended by children of different social classes vary in terms of what proportion of their students study an academic curriculum. They also vary in terms of how much work they expect and demand of their students. Two curricular and teaching practices in particular highlight how school experiences vary by the students' social class, namely, tracking and teachers' expectations.

Tracking

The first recorded instance of tracking was the Harris plan in St. Louis, begun in 1867. Since then, tracking has followed a curious pattern in the United States of alternate popularity and disuse. In the 1920s and 1930s, when many foreign immigrants settled in the United States, tracking increased greatly. Thereafter, it fell into decline until the late 1950s, when it was revived, apparently in response to the USSR's launching of Sputnik and the United States' competitive concern with identifying and educating the gifted.[17] That period was also marked by large migrations of rural southern African Americans to northern cities and by an influx of Puerto Rican and Mexican American migrants into the United States. Tracking today is widespread, particularly in large, diverse school systems and in schools serving primarily lower-class students.[18] It is less prevalent, and less rigid when it occurs, in upper-middle-class suburban and private schools and in parochial schools.[19]

What exactly is tracking? To address this question, we need to examine the distinction between ability grouping and curriculum differentiation. Proponents of ability grouping stress flexible subject-area assignment. By this they mean that students are assigned to learning groups on the basis of their background and achievement in a subject area at any given moment, and that skills and knowledge are evaluated at relatively frequent intervals. Students showing gains can be shifted readily into another group. They might also be in different ability groups in different subjects, according to their own rate of growth in each subject. This practice suggests a common curriculum shared by all students, with only the mix of student abilities being varied. It also assumes that, within that curriculum, all groups are taught the same material.

In fact, it seems that group placement becomes self-perpetuating, that students are often grouped at the same level in all subjects, and that even a shared curriculum may be taught differently to different groups. This is especially likely to happen in large, bureaucratic, urban public schools. Quite often, different ability groups are assigned to different courses of study, resulting in simultaneous grouping by curriculum and ability. Rosenbaum notes that although ability grouping and curriculum grouping may appear different to educators, in fact they share several social similarities: (1) Students are placed with those defined as similar to themselves and are segregated from those deemed different; (2) group placement is done on the basis of criteria such as ability or postgraduate plans that are unequally esteemed. Thus, group membership immediately ranks students in a status hierarchy, formally stating that some students are better than others.[20] Following Rosenbaum, the general term of tracking is applied here to both types of grouping.[21]

On what basis are students assigned to tracks? Three major criteria have been noted in the literature: (1) standardized test scores; (2) teacher grades, recommendations, or opinions about pupils; and (3) pupil race and socioeconomic class. Test scores are usually based on large group-administered aptitude tests, a method considered least valid by test-givers. Teacher opinions about students may be influenced by test scores, pupil social class, or ethnicity, as discussed below. Social class and ethnicity have been found in some research studies to be directly related to track assignments as well, even when ability and teacher recommendations were similar.[22] Thus, the social-class background of students is related to the prevalence of tracking in the schools and to the ways track assignments are made.

Once students are assigned to different tracks, what happens to them? Do they have different educational experiences? The major educational processes that have been observed to vary according to track placement include the unequal allocation of educational resources, the instruction offered, student-teacher interactions, and student-student interactions. Hallinan studied within-class ability grouping in thirty-four elementary school classes. She found that ability grouping affects the learning of students in higher and lower groups because it influences their opportunities for learning, the instructional climate, and the student aptitudes clustered in the different groups. "High-ability" groups spend "more time on tasks" during class; that is, more class time is devoted to actual teaching activities. Also, teachers use more interesting teaching methods and materials. Finally, teachers hold higher expectations, and the other students support learning more in the higher-ability groups. As a result, the aptitude of students in the higher groups tends to develop more than does the aptitude of students in the lower group.[23]

In secondary schools, college-track students consistently receive better teachers, class materials, laboratory facilities, field trips, and visitors than their lower-track counterparts.[24] Oakes observed that teachers of high-track students set aside more time for student learning and devoted more class time to learning activities. Fewer students in these classes engaged in "off-task" activities.[25] Oakes also found that "students are being exposed to knowledge and taught behaviors that differ not only educationally but also in socially important ways. Students at the top are exposed to the knowledge that is highly valued in our culture, knowledge that identifies its possessors as 'educated.' "[26] Similarly, those students are taught critical thinking, creativity, and independence. Students at the bottom are denied access to these educationally and socially important experiences.[27]

Freiberg found that higher-track students received more empathy, praise, and use of their ideas, as well as less direction and criticism, than did lower-track students.[28] Oakes observed that teachers spent more time in low-track classes on discipline and that students in those classes perceived their teachers as more punitive than did students in high-track classes.[29]

Rosenbaum reported that more than one-third of lower-track (noncollege) students mentioned "blatant insults directed at them by teachers and administrators: 'Teachers are always telling us how dumb we are.' " One articulate general-track student in that study reported that he sought academic help from a teacher but was told that he was not smart enough to learn the material. Several students reported that a lower-track student who asks a guidance counselor for a change of classes is not only prevented from changing but is also insulted for being so presumptuous as to make the request. Rosenbaum was told by one teacher, "You're wasting your time asking these kids for their opinions. There's not an idea in any of their heads." As the researcher notes, "This comment was not expressed in the privacy of the teacher's room; it was said at a normal volume in a quiet classroom full of students!"[30]

Students have been observed to pick up on the negative evaluations associated with lower track placement. They may make fun of lower-track students, call them unflattering names, or stop associating with them.[31] Hence, a major result of tracking is differential respect from peers and teachers, with implications for both instruction and esteem.

Further consequences of tracking include segregation of students by social class and ethnicity,[32] unequal learning by students in different tracks,[33] and unequal chances to attend college.[34] The percentage of students in an academic curriculum may be the single most significant structural difference between different types of schools. Noncollege preparatory programs may foreclose future opportunities for young persons by failing to provide them with the courses or training necessary for admission to institutions of higher education, or for pursuing particular college majors.[35]

If tracking has so many negative consequences, why does it persist? Oakes thinks tracking persists because it is "an integral part of the culture of secondary schools: the collection of organizational arrangements, behaviors, relationships, and beliefs that define how things are at a school."[36] She suggests that tracking rests on four unexamined assumptions:

1. Students learn better in groups of those who are academically similar.

2. Slower students develop more positive attitudes about themselves and school when they are not in day-to-day classroom contact with those who are much brighter.

3. Track placements are part of a meritocratic system with assignments 'earned' by students and accorded through fair and accurate means.

4. Teaching is easier when students are grouped homogeneously, and teaching is better when there are not slower students to lower the common denominator.[37]

Oakes's research in 297 classrooms suggests that these assumptions are false. If teachers accept her evidence, they should work to eliminate tracking from schools. However, emerging evidence suggests that educators have not been quick to do so. Finley found that support for the tracking system in the school came from teachers who competed with each other for high-status students.[38]

Teachers' Expectations

Educational structures such as schools that are socioeconomically homogeneous, concepts such as IQ and cultural deprivation, and practices such as tracking go a long way toward shaping the expectations teachers hold about students. Teacher training and textbooks have tended to attribute educational failures to deficiencies in the children.[39] Often, such deficiencies are social characteristics of the pupils, such as their social-class background, ethnicity, language, or behavior. In a review of relevant research, Persell[40] found that student social class was related to teacher expectations when other factors such as race were not more salient, when expectations were engendered by real children, or when teachers had a chance to draw inferences about a student's social class rather than simply being told his or her background. Sometimes social class was related to teacher expectations even when the child's current IQ and achievement were comparable. That is, teachers held lower expectations for lower-class children than for middle-class children even when those children had similar IQ scores and achievement.

Teachers' expectations may also be influenced by the behavior and physical appearance of the children.[41] Social class may influence teacher expectations directly or indirectly through test scores, appearance, language style, speed of task performance, and behavior. All of these traits are themselves culturally defined and are related to class position. Moreover, teacher expectations are influenced more by negative information about pupil characteristics than by positive data.[42] It is important to know this because much of the information teachers gain about low income children seems to be negative.

Another factor that may influence teacher expectations is the operation of the cultural capital possessed by families of higher social classes. As used here, the term *cultural capital* refers to the cultural resources and assets that families bring to their interactions with school personnel. By virtue of their own educational credentials and knowledge of educational institutions, parents, especially mothers, are able to help their children get the right teachers and courses and do extra work at home if necessary.[43]

If teacher expectations are often influenced by the social class of students, do those expectations have significant consequences for students? Research on this question has produced seemingly contradictory results. The controversy began with the publication of *Pygmalion in the Classroom.*[44] That book suggested that the expectations of classroom teachers might powerfully influence the achievement of students. Hundreds of studies on the possibility of "expectancy effects" have been conducted since then.[45] One thing is clear: only expectations that teachers truly believe are likely to affect their behaviors.

When teachers hold higher expectations for pupils, how does this affect their behavior? Their expectations seem to affect the frequency of interaction they have with their pupils and the kinds of behaviors they show toward different children. Teachers spend more time interacting with pupils for whom they have higher expectations.[46] For example, Brophy and Good[47] found that students for whom teachers held high expectations were praised more frequently when correct and were criticized less frequently when wrong or unresponsive than were pupils for whom teachers had low expectations.

Rosenthal[48] believes that teachers convey their expectations in at least four related ways. He bases this judgment on his review of 285 studies of interpersonal influence, including at least 80 in classrooms or other settings. First, he sees a general climate factor, consisting of the overall warmth a teacher shows to children, with more shown to high-expectancy students. Second, he sees students for whom high expectations are held as receiving more praise for doing something right than do students for whom low expectations are held. Third, Rosenthal notes that high-expectancy students are taught more than are low-expectancy students. This is consistent with research by others.[49] Fourth, Rosenthal indicates that expectancy may be affected by a response opportunity factor. That is, students for whom the teacher has higher expectations are called on more often and are given more chances to reply, as well as more frequent and more difficult questions.

A fifth way teachers convey their expectations, which Rosenthal does not mention but which has been observed by others, is the different type of curricula teachers may present to children for whom they have different expectations. One study found that teachers report that they present completely different types of economics to students of differently perceived abilities.[50] Another study reported that teachers use more reading texts and more difficult ones with the top reading group.[51] Clearly, there is evidence that at least some teachers behave differently toward students for whom they hold different expectations. The critical question remains: Do these expectations and behaviors actually affect students? Do the students think differently about themselves or learn more as a result of the expectations teachers hold? Therein lies the heart of the "Pygmalion effect" controversy.

When teachers hold definite expectations and when those expectations are reflected in their behavior toward children, these expectations are related to student cognitive changes, even when pupil IQ and achievement are controlled. Moreover, negative expectations, which can be observed only in natural settings because it is unethical to induce negative expectations experimentally, appear to have even more powerful consequences than do positive expectations.[52] Moreover, socially vulnerable children (i.e., younger, lower-class, and minority children) seem to be more susceptible to lower teacher expectations.[53]

CONSEQUENCES OF SOCIAL CLASS AND EDUCATIONAL INEQUALITY

This profile of social-class differences in education in the United States is oversimplified, but considerable evidence suggests that the general patterns described here do exist. Social-class backgrounds affect where students go to school and what happens to them once they are there. As a result, lower-class students are less likely to be exposed to valued curricula, are taught less of whatever curricula they do study, and are expected to do less work in the classroom and outside of it. Hence, they learn less and are less well prepared for the next level of education.

Although students have many reasons for dropping out of school or for failing to continue, their experiences in school may contribute to their desire to continue or to quit. Coleman, Hoffer, and Kilgore found that 24 percent of public high school students dropped out, compared to 12 percent of Catholic and 13 percent of other private school students.[54]

Similarly, college attendance depends on a number of factors, including access to the necessary financial resources. Nevertheless, it is striking how differently students at different schools fare. Graduation from a private rather than a public high school is related to attending a four-year (rather than a two-year) college,[55] attending a highly selective college,[56] and earning higher income in adult life.[57] Even within the same school, track placement is related to college attendance.[58] College attendance, in turn, is related to the adult positions and earnings one attains.[59] In 1987, women college graduates aged thirty to thirty-four earned 83 percent more than did women with a high school education, and the comparable premium for men was 57 percent more.[60] Thus, educational inequalities help create and legitimate economic and social inequalities.

However, most educators do not want to enhance and legitimate social inequalities. Therefore, it seems reasonable to ask, What can they do to try to change these patterns?

RECOMMENDATIONS FOR ACTION

Teachers, educators, and concerned citizens might consider the following actions:

1. Working politically to increase the educational resources available to all children, not just those in wealthy school districts, and not just the gifted and talented. Those concerned might do this by joining a political party that works to advance the interests of the less advantaged members of society, by attending political meetings, and by holding candidates accountable for their positions on education. We can join other people interested in scrutinizing candidates' records of support for education, and contribute time, money, or both to the campaigns of candidates seeking to defeat incumbents who have not supported quality education for all children.

2. Working to reduce economic inequalities in society. This can be done by supporting income-tax reforms at the national level that benefit hard-working low- and middle-income families, by trying to close tax loopholes for the rich, such as oil-depletion allowances, and by supporting aid for impoverished one-parent families.

3. Working to build economically and racially integrated communities. This can be done by choosing to live in such a community, by supporting federal subsidies for low-income housing in mixed-income areas, and by opposing efforts to restrict access to certain communities by members of particular ethnic or income groups. Such restrictions might take the form of zoning that prohibits the construction of high-rise housing for low-income groups or limits housing lots to a large size, such as two acres.

4. Working to support prenatal care for all pregnant women. Currently, about one-quarter of them receive no prenatal care. Helping all pregnant women could reduce or eliminate perhaps one-third of all learning disorders.[61]

5. Working to support Head Start programs for all eligible children. Only 16 percent of low-income children eligible for the preschool program for four-year-olds are now enrolled in it, yet Head Start has a proven track record. Every dollar invested in quality preschool education yields $4.75 because of lower costs later on for special education and public assistance, and the incarceration of people who commit crimes.[62]

6. Using tests for diagnosing rather than dismissing students. For example, instead of taking a low IQ test score as evidence that a child cannot learn, we can examine what parts of a particular test were difficult for that child. If necessary, we can obtain further, individual testing to identify and analyze what skills the child needs to develop, and devise strategies for teaching those specific skills. We can try alternative teaching strategies with each child until we find one that works. If a child has difficulty learning to read phonetically, for example, we might try teaching that child a different way, perhaps visually. We can help children with various kinds of learning disabilities learn ways to compensate for their difficulties. For example, planning their work in advance, organizing it so that they have enough time to complete the necessary steps, and allowing time for someone else to check their spelling are all compensatory strategies that can be adopted to good effect by children trying to overcome various learning disabilities.

7. Working on finding what abilities students do have, rather than on deciding that they haven't any. For example, if a student has strong artistic, musical, athletic, or auditory talents, but is weaker in the verbal or mathematical areas, we can help that child find ways into the academic subjects through their strengths.

8. Critically examining practices, such as tracking, that may bring teacher and student interests into conflict. Perhaps schools should have someone other than teachers represent the viewpoint and interests of students in the lowest tracks. This role might be filled by community representatives or by university professors who know the research on the negative effects of tracking.

9. Expecting and demanding a lot from students in the way of effort, thought, and work. We can help students take pride in themselves and their work by teaching them what a first-rate job should look like. The written materials students get from teachers and schools and the appearance of the classrooms, hallways, and school should all convey a sense of care, quality, and value. We can carefully check the work students do, suggest constructive ways they might improve it, and expect them to do better the next time.

10. Teaching students content and subject matter. We can show students that we value them and their learning by devoting class time to pedagogically useful tasks, by refusing to waste class time on frivolous activities, and by trying to stick to an annual schedule of curricular coverage.

11. If any form of tracking must be done, we can try to see that it is based on the willingness of students to do more work and on their proficiency in relevant prior areas of study, rather than on general aptitude tests. Systems of grouping should be flexible and easy to change as students progress (or lag behind). They should seek to avoid social evaluation and ranking and should allow students who acquire the necessary competencies to move into more advanced classes.

12. Helping students see how education is relevant and useful for their lives, perhaps by bringing back graduates who have used school as a springboard to better themselves and their worlds. Schools might keep a roster of successful graduates and post pictures and stories about them for current students to see. We can bring in examples that link learning with life accomplishments so students can begin to see connections between school and life. For example, we might invite people who run their own business to talk about how they use math, or bring in people who work in social service organizations to show how they use writing in their daily work.

SUMMARY

This chapter explores how educational structures, beliefs, and practices contribute to unequal educational outcomes. To achieve greater educational equality, educators must understand what social-class differences presently exist in those structures, beliefs, and practices. If these differences are understood, then the educational experiences of children of all social classes might be made more similar.

The higher one's social-class background, the more likely one is to attend a smaller school with more resources, smaller classes, and an academic curriculum. Achieving greater educational equality means making such school experiences available to all students, regardless of their social-class backgrounds.

Two different educational beliefs exist about why some children learn better than others, namely, beliefs about IQ and beliefs about cultural deprivation. Rather than sinking into the controversy over which one provides a better explanation for educational failure, this chapter considers what these beliefs have in common and examines how they both blame the victims for their failure and divert attention from how the social organization of schools may help to create failures. These beliefs also influence the curricular and teaching practices of schools attended by children of different social classes.

The educational process of tracking refers to the segregation of students into different learning or curriculum groups that are unequally ranked in a prestige hierarchy. Whether based on ability grouping or curricular grouping, such tracking tends to reduce learning opportunities for students in the lower groups, while increasing such opportunities for students in higher groups. As a result, this educational practice contributes to educational inequalities. Efforts to create greater educational equality require that the practice of tracking be changed in major ways.

Teachers may unconsciously form different learning expectations about students of different social-class backgrounds. When teachers hold higher expectations for students, they tend to spend more time interacting with those students, praise them more, teach them more, call on them more often, and offer them a more socially valued curriculum. When teachers hold higher expectations, and when those expectations are evident in their behavior, they increase student learning. Thus, achieving greater educational equality means that teachers' expectations for lower-class students need to be raised.

Because the educational structures, beliefs, and practices examined here are related to unequal educational attainment, and because educational success is related to lifetime occupations and earnings, it is important that educational inequalities be reduced. This chapter recommends a number of steps that concerned educators and citizens can take to promote educational and social equality.

QUESTIONS AND ACTIVITIES

1. According to Persell, in what ways do schools contribute to inequality? What evidence does the author give to support her position?

2. Give examples of how each of the following factors contributes to educational inequality: (a) educational structures; (b) beliefs of teachers and administrators; and (c) educational practices.

3. What are the major characteristics of each of the following types of schools: (a) elite private schools and exclusive suburban schools; (b) parochial schools; and (c) large urban public school systems?

4. Why do students from different social-class backgrounds often attend different schools or get assigned to different tracks when they attend the same schools? How does the social-class background of students influence the kind of education they often receive?

5. Visit and observe in (a) a local elite private school; (b) a school in an upper-middle-class suburb; and (c) an inner-city school. How are these schools alike? How are they different? Based on your visits and observations, what tentative generalizations can you make about education, social class, and inequality? To what extent are your generalizations similar to and different from those of Persell?

6. What are some of the major limitations of IQ tests? What cautions should teachers bear in mind when interpreting IQ tests, particularly the scores of lower-class and ethnic minority students?

7. How are the genetic and cultural-deprivation explanations of the low achievement of low-income students alike and different?

8. What is the self-fulfilling prophecy? How does it affect teacher expectations?

9. What is tracking? Why do you think tracking is more widespread in large, diverse school systems and in schools serving primarily lower-class students than in upper-middle-class suburban, private, and parochial schools?

10. How do the school experiences of students in lower and higher tracks differ? How does tracking contribute to educational inequality?

11. How do factors related to social class influence teacher expectations of students?

12. How do teacher expectations influence how teachers and pupils interact, what students are taught, and what students achieve?

NOTES

1. Caroline Hodges Persell, *Understanding Society*, 2d ed (New York: Harper & Row, 1987), p. 204.

2. James S. Coleman, Ernest Q. Campbell, Carol J. Hobson, James McPartland, Alexander M. Mood, Frederic D. Weinfeld, and Robert L. York, *Equality of Educational Opportunity* (Washington, D.C.: U.S. Government Printing Office, 1966); Bernard Goldstein, *Low Income Youth in Urban Areas: A Critical Review of the Literature* (New York: Holt, Rinehart, and Winston, 1967); Torsten Husen, *Social Background and Educational Career* (Paris: Center for Educational Research and Innovation, Organization for Economic Co-Operation and Development, 1972); George W. Mayeske and Carl E. Wisler, *A Study of Our Nation's Schools* (Washington, D.C.: U.S. Government Printing Office, 1972).

3. James S. Coleman, Thomas Hoffer, and Sally Kilgore, *High School Achievement* (New York: Basic Books, 1982), pp. 20–21.

4. Peter W. Cookson, Jr., and Caroline Hodges Persell, *Preparing for Power: America's Elite Boarding Schools* (New York: Basic Books, 1985), p. 58.

5. Ibid., 95.

6. In the Cookson and Persell study, more than half the students at elite boarding schools watched no television during the school week, compared to only 5 percent of public high school students. More than 80 percent of the elite boarding school students did more than 10 hours per week of homework, compared to less than 10 percent of the public high school students.

7. Coleman, Hoffer, and Kilgore, *High School Achievement.*

8. Ibid.

9. David Tyack, *The One Best System* (Cambridge, Mass.: Harvard University Press, 1974).

10. David Rogers, *110 Livingston Street: Politics and Bureaucracy in the New York City School System* (New York: Random House, 1968).

11. Howard Gardner, *Frames of Mind* (New York: Basic Books, 1983).

12. Ivar E. Berg, *Education and Jobs: The Great Training Robbery* (New York: Praeger, 1970); Randall Collins, *The Credential Society* (New York: Academic Press, 1979), Ch. 1; Donald P. Hoyt, *The Relationship between College Grades and Adult Achievement: A Review of the Literature,* Res. Rep. No. 7 (Iowa City: American College Testing Program, 1965); David C. McClelland, Testing for Competence Rather Than for "Intelligence," in Alan Gartner, Colin Greer, and Frank Riessman, eds. *The New Assault on Equality* (New York: Social Policy, 1974), pp. 163–197; C. Taylor, W. R. Smith, and B. Ghiselin, "The Creative and Other Contributions of One Sample of Research Scientists," in C. W. Taylor and F. Barron, eds. *Scientific Creativity: Its Recognition and Development* (New York: Wiley, 1963), pp. 53–76.

13. Arthur R. Jensen, "How Much Can We Boost I.Q. and Scholastic Achievement?" *Harvard Educational Review*, 39:No. 1 (Winter 1969): 1–123.

14. Thomas J. Bouchard, Jr., David T. Lykken, Matthew McGue, Nancy L. Segal, and Auke Tellegen, "Sources of Human Psychological Differences: The Minnesota Study of Twins Reared Apart," *Science* 250 (Oct. 12, 1990): 223–228.

15. Brent Bridgeman and Virginia Shipman, *Predictive Value of Measures of Self-Esteem and Achievement Motivation in Four-to-Nine-Year-Old-Low-Income Children* (ETS-Head Start Longitudinal Study) (Princeton, N.J.: Educational Testing Service, 1975).

16. Quoted in Walter Feinberg, "Educational Equality under Two Conflicting Models of Educational Development," *Theory and Society*, No. 2 (Summer 1975): 183–210.

17. See James B. Conant, *Slums and Suburbs* (New York: McGraw Hill, 1961); Jeannie Oakes, *Keeping Track: How Schools Structure Inequality* (New Haven, Conn.: Yale University Press, 1985).

18. Warren G. Findley and Miriam M. Bryan, *Ability Grouping: 1970–I, Common Practices in the Use of Tests for Grouping Students in Public Schools* (Athens: University of Georgia Center for Educational Improvement, ED 048381, 1970).

19. James D. Jones, Beth E. Vanfossen, and Joan Z. Spade, "Curriculum Placement: Individual and School Effects Using the High School and Beyond Data." Paper presented at the American Sociological Association Annual Meeting, Washington, D.C., 1985.

20. James E. Rosenbaum, *Making Inequality* (New York: Wiley-Interscience, 1976).

21. Rosenbaum, *Making Inequality.*

22. W. B. Brookover, D. J. Leu, and R. H. Kariger, *Tracking.* Unpublished manuscript (mimeo) (Western Michigan University, 1965); Roger B. Kariger, "The Relationship of Lane Grouping to the Socioeconomic Status of the Parents of Seventh-Grade Pupils in Three Junior High Schools." Unpublished doctoral dissertation, (Michigan State University), *Dissertation Abstracts,* 23: 4586, 1962; Ray C. Rist, "Student Social Class and Teacher Expectations: The Self-Fulfilling Prophecy in Ghetto Education," *Harvard Educational Review,* 40: No. 3 (August 1970): 411–451.

23. Maureen T. Hallinan, "Ability Grouping and Student Learning," in Maureen T. Hallinan, ed. *The Social Organization of Schools: New Conceptualizations of the Learning Process* (New York: Plenum, 1987), pp. 41–69.

24. Warren G. Findley and Miriam M. Bryan. *The Pros and Cons of Ability Grouping* (Bloomington, Ind: Phi Delta Kappa, 1975); John I. Goodlad, *A Place Called School* (New York: McGraw-Hill, 1984), pp. 159–160; Barbara Heyns, "Social Selection and Stratification within Schools," *American Journal of Sociology,* 79: No. 6 (May 1974): 1434–1451); Oakes, *Keeping Track;* Rosenbaum, *Making Inequality;* Walter E. Schafer, Carol Olexa, and Kenneth Polk, "Programmed for Social Class: Tracking in American High Schools," in Norman K. Denzin, ed., *Children and Their Caretakers* (New Brunswick, N.J.: Transaction Books, 1973), pp. 200–226.

25. Oakes, *Keeping Track,* 111.

26. Ibid., 91–92.

27. Ibid., 92.

28. Jerome Freiberg, *The Effects of Ability Grouping on Interactions in the Classroom* (ED 053194, 1970).

29. Oakes, *Keeping Track,* 133.

30. Rosenbaum, *Making Inequality,* 179–180.

31. Rist, "Student Social Class and Teacher Expectations"; Rosenbaum, *Making Inequality.*

32. D. Esposito, "Homogeneous and Heterogeneous Ability Grouping: Principal Findings and Implications for Evaluating and Designing More Effective Educational Environments," *Review of Educational Research,* 43: No. 2 (Spring 1973): 163–179; *Hobson v. Hansen Congressional Record* (June 21, 1967): 16721–16766; *Racial and Social Isolation in the Schools* (Albany: New York State Education Department, 1969); Oakes, *Keeping Track.*

33. Warren G. Findley and Miriam M. Bryan, *Ability Grouping: 1970-II The Impact of Ability Grouping on School Achievement, Affective Development, Ethnic Separation and Socioeconomic Separation* (Athens: University of Georgia Center for Educational Improvement), ED 048382, 1970; Oakes, *Keeping Track;* Rosenbaum, *Making Inequality;* Schafer, Olexa, and Polk, "Programmed for Social Class."

34. Karl L. Alexander, Martha Cook, and Edward L. McDill "Curriculum Tracking and Educational Stratification: Some Further Evidence," *American Sociological Review* 43 (1978): 47–66; Karl L. Alexander and Bruce K. Eckland, "Contextual Effects in the High School Attainment Process," *American Sociological Review,* 40, No. 3 (June 1975): 402–416; Abraham Jaffe and Walter Adams, *Academic and Socio-Economic Factors Related to Entrance and Retention at Two- and Four-Year Colleges in the Late 1960's* (New York: Columbia University Bureau of Applied Social Research, 1970); Rosenbaum, *Making Inequality;* James E. Rosenbaum, "Track Misperceptions and Frustrated College Plans: An Analysis of the Effects of Tracks and Track Perceptions in the National Longitudinal Survey," *Sociology of Education,* 53, No. 2 (April 1980): 74–88; James D. Jones, Joan N. Spade, and Beth E. Vanfossen, "Curriculum Tracking and Status Maintenance," *Sociology of Education,* 60, No. 2 (April 1987): 104–122.

35. Maureen T. Hallinan, "The Social Organization of Schools: An Overview," in Maureen T. Hallinan, *The Social Organization of the Schools: New Conceptualizations of the Learning Process* (New York: Plenum, 1987) pp. 1–12.

36. Oakes, *Keeping Track,* 191.

37. Ibid., 192.

38. Merrilee K. Finley, "Teachers and Tracking in a Comprehensive High School," *Sociology of Education,* 57, No. 4 (October 1984): 233–243.

39. Sylvia I. B. Hill, *Race, Class and Ethnic Biases in Research on School Performance of Low Income Youth.* Unpublished doctoral dissertation (University of Oregon, 1971); Annie Stein, "Strategies of Failure," *Harvard Educational Review,* 41, No. 2 (May 1971): 158–204.

40. Persell, *Education and Inequality,* 105–107.

41. Gerald R. Adams and Allan S. Cohen, "Children's Physical and Interpersonal Characteristics That Effect [sic] Student-Teacher Interactions," *Journal of Experimental Education,* 43, No. 1 (Fall 1974): 1–5; Gerald R. Adams and Joseph LaVoie, "The Effect of Student's Sex, Conduct, and Facial Attractiveness on Teacher Expectancy, *Education,* 95, No. 1 (Fall 1974): 76–83; M. Clifford and E. Walster, "The Effect of Physical Attractiveness on Teacher Expectation," *Sociology of Education,* 46, No. 2 (Spring 1973): 248–258; F. X. Lawlor and E. Lawlor, "Teacher Expectations: A Study of Their Genesis," *Science Education,* 57, No. 1 (Jan.–Mar. 1973): 9–14.

42. Emanuel J. Mason, "Teachers' Observations and Expectations of Boys and Girls as Influenced by Biased Psychological Reports and Knowledge of the Effects of Bias," *Journal of Educational Psychology,* 65, No. 2 (October 1973): 238–243.

43. David P. Baker and David L. Stevenson, "Mothers' Strategies for Children's School Achievement: Managing the Transition to High School," *Sociology of Education* 59 (July 1986): 156–166; Annette Lareau, *Home Advantage* (Philadelphia: The Falmer Press, 1989); Elizabeth L. Useem, "Social Class and Ability Group Placement in Mathematics in the Transition to Seventh Grade: The Role of Parental Involvement." Paper presented at the American Educational Research Association Annual Meeting, Boston, Mass., April 1990.

44. Robert Rosenthal and Lenore Jacobson, *Pygmalion in the Classroom* (New York: Holt, Rinehart, and Winston, 1968).

45. See, for example, Harris M. Cooper and Thomas L. Good, *Pygmalion Grows Up* (New York: Longman, 1983), for a review of some of this research.

46. Jere E. Brophy and Thomas L. Good, "Teachers' Communication of Differential Expectations for Children's Classroom Performance: Some Behavioral Data," *Journal of Educational Psychology,* 61, No. 5 (October 1970):365–374; Catherine Cornbleth, O. L. Davis, Jr., and Christine Button, "Expectations for Pupil Achievement and Teacher-Pupil Interaction," *Research in Social Studies Education,* Supplement 9, Vol. 38 (January 1974): 54–58, 1974; Barbara K. Given, "Teacher Expectancy and Pupil Performance: Their Relationship to Verbal and Non-Verbal Communications by Teachers of Learning Disabled Children." Doctoral dissertation, (Catholic University), *Dissertation Abstracts International,* 35: 1529A, 1974; J. T. Jeter, "Can Teacher Expectations Function as Self-Fulfilling Prophecies?" *Contemporary Education,* 46, No. 3 (Spring 1973): 161–165; Patricia L. Kranz, Wilford A. Weber, and Kenneth N. Fishell, "The Relationship between Teacher Perception of Pupils and Teacher Behavior toward Those Pupils." Paper presented at the American Educational Research Association Annual Meeting, Minneapolis, 1970 ED 038346; Rist, "Student Social Class and Teacher Expectations; P. Rubovits and M. Maehr, "Pygmalion Analyzed: Toward an Explanation of the Rosenthal-Jacobson Findings," *Journal of Personality and Social Psychology,* 19, No. 2 (August 1971): 197–203; Melvin L. Silberman, "Behavioral Expression of Teachers' Attitudes toward Elementary Students," *Journal of Educational Psychology,* 60, No. 5 (October 1969): 402–407; Bill J. Willis, "The Influence of Teacher Expectation on Teachers' Classroom Interaction with Selected Children." Doctoral dissertation, (George Peabody College), *Dissertation Abstracts International,* 30: 5072A, 1969.

47. Brophy and Good, "Teachers Communication of Differential Expectations."

48. Robert Rosenthal, "The Pygmalion Effect: What You Expect Is What You Get," *Psychology Today Library Cassette* 12 (New York: Ziff-Davis, 1974).

49. Walter V. Beez, "Influence of Biased Psychological Reports on Teacher Behavior and Pupil Performance," in Mathew B. Miles and W. W. Charters, Jr., eds., *Learning in Social Settings* (Boston: Allyn and Bacon, 1970), pp. 320–334; Ronald M. Carter, "Locus of Control and Teacher Expectancy as Related to Achievement of Young School Children," doctoral dissertation, Indiana University, *Dissertation Abstracts International,* 30: 467A, 1969; David H. Martinez, "A Comparison of the Behavior during Reading Instruction, of Teachers of High and Low Achieving in First Grade Classes." Doctoral dissertation, (*University of Oregon*), *Dissertation Abstracts International,* 34: 7520A, 1973; William M. McQueen, Jr., "The

Effect of Divergent Teacher Expectations on the Performance of Elementary School Children on a Vocabulary Learning Task." Doctoral dissertation, (University of South Carolina), *Dissertation Abstracts International,* 31: 5206A, 1970; Rist, "Student Social Class and Teacher Expectations."

50. Nell Keddie, ed., "Classroom Knowledge," in Michael F. D. Young, ed., *Knowledge and Control* (London: Collier, MacMillan, 1971), pp. 133–160.

51. Judith Landon Alpert, "Do Teachers Adapt Methods and Materials to Ability Groups in Reading?" *California Journal of Education Research,* 26: 3 (May 1975):120–123.

52. Damon Floyd Asbury, "The Effects of Teacher Expectancy, Subject Expectancy, and Subject Sex on the Learning Performance of Elementary School Children." Doctoral dissertation (Ohio State University), *Dissertation Abstracts International,* 31: 4437A, 1970; Paul M. Kohn, "Relationship between Expectations of Teachers and Performance of Students," *Journal of School Health,* No. 4 (Winter 1973): 498–503; Mason, "Teachers' Observations and Expectations"; William B. Seaver, Jr., "Effects of Naturally Induced Teacher Expectancies, *Journal of Personality and Social Psychology,* 28, No. 3 (December 1973): 333–342.

53. Stephen H. Baker, "Teacher Effectiveness and Social Class as Factors in Teacher Expectancy Effects on Pupils Scholastic Achievement." Doctoral dissertation (Clark University), *Dissertation Abstracts International,* 34:2376A, 1973; William P. Krupczak, "Relationships among Student Self-Concept of Academic Ability, Teacher Perception of Student Academic Ability and Student Achievement." Doctoral dissertation (University of Miami), *Dissertation Abstracts International,* 33: 3388A–3389A, 1972; Rosenthal and Jacobson, *Pygmalion in the Classroom;* Albert H. Yee, "Source and Direction of Casual Influence in Teacher-Pupil Relationships," *Journal of Educational Psychology,* 59, No. 4 (August 1968): 275–282.

54. Coleman, Hoffer, and Kilgore, *High School Achievement,* 148.

55. Barbara Falsey and Barbara Heyns, "The College Channel: Private and Public Schools Reconsidered," *Sociology of Education,* 57, No. 2 (April 1984): 111–122.

56. Caroline Hodges Persell and Peter W. Cookson, Jr., "Chartering and Bartering: Elite Education and Social Reproduction," *Social Problems,* 33, No. 2 (December 1985): 114–129.

57. Lionel S. Lewis and Richard A. Wanner, "Private Schooling and the Status Attainment Process," *Sociology of Education,* 52, No. 2, 1979: 99–112.

58. Alexander, Cook, and McDill, "Curriculum Tracking and Educational Stratification: Some Further Evidence"; Karl L. Alexander and Edward L. McDill, "Selection and Allocation within Schools: Some Causes and Consequences of Curriculum Placement," *American Sociological Review,* 41: No. 6 (December 1976): 963–980; Jaffe and Adams, "Academic and Socio-Economic Factors Related to Entrance and Retention"; Rosenbaum, *Making Inequality;* Rosenbaum, "Track Misperceptions and Frustrated College Plans: An Analysis of the Effects of Tracks and Track Perceptions in the National Longitudinal Survey."

59. Steve Brint, "Intra-Occupational Stratification in Six High-Status Occupations: An Analysis of Status and Status Attainment in Academe, Science, Law, and Corporate Management, Engineering and Medicine." Unpublished paper (Yale University, 1985); David Kamens, "Colleges and Elite Formation: The Case of Prestigious American Colleges," *Sociology of Education,* 47, No. 3 (Summer 1974): 354–378; Vincent Tinto, "College Origin and Patterns of Status Attainment," *Sociology of Work and Occupations,* 7, No. 4 (November 1980): pp. 457–486; Michael Useem, *The Inner Circle: Large Corporations and the Rise of Business Political Activity in the U.S. and U.K.* (New York: Oxford University Press, 1984); Michael Useem and Jerome Karabel, "Educational Pathways to Top Corporate Management," *American Sociological Review* 51 No. 2 (April 1986): 184–200.

60. U.S. Department of Education, *The Condition of Education 1990,* Vol. 2, *Postsecondary Education* (Washington, D.C.: United States Government Printing Office, 1990), p. 52.

61. Harold L. Hodgkinson, *The Same Client: The Demographics of Education and Service Delivery Systems* (Washington, D.C.: I.E.L., 1989).

62. David Weikart and Lawrence J. Schweinhart, *Changed Lives: The Effects of the Perry Preschool Program on Youths through Age 19* (Ypsilanti, Mich.: High Scope, 1984); *Children's Defense Fund: A Call for Action* (Washington, D.C.: Children's Defense Fund, 1988).

CHAPTER 5

Religious Diversity and Education

■ JAMES K. UPHOFF

INTRODUCTION

A beautiful new mosque stands with its center dome and twin minarets vivid against the blue sky. Where in the United States is this religious center located? In Washington, D.C., where many nations of the world send their diplomats? In New York City, the home of the United Nations? In Los Angeles? The answer to each of these questions is no.

The mosque is located on the flat, fertile farmland of northwest Ohio, just south of Toledo, deep in the heart of the midwestern United States. Unusual? Yes, but a vivid sign of the changing times as religions in the United States become more diverse.

Watching local law enforcement officers chain and padlock a church door on the television news recently was unsettling to many people. Yet this scenario did happen in rural Nebraska, when a small independent Protestant church decided to defy a state law requiring all teachers in the state to be certified. This church had recently created its own small school, which met in the church. However, the teaching staff did not meet the qualifications set by the law. The minister made national news as he, on behalf of the congregation, defied the law and all attempts of the authorities to reach a compromise.

In California's San Ramone School District, some parents raised objections to an education curriculum because it called for teachers and students to use decision-making techniques and because it was alleged to be the teaching of "secular humanism," considered by some people to be a type of religion.[1] This example is only the tip of a large iceberg of formal objections that have been made in school districts throughout the nation. More than ever before, school materials and teaching methods, standards, and requirements are being challenged on religious grounds as groups and individuals fight back against what they perceive as the antireligious nature of the public schools.

This chapter helps you better understand the religious element of cultural diversity. If the United States is to function as a cohesive unit, it must be able to accommodate the diversity within it. Teachers have a key role to play, but they can perform it only if they fully understand the play and the audiences who will attend.

To help teachers prepare for this theater, this chapter provides definitions of religion, a glimpse at the importance of religion, a brief review of relevant U.S. history, an examination of constitutional issues involved, facts and figures about the religious diversity within the United States, and a focus on the educational implications of all of these factors.

DEFINITIONS OF RELIGION

Before we can discuss religion, we must come to some common agreement about what religion is. The word is a common one that seems easy to define but in fact is difficult to explain. Nearly everyone uses the term, but few have a well-developed idea of what we mean. Wilson contends, "Often, one's definition of 'religion' reveals much more about the point of view or prejudices of the definer than it does about religion itself."[2] He feels that the definition can be either negative or positive depending on the emotions it calls forth in the speaker.

Albanese states, "Everyone knows what religion is—that is, until one tries to define it. It is in the act of defining that religion seems to slip away."[3] She believes that the difficulty exists because religion crosses many boundaries, even though the purpose of most definitions is to establish boundaries.

We provide a definition by describing examples, thus providing each of us with a more common picture on which to build our look at the educational implications of religious diversity. As we focus our camera on this concept, we will need to use both a close-up and a wide-angle lens. These views will give us first the narrow definition most commonly used and then the much broader definition used by the U.S. Supreme Court in several landmark cases regarding church and state.

If we were to play a word-association game using the term *religion*, the responses would probably include at least some of the following: buildings of worship; traditions and festivals; names of organized groups; special objects, symbols, or literature; sets of beliefs; and specific types of persons or roles. Thus, such words as *church, temple, pagoda, shrine, confirmation, bar/bat mitzvah, Hindu, Shinto, Buddhist, Society of Mary, cross, Star of David, clerical collar, Upanishad, Koran, baptism, creed, priest, monk, nun, minister, rabbi, mullah,* and *evangelist* would be commonly stated by people using this narrowly focused view of religion.

The wide-angle view was described by the leaders of the Public Education Religion Studies Center (PERSC) in their 1974 book, *Questions and Answers*[4]:

> The broad definition envisions religion as any faith or set of values to which an individual or group gives ultimate loyalty. . . . Buddhism, Taoism, Ethical Culture, secularism, humanists, scientism, nationalism, money, and power illustrate this concept of religion.

The U.S. Supreme Court has for several decades been using this broader definition as it has made decisions. Thus, Madeline Murray O'Hare, an avowed atheist, has been considered by some to be a very religious person by this broad definition.

Several of the most recent church-state cases currently on appeal in the federal courts involve this broader definition. One federal judge found that secular humanism is a religion, that many textbooks discuss its beliefs, and that other religions such as Christianity do not have their own beliefs included in those same textbooks; thus, more than forty textbooks must be withdrawn from the public schools. Judge William Brevard Hand's ruling in *Smith et al. v. Board of School Commissioners of Mobile County et al.* of March 4, 1987, represented a direct use of the broader definition.

One important aspect of this dual definition is that many individuals use and live by both. Often referred to as *crypto* (hidden) religion, these people use a sectarian (narrow definition) mask to hide an ultimate concern. They often use the same symbols as those whose prime belief is a more traditional form of religion. For instance, such groups as the Ku Klux Klan use the Christian cross as a symbol of their "WASP-supremacy ultimate concern religion." Other people "believe" in the acquisition of power or wealth, doing everything they can to obtain them, even though they outwardly profess belief in the giving, sharing, and serving creeds of a particular church.

Thus, the broad definition, because it so clearly includes values and the valuing process, must also be used as we proceed through this chapter. We can understand the many educational implications of religious diversity in the United States and in the world at large only if we use both views. These views include the traditional notion of religion (being Jewish or Christian, for example) and the idea of religion as any strong faith.

Importance of Religion

For what idea, principle, cause, belief, or value would you be willing to give your life? As each of us answers this question of ultimate commitment, we state the importance of our religion. In the history of humanity, millions of people have answered this question through action. Countless lives have been given in defense of religious beliefs. There has been no shortage of examples, from the earliest hunter who believed in the security of family and died while protecting that family, to those who blow themselves up as they conduct holy war.

It is our own system of values and beliefs that makes each example positive or negative. Such emotion-laden terms as *religious fanatic, heroic,* and *martyr* provide clues as to how we perceive a particular event.

If human beings are willing to die for a belief, then they are even more willing to suffer lesser penalties such as ridicule, separation, torture, imprisonment, fines, or restrictions, on behalf of their beliefs. British and American women of the early twentieth century who fought for women's rights certainly suffered as a result of their beliefs. Today, parents who decide to school their children at home have often found themselves in court facing state charges for disobeying school-attendance laws.

Religion is an important element in the lives of many people; to some, it is the *most* important element. It has been the source of strength in times of trouble. Certainly this has been the case for African Americans in their history in the

United States. African American historian Barbara Green writes of the relationship between the survival skills and the folklore of Blacks. The spirituals they sang provided them with comfort, hope, and strength. Green states, "The performance of work songs and spirituals was just as important as the songs themselves. Singing them sharpened memory skills; taught language skills, religious values, and survival strategy; and cultivated group identity."[5]

Much of the civil rights movement of the last half of this century had a strong foundation within the churches and synagogues of the United States. People opposed to integration were often placed in the position of being opposed to their own church bodies or to religion in general. Churches became divided, and crypto religions developed.

The public schools often became the battleground for these contrasting belief systems. Governors who stood at the schoolhouse door to prevent integration were endorsed by some ministers and condemned by others. The schools were in the middle. Today, the schools are still in the middle. One example is when laws are passed requiring schools to teach sex education while many individuals and churches object with such vigor that they withdraw their children from school and establish new, private schools.

It should be no wonder, then, that public education as an arm of the state should have found itself frequently at odds with first one religious group and then another, as the United States has become ever more diverse and religiously pluralistic.

We Are What We Were

Historically the United States has always had a number of different religions. The similar, yet very different, religions of the Native Americans were well in place when the Europeans arrived. These newcomers brought with them a collection of similar, yet very different, forms of Christianity. Several colonies adopted nearly exclusively a single form of this religion (for example, the Puritans and Congregationalists in Massachusetts, the Catholics in Georgia, and the Anglicans and Episcopalians in Virginia), while others were settled by a variety of groups. Pennsylvania, for instance, became home to Quakers, Lutherans, Baptists, and many others.

Three different types of school systems developed, in part as a result of these patterns of religious settlement. The New England colonies developed public school laws (Massachusetts Laws of 1642 and 1647) that required an elementary school for every 50 families and a grammar school for every 100 families. However, since the government was essentially a *theocracy,* in which the church and state were essentially one, the name of those laws was "Ye Old Deluder Satan Act," and their purpose was to teach the children to read and write so they would be able to read the scriptures on their own and thus "ward off ye old deluder Satan." This *public parochial school* became the model for much of American education.

Because of the geographic size of the Southern colonies and the dominance by the Anglican Church of England, most schooling was done by traveling teachers who would stay for several months, visiting first one plantation and then another. Most children did not attend school; usually only boys from the wealthier families were so privileged. Apprenticeships were widely used for the less well-to-do. Formal education was much more a system of private schooling.

The middle colonies tended to have very diverse settlement patterns. No single religion dominated, but because religion was felt by many people to be a major reason for having formal education, little agreement among the various religious groups was possible. Therefore, a system of parochial schools resulted, with each group establishing its own schools.

Even amid this diversity, however, there was *oneness of religion,* a religious unity among Americans. Albanese says that religious unity refers to the "dominant and public cluster of organizations, ideas, and moral values which, historically and geographically, have characterized this country."[6] Today, this is often referred to as the Judeo-Christian tradition. For some people, this ethic has become a civil religion, in which patriotism and nationalism become an ultimate concern, a cryptoreligion.

As each new wave of immigrants came into the United States, the oneness expanded to accommodate the new arrivals even as the established religions changed and adapted to the new setting. Some geographic areas became closely associated with a particular group, such as the Amish in Pennsylvania. Add to the problems associated with religious differences the difficulties of language, dress, and food, and we can understand the assimilation problems experienced by immigrating groups. Most recently the new immigrants have come from non-Christian lands and are of a different race, thus making for a more difficult assimilation.

The process of assimilation did not always work smoothly. The religious oneness described above was nearly always patterned after the Massachusetts public school model—public parochial schools. Cincinnati's Bible War in 1869–1870 is one example of the assimilation process not working well. The public schools required the reading of the King James version of the Bible, which was objectionable to the large Catholic population, to Jews, and to others. Those in charge argued that the "common schools" were an appropriate place for the "common religion" to be taught. This religion was, however, a generalized Protestant version of Christianity and thus was not acceptable to all students.[7]

From the inception of the United States, the most fundamental question asked about religion and education has been, To what extent should the public schools be an extension of the oneness of religion, an extension of the separateness of the many religions, or no extension of any kind of religion? The many court cases in this century have been part of the process of trying to answer this question. The line separating church and state has always been unclear. Two centuries ago, the framers of the constitution addressed this question; legislative bodies and the courts have tried to clarify it; but it remains an issue very important to many people.

Constitutional Issues

The First Amendment to the U.S. Constitution said clearly: "Congress shall make no law respecting an establishment of religion, or prohibiting the free exercise thereof." The key word here is *Congress,* because not until the Fourteenth Amendment was adopted (1868) and gave to the citizens of the states all of the rights they had as citizens of the nation did the federal separation of church and state have any influence on the schools. In fact, not until the 1830s did the Commonwealth of Massachusetts repeal such laws as mandatory church membership as a requirement for holding a public office.

The constitutional separation of church and state has two key elements: no state support to create or maintain a religion (establishment), and no state laws against the practice of a religion (prohibition). Most constitutional cases regarding religion and the schools have dealt with the "establishment clause"; that is, the state (public school) cannot help to establish a religion by requiring prayer, Bible reading, or devotional moments of silent meditation or by permitting the use of school buildings or funds for religious instruction. Busing children to parochial schools for safety reasons and using public funds to purchase nonreligious textbooks is legal.

The Supreme Court gave strong support to the need for and appropriateness of teaching about religion in the public schools. On June 17, 1963, the Court gave its opinion on the cases of *Abington* v. *Schempp* and *Murray* (son of Madeline Murray O'Hare) v. *Curlett,* which dealt with required prayer and Bible reading in school. Associate Justice Tom Clark wrote the majority opinion, which included the following statement (emphasis mine):

> It might well be said that one's education is not complete without a study of comparative religion or the history of religion and its relationship to the advancement of civilization. It certainly may be said that the Bible is worthy of study for its literary and historic qualities. Nothing we have said here indicates that such study of the Bible or of religion, when presented objectively as part of a secular program of education, may not be effected consistent with the First Amendment.

Because the headlines following this decision were inaccurate and misleading ("Prayer Banned—Bible Banned"), many educators as well as parents and other citizens were angry, perplexed, and concerned. Almost immediately the school curriculum guides and materials were subjected to "self-censoring," first by educators and then by publishers. So much censorship occurred so rapidly that the American Association of School Administrators published a book in 1964 entitled *Religion in the Public Schools.* The association took a strong and clear position in support of the valid academic study of religion in the public schools when it stated:

> A curriculum which ignored religion would itself have serious implications. It would seem to proclaim that religion has not been as real in men's lives as health, or politics, or economics. By omission it would appear to deny that religion has been and is important in man's history—a denial of the obvious. In day by day practice, the topic cannot be avoided. As an integral part of man's culture, it must be included.

Even though the need for and appropriateness of teaching about religion has been strongly shown since 1963, not everyone in the nation concurs. Problems occur when the public feels that schools are teaching about the religions of other lands but are giving little attention to religions of this land. The emotions

schools had hoped to avoid by focusing only on remote and thus less controversial peoples are now in the headlines and in the courts.

Other constitutional issues have addressed how much power the state
actually has to regulate religious schools, to require attendance at an approved
school (religious or public), and to provide aid (what kind, how much, etc.). A
1980s case, for example, that began in Dayton, Ohio, involved the issue of
whether the state civil rights commission had the power to investigate a
teacher's charge that she had been dismissed from a private Christian school
because she exercised her civil right to question an administrative decision. The
school contends that, because the school is a religious institution, civil rights laws
do not apply to how it treats its own personnel. This is one of a new type of
church-state cases focusing on prohibiting the free exercise thereof clause of the
First Amendment.

The founders of the United States had either experienced firsthand or
knew about the unwelcome combination of church and state in Europe. Wars,
inquisitions, and the absence of freedom were fresh in their minds as they
developed the Constitution. The quality of their work is seen today in the fact
that in the more than 200 years that have passed, the United States has
become even more religiously diverse but has avoided the major problems
of lasting and often violent interreligious conflicts too often found elsewhere
in the world.

RELIGIOUS DIVERSITY IN THE UNITED STATES

Lessons from history tell us that religious, ethnic, and language diversity within
a nation or other area often lead to many problems. Such examples as Ireland,
India, Pakistan, Sri Lanka, and Belgium come to mind. Diversity, however, also
exists within particular religions and even within particular denominations of a
religion. Conflicts during the 1980s within the Southern Baptist Convention
and a split in the Lutheran Church Missouri Synod—both separate Christian
denominations—illustrate the point.

If we are to learn from history, we must be more knowledgeable about
our own religious diversity and learn how to respond to it more appropriately.
This section examines the extent of religious diversity within the United States
and within Christianity, the major religious groups.

As a nation, the United States began with a diversity of peoples and their
beliefs. The dominant common Western European heritage, although not one
of peace and goodwill among themselves, was clearly Christian in a general
way. While some early settlers were deeply religious and came to this land in
order to practice their religion, others came for different reasons, including economic gain, adventure, and escape from legal or other problems. It must be
noted that some of those who sought religious freedom were, in turn, unwilling
to grant it to others; Rhode Island was founded by people whose religious
beliefs were not welcome in neighboring Massachusetts.

Specific data on religious diversity in the United States are difficult to find.
One must turn to a variety of sources and sometimes use information from
different studies to gain even a fuzzy picture of how many religions are practiced

today in the United States. There is always a danger that comparisons of religions are being made between apples and oranges.

A massive 1980 survey of Judeo-Christian denominations[8] found more than 228 different church groups. A few, 17 out of 111 who returned surveys, reported having more than one million adherents and another 25 church bodies claimed between 100,000 and one million members. After Roman Catholics, who accounted for 42 percent of the total, the figures dropped dramatically to 14.5 percent for Southern Baptists and 10.3 percent for Methodists. A total of 108 'denominations' were listed for the other 31 percent, with no one group claiming more than 2.6 percent of the total.

Add to these data the fact that there are thousands of local churches not affiliated with any larger body, synod, or organization. Many of these independent churches grew in number of adherents during the 1970s and 1980s. Television evangelists, at least up until their scandals of the late 1980s, experienced large and growing video congregations, which were also outside of the enumerations of the survey cited above.

Still other groups that stand partially or totally outside the Judeo-Christian realm (Unification Church of the Rev. Sun Myung Moon, the Scientologists, and the Hare Krishna movement, for example) experienced growth during the 1970s. Precise numbers for such groups are not available.

Gaustad's data indicate that as the United States has grown over the years, the percentage of the population claiming a religious affiliation has also grown.[9] Another way to say this is that as the United States has become more diverse in the social and religious aspects of its peoples, a larger percentage of people have become affiliated with a religious body. Gaustad reports that in 1865, 26 percent claimed a religious affiliation. This percentage rose over the years to 44 percent in 1930 and 62 percent in 1970, the final year for these data.

Table 5.1, from *Statistical Abstract of the United States,* summarizes data on religious preference, church membership, and attendance from 1957 to 1989 for the noninstitutional population of the United States eighteen years old and over.[10] The table indicates that this population showed the following religious preferences in 1989: Protestant, 56 percent; Catholic, 28 percent; Jewish, 2 percent, and other, 2 percent. Although 90 percent of this population expressed a religious preference, only 69 percent were church or synagogue members and only 43 percent actually attended churches or synagogues.

The 1990 Yearbook of American and Canadian Churches, reporting data from the Gallup organization, found that worship attendance by adults has remained remarkably steady over a fifty-year period, moving from 41 percent in 1939 to only 43 percent in 1989 after a nearly twenty-year decline. However, the worship attendance of U.S. teens has grown significantly from 50 percent in 1980 to 57 percent in 1989.[11] The December 17, 1990, issue of *Newsweek* included a seven-page story entitled "A Time to Seek—with babes in arms and doubts in mind, a generation looks to religion." Noting the clear trend of former baby boomers to return to religion, the article reports the following:

- At one time or another, roughly two-thirds of baby boomers dropped out of organized religion. But in recent years, more than one-third of the dropouts have returned.
- About 57 percent—43 million people now attend church or synagogue.

Table 5.1

Religious Preference, Church Membership and Attendance: 1957 to 1989 [In percent. Covers civilian noninstitutional population, 18 years old and over. Data represent averages of the combined results of several surveys during year. Data are subject to sampling variability; see source.]

Year	Religious Preference					Church/ Synagogue Members	Persons Attending Church/ Synagogue[1]	Age and Region	Church/ Synagogue Members, 1989
	Protestant	Catholic	Jewish	Other	None				
1957	66	26	3	1	3	73	47	18–29 years old	61
1967	67	25	3	3	2	[2]73	43	30–49 years old	66
1975	62	27	2	4	6	[3]71	41	50 years and over	76
1980	61	28	2	2	7	69	40	East[4]	69
1985	57	28	2	4	9	71	42	Midwest[5]	72
1988	56	28	2	2	9	65	42	South[6]	74
1989	56	28	2	4	10	69	43	West[7]	55

Source: U.S. Bureau of the Census, *Statistical Abstract of the United States: 1991* (111 edition) (Washington, D.C.: U.S. Government Printing Office, Table 76), p. 55.

[1] Persons who attended a church or synagogue in the last seven days. [2] 1952 data. [3] 1965 data. [4] ME, NH, RI, NY, CT, VT, MA, NJ, PA, WV, DE, MD, and DC. [5] OH, IN, IL, MI, MN, WI, IA, ND, SD, KS, NE, and MO. [6] KY, TN, VA, NC, SC, GA, FL, AL, MS, TX, AR, OK, and LA. [7] AZ, NM, CO, NV, MT, ID, WY, UT, CA, WA, OR, AK, and HI.

■ More than 80 percent of the boomers consider themselves religious and believe in life after death.

■ The biggest group of returnees (about 60 percent) are married with children.

■ The least likely to have returned are married couples without kids.[12]

According to the *New Book of American Rankings,* the percentage of Christian-Judaic adherents varies greatly by state. Rhode Island leads the list, with 75.5 percent; Utah follows closely, with 75.2 percent; Alaska, with 30.8 percent, and Nevada, with 29.3 percent, are at the bottom of the rankings. In general, the New England area and the Upper Midwest and Plains states have the highest percentages of adherents, and the West has the lowest.

Data for Christians and Jews are much easier to obtain than is accurate and reliable information for other religions. Only the former tend to maintain records and statistics (many of which are less than complete and current). Most information for other religions is based on informed estimates. What follows, then, should be viewed as general patterns rather than as hard data.

Immigration reports provide a basis for enlightened conjecture as to how many adherents there are for each religion. *The World Almanac and Book of Facts: 1987* indicates that the total percentage of European immigrants to the United States went down from 33.8 percent in 1961 to only 17.8 percent for the following decade.[13] In sharp contrast is the number of immigrants from Asia. Figures for these immigrants went up dramatically, from 12.9 percent of total immigrants in the 1960s to 35.3 percent in the 1970s. The figures for African immigrants went from 0.9 percent to 1.8 percent, and those for South and Central America and for Australia both declined a little. The continued emigration of the many refugees from Southeast Asia during the 1980s maintained this pattern and probably increased the influx of persons from non-Christian-Judaic backgrounds, thus further increasing the religious diversity of the United States.

Other data that support these conclusions indicate that in 1957 there were only 10,000 Buddhists in the United States, but in 1970, 100,000 were here.[14] However, the *Handbook of Denominations in the U.S.,* published in 1990, shows 250,000 Buddhists in the United States.[15]

Jacquet's 1990 *Yearbook of American and Canadian Churches* indicates that practicing Jews in the United States numbered 3,750,000, with a more inclusive count totaling 5,935,700 Jewish "adherents."[16] This larger group made up about 2 percent of the total U.S. population according to *Statistical Abstracts of the United States: 1990.*[17] The U.S. Jewish population in 1960 numbered 5,367,000, thus giving a growth rate over thirty years of only about 10.6 percent.[18]

In contrast, U.S. believers of the Muslim faith were estimated to number 3,000,000 in the 1985 *Handbook of Denominations in the U.S.*[19] The 1990 *World Almanac* gives a figure of 6,000,000 Muslim adherents within the United States. Even though these figures are not as precise as those for Christianity and Judaism, they do clearly indicate a significant growth rate for followers of Islam.[20]

Christianity remains the largest religion in the United States, and Judaism may have already been surpassed for its number-two ranking by Muslim followers. This increase in the numbers of Muslims has resulted from immigration from such areas as Lebanon, Iran, Egypt, India, and Pakistan, as well as from the growth of the Black Muslim sect.

Given the fact that U.S. schools and textbooks have paid little attention to the teachings of the Islamic faith, this growth will represent a challenge. According to Uphoff, "William J. Griswold, a key investigator in a thorough study of U.S. textbooks and their treatment of Islam in history, reports that 27 of 45 texts examined either have nothing on the Muslim world, are biased, simplistic, and error-filled, or are scanty and not always dependable in their treatment of Islam."[21]

Such lack of knowledge about the Islamic faith and those who follow it led to major problems following the outbreak of the Persian Gulf War in January 1991. The January 27, 1991, issue of the *Dayton Daily News* ran a front-page story with the following headlines: "Ignorance Turns to Violence: Arab-Americans the Target of Misplaced Anger in Cleveland." The February 4, 1991, issue of *Time* magazine addressed similar violence and then informed its readers that

> *The attacks are one measure of widespread ignorance about the Arab-American community. Few are aware, for example, of the degree to which Arab-Americans have flourished in this country, rising to the ranks of White House chief of staff and Senate majority leader. . . . Arab-Americans are better educated than the U.S. population as a whole, more likely to hold management or professional positions, and wealthier: an average household income of $22,973 is above the U.S. average of $20,973.*[22]

The ABC-TV news program "Nightline" focused its February 8, 1991, show on the backlash against Arab Americans. It reported the frequent use of such derogatory terms as *camel jockey* and said that slogans such as "Arabs Go Home!" were being used much more often along with more violent actions. The show also reported that hate crimes against Arab Americans numbered 41 in all of 1990, but that a total of 36 had been documented in January 1991.

It is obvious that such actions clearly demonstrate ignorance about the religion of Islam and the people who practice it. The problem becomes even more serious when we realize that this religion has the same roots as Christianity and Judaism (all three trace their heritage back to Abraham) and that Islam's adherents make up a sizable porportion of the U.S. population.

A report on languages other than English spoken in the United States is another source of data for our conjecturing about the nation's religious diversity. According to the report, in 1980 the primary languages spoken at home by persons between the ages of five and seventeen were as follows:

- Vietnamese, spoken by 64,000
- Korean, 60,000
- Japanese, 34,000
- Filipino, 63,000
- Chinese, 114,000
- Other non-European, 544,000

(Spanish was the largest, with 2,952,000 speakers, but most of these children are within the Christian tradition, given their cultural heritage.) Hundreds of thousands of children speaking languages other than English at home and coming from nations where religions other than Christianity and Judaism are practiced are now common in the United States and its schools.

The New Book of World Rankings has developed what it calls a homogeneity index to use when comparing nations on a scale of internal diversity. The book's introduction states:

> *Political stability is often associated with linguistic and ethnic homogeneity. While developed societies in the West are moving toward pluralism and multi-culturalism, traditional societies in Asia and Africa are moving toward monocultures. Many governments are striving to create nations from heterogeneous populations and finding the task difficult. Because the primary loyalty of an individual in traditional societies is to his race, language, and religion, ethnicity becomes the basis for factional and separatist tendencies.*[23]

The index includes 135 countries, with the highest ranking indicating the most homogeneity. North and South Korea are tied for first and second place, with a homogeneity percentage of 100. Others in the top ten include South Yemen, Portugal, Japan, Haiti, Puerto Rico, Hong Kong, and Germany. The United States ranks 82:135, with a homogeneity percentage of only 50. These data indicate that the United States is among the most diverse nations in the world in terms of ethnicity, race, language, and religion.

Changes have also taken place within the dominant Christian community of the United States. Membership in many mainline denominations has declined during the past ten to twenty years, while fundamentalist religions have experienced growth. The figures below illustrate these patterns of growth and decline:[24]

Denominations with Their Highest Membership Figures between 1960 and 1970
American Lutheran Church (1970)
Christian Church (Disciples of Christ) (1965)
Church of the Brethren (1960)
Episcopal Church (1965)
Lutheran Church in America (1965)
Lutheran Church—Missouri Synod (1970)
Presbyterian Church (USA) (1965)
Reformed Church in America (1965)
United Church of Christ (1960)
United Methodist Church (1965)

Denominations with Their Highest Membership Figures in 1988
Assemblies of God
Christian and Missionary Alliance
Church of Jesus Christ of Latter-Day Saints (1985, most recent data)

> Church of the Nazarene
> Jehovah's Witnesses
> Roman Catholic Church
> Salvation Army
> Seventh-Day Adventists
> Southern Baptist Convention

Within many mainstream churches, movement also occurred during the 1970s and 1980s. Hill describes it as "the infusion of unfamiliar styles of Christian practice and expression into existing denominations." He talks about many people who remain happily Lutheran or Episcopalian or Roman Catholic "while embracing new forms of spirituality that are more often 'Spirit-filled' than 'pentecostal.'"[25] Hill contends that this movement was away from authority within a church and toward greater individuality. He sees a "moving from tradition to immediacy; from church as authoritative institution to free-form congregations and each individual; from prescribed worship to informal gatherings." Combined with the other growing diversities of religious groups within the United States, schools now face a different public.

This change gave public school leaders many more headaches because they had to deal more frequently with individuals and with individual congregations than with only the local ministerial association. There was more scrutiny of more aspects of public education by more people than ever before in the nation's history.

EDUCATIONAL IMPLICATIONS

The high level of religious diversity in the United States is a fact. The public schools, which at one time were a public extension of a generalized Protestant belief system, can no longer fill that role. On the other hand, these same schools must be sure that they do not move in the opposite direction, to a position of open hostility to religion.

The mission of the public schools is a broad one and may go beyond what some religious groups deem acceptable. For example, people who object to the teaching of critical-thinking skills (and there are some) will most likely have to find an alternative to public education. Although the public schools cannot be all things to all people—they must be sure to be fair to all, respect all, and be open to all.

Specific implications of this state of diversity are focused on the following eight aspects of education:

1. Curriculum resources such as textbooks, library books, films, and speakers

2. Subject matter to be included in the curriculum, whether elective or required, such as values clarification, sex and health education, and religion

3. School rules of all types, such as teacher qualifications, school attendance, discipline, and dress codes, whether from the federal, state, or local level

4. Student services such as psychological counseling, testing, and health care

5. School calendar decisions, historically tied to Christmas and Easter

6. Scheduling of student activities that interfere with the religious observances of some students (e.g., athletic events on Friday nights)

7. Teaching methods that require student behaviors objectionable to some people, such as value clarification, decision-making, and thinking and debating skills

8. School financing, especially where local voters must approve new monies for the school budget, but even at the state level, where legislators are subject to intense political pressure

The factors described above have too often caused significant controversies within a community, a state, or the entire nation. Headlines, television cameras, angry protesters, emotional meetings, and court cases have been too common. To avoid such negative situations, every educator must first become better informed about religion in general, and especially about its influence on human beings now and throughout history. The academic study of religion is vital for both teachers and students. Within the public schools, the best place for this type of study to occur is wherever it logically falls in the regular curriculum. In a home economics unit on food preparation, for example, it would be logical to include how some religions have given their adherents rules to follow regarding the handling and consumption of foods in their daily lives. During a unit on the colonial period of American history, students could study the roles of the various churches and how each affected the geographic area in which it was dominant. The effects of beliefs on the decisions of individual leaders could be examined.

Curriculum resources need to be examined carefully. Earlier in this chapter the lack of appropriate treatment of Islamic peoples and beliefs in U.S. history textbooks was cited. An Associated Press story on May 28, 1986, carried the headline "Most High School Texts Neglect Religion, Group Says." The article quotes People for the American Way as follows: "Students aren't learning about America's rich and diverse religious heritage because textbook publishers are still afraid of offending anyone, from moral majoritarians to civil libertarians."[26]

Another report, by the well-respected Association for Supervision and Curriculum Development, refers to the "benign neglect" of religion by textbooks at all levels. It states that "an elementary student can come away from a textbook account of the Crusades, for example, with the notion that these wars to win the Holy Land for Christendom were little more than exotic shopping expeditions."[27]

It is interesting that liberal and conservative political action groups, as well as educational groups, have arrived at the same conclusions regarding the inappropriate treatment of religion in school textbooks. This was exactly the basis used by Judge William Brevard Hand in his decision to ban dozens of books from use in schools.

In addition to becoming better educated about religion, educators must use appropriate teaching methods. The continuing controversy over the teaching of evolution and the call for the balancing inclusion of "creation science" illustrate the need to use effective and sensitive teaching methods. People who accept the story of creation in Genesis and teach it to their children are highly offended when their children are told by teachers that the parents are wrong. The anger of the parents is understandable.

How a teacher handles the teaching of evolution is crucial. Two possible exam questions illustrate how easy it is to avoid a direct confrontation with these children and their parents, and at the same time continue to teach the prescribed curriculum:

Poor It took millions of years for the earth to evolve to its present state. (True/False)

Better Evolutionists believe that it took millions of years for the earth to evolve to its present state. (True/False)

The first question requires the child to agree with a statement of "fact." The second question allows the child to answer that one group of people has a different set of beliefs than the child has, while at the same time protecting his or her own integrity. The difference is subtle, but powerful. The second question respects diversity of beliefs while teaching scientific information—that is, information about evolutionary theory. No child is forced to go against personal or family beliefs.

Such a change in teaching approaches will help reduce conflict between home and school. However, we need to be aware from the beginning that not everyone will be satisfied. Some people have such a narrow belief system that the public school system will never be able to satisfy them.

Teachers of all subject areas can benefit from the work done on teaching about religion by the National Council for the Social Studies (NCSS). The January 1981 issue of *Social Education* has as its theme "Teaching about Religion: Vistas Unlimited" and includes an article entitled "Instructional Issues in Teaching about Religion." This article calls for teachers to use a wide range of methodologies, including the use of music, skits, art, and role playing.[28] It is next to impossible to teach students to think critically if they are limited to a single source of information, the textbook. A teacher's academic knowledge about religion as distinguished from personal, experiential knowledge is vital. The importance of the teacher's objectivity is also stressed, and specific teacher behaviors to bring this about are presented.

The NCSS in 1984 published its official position, in an article entitled "Including the Study about Religions in the Social Studies Curriculum: A Position Statement and Guidelines."[29] The fourteen guidelines it recommends are specific and helpful. Two guidelines are:

■ Study about religions should stress the influence of religions on history, culture, the arts, and contemporary issues.

■ Study about religions should be descriptive, nonconfessional, and conducted in an environment free of advocacy.

A short booklet entitled *Public Education Religion Studies: Questions and Answers* is available from the National Council on Religion and Public Education (address: c/o Dept. of Religion, University of Kansas, Lawrence, Kansas 66045). The booklet is organized around eleven different questions, such as "How do you study about religion in public schools?" and "What criteria should be used in selecting teaching materials?" This help for educators is based on the work of a diverse advisory committee that helped the Public Education Religion Studies Center at Wright State University, Dayton, Ohio, in the early 1970s.

SUMMARY

The United States is a religiously diverse nation and is becoming more so every day. If the United States is to avoid the fractionalization and inner turmoil that have destroyed other diverse nations, the public schools must lead the nation in being sensitive to the diversity itself, and by helping students to learn about each other as well as about people in other parts of the world.

The old etiquette guide about not discussing religion or politics in mixed company has done more harm than good. It is not an appropriate policy for the schools of the United States as they prepare students for life in the twenty-first century.

QUESTIONS AND ACTIVITIES

1. What is the broad definition of religion developed by the Public Education Religious Studies Center? How is this definition of religion similar to and different from other definitions of religion with which you are familiar? With your own personal definition of religion?

2. What are the educational consequences of broad and narrow definitions of religion?

3. Prepare a report indicating the role religion has played in the history and culture of an ethnic group, such as Jewish Americans or African Americans. Helpful references are Irving Howe's *World of Our Fathers: The Journey of the East European Jews to America and the Life They Found and Made* (New York: Simon and Schuster, 1976); E. Franklin Frazier's *The Negro Church in America* and *The Black Church in the African American Experience* (Durham, N.C.: Duke University Press, 1990) by C. Eric Lincoln and Lawrence H. Mamiya.

4. Uphoff points out that an increasing number of children now in U.S. schools have come from nations where religions other than Christianity and Judaism are common. This means that religious diversity is increasing in U.S. schools. What are the educational implications of the increasing religious diversity in U.S. schools?

5. Controversies have developed in many communities about the way Christmas is celebrated in the schools. In some communities, the school boards have established policies that prevent teachers from using religious songs or symbols in holiday celebrations during the Christmas season. What is your opinion of such school board policies? Give reasons to support your position.

6. According to the author, why is it important for students to study religion in the public schools?

7. Why do textbooks tend to ignore religion? How can teachers supplement the textbook treatment of religion? What guidelines should teachers keep in mind when teaching about religion in public schools? What knowledge and sensitivities should they have?

8. To develop a better understanding of religious and cultural diversity in U.S. society, attend services at several religious institutions within your community or region, such as a synagogue, a Catholic church, an African American Baptist church, a Buddhist temple, and a mosque. How are the services and rituals at these institutions alike and different?

NOTES

1. "Alleged 'Secular Humanism' Courses Attacked," *Education Week* 5 (October 15, 1986): 12.

2. John F. Wilson, Religion: *A Preface* (Englewood Cliffs, N.J.: Prentice-Hall, 1982), p. 18.

3. Catherine L. Albanese, *America: Religions and Religion* (Belmont, Calif.: Wadsworth Publishing Co., 1981), p. 2.

4. Peter Bracher, James V. Panoch, Nicholas Piediscalzi, and James K. Uphoff, *Public Education Religion Studies: Questions and Answers* (Dayton, Ohio: Public Education Religion Studies Center, Wright State University, 1974), p. 5.

5. Barbara L. Green, "Solace, Self-Esteem, and Solidarity: The Role of Afro-American Folklore in the Education and Acculturation of Black Americans," *Texas Tech Journal of Education,* 2, No. 1 (Winter 1984): 94.

6. Albanese, *America,* 10.

7. Robert Michaelsen, *Piety in the Public School* (New York: Macmillan, 1970), pp. 89–98.

8. *The New Book of American Rankings* (New York: Facts on File Publications, 1984), pp. 61–63.

9. Edwin Scott Gaustad, *Historical Atlas of Religion in America,* rev. ed. (New York: Harper & Row, 1976), p. 168.

10. U.S. Bureau of the Census, *Statistical Abstract of the United States: 1990,* 110th ed., (Washington, D.C.: U.S. Government Printing Office, 1990), Table 75, p. 55.

11. Constant H. Jacquet, Jr., ed., *Yearbook of American and Canadian Churches* (Nashville, Tenn.: Abington Press, 1990), p. 292.

12. "A Time to Seek," *Newsweek* (December 17, 1990): 51.

13. *The World Almanac and Book of Facts: 1987* (New York: World Almanac, 1987), p. 226.

14. *Historical Statistics of the United States: Colonial Times to 1970, Part 1* (Washington, D.C.: U.S. Department of Commerce, Bureau of the Census, 1975), p. 391.

15. Samuel S. Hill, ed., *Handbook of Denominations in the U.S.,* 9th ed., (Nashville, Tenn.: Abington Press, 1990), pp. 68, 170.

16. Jacquet, *Yearbook,* 252.

17. *Statistical Abstract,* 1990.

18. *Historical Statistics.*

19. Samuel S. Hill, ed., *Handbook of Denominations in the U.S.,* 8th ed. (Nashville, Tenn.: Abington Press, 1985), pp. 70, 176.

20. Hill, *Handbook of Denominations,*

21. James K. Uphoff, "Religious Minorities: In or Out of the Culturally Pluralistic Curriculum?" *Educational Leadership,* 32, No. 3 (December 1974):199–202.

22. *Time,* February 4, 1991.

23. George Thomas Kurian, *New Book of World Rankings* (New York: Facts on File Publications, 1984), pp. 47–49.

24. Jacquet, *Yearbook,* p. 97.

25. Hill, *Handbook of Denominations in the U.S.,* 262–263.

26. "Most High School Texts Neglect Religion, Group Says," *The Journal Herald,* Dayton, Ohio (May 28, 1986): 16.

27. "Panel of Educators Ask End to 'Neglect' about Religions," *The New York Times* (July 2, 1987): 1, 9.

28. James K. Uphoff, "Instructional Issues in Teaching about Religion," *Social Education,* 45, No. 1 (January 1981): 22–27.

29. National Council for the Social Studies, "Including the Study about Religion in the Social Studies Curriculum: A Position Statement and Guidelines," *Social Education,* 49, No. 5 (May 1985): 413–414.

Students from a wide variety of social classes and religions work and play together in today's schools.

PART THREE

Gender

Social, economic, and political conditions for women have improved substantially since the women's rights movement emerged as part of the civil rights movement of the 1960s and 1970s. However, gender discrimination and inequality still exist in schools and in society at large. In 1988, the median earnings for women who were full-time workers were 70.2 percent of those for men, up from 66.6 percent in 1983. The status of women in the United States within the last two decades has changed substantially. More women are now working outside the home than ever before, and more women are heads of households. In 1988, 56.6 percent of women worked outside the home, making up 45 percent of the total work force. In 1989, 17 percent of households in the United States were headed by women. A growing percentage of women and their dependents constitute the nation's poor. Some writers use the term *the feminization of poverty* to describe this development. Fifty-two percent of the nation's population (32.5 million) living in poverty in the early 1980s were women and their dependent children.

The chapters in this part of the book describe the status of women in the United States, the ways in which schools perpetuate gender discrimination, and strategies that educators can use to create equal educational opportunities for female and male students. As Sadker, Sadker, and Long point out in Chapter 6, both males and females are harmed by sexual stereotypes and gender discrimination. Tetreault describes how school knowledge is dominated by male perspectives and how teachers can infuse their curricula with perspectives from both genders and thereby expand their students' thinking and insights. Butler discusses how women of color have often been ignored by the women's movement, which is predominantly a White, middle-class phenomenon. She describes perspectives and content that will enable teachers to integrate their curricula with the experiences and cultures of women of color.

Gender

CHAPTER 6

Gender and Educational Equality

- ■ **MYRA SADKER, DAVID SADKER,**
  and LYNETTE LONG

INTRODUCTION

"Boys are doctors. Girls are nurses," insisted the kindergarten class. Amazed that young children could be so firm in their stereotype, the teacher took the twenty-two youngsters on a field trip to a nearby hospital. She introduced them to a female doctor and a male nurse who talked with them about their jobs and gave them a tour of the hospital.

Upon returning to the classroom, the teacher emphasized her point, "Now you can see that boys can be nurses. Girls can be doctors."

"No they can't," the students insisted.

"What do you mean?" The teacher was stunned. "We visited the hospital and met a man who is a nurse and a woman who is a doctor. You saw them. They talked with you."

"Yes," chorused the children triumphantly, "but they lied."[1]

As this real-life anecdote shows, sometimes it is easier to split an atom than to change an attitude. The past two decades have seen tremendous strides in abolishing sexism, but entrenched resistance remains. From the books they read, to the role models they see, to the way they are treated in classrooms, girls and boys continue to learn subtle yet powerful messages about separate and unequal opportunities based on gender.

This chapter provides an overview of how sexism operates in school, from curriculum and instruction to administration. Through a report card, it also shows the cost of sex bias: its influence on our nation's children. After highlighting current issues, the chapter concludes with strategies educators can use to make sure their classrooms are fair to all students regardless of gender.

CURRICULAR MATERIALS

Central to academic progress are the textbooks, workbooks, tests, encyclopedias, paperbacks, computer software, and a variety of other instructional materials teachers use *every* day. Administrators and teachers select educational materials based on a variety of criteria, including how well they match the needs of a particular school or group of students, how clearly they present the desired material, and how practical the materials are in terms of affordability and availability. These experts must also consider whether curricular materials reflect equity in their presentation of males and females.

Six Forms of Bias

Below is a description of six forms of sex bias educators can use to evaluate materials for gender equity.[2] The description of each form reviews research and presents historical perspectives on how the form has been manifested in instructional material. Following these six forms of bias, the state of gender equity in curriculum today is assessed.

Linguistic Bias

Referring to the use of masculine terms and pronouns in curriculum materials, linguistic bias is one of the easiest forms of sex bias to detect and eliminate. In history texts, terms such as *caveman, forefathers,* and *mankind* inherently deny the contributions of women. Similarly, masculine occupational titles such as *mailman, policeman,* and *businessman* are labels that deny the participation of women in our society. So does use of the pronoun *he* to refer to all people.

Another form of linguistic bias occurs when women are identified in terms of being someone's wife or possession, as in this sentence: "Winston Williams and his wife and children moved to New York." When this is reworded to read, "The Williams family moved to New York," all members of the family are considered equally.

Stereotyping

Many studies indicate that children and adults have been stereotyped in textbooks. Boys typically are portrayed as exhibiting one set of values, behaviors, and roles, whereas girls are drawn with a different set of characteristics. In reading books, boys routinely have been shown as ingenious, creative, brave, athletic, achieving, and curious. Girls have been portrayed as dependent, passive, fearful, and docile victims. Adults have also been stereotyped in roles and careers. In a study of seventy-seven basal readers published between 1980 and 1982, Britton and Lumpkin found a total of 5,501 careers depicted; 64 percent were attributed to Anglo males, 14 percent to Anglo females, 17 percent to males of color, and 5 percent to females of color. The most common careers shown for Anglo males were soldier, farmer, doctor, and police officer. The most frequently shown role models for males of color were worker, farmer, warrior, Indian chief, and hunter. The most common careers for White women were mother, teacher, author, and princess. For females of color, mother and teacher also headed the list, followed by slave, worker, porter, and artist.[3]

Invisibility

Women have made significant contributions to the growth and development of the United States, yet few have appeared in the history books children are assigned to read. This form of sex bias—invisibility, or omission—has characterized not only history books, but also texts in reading, language arts, mathematics, science, spelling, and vocational education. For example, a 1972 study of science, math, reading, spelling, and social studies textbooks found that only 31 percent of all illustrations included females and that the percentage of females decreased as the grade level increased.[4]

In another study, researchers analyzed 134 elementary readers and found males pictured twice as often as females and portrayed in three times as many occupations.[5] A 1970 study of history texts found that students had to read more than 500 pages before they found one page of information about women.[6] When girls and women are systematically excluded from curricular material, students are deprived of information about half the nation's people. Even though studies in the 1980s showed that significant improvement has been made, women and girls are still underrepresented on textbook pages.

Imbalance

Textbooks perpetuate bias by presenting only one interpretation of an issue, situation, or group of people. Often this one-sided view is presented because the author has limited space or decides that it is not feasible to present all sides of an issue in elementary textbooks. History textbooks contain many examples of imbalance, mostly minimizing the role of women. For example, Janice Trecker studied the most widely used history textbooks and found more information on women's skirt lengths than on the suffragist movement.[7] As a result of such imbalanced presentation, millions of students have been given limited perspectives concerning the contributions, struggles, and participation of women in U.S. society. Although more recent textbook studies show improvement, problems remain.

Unreality

Many textbooks have presented an unrealistic portrayal of U.S. history and contemporary life experience by glossing over controversial topics and avoiding discussion of discrimination and prejudice. For example, almost 50 percent of all marriages end in divorce, and one-third of all children will live with a single parent during part of their lives. Yet many textbooks portray the typical American family as one having two adults, two children, a dog, and a house in suburbia. When controversial issues are not presented, students are denied the information they need to confront contemporary problems.

Fragmentation

Textbooks fragment the contributions of women by treating these contributions as unique occurrences rather than integrating them into the main body of the text. In fragmented textbooks, the contributions of important women are often highlighted in separate boxes or are contained in a separate chapter. Fragmentation communicates to readers that women are an interesting diversion but that their contributions do not constitute the mainstream of history and literature. Fragmentation and isolation also occur when women are depicted as interacting only among themselves and as having little or no influence on society as a whole. For example, textbook discussions of feminism often talk about how women are affected by this contemporary movement, but there is little analysis of the effect of the women's movement on other groups and social issues.

Recent Progress

In 1972, Scott, Foresman, the first company to publish nonsexist guidelines, suggested that the achievements of women be recognized, that women and girls be given the same respect as men and boys, that abilities, traits, interests, and activities should not be assigned on the basis of male or female stereotypes, and that sexist language be avoided. Today most textbook publishers edit books for sexist language and produce guidelines for authors to improve the image of women. By following these guidelines and avoiding the six forms of sex bias presented here, authors can develop nonsexist texts and other curricular materials.

Although bias in educational materials still exists, great gains were made in the 1980s. For example, a study of the story problems in mathematics textbooks from the mid-1930s to the late 1980s found a greater proportion of story problems about women in textbooks used in the 1980s than in the 1970s or before.[8] A study of the Newbery Medal Award books from 1977 through 1984 also found the portrayal of women and girls less stereotypic. Also, compared to a 1971 study, the number of books with girls and women as the main character has increased substantially.[9] Basal science texts are also more sensitive to the issue of sexism. A study of the illustrations of seven elementary science textbook series found that female children are represented with greater frequency than male children.[10] Unfortunately, gains in history have not been as impressive, and a review of thirty-one U.S. history textbooks published in 1986 found that the contributions of women are still minimized.[11] To represent an accurate view of history, textbooks need to portray the role of the average, as well as the exceptional, woman in our nation's history.

The influence of sex bias in curriculum materials is significant. Misrepresentations and omissions can negatively affect the self-image, goals, and philosophy of girls. Children need strong, positive role models for the development of self-esteem. When females are omitted from books, a hidden curriculum is created, one that teaches children that females are less important and less significant in our society than males.

In contrast, studies show that bias-free materials can have a positive influence and can encourage students at various grade levels to change attitudes and behaviors as a result of their reading materials. One researcher found that children in grades 1 through 5 developed less stereotyped attitudes about jobs and activities after reading about people who successfully fought sex discrimination in nontraditional jobs.[12] In a similar study, children who read instructional materials about girls in nontraditional roles were more likely to think that girls could perform the nontraditional activity of the narrative than children who read the same materials with boys as the main characters.[13]

Educators who select gender-fair materials can encourage significant changes in their students. Bias-free materials in literature expand students' knowledge of changing sex roles and encourage greater flexibility in attitudes regarding appropriate behavior for females and males. In science and math, gender-fair materials provide females with encouragement to enter careers in these areas. In history, bias-free materials provide role models and demonstrate contributions of women in the history of this nation.

But gender-fair curricular materials by themselves are not sufficient to create a nonsexist educational environment. Attention must also be paid to the process of instruction.

Instruction

The following scene, a general music class in action, reflects the subtle ways sex bias can permeate the instructional process.[14]

As the bell rings, students take their seats. The girls are clustered in the front and on the right-hand side of the room, while the boys are predominantly on the other side of the room and in the back. This seating arrangement doesn't bother the students—they choose their own seats; and it doesn't seem to bother their teacher, Mrs. Howe, who makes no comment about the segregated arrangement.

Mrs. Howe starts the lesson by playing part of Mozart's *Symphony Concertante* on the record player. After about five minutes, she turns to the class with questions.

Mrs. Howe: Who can tell me the name of this composer?
(A few hands are raised when John shouts out "Bruce Springsteen." After the laughter dies down, Mrs. Howe calls on Mitch.)
    Mitch: Haydn.
    Mrs. Howe: Why do you think so?
    Mitch: Because yesterday you played Haydn.
    Mrs. Howe: Close. Eric what do you think?
    Eric: I don't know.
    Mrs. Howe: Come on, Eric. During the last two weeks we have been listening to various Classical period composers. Out of those we've listened to, who wrote this piece?
(Silence)
    Mrs. Howe: John, can you help Eric out?
    John: Beethoven.
    Mrs. Howe: No, it's not Beethoven. Beethoven was more a Romantic period composer. Think.
(Mrs. Howe finally calls on Pam, who has had her hand half-raised during this discussion.)
    Pam: I'm not sure, but is it Mozart?
    Mrs. Howe: Uh-huh. Anyone else agree with Pam?
    Mitch (calls out):   It's Mozart. It's similar to the Mozart concerto you played yesterday.
    Mrs. Howe: Very good. Can you tell us if this is another concerto he wrote?
    Mitch: Yes, it's a violin concerto.
    Mrs. Howe: That's almost right. It's a special concerto written for two instruments. To help you figure out the other instrument, let's listen to more of the piece.
(Mrs. Howe plays more of the piece and calls on Mitch.)
    Mitch: Another violin.
    Mrs. Howe: Peter?

Peter: A cello.

Mrs. Howe: You're all close. It's another string instrument, but it's not another violin or a cello.

Ruth (calls out):   What about a viola?

Mrs. Howe: Ruth, you know I don't allow shouting out. Raise your hand next time. Peter?

Peter: A viola.

Mrs. Howe: Very good. This is a special kind of concerto Mozart wrote for both the violin and viola called *Symphony Concertante.* One reason why I want you to listen to it is to notice the difference between the violin and the viola. Let's listen to the melody as played first by the violin then the viola. Listen for the similarities and differences between the two.

This scenario demonstrates several important interaction patterns; in this sex-segregated classroom, Mrs. Howe called on the boys more often than the girls and asked them more higher-order and lower-order questions. She gave male students more specific feedback, including praise, constructive criticism, and remediation. Research shows that from grade school to graduate school, most classrooms demonstrate similar instructional patterns.

One large study conducted in the fourth, sixth, and eighth grades in more than 100 classrooms in four states and the District of Columbia found that teachers gave boys more academic attention than girls. They asked them more questions and gave them more precise and clear feedback concerning the quality of their responses. In contrast, girls were more likely to be ignored or given diffuse evaluation of the academic quality of their work.[15] Other research shows that these same patterns are prevalent at the secondary and postsecondary levels.[16]

One reason boys get more teacher attention is that they demand it. Approximately eight times as likely to shout out questions and answers, they dominate the classroom airwaves. However, when boys call out, teachers accept their comments. In contrast, when girls call out teachers are more likely to reprimand them by saying things like, "In this class, we raise our hands before talking."

Another factor allowing boys to dominate classroom interaction is the widespread sex segregation that characterizes classrooms. Occasionally teachers divide their classrooms into sex-segregated lines, teams, work and play areas, and seating arrangements. More frequently, students sex-segregate themselves. Drawn to the sections of the classroom where the more assertive boys are clustered, the teacher is positioned to keep interacting with male students.

The conclusion of most interaction studies is that teachers give more attention—positive, negative, and neutral—to male students. However, some researchers emphasize that low-achieving males get most of the negative attention, while high-achieving boys get more positive and constructive academic contacts. But no matter whether they are high or low achievers, female students are more likely to be invisible and ignored.[17]

The gender difference in classroom communications is more than a mere counting game of who gets the teacher's attention and who doesn't. Teacher attention is a vote of high expectations and commitment to a student. Decades of research show that students who are actively involved in classroom discussion are more likely to achieve and to express positive attitudes toward schools and learning.[18]

Most teachers do not want to be biased in their treatment of students and are completely unaware of inequitable interaction. On the positive side, studies show that with resources, awareness, and training, teachers can eliminate these patterns and achieve equity in how they teach female and male students. Given the crucial nature of this pervasive problem, it is unfortunate that most schools of education still do not include the issue in their teaching-preparation programs.

School Administration

Effective research on schools has highlighted the crucial role of the principal in encouraging student achievement. When principals become instructional leaders, student performance is enhanced. Student achievement scores rise when the principal is visible throughout the school, especially in classrooms; encourages staff to work as a team in meeting school goals; holds high expectations; and is actively involved in observing and analyzing the instructional process. To accomplish these goals, an effective administrator must have extensive teaching experience, a thorough understanding of the teaching-learning process, and positive human relations skills. Although women excel in these areas, the world of school administration still belongs to men.

Almost 70 percent of teachers in the United States are women, yet women account for less than 30 percent of the administrators. Research shows that women who attain positions in administration are as competent as or more competent than their male counterparts.[19] Female administrators excel at the human relations skills essential to effective leadership. More aware of the problems facing teachers and more supportive of their staffs, female administrators create democratic school climates and are rated high in the areas of productivity and morale.

Women as administrators also have a positive influence on students. They focus more energy on the teaching-learning process and monitor student learning more carefully than their male colleagues do. One study showed that students of all socioeconomic levels achieved more in schools with female principals.[20] Given this research-based demonstration of competence, the question remains, Why are so few women managing schools?

Historical Perspective

During the 1920s, women were well represented as leaders in educational administration. Two-thirds of the nation's superintendents in the West and Midwest were women. In 1928, 55 percent of all elementary school principals were women. But many of these early small schools served grades 1 through 8, and typically the eighth-grade teacher was also designated as the principal. As schools grew and full-time administrators became the norm, the number of women in administrative positions dropped precipitously. By the mid-1970s only 13 percent of the nation's principalships were filled by women. In terms of school level, only 18 percent of elementary school principals, 3 percent of junior high school principals, and less than 2 percent of senior high principals were female. By the early 1980s, some gains had been achieved, with women comprising 23 percent of elementary principals and 10 percent of secondary principals.[21]

Today women have higher career aspirations and have attained higher levels of education and training than ever before. By 1980, women had earned one-third of all doctorates and one-half of all masters degrees in educational administration. More than 50 percent of female teachers now express interest in educational administration.

Prejudice

Although the 1980s saw more female principals than the previous decades, problems remain. Women still are not selected as frequently as men: the higher the rung on the ladder, the fewer the women in administration. Study after study has demonstrated that when an equally qualified man and woman apply for the same administrative position, the man is more likely to get the job.[22] Women must be more qualified, more experienced, and more skilled than their male colleagues to secure the administrative appointment. Male superintendents often view women through stereotypic lenses. They see them as too emotional and indecisive for administration, unable to manage budgets and finance, and plagued with problems related to menstruation and pregnancy.

Besides these blatant discriminatory attitudes, other informal barriers inhibit the entrance and promotion of women in educational administration. Job descriptions are often written in sex-stereotyped language that discourages women from applying. Women who decide to apply may find application forms that request personal information, such as marital status or number of children, questions implying that women are too busy with family responsibilities to do an adequate job. Female candidates for administrative positions find themselves facing screening committees comprised primarily of male personnel. Often these committees have a pro-male bias and favor applicants with so-called preadministrative experience, such as coaching.

Women also apply less often than men for administrative positions. Another barrier to administrative advancement is that most women enter teaching not as a stepping-stone to management but rather to work closely with children. Administrative duties away from the classroom are less attractive to these women who view their role primarily as working with children. Some women are also concerned about time commitments that may impinge on home and family responsibilities.

The result of prejudice as well as personal constraint is a dearth of women in administrative roles. Students are denied appropriate role models as well as the opportunity to be led by some of the best talent available to U.S. schools. When politics and prejudice control the selection process, schools and children lose access to the best leadership available.

REPORT CARD: THE COST OF SEXISM IN SCHOOL

Below is a report card you will not find in any elementary or secondary school.[23] Nevertheless, it is an important evaluation. It reflects the loss that both girls and boys suffer because of sex bias in society and in education. Years after the passage of Title IX of the Education Amendments of 1972, the law that prohibits sex discrimination in schools receiving federal financial assistance, gender inequities continue to permeate schools.

Academic

Girls

- Girls start out ahead of boys in speaking, reading, and counting. In the early grades, their academic performance is equal to that of boys in math and science. However, as they progress through school, their achievement test scores show significant decline. The scores of boys, on the other hand, continue to rise and eventually reach and surpass those of their female counterparts, particularly in the areas of math and science. Girls are the only group in our society that begins school ahead and ends up behind.

- Sex differences in mathematics become apparent at the junior high school level. Male superiority increases as the level of mathematics becomes more difficult and is evident even when the number of mathematics courses taken by males and females is the same.

- Between 1970 and 1984 the National Assessment of Educational Progress conducted three assessments of reading achievement. Although girls continue to outperform boys at the 9-, 14-, and 17-year-old levels, the achievement gap between the sexes has narrowed; as girls' performance has remained stable, boys continue to make achievement gains. A 1985 National Assessment of Educational Progress showed that by ages 21–25, males have caught up with females in reading proficiency and literacy.

- Males outperform females substantially on all subsections of the Scholastic Aptitude Test (SAT) and the American College Testing Program Examination (ACT). The largest gap is in the math section of the SAT, followed by the ACT natural science reading, the ACT math usage, and the ACT social studies reading.

- The College Board Achievement Tests are required for admission to more selective colleges and universities. On these achievement tests, males outperform females in European history, American history, biology levels 1 and 2, and mathematics.

- Girls attain only 36 percent of the more than 6,000 National Merit Scholarships awarded each year. These awards are based on the higher Preliminary Scholastic Aptitude Tests (PSAT) scores attained by boys.

- On tests for admission to graduate and professional schools, males outperform females on the Graduate Record Exam (GRE), the Medical College Admissions Test (MCAT), and the Graduate Management Admissions Test (GMAT).

- In spite of performance decline on standardized achievement tests, girls frequently receive better grades in school. This may be one of the rewards they get for being more quiet and docile in the classroom. However, their silence may be at the cost of achievement, independence, and self-reliance.

- Girls are more likely to be invisible members of classrooms. They receive fewer academic contacts, less praise and constructive feedback, fewer complex and abstract questions, and less instruction on how to do things for themselves.

■ Girls who are gifted are less likely to be identified than are gifted boys. Those girls who *are* identified as gifted are less likely to participate in special or accelerated programs to develop their talent. Girls who suffer from learning disabilities are also less likely to be identified or to participate in special-education programs than are learning-disabled boys.

Boys

■ Boys are more likely to be scolded and reprimanded in classrooms, even when the observed conduct and behavior of boys and girls does not differ. Also, boys are more likely to be referred to school authorities for disciplinary action than are girls.

■ Boys are far more likely to be identified as exhibiting learning disabilities, reading problems, and mental retardation.

■ Not only are boys more likely to be identified as having greater learning and reading disabilities, but they also receive lower grades, are more likely to be grade repeaters, and are less likely to complete high school.

■ The National Assessment of Educational Progress indicates that males perform significantly below females in writing achievement.

Psychological and Physical

Girls

■ Although women achieve better grades than men, they are less likely to believe they can do college work. Females exhibit lower self-esteem than do males during secondary and postsecondary education.

■ Girls have less confidence than boys in their mathematical ability. The sex typing of mathematics as a masculine discipline may also be related to low female confidence and performance.

■ Girls have a less positive attitude toward science than do boys. High school girls view science, especially physical science, as a masculine subject.

■ In athletics, females also suffer from sex bias. For example, although there has been some progress, women's athletic budgets in the nation's colleges are only a modest percentage of men's budgets.

■ One in ten teenage girls becomes pregnant every year. More than 40 percent of all adolescent girls who drop out of school do so because of pregnancy. Teenage pregnancy is related to a constellation of factors, including poverty, low self-esteem, academic failure, and the perception of few life options.

Boys

■ Society socializes boys into an active, independent, and aggressive role. But such behavior is incongruent with school norms and rituals that stress quiet behavior and docility. This results in a pattern of role conflict for boys, particularly during the elementary years.

■ Hyperactivity is estimated to be nine times more prevalent in boys than in girls. Boys are more likely to be identified as having emotional problems, and statistics indicate a higher suicide rate among males.

■ Boys are taught stereotyped behaviors earlier and more harshly than girls; there is a 20 percent greater probability that such stereotyped behavior will stay with them for life.

■ Conforming to the male sex-role stereotype takes a psychological toll. Boys who score high on sex-appropriate behavior tests also score highest on anxiety tests.

■ Males are less likely than females to be close friends with one another. When asked, most men identify women as their closest friends.

■ Until recently, programs focusing on adolescent sexuality and teen pregnancy were directed almost exclusively at females. Males were ignored, and this permissive "boys will be boys" attitude translated into sexual irresponsibility.

■ Family planning experts say that 50 percent of sexually active single males will contract a sexually transmitted disease by the time they are 25. The highest incidence of venereal disease occurs in young men between 15 and 25.

■ Males are more likely to succumb to serious disease and be victims of accidents or violence. The average life expectancy of men is approximately eight years shorter than that of women.

Career and Family Relationships

Girls
■ When elementary school girls are asked to describe what they want to do when they grow up, they are able to identify only a limited number of career options, and these fit stereotypic patterns. Boys, on the other hand, are able to identify many more potential occupations.

■ Starting at the junior high school level, girls say that mathematics are less important and useful to career goals. The majority of girls enter college without completing four years of high school mathematics. This lack of preparation in math serves as a "critical filter" inhibiting or preventing girls from entering many careers in science, math, and technology.

■ Girls from lower socioeconomic backgrounds are less likely to have plans for college than are those from more affluent families. Family finances are less likely to affect the college options of males.

■ Teenagers who become mothers earn only about half the income of females who delay childbearing. When families are headed by young mothers, they are six times as likely to be in poverty. The National Research Council indicates that it costs $18,130 a year to support a 15-year-old mother and her baby.

■ In urban areas, many young males who drop out of school are likely to return to school. For young females who drop out, the return rate is very low.

■ The preparation and counseling girls receive in school contribute to the economic penalties that they encounter in the workplace. Although over 90 percent of the girls in U.S. classrooms will work in the paid labor force for all or part of their lives, the following statistics reveal the cost of the bias they encounter.

■ More than one-half of families headed by women live below the poverty level.

■ A woman with a college degree will typically earn less than a male who is a high school dropout.

■ The typical working woman will earn 65 cents for every dollar earned by a male worker.

■ Minority women earn even less, averaging approximately 50 percent of the wages earned by White males.

■ Approximately 77 percent of employed women are in nonprofessional jobs. Only 11 percent are in traditionally male occupations.

■ A majority of women work not for "extra" cash, but because of economic necessity. Nearly two-thirds of all women in the labor force are single, widowed, divorced, or separated, or are married to spouses earning less than $11,000 a year.

Boys

■ Teachers and counselors advise boys to enter sex-stereotyped careers and limit their potential in occupations such as kindergarten teacher, nurse, or secretary.

■ Many boys build career expectations that are higher than their abilities. This results in later compromise, disappointment, and frustration.

■ Both at school and at home, boys are taught to hide or suppress their emotions; as adults, they may find it difficult or impossible to show feelings toward their family and friends.

■ Boys are actively discouraged from playing with dolls (except those that play sports or wage war). Few schools provide programs that encourage boys to learn about the skills of parenting. Many men, through absence and apathy, become not so much parents as "transparents." In fact, the typical father spends only twelve minutes a day interacting with his children.

■ Men and women vary in their beliefs of the important aspects of a father's role. Men emphasize the need for the father to earn a good income and to provide solutions to family problems. Women, on the other hand, stress the need for fathers to assist in caring for children and in responding to the emotional needs of the family. These differing perceptions of fatherhood lead to family strain and anxiety.

■ Scientific advances involving the analysis of blood and other body fluids now make possible genetic testing for paternity. Such testing, along with the passage of stricter laws and enforcement procedures for child support, have major implications for the role of males in parenting.

Even as this report card calls attention to remaining sex disparities in academic achievement, research in this area is undergoing a great deal of activity and change. Meta-analyses conducted at the end of the 1980s and in the early 1990s hold hope that these disparities are shrinking.[24] The gender gap is disappearing in verbal abilities and has decreased significantly in mathematics and spatial skills. This decrease is occurring extremely quickly and at a time when equal treatment of males and females has been encouraged. Such rapid change suggests that the academic gender gap has been caused more by socialization than by biological factors.[25] You will need to keep up with current research for the most up-to-date information on differences in how boys and girls achieve in school.

ONGOING PROBLEMS AND NEW ISSUES

The cost of sexism is obvious. As educators and other professionals fight the traditional barriers to female achievement, new issues are emerging for the 1990s. Many topics have attracted current attention, including nonsexist parenting and the role of fathers, and the potential conflict between cultural background and gender equity. In this chapter, two issues are explored in greater detail. It is important to note current developments related to single-sex schools, since research in the late 1980s demonstrated how viable these are for girls' achievement. Even as the evidence mounts in favor of these schools, they face extinction during the decade of the nineties. Also, since legal decisions in the 1980s threatened the power and coverage of Title IX (which prohibits sex discrimination in education) developments surrounding this law are discussed.

Single-Sex Schools

The past decades have witnessed a precipitous decline in U.S. single-sex secondary and postsecondary schools. The number of women's colleges has dwindled from almost 300 to fewer than 100. The widespread belief that single-sex education is an anachronism has caused many schools to become coeducational institutions—or to close their doors. Single-sex high schools, typically private and parochial, are also vanishing. Further, Title IX, with good intention, has encouraged coeducation in all but the most limited public school situations, such as contact sports and sex education.

The trend toward coeducation continues on a national scale despite research suggesting the benefits of single-sex schools, especially for female students. These benefits include increased academic achievement, self-esteem, and career salience, as well as a decrease in sex-role stereotyping. One study found that students in girls' schools in the United States expressed greater interest in both mathematics and English, took more mathematics courses, did more homework, and had more positive attitudes toward academic achievement.[26] Finally, research shows that girls in single-sex schools show more interest in the feminist movement and are less sex-role stereotyped than are their peers in coeducational schools.[27] Despite these impressive findings, single-sex education is becoming a vanishing option.

Title IX

By the mid-1970s, Title IX of the 1972 Educational Amendments was being implemented, with varying degrees of success in the nation's 16,000 school districts. The Title IX legislation prohibits sex discrimination in all educational programs receiving federal assistance. Widely known for its application to sports, Title IX also prohibits sex discrimination in counseling, discipline, testing, admissions, medical facilities, the treatment of students, financial aid, and a host of educational activities. Although theoretically the vast majority of programs should have eliminated sex bias in the past decade, the reality has been less positive. Too often sexist practices continue because of the unwillingness of parents and students to lodge complaints, or because of the slow pace of federal enforcement practices.

In the 1980s, the *Grove City College* case dealt Title IX a serious blow. The Supreme Court ruled that federal funds must be traced directly to the discriminatory activity before Title IX can be enforced. This decision meant that elementary and secondary schools as well as colleges and vocational programs could practice sex discrimination in all their programs except those directly receiving federal support. If a library was built with federal funds, for example, Title IX would prohibit sex discrimination in the library only. On the same campus or school, however, financial aid could be given legally only to male students without violating federal law. The *Grove City College* case jeopardized not only Title IX, but also much of the civil rights legislation currently on the books. At the end of the 1980s, Congress passed the Civil Rights Restoration Act, which nullified the *Grove City College* case. This new legislation should revitalize Title IX and protect all students and educators from sex discrimination if any school program receives federal assistance.

Creating Gender-Fair Education

Although the struggle against a sexist educational system is long and difficult, change is already taking place. Consider the following:

■ Although both girls and boys typically picture sex-stereotyped occupations, girls are beginning to view more prestigious and lucrative professional careers as both attainable and desirable.[28]

■ In 1960 women comprised 35 percent of students in higher education. Today they are the majority.[29]

■ In 1958 the labor force participation rate of women stood at 33 percent; by 1990 it had reached 45 percent. Although most women are still overrepresented in low-paying jobs, barriers are falling as some women are entering higher-level positions previously held only by men.[30]

■ More than 600,000 students participated in a *Weekly Reader* national survey on the future. From ten statements describing the future, the largest number of students strongly agreed with the item predicting equal treatment of the sexes. Overwhelmingly, our nation's young people express egalitarian attitudes about roles for women and men.[31]

While change is possible, it takes time, effort, and commitment to break down barriers that have been in place for centuries. Following are ten key steps you can take to build nonsexist classrooms today.[32]

1. If the textbooks you are given to use with students are biased, you may wish to confront this bias rather than ignore it. Discuss the issue directly with your students. It's entirely appropriate to acknowledge that texts are not always perfect. By engaging your students in a discussion about textbook omission and stereotyping, you can introduce them to important social issues and develop critical reading skills as well.

2. Supplementary materials can offset the influence of unrepresentative textbooks. Often school, university, and local libraries have information on the lives and contributions of women and minority-group members.

3. Have your students help you assemble bulletin boards and other instructional displays. Teach them about the forms of bias and make sure that the displays they assemble are bias free.

4. Analyze your seating chart to determine whether there are pockets of race or gender segregation in your classroom. When your students work in groups, check to see if they are representative of the different populations in the class.

5. When students themselves form segregated groups, you may need to intervene. Establish ground rules to ensure that work and play groups and teams are representative. Explain to students why segregation on any basis—race, religion, national origin, or gender—is harmful to learning and the principles of a democratic society.

6. Reinforcement can be effective for increasing the amount of time boys and girls work and play in coeducational arrangements. In one study, teachers made a consistent effort to praise girls and boys who were working and playing cooperatively together. When teachers praised in this way, the amount of time girls and boys spent working and playing cooperatively increased.

7. Peer tutoring and cooperative learning can encourage gender integration. Moreover, these techniques increase achievement not only for the students being helped, but for those doing the helping as well. Even though the research shows that peer tutoring and cooperative learning are effective techniques, they should be used as supplements to (not replacements for) teacher-led instruction. Also, both peer tutoring and cooperative learning are much more powerful when students receive training in how to tutor and work constructively with others.

8. Most teachers find it difficult to track their own questioning patterns while they are teaching. Try to have someone do this for you. Make arrangements to have a professional whose feedback you value—a supervisor, your principal, another teacher—come into your classroom and observe. Your observer can tally how many questions you ask boys and how many you ask girls, how many questions you ask majority and how many you ask minority students. Then you can consider the race and sex of your involved and silent students and determine whether one sex or race is receiving more than its fair share of your time and attention.

9. Because teachers may find it difficult to have professional observers come into their classrooms on a regular basis, many have found it helpful to have students keep a tally of questioning patterns. Before you do this, you may want to explain to the class how important it is for all students to get involved in classroom discussion.

10. Because research on sex equity in education is occurring at a rapid pace, it is important to continue your reading and professional development in this area. Be alert for articles and other publications on the topic, and be careful that your own rights are not denied because of sex discrimination.

When teachers become aware of the nature and cost of sex bias in schools, they can make an important difference in the lives of their students. Teachers can reduce sexism in schools or even make it obsolete. They can make sex equity a reality for children in our schools. Then tomorrow's children, boys and girls, need not suffer from the limiting effects of sexism in school.

QUESTIONS AND ACTIVITIES

1. The authors of this chapter list six forms of gender bias that you can use when evaluating instructional materials: (a) linguistic bias, (b) stereotyping, (c) invisibility, (d) imbalance, (e) unreality, and (f) fragmentation.

   Define each form of bias. Examine a sample of social studies, language arts, reading, science, or mathematics textbooks (or a combination of two kinds of textbooks) to determine whether they contain any of these forms of gender bias. Share your findings with your classmates or workshop participants.

2. Give some examples of how teachers can supplement textbooks to help to eliminate the six forms of gender bias identified in activity 1 above.

3. What are some of the behavioral and attitudinal consequences for students of gender bias in curriculum materials? Of gender-fair curriculum materials?

4. In what ways do Mrs. Howe's interactions with the boys and girls during the music lesson indicate gender bias? How can Mrs. Howe be helped to change her behavior and to make it more gender fair?

5. Observe lessons being taught in several classrooms that include boys and girls and students from different racial and ethnic groups. Did the ways the teachers interacted with males and female students differ? If so, in what ways? Did the teachers interact with students from different ethnic groups differently? If so, in what ways? Did you notice any ways that gender and ethnicity combined to influence the ways the teachers interacted with particular students? If so, explain.

6. What are the major reasons there are fewer women than men who are educational administrators? Are more women likely to become educational administrators in the future? Why or why not?

7. Girls start out in school ahead of boys in speaking, reading, and counting. Boys surpass girls in math performance by junior high school. Why do you think this happens? Recent research indicates that the disparities in the academic achievement of boys and girls are declining. Why do you think they are?

8. In what ways, according to the authors, are single-sex schools beneficial for females? Why do you think all-girls schools are vanishing? Do you think this trend should be halted? Why or why not?

9. After reading this chapter, do you think there are some ways you can change your behavior to make it more gender fair? If yes, in what ways? If no, why not?

NOTES

1. Myra Sadker, David Sadker, and Susan Klein, "Abolishing Misperceptions about Sex Equity in Education," *Theory into Practice,* 25 (Autumn 1986): 220–226.

2. Myra Sadker and David Sadker, *Sex Equity Handbook for Schools* (New York: Longman, 1982).

3. Gwyneth Britton and Margaret Lumpkin, "Females and Minorities in Basal Readers," *Interracial Books for Children Bulletin,* 14, No. 6 (1983): 4–7.

4. Lenore Weitzman and Diane Rizzo, *Biased Textbooks* (Washington, D.C.: The Resource Center on Sex Roles in Education, 1974).

5. Women on Words and Images, *Dick and Jane as Victims: Sex Stereotyping in Children's Readers* (Princeton, N.J.: Women on Words and Images, 1975).

6. Janice Law Trecker, "Women in U.S. History High-School Textbooks," in Janice Pottker and Andrew Fishel, eds. *Sex Bias in the Schools: The Research Evidence* (Cranbury, N.J.: Associated University Presses, 1977), pp. 146–161.

7. Ibid.

8. William Nibbelink, Susan Stockdale, and Matadial Mangru, "Sex Role Assignments in Elementary School Mathematics Textbooks," *The Arithmetic Teacher* 34 (October 1986): 19–21.

9. Judith Kinman and Darwin Henderson, "An Analysis of Sexism in Newbery Medal Award Books from 1977 to 1984," *The Reading Teacher* 38 (May 1985): 885–889.

10. Richard Powell and Jesus Garcia, "The Portrayal of Minorities and Women in Selected Elementary Science Series," *Journal of Research in Science Teaching* 22, No. 6 (1985): 519–533.

11. O. L. Davis, Jr., Gerald Ponder, Lynn Burlbaw, Maria Garza-Lubeck, and Alfred Moss, "A Review of U.S. History Textbooks," *Looking at History: A Review of Major U.S. History Textbooks* (Washington, D.C.: People for the American Way, 1986).

12. Kathryn Scott, "Elementary Pupils' Perceptions of Reading and Social Studies Materials: Does the Sex of the Main Character Make a Difference?" *Dissertation Abstracts* 780973 (Ann Arbor: University of Michigan, 1977).

13. Kathryn Scott, "Effects of Sex-Fair Reading Materials on Pupils Attitudes, Comprehension, and Interest, *American Educational Research Journal* 23 (Spring 1986): 105–116.

14. Robin Carter, Unpublished class paper, American University, Washington, D.C., 1987. Used with permission.

15. David Sadker and Myra Sadker, "Is the O.K. Classroom O.K.?" *Phi Delta Kappan* 66 (January 1985): 358–361.

16. Myra Sadker and David Sadker, *Effectiveness and Equity in College Teaching: Final Report* (Washington, D.C.: Fund for the Improvement of Postsecondary Education, 1985).

17. Jere Brophy and Thomas Good, *Teacher-Student Relationships: Causes and Consequences* (New York: Holt, Rinehart and Winston, 1974); see also G. Jones, "Gender Bias in Classroom Interactions," *Contemporary Education* 60 (1989): 216–222.

18. Ned Flanders, *Analyzing Teaching Behaviors* (Reading, Mass.: Addison-Wesley, 1970).

19. N. Gross and A. Trask, *Men and Women as Elementary School Principals* (Cambridge, Mass.: Harvard University Press, 1965).

20. Ibid.

21. Myra Sadker, "Women in Educational Administration," (Washington, D.C.: The Mid-Atlantic Center for Sex Equity, 1985).

22. M. Smith, J. Kalvelage, and P. Schmuck, *Women Getting Together and Getting Ahead* (Washington, D.C.: Women's Educational Equity Act Program, 1982).

23. Myra Sadker and David Sadker, adapted from "Cost of Sex Bias in Schools," *Sex Equity Handbook for Schools* (New York: Longman, 1982). Copyright © 1987 David and Myra Sadker. All rights reserved. (pp. 114–117.) Reprinted, Carnegie Foundation, 1990.

24. Myra Sadker, David Sadker, and Susan Klein, "The Issue of Gender in Elementary and Secondary Education," *Review of Research in Education* (Washington, D.C.: American Educational Research Association, 1991).

25. Janet Hyde and Marsha Lynn, "Gender Differences in Verbal Activity: A Meta-Analysis," *Psychological Bulletin* 104 (1988): 53–69; see also J. Hyde, E. Fenneman, and S. Lamon, "Gender Differences in Mathematical Performance: A Meta-Analysis," *Psychological Bulletin* 107 (1990): 139–155.

26. Valerie Lee and Anthony Bryk, "Effects of Single-Sex Secondary Schools on Student Achievement and Attitudes," *Journal of Educational Psychology* 78, No. 5 (October 1986): 381–395.

28. Kathleen Lenerz, "Factors Related to Educational and Occupational Orientations in Early Adolescence." Paper presented at the American Educational Research Association, Washington, D.C., 1987.

29. Karen Bogart, "Improving Sex Equity in Postsecondary Education," in Susan Klein, ed., *Handbook for Achieving Sex Equity through Education* (Baltimore: Johns Hopkins University Press, 1984)

30. National Commission on Working Women, "An Overview of Women in the Workforce" (Washington, D.C.: 1986); see also National Commission on Working Women of Wider Opportunities for Women, "Women and Work," (Washington, D.C.: 1990).

31. Lynell Johnson, "Children's Visions of the Future," *The Futurist,* 21, No. 3, (May–June 1987): 36–40.

32. Myra Sadker and David Sadker, *PEPA (Principal Effectiveness—Pupil Achievement): A Training Program for Principals and Other Educational Leaders* (Washington, D.C.: American University, 1986). Ten steps copyright © David and Myra Sadker. All rights reserved.

CHAPTER 7

Classrooms for Diversity: Rethinking Curriculum and Pedagogy

■ MARY KAY THOMPSON TETREAULT

We are presently in a period of rethinking the aims of public education. New directions for public education are emerging. These new directions include challenging the male dominance over curricular content and over the substance of knowledge itself. Evidence of that challenge is our new understanding of the extent to which the curriculum we learned excluded (or included) women's traditions, history, culture, values, visions, and perspectives. We are beginning to envision a curriculum that includes content about women and gender, one that interweaves issues of gender with ethnicity, race, and class.

There is also widespread concern about the quality of teaching in our nation's classrooms, particularly the predominance of passive modes of student learning. Beginning with questions about the silence and alienation of women students, some faculty members worry that traditional ways of teaching no longer serve our increasingly diverse student body.

FEMINIST PHASE THEORY

One of the most effective ways I have found to set a frame for envisioning a gender-balanced, multicultural curriculum, while at the same time capturing the reforms that have occurred over the past twenty years, is feminist phase theory. Conceptually rooted in the scholarship on women, feminist phase theory is a classification system of the evolution in thought during the past twenty years about the incorporation of women's traditions, history, and experiences into selected disciplines. The model I have developed identifies five common phases of thinking about women: *male-defined curriculum, contribution curriculum, bifocal curriculum, women's curriculum,* and *gender-balanced curriculum.*[1]

The language of this system or schema, particularly the word *phase,* and the description of one phase and then another, suggests a sequential hierarchy, in which one phase supplants another. Before presenting the schema, please refrain from thinking of these phases in a linear fashion and envision them as a series of intersecting circles, or patches on a quilt, or threads in a tapestry, which interact and undergo changes in response to one another. It is more accurate to view the phases as "different emphases that co-exist in feminist research."[2] The important thing is that teachers, scholars, and curriculum developers ask and answer certain questions at each phase. In the section that follows, I identify key concepts and questions articulated initially at each phase, using examples from history, literature, and science, and then discuss how the phases interact and undergo changes in response to one another.[3] The final part of this chapter suggests some implications of feminist theory for classroom pedagogy and concludes with specific objectives, practices, and teaching suggestions for incorporating content about women into the K–12 curriculum in social studies, language arts, and science.

Male-Defined Curriculum

Male-defined curricula rest on the assumption that the male experience is universal, that it is representative of humanity, and that it constitutes a basis for generalizing about all human beings. The knowledge that is researched and taught, the substance of learning, is knowledge articulated by and about men. There is little or no consciousness in it that the existence of women as a group is an anomaly calling for a broader definition of knowledge. The female experience is subsumed under the male experience. For example, a well-known scientist cited methodological problems in some research about sex differences that draws conclusions about females based on experiments done only on males or that uses limited (usually White, middle-class) experimental populations from which scientists draw conclusions about all males and females.[4]

The incorporation of women into the curriculum has not only taught us about women's lives but has also led to questions about our lopsided rendition of men's lives, wherein we pay attention primarily to men in the public world and conceal their lives in the private world. Historians, for example, are posing a series of interesting questions about men's history: What do we need to unlearn about men's history? What are the taken-for-granted truths about men's history that we need to rethink? How do we get at the significant masculine truths? Is man's primary sense of self defined in relation to the public sphere only? How does it relate to boyhood, adolescence, family, life, recreation, and love? What does this imply about the teaching of history?[5]

Feminist scholarship, like African American, Native American, Latino, and Asian scholarship, reveals the systematic and contestable exclusions in the male-defined curriculum. When we examine it through the lens of this scholarship, we are forced to reconsider our understanding of the most fundamental conceptualization of knowledge and social relations within our society. We understand in a new way that knowledge is a social construction, written by individual human beings who live and think at a particular time and within a particular social framework. All works in literature, science, and history, for example, have an author—male or female, White or ethnic or racial minority, elite or middle-class or occasionally poor—with motivations and beliefs. The scientist's questions and activities, for instance, are shaped, often unconsciously, by the great social issues of the day (see Table 7.1). Different perspectives on the same subject will change the patterns discerned.

TABLE 7.1
Male-Defined Curriculum

Characteristics of Phase	Questions Commonly Asked about Women in History*	Questions Commonly Asked about Women in Literature*	Questions Commonly Asked about Women in Science*
The absence of women is not noted. There is no consciousness that the male experience is a "particular knowledge" selected from a wider universe of possible knowledge and experience. It is valued, emphasized, and viewed as the knowledge most worth having.	Who is the author of a particular history? What is her or his race, ethnicity, religion, ideological orientation, social class, place of origin and historical period? How does incorporating women's experiences lead to new understandings of the most fundamental ordering of social relations, institutions, and power arrangements? How can we define the content and methodology of history, so it will be a history of us all?	How is traditional humanism, with an integrated self at its center and an authentic view of life, in effect part of patriarchal ideology? How can the objectivist illusion be dismantled? How can the idea of a literary canon of "great literature" be challenged? How are writing and reading political acts? How do race, class, and gender relate to the conflict, sufferings, and passions that attend these realities? How can we study language as specific *discourse,* that is, specific linguistic strategies in specific situations, rather than as universal language?	How do scientific studies reveal cultural values? What cultural, historical, and gender values are projected onto the physical and natural world? How might gender be a bias that influences choice of questions, hypotheses, subjects, experimented design, or theory formation in science? What is the underlying philosophy of an androcentric science that values objectivity, rationality, and dominance? How can the distance between the subject and the scientific observer be shortened so that the scientist has some feeling or empathy with the organism? How can gender play a crucial role in transforming science?

*New questions generated by feminist scholars.

Contribution Curriculum

Early efforts to reclaim women's rightful place in the curriculum were a search for missing women within a male framework. Although there was the recognition that women were missing, men continued to serve as the norm, the representative, the universal human being. Outstanding women emerged who fit this male norm of excellence or greatness or conformed to implicit assumptions about appropriate roles for women outside the home. In literature, female authors were added who performed well within the masculine tradition, internalizing its standards of art and its views on social roles. Great women of science, who have made it in the male scientific world, most frequently Marie Curie, for example, were added.

Examples of contribution history can be seen in U.S. history textbooks. They now include the contributions of notable American women who were outstanding in the public sphere as rulers or as contributors to wars or reform movements to a remarkable degree. Queen Liliuokalani, Hawaii's first reigning queen and a nationalist, is included in the story of the kingdom's annexation. Molly Pitcher and Deborah Sampson are depicted as contributors to the Revolutionary War, as is Clara Barton to the Civil War effort. Some authors have also included women who conform to the assumption that it is acceptable for women to engage in activities outside the home if they are an extension of women's nurturing role within the family. Examples of this are Dorothea Dix, Jane Addams, Eleanor Roosevelt, and Mary McLeod Bethune.[6]

The lesson to be learned from understanding these limitations of early contribution history is not to disregard the study of notable women, but to include those who worked to reshape the world according to a feminist reordering of values. This includes efforts to increase women's self-determination through a feminist transformation of the home, increased education, women's rights to control their bodies, to increase their political rights, and to improve their economic status. A history with women at the center moves beyond paying attention to caring for the unfortunate in the public sphere to how exceptional women influenced the lives of women in general (see Table 7.2). Just as Mary McLeod Bethune's role in the New Deal is worth teaching to our students, so is her aggressive work to project a positive image of Black women to the nation through her work in Black women's clubs and the launching of the *Afro-American Woman's Journal.*

Bifocal Curriculum

In bifocal curricula, feminist scholars have made an important shift, from a perspective that views men as the norm to one that opens up the possibility of seeing the world through women's eyes. This dual vision, or bifocal perspective, generated global questions about women and about the differences between women and men. Historians investigated the separation between the public and the private sphere and asked, for example, how the division between them explains women's lives. Some elaborated on the construct by identifying arenas of female power in the domestic sphere. Literary critics aimed to provide a new understanding of a distinctively female literary tradition and a theory of women's literary creativity. They sought to provide models for understanding the dynamics of female literary response to male literary assertion and coercion.[7] Scientists grapple with definitions of woman's and man's nature by asking how the public and private, biology and culture, and personal and impersonal inform each other and affect men and women, science, and nature.

Scholars have pointed out some of the problems with bifocal knowledge. Thinking about women and men is dualistic and dichotomized. Women and men are thought of as having different spheres, different notions of what is of value in life, different ways of imagining the human condition, and different associations with nature and culture. But both views are valued. In short, women are thought

TABLE 7.2
Contribution Curriculum

Characteristics of Phase	Questions Commonly Asked about Women in History	Questions Commonly Asked about Women in Literature	Questions Commonly Asked about Women in Science
The absence of women is not noted. There is a search for missing women according to a male norm of greatness, excellence, or humanness. Women are considered exceptional, deviant, or other. Women are added into history, but the content and notions of historical significance are not challenged.	Who are the notable women missing from history and what did they and ordinary women contribute in areas or movements traditionally dominated by men, for example, during major wars or during reform movements like abolitionism or the labor movement? What did notable and ordinary women contribute in areas that are an extension of women's traditional roles, for example, caring for the poor and the sick? How have major economic and political changes like industrialization or extension of the franchise affected women in the public sphere? How did notable and ordinary women respond to their oppression, particularly through women's rights organizations? *Who were outstanding women who advocated a feminist transformation of the home, who contributed to women's greater self-determination through increased education, the right to	Who are the missing female authors whose subject matter and use of language and form meet the male norm of "masterpiece?" What primary biographical facts and interpretations are missing about major female authors?	Who are the notable women scientists who have made contributions to mainstream science? How is women's different (and inferior) nature related to hormones, brain lateralization, and sociobiology? Where are the missing females in scientific experiments? What is the current status of women within the scientific profession? *How does adding minority women into the history of science reveal patterns of exclusion and recast definitions of what it means to practice science and to be a scientist? *How is the exclusion of women from science related to the way science is done and thought? *What is the usual pattern of women working in science? How is it the same as or different from the pattern of notable women? *How do our definitions of science need to be broadened to evaluate women's contributions to science? Do

(continued)

TABLE 7.2
Continued

Characteristics of Phase	Questions Commonly Asked about Women in History	Questions Commonly Asked about Women in Literature	Questions Commonly Asked about Women in Science
	control their bodies, to increase their political rights, and to improve their economic status? *What did women contribute through the settlement house and labor movements?		institutions of science need to be reshaped to accommodate women? If so, how?

*New questions generated by feminist scholars.

of as a group that is complementary but equal to men; there are some truths for men and there are some truths for women. General analyses of men's and women's experiences often come dangerously close to reiterating the sexual stereotypes scholars are trying to overcome. Because many believe that the public sphere is more valuable than the private sphere, there is a tendency to slip back into thinking of women as inferior and subordinate.

The generalized view of women and men that predominates in the bifocal curriculum often does not allow for distinctions within groups as large and as complex as women and men. Important factors like historical period, geographic location, structural barriers, race, paternity, sexual orientation, and social class, to name a few, clearly make a difference.

Other common emphases in the bifocal curriculum are the oppression of women and exploration of that oppression. Exposés of woman-hating in history and literature are common. Kate Millett's analysis of male writers like Norman Mailer, Arthur Miller, and D. H. Lawrence was one of the first literary exposés.[8] The emphasis in her analysis is on the misogyny (the hatred of women) of the human experience, particularly the means men have used to advance their authority and to assert or imply female inferiority. The paradoxes of women's existence are sometimes overlooked with this emphasis on oppression. For example, although women have been excluded from positions of power, a few of them as wives and daughters in powerful families were often closer to actual power than were men. If some women were dissatisfied with their status and role, most women adjusted and resisted efforts to improve women's lot.[9] Too much emphasis on women's oppression perpetuates a patriarchal framework presenting women as primarily passive, reacting only to the pressures of a sexist society. In the main, it emphasizes men thinking and women being thought about.[10]

Women's scholarship during the 1970s and 1980s has helped us see that understanding women's oppression is more complex than we initially thought. We do not yet have adequate concepts to explain gender systems, founded on a division of labor and sexual asymmetry. To understand gender systems, it is necessary to take a structural and experiential perspective that asks from a woman's point of view where we are agents and where we are not; where our relations with men are egalitarian and where they are not. This questioning may lead to explanations of why women's experiences and interpretations of their world can differ significantly from men's.

Further, the concepts with which we approach our analysis need to be questioned. Anthropologists have pointed out that our way of seeing the world— for instance, the idea of complementary spheres for women (the private sphere) and men (the public sphere)—is a product of our experience in a Western, modern, industrial, capitalistic state with a specific history. We distort our understanding of other social systems by imposing our world view on them. Feminist critics are calling for rethinking, not only of categories like the domestic versus the public sphere, and production and reproduction but even of categories like gender itself.[11]

Feminist scholars have helped us see the urgency of probing and analyzing the interactive nature of the oppressions of race, ethnicity, class, and gender. We are reminded that we can no longer take a liberal reformist approach that does not probe the needs of the system that are being satisfied by oppression. We have to take seriously the model of feminist scholarship that analyzes women's status within the social, cultural, historical, political, and economic contexts. Only then will issues of gender be understood in relation to the economic needs of both male dominance and capitalism that undergird such oppressions.[12]

One of the most important things we have learned about a bifocal perspective is the danger of generalizing too much, of longing for women's history, instead of writing histories about women. We must guard against establishing a feminist version of great literature and then resisting any modifications or additions to it. We have also learned that the traditional disciplines are limited in their ability to shed light on gender complexities, and it becomes apparent that there is a need for an interdisciplinary perspective (see Table 7.3).

Women's Curriculum

The most important idea to emerge in women's scholarship is that women's activities, not men's, are the measure of significance. What was formerly devalued, the content of women's everyday lives, assumes new value as scholars investigate female rituals, housework, childbearing, child rearing, female sexuality, female friendship, and studies of the life cycle. For instance, scientists investigate how research on areas of primary interest to women—menstruation, childbirth, and menopause—challenge existing scientific theories. Historians document women's efforts to break out of their traditional sphere of the home in a way that uses women's activities, not men's, as the measure of historical significance. These activities include women's education, women's paid work and volunteer work outside the home, particularly in women's clubs and associations. Of equal importance is the development of a collective feminist consciousness, that is, of women's consciousness of their own distinct role in society. Analyses begun in the bifocal phase continue to explore what sex and gender have meant for the majority of women.

TABLE 7.3
Bifocal Curriculum

Characteristics of Phase	Questions Commonly Asked about Women in History	Questions Commonly Asked about Women in Literature	Questions Commonly Asked about Women in Science
Human experience is conceptualized primarily in dualist categories: male and female, private and public, agency and communion. Emphasis is on a complementary but equal conceptualization of men's and women's spheres and personal qualities There is a focus on women's oppression and on misogny. Women's efforts to overcome the oppression are presented. Efforts to include women lead to the insight that the traditional content, structure, and methodology of the disciplines are more appropriate to the male experience.	How does the vision between the public and the private sphere explain women's lives? Who oppressed women, and how were they oppressed? *What are forms of power and value in women's worlds? *How have women been excluded from and deprived of power and value in men's spheres? *How do gender systems create divisions between the sexes such that experience and interpretations of their world can differ significantly from men's? *How can we rethink categories like public and private, productive and reproductive, sex and gender?	Who are the missing minor female authors whose books are unobtainable, whose lives have never been written, and whose works have been studied casually, if at all? How is literature a record of the collective consciousness of patriarchy? What myths and stereotypes about women are present in male literature? How can we critique the meritocratic pretensions of traditional literary history? How can we pair opposite-sex texts in literature as a way of understanding the differences between women's and men's experiences? How is literature one of the expressive modes of a female subculture that developed with the distinction of separate spheres for women and men? *How can feminist literary critics resist establishing their own great canon of literature and any additions to it?	How have the sciences defined (and misdefined) the nature of women? Why are there so few women scientists? What social and psychological forces have kept women in the lower ranks or out of science entirely? How do women fit into the study of history of science and health care? How do scientific findings, originally carried out on males of a species, change when carried out on the females of the same species? How do the theories and interpretations of sociobiology require constant testing and change to fit the theory for males and females with regard to competition, sexual selection, and infanticide? How does the science/gender system—the network of associations and disjunctions between public and private, personal and impersonal, and masculine and feminine—inform each other and affect men and women, science and nature? *What are the structural barriers to women in science?

*New questions generated by feminist scholars

As scholars look more closely at the complex patterns of women's lives, they see the need for a pluralistic conceptualization of women. Although thinking of women as a monolithic group provides valuable information about patterns of continuity and change in those areas most central to women's lives, generalizing about a group as vast and diverse as women leads to inaccuracies. The subtle interactions among gender and other variables are investigated. Historians ask how the particulars of race, ethnicity, social class, marital status, and sexual orientation challenge the homogeneity of women's experiences.

Questions about sex and gender are set within historical, ideological, and cultural contexts, including culture's definition of the facts of biological development and what they mean for individuals. Researchers ask, for example, Why are these attitudes toward sexuality prevalent at this time in history? What are the ways in which sexual words, categories, and ideology mirror the organization of society as a whole? What are the socioeconomic factors contributing to them? How do current conceptions of the body reflect social experiences and professional needs?[13]

Life histories and autobiographies shed light on societies' perceptions of women and women's perceptions of themselves. Women's individual experiences are revealed through these stories and contribute to the fashioning of the human experience from the perspective of women.

Scholars find it necessary to draw on other disciplines for a clearer vision of the social structure and culture of societies as individuals encounter them in their daily life. Likewise, there are calls for new unifying frameworks and different ways to think of periods in history and literature to identify concepts that accommodate women's history and traditions. There is also a more complex conceptualization of historical time. The emphasis in much history is on *events,* a unit of time too brief to afford a sense of structural change, changes in the way people think about their own reality, and the possibilities for other realities. *L'Ecole des Annales* in France (a group of historians who pioneered the use of public records such as birth, marriage, and death certificates in historical analysis) has distinguished between events and what they call the *longue durée.*[14] By the *longue durée* they mean the slow, glacial changes, requiring hundreds of years to complete, that represent significant shifts in the way people think.

Examples of areas of women's history that lend themselves to the concept are the structural change from a male-dominated to an egalitarian perspective, the transformation of women's traditional role in the family to their present roles as wives, mothers, and paid workers outside the home. Also important is the demographic change in the average number of children per woman of childbearing age from seven to fewer than two children between 1800 and 1990 (see Table 7.4).

Gender-Balanced Curriculum

This phase continues many of the inquiries begun in the women's curriculum phase but articulates questions about how women and men relate to and complement one another. Conscious of the limitations of seeing women in isolation and aware of the relational character of gender, researchers search for the nodal points at which women's and men's experiences intersect. Historians and literary critics ask if the private, as well as the public, aspects of life are presented as a continuum in women's and men's experience.

TABLE 7.4
Women's Curriculum

Characteristics of Phase	Questions Commonly Asked about Women in History	Questions Commonly Asked about Women in Literature	Questions Commonly Asked about Women in Science
Scholarly inquiry pursues new questions, new categories, and new notions of significance that illuminate women's traditions, history, culture, values, visions, and perspectives.	What were the majority of women doing at a particular time in history? What was the significance of these activities?	What does women's sphere—for example, domesticity and family, education, marriage, sexuality, and love—reveal about our culture?	How do the cultural dualisms associated with masculinity and femininity permeate scientific thought and discourse?
A pluralistic conception of women emerges that acknowledges diversity and recognizes that variables besides gender shape women's lives—for example, race, ethnicity, and social class.	How can female friendship between kin, mothers, daughters, and friends be analyzed as one aspect of women's overall relations with others?	How can we contrast the fictional image of women in literature with the complexity and variety of the roles of individual women in real life as workers, housewives, revolutionaries, mothers, lovers, and so on?	How does women's actual experiences, as compared to the physician's analysis or scientific theory, challenge the traditional paradigms of science and of the health care systems?
Women's experience is allowed to speak for itself. Feminist history is rooted in the personal and the specific; it builds from that to the general.	What kind of productive work, paid and unpaid, did women do and under what conditions?	How do the particulars of race, ethnicity, social class, marital status, and sexual orientation, as revealed in literature, challenge the thematic homogeneity of women's experiences?	How does research on areas of primary interest to women, for instance, menopause, childbirth and menstruation/estrus, challenge existing scientific theories?
The public and the private are seen as a continuum in women's experiences.	What were the reproductive activities of women? How did they reproduce the American family?	How does literature portray what binds women together and what separates them because of race, ethnicity, social class, marital status, and sexual orientation?	How do variables other than sex and gender, such as age, species, and individual variation, challenge current theories?
Women's experience is analyzed within the social, cultural, historical, political, and economic contexts.	How did the variables of race, ethnicity, social class, marital status, and sexual preference affect women's experience?	How does the social and historical context of a work of literature shed light on it?	How do the experience of female primates and the variation among species of primates, for example, competition among women, female agency in sexuality, and infanticide, test the traditional paradigms?
Efforts are made to reconceptualize knowledge to encompass the female experience. The conceptualization of knowledge is not characterized by disciplinary thinking but becomes multidisciplinary.	What new categories need to be added to the study of history, for instance, housework, childbearing, and child rearing?		
	How have women of different races and classes interacted throughout history?		
	What are appropriate ways of organizing or periodizing women's history? For example, how will examining women's experiences at each stage of the life span help us to understand women's experiences on their own terms?		

The pluralistic and multifocal conception of women that emerged in the women's curriculum phase is extended to human beings. A central idea in this phase is positionality.[15] Positionality means that important aspects of our identity (for example, our gender, our race, our class, our age, and so on) are markers of relational positions rather than essential qualities. Their effects and implications change according to context. Recently, feminist thinkers have seen knowledge as valid when it comes from an acknowledgement of the knower's specific position in any context, one always defined by gender, race, class, and other variables.

Scientists ask explicit questions about male-female relations in animals and inquire about how such variables as age, species, and individual variation challenge current theories. Accompanying this particularistic perspective is attention to the larger context, for example, the interplay among situation, meaning, economic systems, family organization, and political systems. Thus, historians ask how gender inequities are linked to economics, family organization, marriage, ritual, and politics. Research scientists probe how differences between the male and female body have been used to justify a social agenda that privileges men economically, socially, and politically. In this phase, a revolutionary relationship comes to exist between things traditionally treated as serious, primarily the activities of men in the public sphere, and those things formerly perceived as trivial, namely the activities of women in the private sphere.

This new relationship leads to a recentering of knowledge in the disciplines, a shift from a male-centered perspective to one that includes both females and males. This reconceptualization of knowledge works toward a more holistic view of human experience. As in the previous stage, the conceptualization of knowledge is characterized by multidisciplinary thinking.

Feminist scholars have cautioned against moving too quickly from women's curricula to gender-balanced curricula. As the historian Gerda Lerner once observed, our decade-and-a-half-old investigation of women's history is only a speck on the horizon compared to the centuries-old tradition of male-defined history.[16] By turning too quickly to studies of gender, we risk short-circuiting important directions in women's studies and again having women's history and experiences subsumed under those of men. It remains politically important for feminists to defend women as women in order to counteract the male domination that continues to exist. French philosopher Julia Kristeva, however, pushes us to new considerations when she urges women (and men) to recognize the falsifying nature of masculinity and femininity, to explore how the fact of being born male or female determines one's position in relation to power, and to envision more fluid gender identities that have the potential to liberate both women and men to a fuller personhood (see Table 7.5).[17]

CHANGING TRADITIONAL WAYS OF TEACHING

Two forces are pushing us to rethink our traditional ways of teaching. The first is our changing student population and the concurrent revolution in the disciplines, a revolution in which feminist scholarship has played a central role. The students we find in our classrooms are increasingly likely to be of an ethnic or racial minority. There is widespread concern for the high percentage of students who drop out, often because of dissatisfaction with their education. Even students who succeed often feel they have "made it in an institution that wasn't made for us."[18]

TABLE 7.5
Gender-Balanced Curriculum

Characteristics of Phase	Questions Commonly Asked about Women in History	Questions Commonly Asked about Women in Literature	Questions Commonly Asked about Women in Science
A multifocal, gender-balanced perspective is sought that weaves together women's and men's experiences into multilayered composites of human experience. At this stage, scholars are conscious of positionality.

Positionality represents the insight that all women and men must be located in historical contexts, contexts defined in terms of race, class, culture, and age, as well as gender, and that they gain their knowledge and their power from the specifics of their situations.

Scholars must begin to define what binds together and what separates the various segments of humanity.

Scholars have a deepened understanding of how the private as well as the public form a continuum in individual experience. They search for the nodal points at which comparative treatment of men's and women's experience is possible. | What is the knower's specific position in this historical context?

How is gender asymmetry linked to economic systems, family organizations, marriage, ritual, and political systems?

How can we compare women and men in all aspects of their lives to reveal gender as a crucial historical determinant?

Are the private, as well as the public, aspects of history presented as a continuum in women's and men's experiences?

How is gender a social construction? What does the particular construction of gender in a society tell us about the society that so constructed gender?

What is the intricate relation between the construction of gender and the structure of power?

How can we expand our conceptualization of historical time to a pluralistic one that conceives of three levels of history: structures, trends, and events?

How can we unify approaches and types of knowledge of all social | How does the author's specific position, as defined by gender, race, and class, affect this literary work?

How can we validate the full range of human expression by selecting literature according to its insight into any aspect of human experience rather than according to how it measures up to a predetermined canon?

Is the private as well as the public sphere presented as a continuum in women's and men's experiences?

How can we pair opposite-sex texts in literature as a way of understanding how female and male characters experience "maleness" and "femaleness" as a continuum of "humanness"?

How do the variables of race, ethnicity, social class, marital status, and sexual orientation affect the experience of female and male literary characters?

How can we rethink the concept of periodicity to accentuate the continuity of life and to contain the multitude of previously ignored literary works, for example, instead of | What explicit questions need to be raised about male-female relations in animals? How do variables such as age, species, and individual variation challenge current theories?

What are the limits to generalizing beyond the data collected on limited samples to other genders, species, and conditions not sampled in the experimental protocol?

How have sex differences been used to assign men and women to particular roles in the social hierarchy?

How have differences between the male and female body been used to justify a social agenda that privileges men economically, socially, and politically? |

TABLE 7.5
Continued

Characteristics of Phase	Questions Commonly Asked about Women in History	Questions Commonly Asked about Women in Literature	Questions Commonly Asked about Women in Science
Efforts are made to reconceptualize knowledge to reflect this multilayered composite of women's and men's experience. The conceptualization of knowledge is not characterized by disciplinary thinking but becomes multidisciplinary.	sciences and history as a means of investigating specific problems in relational history?	Puritanism, the contexts for and consequences of sexuality? How can we deconstruct the opposition between masculinity and femininity?	

The second force is feminist scholarship. Feminist scholarship has helped us understand that all knowledge, and therefore all classroom knowledge, is a social construction. The male-dominated disciplines have given us a discourse that silences or marginalizes other ways of knowing. One book, *Women's Ways of Knowing,* evoked a deep and widespread response, in part because the authors pointed out that education rewards certain kinds of learners and particular perspectives on knowledge.[19] To educate students for a complex, multicultural, multiracial world, we need to include the perspectives and voices of those who have not been traditionally included—women of all backgrounds, people of color, and females and males who perceive their education as not made for us.

In collaboration with Dr. Frances Maher of Wheaton College, I am engaged in an ethnographic study of feminist teachers who are committed to improving the education of women and minorities. By going inside the classrooms of these teachers, we have discovered four themes that may help you as you observe others teach and imagine new ways for your own teaching. These themes are, first, mastery of the course content and what constitutes knowledge. Mastery has traditionally meant the goal of rational comprehension of the material on the teacher's and expert's terms. In some classrooms we observed, students seek mastery on their own terms as well as in concert with others. Individual mastery is embedded and folded into the social construction of knowledge—it becomes collaborative rather than hierarchical. Rather than achieving rational comprehension of the material on the teacher's or expert's terms, students make increasingly more sophisticated connections with the topics. Universal notions of the right answer embedded in this term give way to an idea of mastery as empowerment—an instrument for previously silenced students to "claim an education."[20]

The second theme is voice, the awakening of the students' own responses. Voice means speaking for yourself and bringing your own questions and perspectives to the material. It connotes an interchange at both the rational and the unconscious levels among the teacher and the learners that connects one's education to one's own experience, as well as the fashioning of perspectives that are gender-balanced and multifocal. Women (and other oppressed groups) must often give up their voices when they seek mastery on the terms of the dominant discourses.[21]

The third theme is authority. In the traditional classroom, teachers and students stand in a hierarchical relationship to knowledge and to scholarly expertise. The teacher's authority comes from her role as interpreter of the experts' knowledge, as the experts are believed to be the closest people to the ultimate truth of any event or idea. With new paradigms of knowledge construction that occur from the intersection of multiple perspectives, some feminist teachers are reevaluating the source and implications of their authority. They see themselves as facilitators and resources, and they view their expertise as derived from their own experience, both individual and collective, rather than as from a superior access to truth. These teachers also see their authority as grounded in their own various commitments as feminists, seeing their stance as necessarily both a partial and a legitimate world view.

Our fourth theme is positionality, which was defined in the section above on gender-balanced curriculum. Recently, feminist thinkers have seen knowledge as valid when it comes from an acknowledgment of the knower's specific position in any context—a position always defined by gender, race, class, and other variables. We have observed feminist teaching practices that reposition the relationships among the professors, their students, and the materials, thus producing the epistemological shift away from the teacher as the sole authority and transforming the students' experiences of mastery and voice.

In the lessons that follow, I attempt to model teaching that is constructed to reveal the particular and the common denominators of human experience. These sample lessons are organized by the subject areas of language arts, science, and social studies, but they can be adapted to other subject areas as well.

Language Arts

Analyzing Children's Literature

SUGGESTED ACTIVITIES.   Ask students to locate five of their favorite children's books, to read or reread them, and to keep a written record of their reactions to the books. Either on the chalkboard or on a sheet of newsprint, keep a record of the students' (and your) book choices. Divide the class into small groups according to the same or similar favorite books, and have students share their written reactions to the books. Ask the groups to keep a record of the most noteworthy ideas that emerge from their small-group discussions. When you bring the small groups together, ask each group to present their noteworthy ideas. Ideas that may emerge may be as follows:

How differently they read the book now than at the time of their first reading

The differences and similarities in so-called girls books and boys books

The importance of multicultural or international perspectives

What the stories reveal about the culture in which the stories are set.

A follow-up activity could be to interview grandparents, parents, teachers, and other adults about characters and stories they remember from childhood. Questions to ask include, How do they recall feeling about those stories? Have images of female and male behavior or expectations in children's stories changed? Is race or ethnicity treated similarly or differently?

Pairing Female and Male Autobiographies

SUGGESTED ACTIVITIES.   Pairings of autobiographies by male and female authors can contribute greatly to students' multifocal, relational understanding of the human experience. Two pairings I have found to be particularly illuminating are *Black Boy*[22] by Richard Wright and *Woman Warrior* by Maxine Hong Kingston.[23] Another interesting pairing is Maya Angelou's *I Know Why the Caged Bird Sings*[24] and Mark Twain's *Huckleberry Finn.*[25] When I teach these books, I have students keep journals. I ask several students to write about a particular section of the book or in response to a specific question. I then begin class by asking these students to read from their journals. Their questions and insights thus become a basis for discussion. At other times, I might ask students to build a list of the things we need to talk about in relation to our common reading. I record their list on the chalkboard, adding my own questions and ideas where appropriate. The list we have built together then guides our discussion.[26]

Autobiographies of this nature are a rich stimulus for discussions of the many factors that intersect to shape human experience—time in history, geographic location, social class, gender, race, and ethnicity.

Science

Fear of Science: Fact or Fantasy?

SUGGESTED ACTIVITIES.   Fear of science and math contributes to the limited participation of some students, most often female, in math and science classes. Their inadequate participation limits their choice of most undergraduate majors that depend on a minimum of three years of high school mathematics. The following exercise was designed by the Math and Science Education for Women Project at the Lawrence Hall of Science (University of California, Berkeley).[27] The purpose of the exercise is to decrease female and male students' fear of science by enabling them to function as researchers who define the problem and generate solutions to it.

Ask students to complete the following sentence by writing for about fifteen minutes:

When I think about science, I . . .

When they are finished, divide students into groups of five or six to discuss their responses to the cue. Ask each group to state the most important things they have learned. Discuss fear of science with the class and whether there is a difference in how girls and boys feel about science. What could be some reasons for these differences or similarities? When the findings from this exercise are clear, suggest to students that they broaden their research to include other students and teachers in the school. Have each group brainstorm questions that might appear on a science attitude questionnaire. Put the questions on the chalkboard. Analyze the questions and decide on the ten best questions.

Decide with the class what group of students and teachers you will research and how you will do it; for example, other science classes, all ninth-grade science classes, or the entire school during second period. Obtain permission to conduct the survey from the administration and other teachers or classes involved in your research project. Have the class do the survey or questionnaire as a pilot activity. Analyze the questions for sex differences and make minor revisions before giving the survey and questionnaire to your research group. Distribute the survey or conduct interviews. Have the students decide how to analyze the information. Let each group decide how it will display findings and information. Have each group give (1) a report to the class on what it found, using graph displays to convey their information; and (2) recommendations for decreasing science anxiety in their school. Place the entire student research project in the school library, main office, or gymnasium, where the rest of the school population can see the results. Have a student summarize and write an article for the school paper.

Doing Science

SUGGESTED ACTIVITIES.   Evelyn Fox Keller's biography of Barbara McClintoch, *A Feeling for the Organism,* allows students to explore the conditions under which dissent in science arises, the function it serves, and the plurality of values and goals it reflects. Questions her story prompts are, What role do interests, individual and collective, play in the evolution of scientific knowledge? Do all scientists seek the same kinds of explanations? Are the kinds of questions they ask the same? Do differences in methodology between different subdisciplines ever permit the same kinds of answers? Do female and male scientists approach their research differently?

This book is difficult reading for high school or college students, but is manageable if they read carefully and thoroughly. The best way I have found to help them manage is to ask them to read a chapter or section and to come to class with their questions about the reading and to propose some answers.

Social Studies

My Family's Work History

SUGGESTED ACTIVITIES.   Women and men of different social classes, ethnic groups, and geographic locations have done various kinds of work inside and outside their homes in agricultural, industrial, and postindustrial economies. Before introducing students to the history of work, I pique their interest by asking them to complete a Family Work Chart (see Table 7.6). When their charts are complete, the students and I build a work chronology from 1890 to the present. Our work chronology contains information gleaned from the textbook and library sources about important inventions, laws, demographics, and labor history.

I then reproduce the work chronology on a chart so they can compare their family's history. By seeing their families' histories alongside major events in our collective work history, students can see how their family was related to society. A sample of items from our chart looks like this:[28]

TABLE 7.6
Family Work Chart

| | | Work Experience | | |
| | | | After Marriage | |
	Year of Birth	Before Marriage	While Children Were Young?	When Children Were Grown?
Your Maternal Side				
Mother				
Grandmother				
Grandfather				
Great-grandmother				
Great-grandfather				
Great-grandmother				
Great-grandfather				
Your Paternal Side				
Father				
Grandmother				
Grandfather				
Great-grandmother				
Great-grandfather				
Great-grandmother				
Great-grandfather				

This activity was developed by Carol Frenier. Reprinted with permission from the Education Development Center from Adeline Naiman, Projector Director, *Sally Garcia Family Resource Guide,* Unit 3 of *The Role of Women in American Society* (Newton, Mass.: Education Development Center, Inc., 1978), p. 62.

Historical Events	**Your Family History**
1890 Women are 17 percent of labor force	
1915 Telephone connects New York and San Francisco	
1924 Restriction of immigration	

Students conclude this unit by writing about a major theme in their family's work history. They might focus on how the lives of the women in the family differed from the lives of the men. They might focus on how their family's race or ethnicity shaped their work history.

Integrating the Public and Private Spheres
SUGGESTED ACTIVITIES.   Human life is lived in both the public and the private spheres in wartime as well as in peacetime. By asking students consciously to examine individuals' lives as citizens, workers, family members, friends, members of social groups, and individuals, they learn more about the interaction of these roles in both spheres. War is an extraordinary time when the nation's underlying assumptions about these roles are often put to the test. By having students examine the interaction of these roles in wartime, they can see some of our underlying assumptions about the roles and how they are manipulated for the purposes of war. Through researching the histories of their families, and by reading primary source accounts, viewing films, and reading their textbook, they will see the complexity and variety of human experiences in the United States during World War II.

Students research their family's history during World War II by gathering family documents and artifacts and by interviewing at least one relative who was an adult during World War II. Students draw up questions beforehand to find out how the individual's social roles were affected by the war. During the two weeks they are researching their family's history, two class periods are spent on this project. During the first period, students give oral reports to a small group of fellow students in read-around groups.

Appropriate readings and films on World War II are widely available. Studs Terkel's book *The Good War* is particularly useful because of the variety of people the author interviewed.[29] For instance, students can read about the internment of Japanese Americans and can role-play an account read. Their textbook may provide good background information. My students answer two questions in this unit: World War II has been described as a 'good war.' From the materials you have examined, was it a good war for individuals' lives as citizens, workers, family members, friends, and members of social groups? How were their experiences similar to or different from those of your relatives?

SUMMARY

This chapter has illustrated how women's studies is challenging male domination over curricular content. The evolution of that challenge is illuminated by understanding the different emphases that coexist in male-defined, contribution, bifocal, women's and gender-balanced curricula. We now have a conceptual framework for a curriculum that interweaves issues of gender with ethnicity, race, and class. This framework acknowledges and celebrates a multifocal, relational view of the human experience.

The idea of the phases of feminist scholarship as a series of intersecting circles, or patches on a quilt, or threads on a tapestry suggests parallel ways to think about a class of students. Each student brings to your classroom a particular way of knowing. Your challenge as a teacher is to interweave the individual truths with course content into complex understandings that legitimate students' voices.

This relational knowledge, with the authority of the school behind it, has the potential to help students analyze their own social, cultural, historical, political, and economic contexts. The goal of relational knowledge is to build a world in which the oppressions of race, gender, and class, on which capitalism and patriarchy depend, are challenged by critical citizens in a democratic society.

QUESTIONS AND ACTIVITIES

1. What is a gender-balanced, multicultural curriculum?

2. What is feminist phase theory?

3. Define and give an example of each of the following phases of the feminist phase theory developed and described by the author: (a) male-defined curriculum; (b) contribution curriculum; (c) bifocal curriculum; (d) women's curriculum; (e) gender-balanced curriculum.

4. What problems do the contribution and bifocal phases have? How do the women's curriculum and gender-balanced curriculum phases help solve these problems?

5. The author states that "knowledge is a social construction." What does this mean? In what ways is the new scholarship on women and ethnic groups alike? In what ways does the new scholarship on women and ethnic groups challenge the dominant knowledge established in the society and presented in textbooks? Give examples.

6. Examine the treatment of women in a sample of social studies, language arts, mathematics, or science textbooks (or a combination of two types of textbooks). Which phase or phases of the feminist phase theory presented by the author best describe the treatment of women in the textbooks you examined?

7. What is the *longue durée?* Why is it important in the study of social history, particularly women's history?

8. Research your family history, paying particular attention to the roles, careers, and influence of women in your family's saga. Also describe your ethnic heritage and the influence of ethnicity on your family's past and present. Share your family history with a group of your classmates or workshop participants.

NOTES

1. A gender-balanced perspective, one that is rooted in feminist scholarship, takes into account the experiences, perspectives, and voices of women as well as men. It examines the similarities and differences between women and men but also considers how gender interacts with such factors as ethnicity and class.

2. Jane Atkinson, "Gender Studies, Women's Studies, and Political Feminism" (unpublished paper, Lewis and Clark College: Portland, Ore.: 1986).

3. My thinking about women, gender, and science was influenced by Sue Rosser's work, particularly "The Relationship between Women's Studies and Women in Science," in Ruth Bleier, ed., *Feminist Approaches to Science* (New York: Pergamon Press, 1986) and Londa Schiebinger, "The History and Philosophy of Women in Science," *Signs* 12, No. 2 (Winter 1987): 276–292.

4. Carole Jacklin, "Methodological Issues in the Study of Sex-Related Differences," *Developmental Review* 1 (1981): 266–273. Cited in Anne Fausto-Sterling, *Myths of Gender* (New York: Basic Books, 1985).

5. Peter Filene, "The Secrets of Men's History." Unpublished Paper (Chapel Hill: University of North Carolina, no date).

6. Mary Kay Thompson Tetreault, "Integrating Women's History: The Case of United States History Textbooks," *The History Teacher* 19, No. 2 (February 1986): 211–262.

7. Sandra M. Gilbert and Susan Gubar, *The Madwoman in the Attic: The Woman Writer and the Nineteenth-Century Literary Imagination* (New Haven: Yale University Press, 1979).

8. Kate Millett, *Sexual Politics* (London: Virago, 1977).

9. Gerda Lerner, *The Majority Finds Its Past* (New York: Oxford University Press, 1979).

10. Carolyn Lougee, "Women's History and the Humanities: An Argument in Favor of the General Curriculum," *Women's Studies Quarterly* 9 (Spring 1981): 4–7.

11. Atkinson, "Gender Studies," 9–10; see also Sandra Coyner, "The Idea of Mainstreaming: Women's Studies and the Disciplines," *Frontiers* 8, No. 23 (1986): 87–95.

12. I am grateful to Patti Lather for this emphasis. Personal correspondence with Patti Lather, September 10, 1985.

13. Carroll Smith-Rosenberg, *Disorderly Conduct* (New York: Oxford Press, 1985).

14. For an excellent bibliographic review of the Annales School of History, see "Letters to the Editor," *Social Education* (October 1982) Vol. 46: 378, 380.

15. Linda Alcoff, "Cultural Feminism versus Post-Structuralism: The Identity Crisis in Feminist Theory," *Signs* 13, (Spring 1988): 405–436; Donna Haraway, "Situated Knowledges: The Science Question in Feminism and the Privilege of Partial Perspective," *Feminist Studies* 14, 3 (Fall 1988): 575–599; Sandra Harding, *The Science Question in Feminism* (Ithaca, N.Y.: Cornell University Press, 1987).

16. Gerda Lerner is reputed to have said this at a conference on women's history in 1982. Private conversation with Peggy McIntosh.

17. Toril Moi, *Sexual/Textual Politics* (New York: Methuen, 1985).

18. Richard Rodriguez, *Hunger of Memory: The Education of Richard Rodriguez* (New York: Bantam Books, 1982).

19. Mary Belenky, Blythe Clinchy, Nancy Goldberger, and Jill Tarule, *Women's Ways of Knowing: the Development of Self, Body and Mind* (New York: Basic Books, 1986).

20. Adrienne Rich, "Claiming an Education," in *On Lies, Secrets and Silences: Selected Prose 1966–1978.* (New York: Norton, 1979).

21. Our thinking about voice was influenced by Laurie Finke, *Knowledge as Bait: Feminism, Voice, and the Pedagogical Unconscious*. Unpublished paper (Portland, Ore: Lewis and Clark College, 1991).

22. Richard Wright, *Black Boy* (New York: Harper and Brothers, 1945).

23. Maxine Hong Kingston, *The Woman Warrior* (New York: Alfred Knopf, 1976).

24. Maya Angelou, *I Know Why the Caged Bird Sings* (New York: Bantam Books, 1969).

25. Samuel Clemens, *The Adventures of Huckleberry Finn* (New York: Collier, 1912).

26. These ideas about teaching literature are drawn from my observations of a colleague in the English Department at Lewis and Clark College, Dr. Dorothy Berkson. I observed her classes as part of an ethnographic study of feminist teachers.

27. Reprinted with permission from *Fact or Fantasy* (adapted from *Spaces: Solving Problems of Access to Careers in Engineering and Science),* Sherry Fraser, Project Director. Copyright © 1982 by the Lawrence Hall of Science, Regents of the University of California.

28. This chart appears in *Approaches to Women's History,* Ann Chapman, ed. (Washington, D.C.: American Historical Association, 1979).

29. Studs Terkel, *The Good War: An Oral History of World War II* (New York: Pantheon Books, 1984).

CHAPTER 8

Transforming the Curriculum: Teaching about Women of Color

■ **JOHNNELLA E. BUTLER**

Until very recently, teaching about women of color and incorporating material on women of color into the curriculum have been virtually ignored. At best, attention was paid to women of color from a global, culturally different perspective.[1] However, now, due to various national and state efforts, race, class, gender, and ethnicity, as categories of analysis in scholarship, are receiving more serious attention. Central to this curriculum revision are the history and experiences of women of color.

Many efforts to include women and issues of gender into what is called the mainstream curriculum focus on White, middle-class women from the United States and on women from other nations and cultures. Generally, we have taken the White, middle-class woman's experience as the norm when examining and talking about women's lives. When we want to know about women's lives that differ from that norm, we generally have explored the global experience. Curiously, when we deal with cultures of other nations, we seem to grasp that before we can have a proper understanding of the women in these cultures, we must adopt a multicultural perspective. It seems less apparent to us that to understand the lives of women in the United States, a cross-ethnic, multiethnic perspective that takes into account the structures of racism and their effects is necessary.

This chapter focuses on teaching about women of color in the United States and also describes an approach useful for studying and teaching about all women in U.S. society.

The discussion is rooted in the method of critical pedagogy developing in this country that is influenced, but certainly not totally defined, by Brazilian educator and activist Paulo Friere. I see feminist pedagogy as an evolution of this critical pedagogy, as well as the pedagogy implicit in ethnic studies. Examples are provided throughout to keep the theory from seeming only abstract and unrelated to teaching. Although I do not provide suggested activities for kindergarten and grades 1 through 12, I do provide information and a conceptual framework, the appropriate starting point for such activities. Readers are made aware of the teaching process as they convey the content on women of color. The appendix of this book includes bibliographic resources for content about the lives of women of color. They provide a starting point. Much work has yet to be done to make this information available to most teachers.

WHY *WOMEN OF COLOR*?

The phrase *women of color* came into use gradually during the past fifteen years. It immediately brings to mind differences of race and culture. It also makes clear that African American women are not the only women of color. In an ostensibly democratically structured society, with a great power imbalance signified by race and class privilege, labels representative of reality for those outside the realm of power are difficult to determine. This form of that power is both cultural and political and consequently further complicates labeling. Selecting the phrase *women of color* by many women of U.S. ethnic groups of color is part of their struggle to be recognized with dignity for their humanity, racial heritage, and cultural heritage as they work within the women's movement of the United States. The effort of women of color to name themselves is similar to attempts by African Americans and other ethnic groups to define with dignity their race and ethnicity and to counter the many stereotypical names bestowed on them. Because we tend to use the word *women* to be all-inclusive and general, we usually obscure both the differences and the similarities among women.

With the decline of the civil rights movement of the 1960s, the women's movement in the second half of the twentieth century got under way. Not long after, African American women began to articulate the differences they experienced as African American women, not only because of the racism within the women's movement or the sexism within the African American community, but also because of their vastly differing historical reality. One major question posed by Toni Cade's pioneering anthology, *The Black Woman,* remains applicable: "How relevant are the truths, the experiences, the findings of White women to Black women? Are women after all, simply women?" Cade answers the question then as it might still be answered today: "I don't know that our priorities are the same, that our concerns and methods are the same, or even similar enough so that we can afford to depend on this new field of experts (White, female). It is rather obvious that we do not. It is obvious that we are turning to each other."[2] This anthology served as a turning point in the experience of the African American woman. Previously, White males, for the most part, had interpreted her realities, her activities, and her contributions.[3]

Although we are beyond the point of the complete invisibility of women of color in the academic branch of the women's movement (women's studies), African American women must still demand to be heard, must insist on being dealt with from the perspective of the experiences of women of color, just as they did in 1970, as the blurb in the paperback *The Black Woman* implies: "Black Women Speak Out. A Brilliant and Challenging Assembly of Voices That Demand to Be Heard." By the latter part of the 1970s, the logic of a dialogue among women of color became a matter of course. We find, as in Cade's *The Black Woman,* Black women speaking to one another in publications such as *Conditions: Five, The Black Women's Issue,* and women of color speaking in the pioneering *This Bridge Called My Back: Writings by Radical Women of Color.*[4] The academic community began to recognize U.S. women of color who identify with the Third World, both for ancestral heritage and for related conditions of colonization; in 1980 we see, for example, the publication of Dexter Fisher's anthology *The Third Woman: Minority Women Writers of the United States.*[5]

destinies of women and men of color are linked. This reality poses a special problem in the relationship between White women and women of color. Moreover, in emphasizing the commonalities of privilege between White men and women, the oppressive relationship between men of color and White men, women of color and White men, and men of color and White women—all implied in Anna J. Cooper's observation[10]—the teaching about women of color provides the naturally pluralistic, multidimensional catalyst for transformation. As such, women of color are agents of transformation.

This section defines transformation and provides the theoretical framework for the pedagogy and methodology of transformation. The final section discusses aspects of the process of teaching about women of color, which, though closely related to the theoretical framework, manifest themselves in very concrete ways.

A review of feminist pedagogy over the past twenty years or so reveals a call for teaching from multifocal, multidimensional, multicultural, pluralistic, interdisciplinary perspectives. This call, largely consistent with the pedagogy and methodology implied thus far in this chapter, can be accomplished only through transformation. Although many theorists and teachers now see this point, the terminology has still to be corrected to illustrate the process. In fact, we often use the words *mainstreaming, balancing, integration,* and *transformation* interchangeably. Mainstreaming, balancing, and integration imply adding women to an established, accepted, and unchangeable body of knowledge. The experience of White, middle-class women has provided a norm in a way that White Anglo-American male ethnicity provides a norm. All other women's experience is added to and measured by those racial, class, ethnic, and gender roles and experiences.

Transformation, which does away with the dominance of norms, allows us to see the many aspects of women's lives. Understanding the significance of naming the action of treating women's lives through a pluralistic process—transformation—leads naturally to a convergence between women's studies and ethnic studies. This convergence is necessary to give us the information that illuminates the function and content of race, class, and ethnicity in women's lives and in relation to gender. In similar fashion, treating the lives of people of color through a pluralistic process leads to the same convergence, illuminating the functions and content of race, class, and gender in relation to lives of ethnic Americans and in relation to ethnicity.

We still need to come to grips with exactly what is meant by this pluralistic, multidimensional, interdisciplinary scholarship and pedagogy; much of the scholarship on, about, and even frequently, by, women of color renders them systematically invisible, erasing their experience or part of it. White, middle-class, male, and Anglo-American are the insidious norms corresponding to race, class, gender, and ethnicity. In contrasting and comparing experiences of pioneers, White males and females when dealing with Native Americans, for example, often speak of "the male," "the female," and "the Indian." Somehow, those of a different ethnicity and race are assumed to be male. Therefore, both the female and the male Indian experience is observed and distorted. They must be viewed both separately and together to get a more complete view, just as to have a more complete view of the pioneer experience, the White male and White female experiences must be studied both separately and together. Thus, even in our attempts to correct misinformation resulting from measurement by one norm, we can reinforce measurement by others if we do not see the interaction of the categories, the interaction of the -isms, as explained in the previous section. This pluralistic process and eye are demanded in order to understand the particulars and the generalities of people's lives.

Why is it so easy to impose these norms, effectively to erase the experience of others? I do not think erasing these experiences is always intentional. I do, however, think that it results from the dominance of the Western cultural norms of individuality, singularity, rationality, masculinity, and Whiteness at the expense of the communal, the plural, the intuitive, the feminine, and people of color. A brief look at Elizabeth Spelman's seminal work, "Theories of Race and Gender: The Erasure of Black Women," explains the important aspects of how this erasure comes about.[11] Then, a consideration of the philosophical makeup of transformation both tells us how our thinking makes it happen and how we can think to prevent it from happening.

Spelman gives examples of erasure of the Black woman, similar to the examples I have provided. She analyzes concepts that assume primacy of sexism over racism. Furthermore, she rejects the additive approach to analyzing sexism, an approach that assumes a sameness of women modeled on the White, middle-class, Anglo-oriented woman. Spelman shows that it is premature to argue that sexism and racism are either mutually exclusive, totally dependent on one another, or in a causal relationship with one another. She discusses how women differ by race, class, and culture or ethnicity. Most important, she demonstrates that Black does not simply indicate victim. Black indicates a culture, in the United States the African American culture. She suggests, then, that we present women's studies in a way that makes it a given that women are diverse, that their diversity is apparent in their experiences with oppression and in their participation in U.S. culture. To teach about women in this manner, our goal must not be additive, that is, integrating, mainstreaming or balancing the curriculum. Rather, transformation must be our goal.

Essentially, transformation is the process of revealing unity among human beings and the world, as well as revealing important differences. Transformation implies acknowledging and benefiting from the interaction among sameness and diversity, groups and individuals. The maxim on which transformation rests may be stated as an essential affirmation of the West African proverb, "I am because we are. We are because I am." The communality, the human unity implicit in the proverb, operates in African traditional (philosophical) thought in regard to human beings, other categories of life, categories of knowledge, ways of thinking and being.[12] It is in opposition to the European, Western pivotal axiom, on which integration, balancing, and mainstreaming rest (as expressed through the White, middle-class, Anglo norm in the United States), "I think; therefore, I am," as expressed by Déscartes.

The former is in tune with a pluralistic, multidimensional process; the latter with a monolithic, one-dimensional process. Stated succinctly as "I am we," the West African proverb provides the rationale for the interaction and modulation of the categories of race, class, gender, and ethnicity, for the interaction and modulation of their respective -isms, for the interaction and modulation of the objective and subjective, the rational and the intuitive, the feminine and the masculine, all those things which we, as Westerners, see as either opposite or standing rigidly alone. This is the breakdown of what is called variously critical pedagogy, feminist pedagogy, multifocal teaching, when the end is the comprehension of and involvement with cultural, class, racial, and gender diversity toward the end not of tolerance, but rather of an egalitarian world based on communal relationships within humanity.

To realize this transformation, we must redefine categories and displace criteria that have served as norms in order to bring about the life context (norms and values) as follows:

1. Nonhierarchical terms and contexts for human institutions, rituals, and action

2. A respect for the interaction and existence of both diversity and sameness (a removal of measurement by norms perpetuating otherness, silence, and erasure)

3. A balancing and interaction between the individual and the group

4. A concept of humanity emanating from interdependence of human beings on one another and on the world environment, both natural and human-created

5. A concept of humanity emanating from a sense of self that is not abstract and totally individually defined (I think; therefore, I am), but that is both abstract and concrete, individually and communally defined (I am we; I am because we are; we are because I am)

Such a context applies to pedagogy and scholarship, the dissemination and ordering of knowledge in all disciplines and fields. Within this context (the context in which the world does operate and against which the Western individualistic, singular concept of humanity militates), it becomes possible for us to understand the popular music form rap as an Americanized, Westernized version of African praise singing, functioning, obviously, for decidedly different cultural and social reasons. It becomes possible to understand the syncretization of cultures that produced Haitian voudon, Cuban santería, and Brazilian candomblé from Catholicism and the religion of the Yoruba. It becomes possible to understand what is happening when a Japanese American student is finding it difficult to reconcile traditional Buddhist values with her American life. It becomes possible to understand that Maxine Hong Kingston's *Woman Warrior* is essentially about the struggle to syncretize Chinese ways within the United States, whose dominant culture devalues and coerces against syncretization, seeking to impose White, middle-class conformity.

Thinking in this manner is foreign to the mainstream of thought in the United States, although it is alive and well in Native American traditional philosophy; in Taoist philosophy; in African traditional philosophy, and in African American folklore. It is so foreign, in fact, that I realized that in order to bring about this context, we must commit certain sins. Philosopher Elizabeth Minnich suggested that these sins might be more aptly characterized as heresies, because they are strongly at variance with established modes of thought and values.[13]

The following heresies challenge and ultimately displace the ways in which the Western mind orders the world.[14] They emanate from the experiences of people of color, the nature of their oppression, and the way the world operates. Adopting them is a necessity for teaching about women of color. Using the heresies to teach women's studies, to teach about the lives of all women, becomes natural when we study women of color and leads naturally to the transformation of the curriculum to a pluralistic, egalitarian, multidimensional curriculum.

Heresy #1 The goal of interaction among human beings, action, and ideas must be seen not only as synthesis, but also as the identification of opposites and differences. These opposites and differences may or may not be resolved; they may function together by virtue of the similarities identified.

Heresy #2 We *can* address a multiplicity of concerns, approaches, and subjects, without a neutral or dominant center. Reality reflects opposites as well as overlaps in what are perceived as opposites. There exist no pure, distinct opposites.

Heresy #3 It is not reductive to look at gender, race, class, and culture as part of a complex whole. The more different voices we have, the closer we are to the whole.

Heresy #4 Transformation demands an understanding of ethnicity that takes into account the differing cultural continua (in the United States, Western European, Anglo-American, African, Asian, Native American) and their similarities.

Heresy #5 Transformation demands a relinquishing of the primary definitiveness of gender, race, class or culture, and ethnicity as they interact with theory, methodology, pedagogy, institutionalization, and action, both in synthesis and in a dynamic that functions as opposite and same simultaneously.
A variation on this heresy is that although all -isms are not the same, they are unified and operate as such; likewise their correctives.

Heresy #6 The Anglo-American, and ultimately the Western, norm must be seen as only one of many norms, and also as one that enjoys privilege and power that has colonized, and may continue to colonize, other norms.

Heresy #7 Feelings are direct lines to better thinking. The intuitive as well as the rational is part of the process of moving from the familiar to the unfamiliar in acquiring knowledge.

Heresy #8 Knowledge is identity and identity is knowledge. All knowledge is explicitly and implicitly related to who we are, both as individuals and as groups.

TEACHING ABOUT WOMEN OF COLOR

The first six heresies essentially address content and methodology for gathering and interpreting content. They inform decisions such as the following:

1. Not teaching Linda Brent's *Narrative* as the single example of the slave experience of African American women in the nineteenth century, but rather presenting it as a representative example of the slave experience of African American women that occurs within a contradictory, paradoxical world that had free Black women such as Charlotte Forten Grimke and African American abolitionist women such as Sojourner Truth. The picture of Black women that emerges, then, becomes one that illuminates their complexity of experiences and their differing interactions with White people.

2. Not simply teaching about pioneer women in the West, but teaching about Native American women, perhaps through their stories, which they have passed on to their children and their children's children using the word to advance those concepts crucial to cultural survival. The picture of settling the West becomes more balanced, suggesting clearly to students the different perspectives and power relationships.

3. Not choosing biographies for children of a White woman, an Asian American woman, and an African American woman, but rather finding ways through biography, poetry, and storytelling to introduce children to different women's experiences, different according to race, class, ethnicity, and gender roles. The emphases are on the connectedness of experiences and on the differences among experiences, the communality among human beings, and the interrelatedness among experiences and ways of learning.

The last two heresies directly address process. After correct content, process is the most important part of teaching. Students who learn in an environment that is sensitive to their feelings and that supports and encourages the pursuit of knowledge will consistently meet new knowledge and new situations with the necessary openness and understanding for human development and progress. If this sounds moralistic, we must remember that the stated and implied goal of critical pedagogy and feminist pedagogy, as well as of efforts to transform the curriculum with content about women and ethnicity, is to provide an education that more accurately reflects the history and composition of the world, that demonstrates the relationship of *what* we learn to *how* we live, that implicitly and explicitly reveals the relationship between knowledge and social action. Process is most important, then, in helping students develop ways throughout their education to reach the closest approximation of truth toward the end of bettering the human condition.

The key to understanding the teaching process in any classroom in which teaching about women of color from the perspective of transformation is a goal is recognizing that the content alters all students' perceptions of themselves. First, they begin to realize that we can never say *women* to mean all women, that we must particularize the term as appropriate to context and understanding (for example, White, middle-class women; Chinese American, lower-class women; middle-class, Mexican American women). Next, students begin to understand that using White, middle-class women as the norm will seem distortingly reductive. White women's ethnic, regional, class, and gender commonalities and differences soon become apparent, and the role in oppression of the imposed Anglo-American ethnic conformity stands out. Student reactions may range from surprise, to excitement about learning more, to hostility and anger. In the volume

Gendered Subjects, Margo Culley details much of what happens. Her opening paragraph summarizes her main thesis:

> *Teaching about gender and race can create classrooms that are charged arenas. Students enter these classrooms imbued with the values of the dominant culture: they believe that success in conventional terms is largely a matter of will and that those who do not have it all have experienced a failure of will. Closer and closer ties between corporate America and higher education, as well as the "upscaling" of the student body, make it even harder to hear the voices from the margin within the academy. Bringing those voices to the center of the classroom means disorganizing ideology and disorienting individuals. Sometimes, as suddenly as the fragments in a kaleidoscope rearrange to totally change the picture, our work alters the ground of being for our students (and perhaps even for ourselves). When this happens, classrooms can become explosive, but potentially transformative arenas of dialogue.* [15]

"Altering the ground of being" happens to some extent on all levels. The White girl kindergarten pupil's sense of the world is frequently challenged when she discovers that heroines do not necessarily look like her. Awareness of the ways in which the world around children is ordered occurs earlier than most of us may imagine. My niece, barely four years old, told my father in a definitive tone as we entered a church farther from her home than the church to which she belongs, "Gramps, this is the Black church." We had not referred to the church as such, yet clearly that Catholic congregation was predominantly Black and the girl's home congregation predominantly White. Her younger sister, at age three, told her mother that the kids in the day school she attended were "not like me." She then pointed to the brown, back side of her hand. Young children notice difference. We decide what they do with and think of that difference.

Teaching young children about women of color gives male and female children of all backgrounds a sense of the diversity of people, of the various roles in which women function in American culture, of the various joys and sorrows, triumphs and struggles they encounter. Seeds of awareness of the power relationships between male and female, among racial, ethnic, and class groups are sown and nurtured.

Teaching about women of color early in students' academic experience allows the voices of the margin to be heard and to become a part of the matrix of reality. Teaching about women of color reveals race, ethnicity, gender, and class as essential components of human identity and also questions ideology and ways of being. Furthermore, however, it encourages an openness to understanding, difference and similarity, the foreign and the commonplace, necessary to the mind-set of curiosity and fascination for knowledge that we all want to inspire in our students no matter what the subject.

Culley also observes that "anger is the energy mediating the transformation from damage to wholeness," the damage being the values and perspectives of the dominant culture that have shaped opinions based on a seriously flawed and skewed American history and interpretation of the present. [16] Certain reactions occur and are part of the process of teaching about women of color. Because they can occur at all levels to a greater or lesser extent, it is useful to look for variations on their themes.

It is important to recognize that these reactions occur within the context of student and teacher expectations. Students are concerned about grading, teachers about evaluations by superiors and students. Frequently, fear of, disdain for, or hesitancy about feminist perspectives by some students may create a tense, hostile atmosphere. Similarly, fear of, disdain for, or hesitancy about studying people different from you (particularly by the White student) or people similar to you (particularly by the student of color or of a culture related to people of color) also may create a tense, hostile atmosphere. Student expectations of teachers, expectations modulated by the ethnicity, race, class, and gender of the teacher, may encourage students to presume that a teacher will take a certain position. The teacher's need to inspire students to perform with excellence may become a teacher's priority at the expense of presenting material that may at first confuse the students or challenge their opinions. It is important to treat these reactions as though they are as much a part of the process of teaching as the form of presentation, the exams, and the content, for indeed, they are. Moreover, they can affect the success of the teaching of the material about women of color.

Specifically, these reactions are part of the overall process of moving from the familiar to the unfamiliar. As heresy #7 guides us, "Feelings are direct lines to better thinking." Affective reactions to content, such as anger, guilt, and feelings of displacement, when recognized for what they are, lead to the desired cognitive reaction, the conceptualization of the facts so that knowledge becomes useful as the closest approximation to the truth. As Japanese American female students first read accounts by Issei women about their picture bride experiences, their reactions might at first be mixed.[17] Raising the issue of Japanese immigration to the United States during the late nineteenth century may not only challenge the exotic stereotype of the Japanese woman, but it may also engender anger toward Japanese males, because of students' incomplete access to history. White students may respond with guilt or indifference because of the policy of a government whose composition is essentially White, Anglo-oriented, and with which they identify. Japanese American male students may become defensive, desirous of hearing Japanese American men's stories about picture bride marriages. African American male and female students may draw analogies between the Japanese American experience and the African American experience. Such analogies may be welcomed or resented by other students. Of course, students from varied backgrounds may respond to learning about Issei women with a reinforced or instilled pride in Japanese ancestry or with a newfound interest in immigration history.

Teacher presentation of Issei women's experience as picture brides should include, of course, lectures, readings, audiovisuals about the motivation, the experience, the male-female ratio of Japanese Americans at the turn of the century, and the tradition of arranged marriage in Japan. Presentations should also anticipate, however, student reaction based on their generally ill-informed or limited knowledge about the subject.[18] Discussion and analysis of the students' initial perspectives on Issei women, of how those perspectives have changed given the historical, cultural, and sociological information, allow for learning about and reading Issei women's accounts to become an occasion, then, for expressing feelings of guilt, shame, anger, pride, interest, and curiosity, and for getting at the reasons for those feelings.

Understanding those feelings and working with them to move the student from damage, misinformation, and even bigotry to a balanced understanding sometimes become major portions of the content, especially when anger or guilt is directed toward a specific group—other students, the teacher, or perhaps even the self. Then it becomes necessary for the teacher to use what I call pressure-release sessions. The need for such sessions may manifest itself in many ways. For example,

> the fear of being regarded by peers or by the professor as racist, sexist or "politically incorrect" can polarize a classroom. If the [teacher] participates unconsciously in this fear and emotional self-protection, the classroom experience will degenerate to hopeless polarization, and even overt hostility. He or she must constantly stand outside the classroom experience and anticipate such dynamics. . . . "Pressure-release" discussions work best when the teacher directly acknowledges and calls attention to the tension in the classroom. The teacher may initiate the discussion or allow it to come about in whatever way he or she feels most comfortable.[19]

The hostility, fear, and hesitancy "can be converted to fertile ground for profound academic experiences . . . 'profound' because the students' knowledge is challenged, expanded, or reinforced"[20] by a subject matter that is simultaneously affective and cognitive, resonant with the humanness of life in both form and content. Students learn from these pressure-release sessions, as they must learn in life, to achieve balance and harmony in whatever pursuits, that paradoxes and contradictions are sometimes resolved and sometimes stand separately yet function together (recall heresy #1).

Teaching about women of color can often spark resistance to the teacher or cause students to question subject veracity. Students usually are taught that the latter part of the nineteenth century and the turn of the century was a time of expansion for the United States. Learning of the experiences of Native American and Mexican women who were subjected to particular horrors as the United States pushed westward, or reading about restrictions on Chinese immigrant women who were not allowed to enter the United States with the Chinese men who provided slave labor for the building of the railroads, students begin to realize that this time was anything but progressive or expansive.

Teaching about Ida Wells-Barnett, the African American woman who waged the antilynching campaigns at the end of the nineteenth century and well into the twentieth century, also belies the progress of that time. Ida Wells-Barnett brings to the fore the horror of lynchings of African American men, women, and children, the inhuman practice of castration, the stereotyped ideas of African American men and women, ideas that were, as Giddings reminds us, "older than the Republic itself—for they were rooted in the European minds that shaped America."[21] Furthermore, Wells-Barnett's life work reveals the racism of White women in the suffragist movement of the early twentieth century, a reflection of the racism in that movement's nineteenth-century manifestation.

The ever-present interaction of racism and sexism, the stereotyping of African American men and women as bestial, the unfounded labeling of African American men as rapists in search of White women, and the horrid participation in all of this by White men and women in all stations of life, make for difficult history for any teacher to teach and for any student to study. The threat to the founding fathers and Miss Liberty versions are apparent. Such content is often resisted by African American and White students alike, perhaps for different reasons, including rage, anger, or shame that such atrocities were endured by people like them; indifference in the face of reality because "nothing like that will happen again"; and anger, guilt, or shame that people of their race were responsible for such hideous atrocities. Furthermore, all students may resent the upsetting of their neatly packaged understandings of U.S. history and of their world.

The teacher must know the content and be willing to facilitate the pressure-release sessions that undoubtedly will be needed. Pressure-release sessions must help students sort out facts from feelings and, most of all, must clarify the relevance of the material to understanding the world in which we live and to preventing such atrocities from recurring. Also, in teaching about the Issei women and about the life of Ida Wells-Barnett, teachers must never let the class lose sight of the vision these women had, how they dealt with joy and sorrow, the triumphs and struggles of their lives, the contributions to both their own people and to U.S. life at large.

In addition to variations on anger, guilt, and challenges to credibility in learning about women of color, students become more aware of the positive aspects of race and ethnicity and frequently begin to take pride in their identities. As heresy #8 states, "Knowledge is identity and identity is knowledge. All knowledge is explicitly and implicitly related to who we are, both as individuals and as groups." The teacher, however, must watch for overzealous pride as well as unadmitted uneasiness with one's ethnic or racial identity. White students, in particular, may react in a generally unexpected manner. Some may predictably claim their Irish ancestry; others may be confused as to their ethnicity, for they may come from German and Scottish ancestry, which early on assumed Anglo-American identity. Students of Anglo-American ancestry, however, may hesitate to embrace that terminology, for it might suggest to them, in the context of the experiences of women and men of color, an abuse of power and "all things horrible in this country," as one upset student once complained to me. Here teachers must be adept not only at conveying facts, but also at explaining the effects of culture, race, gender, and ethnicity in recording and interpreting historical facts. They also must be able to convey to students both the beautiful and the ugly in all of us. Thus, the African American teacher may find himself or herself explaining the cultural value of Anglo-American or Yankee humor, of Yankee precision in gardening, of Yankee thriftiness, and how we all share, in some way, that heritage. At whatever age this occurs, students must be helped to understand the dichotomous, hierarchical past of that identity and to move toward expressing their awareness in a pluralistic context.

Now that we have explored the why of the phrase *women of color,* identified the essence of what we learn when we study women of color, discussed the theory of transformation, and identified and discussed the most frequent reactions of students to the subject matter, we now focus on the teacher.

CONCLUSION

Teaching about women of color should result in conveying information about a group of people largely invisible in our curricula in a way that encourages students to seek further knowledge and ultimately begin to correct and reorder the flawed perception of the world based on racism, sexism, classism, and ethnocentrism. To do so is no mean feat. Redefining one's world involves not only the inclusion of previously ignored content, but also the revision, deletion, and correction of accepted content in light of missing and ignored content. As such, it might require a redesignation of historical periods, a renaming of literary periods, and a complete reworking of sociological methodology to reflect the ethnic and cultural standards at work. This chapter, then, is essentially an introduction to the journey that teachers must embark on to begin providing for students a curriculum that reflects the reality of the past, prepares students to deal with and understand the present, and creates the basis for a more humane, productive, caring future.

The implications of teaching about women of color are far-reaching, involving many people in many different capacities. New texts need to be written for college-level students. Teacher education must be restructured to include not only the transformed content but also the pedagogy that reflects how our nation and the world are multicultural, multiethnic, multiracial, multifocal, and multidimensional. College texts, children's books, and other materials need to be devised to help teach this curriculum. School administrators, school boards, parents, and teachers need to participate and contribute to this transformation in all ways that influence what our children learn.

For teachers and those studying to be teachers, the immediate implications of a transformed curriculum can seem overwhelming, for transformation is a process that will take longer than our lifetimes. Presently, we are in the formative stages of understanding what must be done to correct the damage in order to lead to wholeness. I suggest that we begin small. That is, decide to include women of color in your classes this year. Begin adding some aspect of that topic to every unit. Pay close attention to how that addition relates to what you already teach. Does it expand the topic? Does it present material you already cover within that expansion? Can you delete some accepted, repetitive material and still meet your objectives? Does the new material conflict with the old? How? Is that conflict a valuable learning resource for your students? Continue to do this each year. Gradually, other central topics will emerge about men of color, White men, White women, class, race, ethnicity, and gender. By beginning with studying women of color, the curriculum then will have evolved to be truly pluralistic.

This chapter pays the most attention to the student. The teacher, who embarks on this long journey, must be determined to succeed. Why? Because all the conflicting emotions, the sometimes painful movement from the familiar to the unfamiliar, are experienced by the teacher as well. We have been shaped by the same damaging, ill-informed view of the world as our students. Often, as we try to resolve their conflicts, we are simultaneously working through our own. Above all, we must demand honesty of ourselves before we can succeed.

The difficulty of the process of transformation is one contributing factor to the maintenance of the status quo. Often we look for the easiest way out. It is easier to work with students who are not puzzled, concerned, or bothered by what they are studying. We, as teachers, must be willing to admit that we do not know everything, but that we do know how to go about learning in a way that reaches the closest approximation of the truth. Our reach must always exceed our grasp, and in doing so, we will encourage the excellence, the passion, the curiosity, the respect, and the love needed to create superb scholarship and encourage thinking, open-minded, caring, knowledgeable students.

QUESTIONS AND ACTIVITIES

1. When Butler uses the phrase *women of color,* to what specific ethnic groups is she referring? Why did this phrase emerge, and what purpose does it serve?

2. How can a study of women of color help broaden our understanding of White women? Of women in general?

3. In what ways, according to Butler, is ethnicity an important variable in women's lives? Give specific examples from this chapter to support your response.

4. How does racism, combined with sexism, influence the ways in which people view and respond to women of color?

5. What does the author mean by *transformation* and a *transformed curriculum*? How does a transformed curriculum differ from a mainstream or balanced curriculum?

6. How can content about women of color serve as a vehicle for transforming the school curriculum?

7. The author lists eight heresies, or assumptions, about reality that differ fundamentally from dominant modes of thought and values. Why does she believe these heresies are essential when teaching about women of color?

8. The author states that teaching about women of color may spark resistance to the teacher, the subject, or both. What examples of content does she describe that may evoke student resistance? Why, according to Butler, might students resist this content? What tips does she give teachers for handling student resistance?

9. Develop a teaching unit in which you incorporate content about women of color, using the transformation approach described in this chapter. Useful references on women of color are found in the appendix ("Gender" section).

NOTES

1. Susan Hill Gross, "Women's History for Global Learning," *Social Education* 51, No. 3 (March 1987): 194–198.

2. Toni Cade, *The Black Woman: An Anthology* (New York: New American Library, 1970), p. 9.

3. The Moynihan Report of 1965, the most notable of this scholarship, received the widest publicity and acceptance by U.S. society at large. Blaming African American social problems on the Black family, Moynihan argues that Black families,

dominated by women, are generally pathological and pathogenic. In attempting to explain the poor social and economic condition of the Black lower class, Moynihan largely ignores the history of racism and ethnocentrism and classism in American life and instead blames their victims. His study directly opposes the scholarship of Billingsley and others, which demonstrates the organizational differences between Black and White family units as well as the existence of a vital African American culture on which to base solutions to the social problems Moynihan identifies. See Daniel Moynihan, *The Negro Family* (Washington, D.C.: U.S. Dept. of Labor, 1965); Joyce Ladner, ed. *The Death of White Sociology* (New York: Vintage, 1973); Andrew Billingsley, *Black Families in White America* (Englewood Cliffs, N.J.: Prentice-Hall, 1968); and Harriet McAdoo, ed., *Black Families* (Beverly Hills, Calif: Sage Publications, 1981).

4. *Conditions, Five: The Black Woman's Issue* 2, No. 3 (Autumn 1979); Cherríe Moraga and Gloria Anzaldúa, eds. *This Bridge Called My Back: Writings by Radical Women of Color* (Watertown, Mass., Persephone Press, 1981).

5. Dexter Fisher, ed., *The Third Woman* (Boston: Houghton Mifflin, 1980).

6. Peggy McIntosh, associate director of the Wellesley Center for Research on Women, directed a training workshop in June 1987 for faculty at participating independent schools to prepare them for running faculty-development workshops in women's studies on their respective campuses. Dr. McIntosh's definition of transformation is similar to mine. I am grateful to work with her periodically, sharing and developing ideas.

7. See "On Being White: Toward a Feminist Understanding of Race and Race Supremacy" in Marilyn Frye's *The Politics of Reality: Essays in Feminist Theory* (Trumansburg, N.Y.: The Crossing Press, 1983), pp. 110–127. Also see "Understanding Correspondence between White Privilege and Male Privilege through Women's Studies Work." Unpublished paper presented by Peggy McIntosh at the 1987 National Women's Studies Association Annual Meeting, Atlanta, Ga. Available through Wellesley Center for Research on Women, Washington St., Wellesley, Mass., 02181. These works illuminate race and class power relationships and the difference between race and skin privileges. They emphasize not the rejection of privilege but the awareness of its function in order to work actively against injustice.

8. Elizabeth V. Spelman, "Theories of Gender and Race: The Erasure of Black Women," *Quest: A Feminist Quarterly* 5, No. 4 (1982): 36–62. Also see Renate D. Klein, "The Dynamics of the Women's Studies Classroom: A Review Essay of the Teaching Practice of Women's Studies in Higher Education," *Women's Studies International Forum* 10, No. 2 (1987): 187–206.

9. Paula Giddings, *When and Where I Enter: The Impact of Black Women on Race and Sex in America* (New York: William Morrow, 1984).

10. See Lillian Smith, *Killers of the Dream* (New York: Norton, 1949, 1961). Smith provides a useful and clear description of the interaction between racism and sexism and its legacy.

11. Spelman, *Theories of Gender and Race*, 57–59.

12. See John Mbiti, *Introduction to African Religion* (London: Heinemann, 1975); Basil Davidson, *The African Genius* (Boston: Little, Brown, 1969).

13. I began to conceptualize this framework while doing consulting work with college faculty to include Black studies and women's studies content in their syllabi. They were first presented as heresies at the First Working Conference on Critical Pedagogy at the University of Massachusetts, Amherst, February 1985. The concept of heresy here implies a reworking of the way that Westerners order the world, essentially by replacing individualism with a sense of communality and interdependence.

14. See Paulo Friere, *Pedagogy of the Oppressed* (New York: Seabury, 1969); *Education for Critical Consciousness* (New York: Seabury, 1973).

15. Margo Culley, "Anger and Authority in the Introductory Women's Studies Classroom" in Margo Culley and Catherine Portuges, eds., *Gendered Subjects: The Dynamics of Feminist Teaching* (Boston: Routledge and Kegan Paul, 1985), p. 209.

16. Ibid., 212. Also see in same volume, Butler, "Toward a Pedagogy of Everywoman's Studies," 230–239.

17. *Sei* in Japanese means "generation." The concepts of first-, second-, and third-generation Japanese Americans are denoted by adding a numerical prefix. Therefore, Issei is first generation, Nisei, second, and Sansei, third. Most Issei immigrated to the United States during the first quarter of the twentieth century to provide cheap, male manual labor, intending to return to Japan after a few years. However, their low wages did not

provide enough money for them to return. In 1900, out of a total of 24,326 in the United States, 983 were women. Through the immigration of picture brides by 1920, women numbered 38,303 out of a population of 111,010. Because of racist, anti-Japanese agitation, the U.S. government helped bring these brides to the United States. For a complete discussion, see the Introduction and "Issei Women" in Nobuya Tsuchida, ed., *Asian and Pacific American Experiences: Women's Perspectives* (Minneapolis: University of Minnesota, 1982).

18. An important rule in the scholarship of critical pedagogy is that the teacher should build on the ideas and feelings that students bring to a subject, helping them understand how they might be useful, in what ways they are flawed, correct, or incorrect. Sometimes this simply means giving the student credit for having thought about an idea, or helping the student become aware that he or she might have encountered the idea or aspects of material studied elsewhere. Generally this process is referred to as moving the student from the familiar to the unfamiliar.

19. Butler, "Toward a Pedagogy," 236.

20. Ibid.

21. Giddings, *When and Where I Enter,* 31.

Ethnic, cultural, and language diversity present challenges as well as opportunities to today's educators.

PART FOUR

Ethnicity and Language

The drastic increase in the percentage of students of color and language minority students in the nation's schools is one of the most significant developments in education in the last several decades. The growth in the percentage of students of color and language minority students in the nation's schools results from several factors, including the new wave of immigration that began after 1968 and the aging of the White population. The nation's classrooms are experiencing the largest influx of immigrant students since the turn of the century. The United States received nearly one million immigrants in 1980, more than in any year up to that time since 1914. Today, more than 600,000 people make the United States their home each year, most of whom come from nations in Asia and Latin America.

Demographers predict that if current trends continue, about 46 percent of the nation's school-age youths will be of color by the year 2020. Students of color now make up the majority of the student population in twenty-five of the nation's largest school districts. They make up a majority of the public school students in California, the nation's most populous state. Another important characteristic of today's students is the large percentage who are poor and who live in female-headed households. Today, about one out of every five students lives in a poor family. Fifteen million children in the United States live in households headed by females.

While the percentage of students of color in the nation's schools is increasing rapidly, the percentage of teachers of color is decreasing sharply. In 1980, teachers of color made up 12.5 percent of the nation's teachers. If current declining trends continue, they will make up about 5 percent of the nation's teachers by the turn of the century. In the year 2000, most students in the nation's cities and a significant percentage of those in suburban school districts will be students of color, and more of the teachers than today will be White and mainstream. This development underscores the need for all teachers to develop the knowledge, attitudes, and skills needed to work effectively with students from diverse racial, ethnic, social-class, and language groups.

CHAPTER 9

Ethnic Minorities and Educational Equality

■ GENEVA GAY

The most popularly understood meaning of educational equality in the United States is the access of African Americans, Hispanics, Asians, and Indians to the same schools and instructional programs as middle-class Anglo students. The prevailing assumption is that when ethnic minorities become students in majority schools, equal educational opportunity is achieved. Little attention is given to the quality of the content and processes of schooling itself. The possibility that what happens within schools might not be equal or comparable in quality for all students tends to be overlooked.

For those who accept this conception of educational equality, the issue of inequality is largely resolved. After all, they argue, federal and state laws now exist prohibiting educational discrimination on the basis of race, color, creed, gender, nationality, and social class. For these people, the persisting discrepancies between the academic achievement, quality of school life, and other indicators of school success for ethnic minority and majority students are not a result of differences in educational opportunities at all. Rather, these problems are matters of personal and individual abilities. Poor students and ethnic minorities do not do as well in school as their middle-class, Anglo counterparts because of individual deficiencies, not because of some disparities in the experiences and opportunities available to them in schools. African American, Hispanic, and Indian youths drop out and experience school failure at a higher rate because of their own personality traits and family backgrounds, not because aspects within the schooling process function systematically to their detriment.

In addition to being overly simplistic, these notions of what educational equality means for ethnic minorities are culturally chauvinistic. They assume that the education White students are receiving is universally desirable, and that the only way for minority youths to get a comparable education is to imitate Whites. Given the great diversity in quality of the teachers, facilities, resources, and instruction that exists in U.S. schools, including predominantly White ones, these conceptions are inadequate. Any viable definitions of and approaches to educational equality must take into consideration the quality of the opportunities, not merely the presence or absence of opportunity. Legal mandates guaranteeing the accessibility of schooling to all students do not ensure quality unless the opportunities themselves are of equal quality.[1] And under no circumstances can identical educational opportunities for very diverse groups and individuals (whether that diversity stems from class, gender, race, ethnicity, nationality, or personal traits) constitute equality.

Ideas that equate sameness of opportunity and open access to all schools for all students with educational equality ignore some of the more fundamental issues of equality of opportunity and access to the processes of schooling. How can *equality* be understood to mean equity and comparability of treatment based on diagnosed needs as opposed to the misconception of sameness of treatment for all students? What elements of the process of schooling should be considered in a more comprehensive and realistic approach to achieving educational equality for ethnic minority students? In other words, how can we assure that the quality of provision and substance of educational experiences available to ethnic minority youths receive priority over mere access measures of educational equality? Or, as Grant and Sleeter might ask, what happens "after the school bell rings"[2] for ethnic minorities in U.S. schools? These issues are explored in this chapter.

CURRENT EDUCATIONAL STATUS OF ETHNIC MINORITIES

Contrary to the misconceptions of some people, legal access of ethnic minorities to all schools was the mere beginning, not the end, of the resolution of educational inequality. The issue prevails at crisis levels today. In its 1983 report, *Equality and Excellence: the Educational Status of Black Americans*, the College Entrance Examination Board concluded that "although many of the legal barriers to educational opportunity have been removed, education—to a large extent—remains separate and unequal in the United States."[3] This inequality becomes clearer when we analyze the current educational status of ethnic minorities, especially African Americans, Mexican Americans, Puerto Ricans, and American Indians, and the pervasiveness of the problems these groups encounter in schools. The situation is not quite as serious for Asian Americans, at least on some standardized test measures of school achievements, school attendance, and graduation records.

Unquestionably, some progress has been made in the last twenty years in the social conditions of schooling for and academic achievement of ethnic minorities. During the 1970s through the 1980s we also saw:

■ The number of high school graduates for all ethnic minority groups increase dramatically.

■ The gap between standardized test scores in reading and mathematics for Hispanics, African Americans, and Whites narrow somewhat. This was a result of the greater relative gains minorities made in academic achievement compared to Whites.

■ The Bilingual Education Act, the Indian Education Act, and Title IX improve educational opportunities for millions of non-English speakers, Indians, and females, respectively.

■ The Education for All Handicapped Children Act (PL 94–142), which allows many children with disabilities to be educated in regular classes.[4]

■ The creation of a variety of pullout programs for special needs instruction to help students in basic skills and to aid in the development of the gifted and talented.

During the 1980s, many of these beginnings toward equalizing access to educational resources were minimized by an unsympathetic national administration and a general social climate of conservatism toward social service programs. For instance:

■ The cutting of more than 750,000 children from Chapter 1 programs (the programs of federal educational assistance for economically deprived children).

■ Relaxation of requirements for schools receiving federal funds to comply with antidiscrimination laws.

■ New funding arrangements that benefit rural and private schools at the expense of urban and inner-city schools.

■ Drastic cuts in bilingual, migrant, Indian, and women's equity educational funding and programs.[5]

Other serious problems that negatively affect minority students' educational opportunities and testify to the persistence of educational inequality prevail. Most elementary and secondary schools in the United States continue to be racially segregated. Racial minorities now constitute the majority student population in the nation's twenty-five largest school districts, and that ratio is increasing yearly. In many of these school systems, the minority enrollment exceeds 75 percent. In 1980, 6.8 percent of all Hispanic children attended schools in which 50 percent or more of the total student enrollment was minority, and one-fourth were enrolled in schools with a minority population of 90 to 100 percent. Together, African Americans, Hispanics, American Indians/Alaskan Natives, and Asian/Pacific Islanders comprised 27 percent of the total number of public school students in 1987. This percentage is expected to continue to increase in the 1990s.[6]

Yet, the ethnicity of teachers, administrators, and policymakers in these districts is the reverse. Whites far outnumber minorities in all school leadership and instructional positions. In fact, the numbers of ethnic minority teachers and school administrators have been steadily declining in the last fifteen years. The percentage of African American teachers declined from 12 percent in 1970 to 6.9 percent in 1987 and is projected to drop to a low of 5 percent in the 1990s. In 1980, Hispanics represented only 2.6 percent of all the elementary and 1.7 percent of the secondary teachers in the United States. In 1987 their combined representation was 1.9 percent. The number of American Indian/Alaskan Native and Asian/Pacific Islander teachers in the same year was 0.6 and 0.9 percent, respectively.[7] Traditionally, urban schools have had less money, fewer resources and poorer facilities, larger numbers of inexperienced teachers, greater management problems, and higher turnover rates among teachers, administrators, and students (see Chapter 4). Moreover, few systematic and sustained high-quality teacher and leadership training programs exist to prepare educators to work effectively with urban ethnic minorities.

Although the levels of educational attainment of ethnic minorities, as measured by median years of schooling completed, high school graduation, and daily attendance records, are increasing for successive generations, the dropout rates continue to be a major problem. The median years of schooling completed by African Americans increased from 8.0 years in 1970 to 12.0 in 1985. For Whites in the same period, the medians were 10.9 and 12.5, respectively. By 1985 the median years of schooling completed for Hispanics had reached 10.8. The dropout rate for African Americans declined between 1970 and 1988 from 30 to 11.5 percent, compared to 15.2 and 11.3 percent for Whites. The overall high school completion rates of Whites in 1987 was 86 percent compared to 83 percent for African Americans and 60 percent for Hispanics. These percentages represent virtually no increase for Whites but an 18 percentage point gain for African Americans and 8 percent increase for Hispanics between 1974 and 1987.

Yet the overall average dropout rate for African Americans in 1988 (12.6 percent) was still higher than the national average (10.9 percent), and the average for Whites (11.3 percent).[8]

The situation is even worse for Hispanics. In 1978, Hispanics between the ages of fourteen and nineteen were more than twice as likely as Whites to drop out of school, and nearly 40 percent of those between the ages of eighteen and twenty-four were dropouts compared to 14 percent of a comparable White population. A 1986 California State University System Advisory Council on Educational Equity reported that Hispanics have the highest dropout rate of all ethnic groups in California. Some school districts indicated that as many as 40 percent of Hispanic students left school before grade 10. Nationwide, the overall dropout rate for Hispanics was 32.2 percent in 1986. However, approximately 50 percent of Mexican Americans and Puerto Ricans drop out of high school before graduation. In some urban school districts, such as Chicago and New York, the Puerto Rican high school dropout rates exceed 70 percent.[9]

Another school attendance factor that helps explain educational inequality for ethnic minority students is *school delay.* Defined by Nielsen as "the discrepancy between the educational level reached by students and the normal level corresponding to their age,"[10] school delay rates are substantially greater for Blacks, Hispanics, and Indians than for Whites. These groups repeat grades more often and generally take longer to complete school. Since 1980 the percentage of minority students below modal grade (the grade in which most children of a certain age are enrolled) has increased substantially. African American males have the highest below modal grade averages. In 1985 their representation in this category was 32.4 percent for eight-year-olds and 44.2 percent for thirteen-year-olds, compared to 24 and 29.1 percent for White eight- and thirteen-year old males, and 19.9 and 35 percent for eight- and 13-year-old African American females.[11] This situation is more serious than it might first appear. It may initiate a cumulative process that ultimately results in the child's leaving school completely. Delayed students are likely to be judged academically inadequate and assigned to special category, low academic, or vocational-track curricula. As these students fall behind their age group, they become stigmatized as slow learners and socially isolated in schools, and teachers tend to have low expectations of achievement for delayed students.

Dropout rates for American Indians, Native Alaskans, and Asian Americans are not reported as systematically as for African Americans and Hispanics. But, given the general educational status of American Indians on other measures of school success that indicate that their situation is even worse than that for African Americans and Hispanics, we can assume that the dropout rates for American Indians are as high or higher. The 1980 Bureau of Census data indicate that Asian American students' school enrollment and attendance are at parity with that of Anglo-Americans. At all age levels the percentages of Asian Americans enrolled in schools and colleges exceed those of Anglo-Americans (see Table 9.1).[12] Although the magnitude of the high school dropout problem is far less for Asian Americans than for other racial minority groups, the gender pattern is similar. More Asian males leave school prior to graduation than do females.[13]

Even for minority students who remain in school and attend racially mixed schools, the likelihood of the greater number of them receiving educational equality is dubious. The academic achievement levels of all ethnic minority groups, except Asian Americans, is significantly lower than for Whites. These differences exist on all measures for every age group at all levels of schooling, in every region of the country, and at every socioeconomic level.[14] Despite reports by the National Assessment of Educational Progress (NAEP), the College Board, and the National Center for Educational Statistics indicating that the reading and mathematics test performance of African Americans and Hispanics improved during the 1970s, their average achievement levels continue to be lower than those of Whites.

On closer inspection, these improvements are not as positive as we might hope, for several reasons. First, the overall performance of all students on standardized tests declined in the 1980s and early 1990s compared to the 1970s. For example, the national averages on SAT scores dropped from 903 in 1975 to 900 in 1990. Average ACT scores during the same period dropped from 18.9 to 18.6. As Table 9.2 shows, the scores of minority students on the SAT were consistently lower than those of Whites and the national average, with the exception of Asian Americans, whose scores were comparable or higher. Although African Americans made a gain of 51 points, their overall performance continues to be lower than that of any other groups. A 1987 study, based on a nationwide survey of 7,812 high school juniors, funded by the National Endowment for the Humanities and conducted by the National Assessment of Educational Progress, gave failing marks to the nation's seventeen-year-olds in literature and history. More than two-thirds of the students were unable to locate the Civil War within the correct half century, or to identify the Reformation and the *Magna Carta*. The vast majority were unfamiliar with such classic writers as Dante, Chaucer, Dostoevsky, Whitman, and Hawthorne. Even students who performed adequately did not display exemplary performance levels. In the 1986 assessments of eleventh graders' performance in history and literature, African Americans and Hispanics scored similarly, but significantly lower than the

TABLE 9.1
Percentage of Persons Enrolled in School by Age for Selected Ethnic Groups in the United States (1980)

	Whites	**Chinese**	**Japanese**	**Koreans**	**Vietnamese**
Five- and Six-Year-Olds	86.1	91.4	94.6	88.4	–
Sixteen- and Seventeen-Year-Olds	89.0	96.0	96.2	94.9	90.2

Source: 1980 Census of Population. Volume 1, *Characteristics of the Population,* Chapter C, *Social and Economic Characteristics,* Part I, *United States Summary,* Report Number PC–80–1–C1 (Washington, D.C.: Bureau of the Census, U.S. Department of Commerce, December 1983).

TABLE 9.2
Scholastic Aptitude Test (SAT) Scores by Selected Ethnicity for 1975 and 1988

Group	SAT Composite (Verbal and Math) Scores		
	1975	*1988*	*Point Difference*
African Americans	686	737	+51
American Indians	802	828	+26
Asian Americans	932	932	0
Mexican Americans	781	810	+29
Puerto Ricans	765	755	−10
Whites	944	935	−9
All students	903	904	+1

Source: Digest of Education Statistics, 25th edition (Washington, D.C.: National Center for Education Statistics, U.S. Department of Education, Office of Educational Research and Improvement, 1989).

national average. Whites scored slightly higher. For African Americans the difference was 21.9 points lower on history and 14.5 on literature, compared to Hispanic differences of 22.5 for history and 20.2 for literature. The 1988 assessments of geographic proficiency indicated that African Americans achieved an average score of 258.4, which was 13.4 points lower than Hispanics, and 42.7 points less than Whites.[15]

Second, the performance patterns across all the subscales of standardized tests are not the same across and within ethnic groups. A case in point is Asian Americans. Often considered the model minority, Asian Americans are commonly considered high achievers who perform well in all aspects of schooling and on all measures of achievement. This positive stereotype overlooks the immense diversity of the Asian American subgroups, the serious language and adjustment problems that recent Southeast Asian refugees and new immigrants encounter, the disparity between educational attainment and income, and the special educational needs of individual Asian students.

When school performance, income, and employment data are analyzed carefully, a bimodal pattern of achievement for Asian Americans emerges. It suggests that Asian American students are more likely than other students to enroll in college preparatory programs, to maintain heavier high school course loads, to take more foreign languages and more high-level mathematics and science, to spend more time on homework, and to have higher educational aspirations. Although Japanese, Chinese, Filipino, and Korean Americans equal or surpass White Americans in median number of school years completed, they also have a higher percentage of adult population with less than five years of education. They hold more professional and technical jobs than do Anglos, and more low-paying jobs. A larger proportion of Asian Americans have four or more years of college, yet they earn less money and experience higher rates of education-occupation mismatches than do Whites. Some Asian American students (principally Japanese and Chinese) are high achievers on some aspects of standardized school achievement tests (science and math), and others (recent immigrants and refugees) are low achievers. Although in 1988 the nationwide average SAT math scores of Asian American students exceeded those of White students by more than 32 points, their verbal scores were more than 37 points lower. As family income levels increase, these differences decrease, but the White advantage never disappears. Furthermore, high academic achieving Asian American students are not necessarily socially and emotionally well adjusted. For instance, they do not feel as positive about their physical features and stature as do their White peers. Other psychological problems they may experience include stress associated with pressure for high performance, learning to cope with failure, the perceptions and expectations teachers have for students they consider model minorities, and ethnic identity[16] conflict.

Third, the improvement pattern on standardized tests is not consistent for all age groups of African American, Hispanic, Asian, and American Indian students. NAEP reports achievement data for nine-, thirteen-, and seventeen-year-olds. The most recent NAEP test scores show that nine-year-old African Americans increased their average reading proficiency scores by 7.2 points between 1975 and 1988, compared to a 1.1 point gain for Whites. African American thirteen-year-olds improved 17.2 points compared to a 0.8 point decline for Whites. The reading proficiency scores of seventeen-year-old African Americans increased by 34 points, while those of their White counterparts improved by only 1.7 points. The overall performance of all students in writing declined slightly between 1984 and 1988, but that of African Americans and Hispanics increased somewhat at all grades (4, 8, 11) tested. Yet, Whites continue to score significantly higher than these two minority groups at all grade levels.

Mathematics test scores between 1977 and 1986 showed an increase of 10 percentage points for nine-year-old African Americans and 2 percentage points for Hispanics compared to a 3.0 percent increase for Whites. Test scores for African American and Hispanic thirteen-year-olds increased by 19 and 16 points respectively, but only 3.7 points for Whites. The math performance of seventeen-year-olds was less encouraging. African Americans increased by 7 percentage points from 1977 to 1986, and Hispanics by 11 percentage points. The math achievement of White seventeen-year-olds during the same period increased by only 2 percentage points. African Americans in all three age groups performed better in areas of mathematical knowledge (recalling and recognizing facts) than in areas of mathematical skills (performing computations and manipulations) and applications (reasoning and problem solving). According to the 1988 reports on science achievement, Native Americans (46.9 percent), African Americans (47.7 percent), and Hispanics (37.8 percent) were more highly represented in the lowest quartile, and more underrepresented in the upper quartile (8.3, 10.3, and 6.3 percent, respectively). By comparison, Asian American students (30.3 percent) slightly outnumbered Whites (29.6 percent) in the upper quartile, as well as in the lower one (22.0 percent for Asians and 19.2 percent for Whites).[17]

In its 1986 *Writing Report Card* NAEP reported that writing achievement correlates highly with reading achievement. Better readers also are better writers. In all grades (4, 8, and 11), African American and Hispanics and students from disadvantaged urban communities performed at a substantially lower level than did Whites, Asians and advantaged urban students on all writing skills assessed (informative, persuasive, and imaginative). On all measures, Whites and Asians performed identically at grades 4 and 8, but Whites were slightly higher than Asians at grade 11. Writing achievement for Hispanics was slightly higher than for African Americans at grades 4 and 8, but the performance of the two groups was identical at grade 11. African American and Hispanic eleventh-grade writing achievement was lower than that of White and Asian eighth-graders. All students in all ethnic groups and grade levels were deficient in higher-order thinking skills, as evidenced by difficulty in performing adequately on analytical and persuasive writing tasks. Although some slight improvements at all three grade levels were evident for African Americans and Hispanics in 1988, the differences were not statistically significant, and the overall patterns of performance across all groups prevailed.[18] No data were reported for American Indians/Alaskan Natives.

These test scores present mixed messages. It is encouraging to see younger minority students making recognizable gains in reading and mathematics achievement, but it is disheartening that this pattern is not true for older students. How can we explain these mixed results? One possible explanation is that teachers and instructional programs are beginning to be more responsive to the educational needs and learning styles of ethnic minorities, and this responsiveness is having effects on students outcomes. Given what we know about patterns of school failure for minority students, a more plausible explanation is that the cumulative negative effects of schooling for these students are not yet fully in force for nine-year-olds. It is in about fourth grade (age nine or ten) that school failure for minority students crystallizes. From that point on, the longer African American, Hispanic, and American Indian youths stay in school, the further they fall behind academically. The decreasing levels of recent improvement on NAEP standardized tests for thirteen- and seventeen-year-olds may be a substantiation of this failure pattern.

Another explanation is that standardized achievement test scores, despite their frequent use, are not valid measures of educational equality. Measures of educational equality need to concentrate more on multidimensional inputs into the schooling process, such as curriculum content and substance, and the quality of classroom instructional interactions. Although recent improvements by ethnic minorities on standardized tests show that they are making some gains on low-level cognitive skills, such as decoding, computation, factual recognition, and recall, they are not developing high-level skills, such as making inferences, critical thinking, analyzing and synthesizing information, logical reasoning, and creative expression. These findings may be a direct result of the curriculum differentiations that exist for ethnic minority and Anglo students in elementary and secondary schools.

An unequal curriculum and instruction system exists in U.S. schools—the substance of education, access to knowledge, classroom climates, and the quality of instructional interactions are qualitatively different for ethnic minority and Anglo students. In its *Mexican-American Education Study*, conducted between 1971 and 1974, the U.S. Civil Rights Commission attributed quality and equality of educational experiences to the opportunities different students receive to participate in classroom interactions with teachers. It found that Mexican Americans were not receiving as many opportunities as Whites to participate in classroom interactions, as evidenced by fewer and lower-level questions asked of them, the time allowed to give responses, and the praise and encouragement teachers gave for students' efforts.

In 1974, Gay's similar findings for African American students' interactions with both African American and White teachers led her to conclude that minority and White teachers act more alike than differently in their classroom treatment of students. All teachers tend to give preferential treatment and more quality opportunities to participate in the substance of instruction to Anglo students. These patterns of interactional and instructional inequalities between ethnic minority and Anglo students have not changed significantly in the years since these studies were conducted.[19]

Minority students are disproportionally enrolled in special-education programs, vocational courses, and low-track classes and are underrepresented in high-track and college preparatory programs (see Chapter 15). Furthermore, the placement of ethnic minorities in vocational courses occurs earlier, and the programs differ substantially in kind and content from those for Whites. Minority students are assigned to vocational programs that train specifically for low-status occupations (e.g., cosmetology, mill and cabinet shop, building maintenance, television repair, retail sales, clerical jobs). By comparison, White students enroll more often in vocational courses that offer managerial training, business finance, and general industrial arts skills. To receive their training, minority youths must leave the school campus more often than Whites, thus isolating them from many of the social activities of the school.[20]

The enrollment of ethnic minority students in academic programs also indicates unequal distributions. Minorities are highly underrepresented in college preparatory and in gifted and talented programs. In its 1985 report on the educational status of African Americans, the College Entrance Examination Board found that most African American seniors in 1981 had taken fewer years of coursework in mathematics, physical sciences, and social studies than had Whites. Even in subjects in which the years of coursework are similar, the content of the courses differs substantially for African Americans and Whites. Although college-bound African American seniors in 1980 were as likely as Whites to have taken three or more years of mathematics, they were less likely to have taken algebra, geometry, trigonometry, and calculus and were more likely to have taken general and business math. Furthermore, students in low-income and predominantly minority schools have less access to microcomputers, have fewer qualified teachers trained in the use of computers, and tend to use microcomputers more for drill and practice in basic skills than for conceptual knowledge or programming instruction.[21]

The routinely used system of tracking to organize students for instruction is probably the most effective means of denying educational equality to ethnic minority students (see Chapter 4). In general, tracking differentiates access to knowledge, content and quality of instruction, expectations of teachers, and classroom climates for learning between upper and lower tracks. The studies of school tracking conducted by Oakes, Goodlad, Rosenbaum, Morgan, and others present convincing and devastating proof of the extent to which this practice perpetuates educational inequities along race, ethnic, and socioeconomic lines. For example:

■ In low-track classes a greater share of instructional time than in high tracks is devoted to developing compliance-type social behaviors and attitudes, classroom management and discipline, and generally dull, unimaginative teaching strategies. High-track and college preparatory students have better teachers, materials and laboratory equipment, field trips and classroom visitors, information about educational and occupational consequences, validations of personal worth, and self-direction.

■ The quality of knowledge students receive is differentiated by tracks. For example, high-track students get math concepts, low tracks get computational exercises.

■ The fostering of lower self-esteem and lower educational aspirations for low-track students.

■ Differences in the intellectual processes and cognitive levels of learning tasks. High-track students do activities that demand critical thinking, problem solving, making generalizations, drawing inferences, and synthesizing knowledge. Instruction in low-track classes focuses on memory and comprehension tasks.

■ Denial of opportunity for low-track students to learn content and materials that are essential for mobility among tracks.

■ High-track students are exposed to high-value social and academic knowledge—knowledge that permits access to advanced education, upper-level social and economic positions, and leadership roles. Low-track students are exposed to knowledge that is of low status and does not permit special access, and to social skills such as following directions, good work habits, punctuality, compliance to authority, and rules of social decorum.

■ In high-track classes, greater portions of the time allocated for instruction are actually used to engage students in learning tasks.

■ Differences in classroom relationships among students and types of involvement exist between low- and high-track classes. For example, stronger feelings of friendliness, cooperation, involvement, trust and goodwill, and positiveness exist in high tracks than in low tracks.

■ Students enrolled in general track and heterogeneously grouped classes are treated more like those in high and academic tracks than are those in homogeneously grouped low-track and vocational courses.[22]

African Americans, Hispanics, and American Indians are overrepresented in lower-track curriculum programs. Because low-track students do not experience comparable curriculum content, instructional practices, classroom climates, and classroom interactions and relationships as do general (average) and high-track students, these ethnic groups are consistently and systematically denied equal access to the substance of quality education. *In effect, tracking is a process for the legitimation of the social inequalities that exist in the larger society.* It serves the instrumental functions of social selection, creating castes among students and closing off paths for personal advancement for students in the lower levels.[23] Through this practice, students learn to accept the unequal patterns of social and political participation in society and all its institutions as the natural order of things.

Ethnic minority students' underenrollment in high-track and academic programs exists at every educational attainment level—high school completion, baccalaureate degrees, and graduate degrees. The higher the level of education, the greater is the degree of underrepresentation. Although minority college enrollments increased in the 1970s, they declined in the 1980s to the extent that the enrollment gap between Whites and African Americans and Hispanics was 15 percentage points in 1987.

Attrition rates continue to be substantially greater than for Anglos. Minorities also are underrepresented in all fields of college study, except the social sciences and education. The greatest minority underrepresentation is in the areas of engineering, biological sciences, and physical sciences. However, in 1987 there was an increase in math, business, and science-related degrees granted to African Americans, but a decline in education and the social sciences. The degrees Hispanics received in computer science, engineering, business, and natural sciences also increased slightly.[24]

In the final analysis, it is the kinds of access ethnic minority students have to the content and substance of education, and the interactions between students and teachers in individual schools and classrooms that define educational quality and equality, not with whom the students attend school. These processes are what ultimately determine which students are educated for self-determination and social empowerment and which ones are trained for a life of dependency in the economic and social underclass.[25] The current educational status of ethnic minorities in the United States suggests that too many of them are being trained for the underclass.

WHY EDUCATIONAL INEQUALITY EXISTS FOR ETHNIC MINORITIES

Wherever ethnic minorities attend school, whether in predominantly minority or racially mixed settings, in urban or suburban environments, in poor or middle-class communities, in the Northern, Eastern, Southern, or Western United States, issues of educational inequality prevail. These issues concern access to excellence and equity of educational opportunities and experiences, with the focus of access being the substance of the educational process. The pivotal question is how to make the total educational enterprise more responsive to the histories, heritages, life experiences, and cultural conditioning of ethnic minorities in all of its policy-making, program-planning, and instructional practices.

The quality of the various resources used in the educational process has a direct effect on the level and quality of student achievement. When different groups of students are exposed to qualitatively different resources, their achievements also differ. In the debate on educational equality, a crucial question is whether the resources used in teaching ethnic minority students are comparable to those used with Whites on measures of accuracy, technical quality, relevance, and appropriateness. These resources include facilities, personnel, financing, instructional materials and programs, and environmental settings.

The relative value of instructional resources cannot be determined independently of environmental context, intended users, and expected outcomes. School resources are preferentially allocated to high-track and academic programs and to middle-class, Anglo students. Even when ethnic minority students receive the same educational resources as Anglo students, the effects are not identical. Although these resources may benefit and facilitate Anglo development they can block or retard the development of ethnic minorities. How is this possible?

We have seen how the overrepresentation of ethnic minorities in low-track programs, vocational courses, and special-education classes minimizes their educational opportunities in several ways. One way is how school systems and personnel generally perceive and treat these program options relative to expected performance and resource allocations. They receive fewer laboratory facilities, fewer out-of-classroom learning experiences, lesser qualified teachers, and less commitment, concern, and effort from teachers.

But not all ethnic minorities are enrolled in these programs. Most are enrolled in regular classrooms and programs across a wide spectrum of curriculum options, including general education, academic, and college preparatory courses. If educational resources are allocated by programs and if these programs receive the best, how is it possible to claim that the ethnic minority students enrolled in them are being denied comparable access to quality resources? Several ways are possible. First, the sameness of educational resources for diverse individuals and groups does not constitute comparability of quality or opportunity. Teachers, materials, and teaching environments that work well for Anglo students do not necessarily work equally well for ethnic minorities. To believe that they do is to assume that African American, Hispanic, American Indian, Asian American, and Anglo students are identical in personal, social, cultural, historical, and family traits.

Second, most graduates of typical teacher-education programs know little about the cultural traits, behaviors, values, and attitudes different ethnic minority groups bring to the classroom, and how they affect the ways these students act and react to instructional situations. They do not know how to understand and use the school behaviors of these students, which differ from their normative expectations, as aides to teaching. Therefore, they tend to misinterpret them as deviant and treat them punitively. Because teachers' cultural backgrounds and value orientations are highly compatible with middle-class and Anglo-American culture, they can use these cultural connections to facilitate learning for Anglo students.

Third, like teacher training, most curriculum designs and instructional materials are Eurocentric. As such they reflect middle-class, Anglo experiences, perspectives, and value priorities. They are likely to be more readily meaningful and to have a greater appeal to the life experiences and aspirations of Anglo students than to those of ethnic minorities. Thus, when attempting to learn academic tasks, Anglo students may not have the additional burden of working across irrelevant instructional materials and methods. More of their efforts and energies can be directed toward mastering the substance of teaching. Ethnic minority students are often placed in double jeopardy. That is, they must divide their energies and efforts between coping with curriculum materials and instructional methods that are not culturally relevant to their learning styles or reflective of their life experiences and also to mastering the academic knowledge and tasks being taught. Because this division of efforts dissipates their concentration on learning tasks, they do not receive the quality educational opportunities to learn the substance of teaching that Anglo students do.

Fourth, the school environments in which students live and learn are not comparable for Anglo and ethnic students. When students and teachers arrive at school they do not leave their cultural backgrounds at home. This is not a problem for most Anglo students, since school culture and rules of behavior are reflections and extensions of their home cultures. A high degree of cultural congruency exists between middle-class Anglo student culture and school culture. These students do not experience much cultural discontinuity, social-code incompatibility, or need for cultural style shifting to adjust to the behavioral codes expected of them in school. The converse is true for ethnic minority students. Many of the social codes for succeeding in school are unfamiliar to them or are diametrically opposed to the codes they have learned in their home cultures. When learning situations do not reflect the cultures of the students, gaps exist "between the *contexts of learning and the contexts of performing.* "[26] These gaps are greatest for students from ethnic-group cultures and communities that are not part of the mainstream culture. Many of the inequities that exist between the educational opportunities of Anglo and ethnic minority students are situated in these contextual incompatibilities.

Most educators do not teach ethnic minority students how to survive and succeed in school, for example, how to study across ethnic learning styles, how to adjust talking styles to accommodate school expectations, how to interact appropriately with school administrators and classroom teachers, and how to identify and adjust to the procedural rules for functioning in different instructional classrooms. Educators operate on the assumption that school codes of behavior are common knowledge acquired from living in the broader culture that surrounds schools. What most educators forget is that many ethnic minorities live only marginally in mainstream culture and that they do not have a heritage and tradition of success in predominantly White schools.

The effect of these differences in socialization of Anglo and ethnic minority students in how to survive in school is another example of the differential use of personal energies and efforts. Minority students have to learn how to survive in school while simultaneously learning what is taught. When they fail to master the social codes, they never get a chance to try the academic tasks, because mastery of the social protocols of schooling is a prerequisite to learning itself.

The school failure of ethnic minorities because of their inability to master social codes of behavior is much more frequent than for Whites. In-class success for minorities also is measured by social skill mastery more often than for Anglos. Teachers evaluate minority students more on criteria such as "he is a nice boy," "she is cooperative," "I feel sorry for these students," and "their work is very neat." Anglo students' performance is assessed more on academic criteria ("he studies hard," "she is an overachiever," "they are very attentive in class," "she asks provocative questions"). Inequalities exist in these situations because the bases for determining school success and failure for Anglo and ethnic minority students are frequently not similar. For the former, reasons for failing tend to be academic incompetence; for the latter they are often social incompetence.

Closely related to the issue of comparable quality resources is the role of teacher attitudes, expectations, and competencies in perpetuating educational inequality for ethnic minorities. The essence of this issue is, How can teachers who have grown up in ethnically isolated communities and in a racist society teach ethnic minorities as well as they can Anglos? This question is crucial in equations of educational equality, especially when most teachers are racially

White, culturally Eurocentric, middle class, and trained in White, Eurocentric colleges and universities to teach White, Eurocentric students.

Most teachers know little about different ethnic groups' life-styles or learning habits and preferences. They tend to be insecure and uncertain about working with African American, Hispanic, Asian, and American Indian students and to have low expectations of achievement for these students. Too many teachers still believe that minority students either are culturally deprived and should be remediated by using middle-class Whites as the appropriate norm or do not have the capacity to learn as well as Anglos. "Teachers form expectations about children based directly upon race and social class, . . . pupil test scores, appearance, language style, speed of task performance, and behavior characteristics which are themselves culturally defined. Moreover, teacher expectations are more influenced by *negative* information about pupil characteristics than positive data."[27] Teachers transmit these attitudes and expectations in everything they say and do in the classroom. Ethnic minority students' responses to these expectations become self-fulfilling prophesis. They come to believe that they are destined to fail, and they act accordingly. Anglo students internalize the high expectations teachers have of them and accordingly believe they are destined to succeed.

Educators tend to discriminate their school behaviors according to their performance expectations of different students. For example, teachers who do not have high academic expectations for ethnic minority students ask them low-level memory, recall, and convergent questions, do not praise or encourage them as often as Anglos, use lower standards for judging the quality of their work, and do not call on them as frequently. Guidance counselors who do not believe minority students can master high-level math and science skills do not schedule them into these classes. School administrators who expect greater discipline problems from ethnic minorities tend to treat their rule infractions with harsher punishment. In general, low expectations of educators cause them to feed African Americans, Hispanics, and American Indians academic pablum. They then wonder why these students do not do well on standardized measures of school achievement.

Special-purpose instruction for minorities tends to be remediation; for Anglos, it tends to be enrichment. Minority students for whom educators have low expectations are suspected of dishonesty and cheating when they defy these expectations by performing well. When they live down to these expectations, their teachers make comments such as "What else can you expect?" Presumed high-achieving Anglo students who do not live up to expectations are described as underachievers, and low-performing Anglos who exceed expectation are called overachievers. These attitudes and expectations cause wide disparities in how educators interact with Anglo and minority students in the day-to-day operations of schools and thereby perpetuate educational inequalities among them.

The educational inequities in school resources, teacher attitudes, and classroom interactions are reinforced further by culturally biased tests and procedures used to diagnose students' needs and to evaluate their performance. Whether standardized achievement measures, minimum-competency tests, teacher-made tests, classroom observations, or even criterion-referenced tests, most assessment approaches currently used discriminate against ethnic minorities in content, standardization norms, and administration procedures. By their nature they contribute to the social stratification of students. Because they are designed and used to discriminate differences among and to rank students according to competence, even the most content bias-free tests—especially norm-referenced ones—are tools for sorting students into unequal categories.[28]

Schools prize verbal learning and written demonstrations of achievement. These styles of demonstrating achievement are consistent with mainstream American and Anglo students' cultures, but they are contrary to the performance styles of many ethnic minority groups. For African Americans, whose cultural socialization emphasizes aural, verbal, and participatory learning, and for American Indians who are accustomed to imitative learning in their home cultures, it is difficult to transform what they know from one performance style to another. When they have to demonstrate their achievement on written tests, the format may be more of a problem for them than are the content and substance of the learning tasks. While they are struggling to translate their knowledge and skill mastery into an unfamiliar expressive style, Anglo students are busy demonstrating their knowledge of the content. These differences in performance starting points mean that ethnic minority students are at a disadvantage from the beginning of formal schooling. Not understanding the problems they are having with performance formats and styles, teachers conclude that their failure is due totally to their failure to master the instructional content and substance. The effects of these misdiagnoses and misevaluations become cumulatively greater for ethnic minority students as they advance in school. Until they receive starting points comparable to those of Anglo students in terms of diagnosis, and until evaluation assessments tools and techniques are more compatible with their cultural and learning styles, inequities in educational opportunities will continue to exist for African Americans, Hispanics, and American Indians.

A similar argument holds for the content and substance of student evaluations. All achievement tests are designed to determine what students know. Presumably they reflect what is taught in schools. This is a reasonable expectation, and there would be no issue of ethnic inequality if schools taught equally relevant curricula equally well to all students. But they do not. Although progress has been made in the last two decades to make school curricula more inclusive of ethnic and cultural diversity, most of the knowledge content taught, and consequently achievement tests, continue to be Eurocentric. Even skill mastery is transmitted through Eurocentric contexts. For instance, achievement tests may embed skills in scenarios about situations that are not relevant to the cultural backgrounds and life experiences of ethnic minorities. These students then have to decipher the contexts in order to extrapolate the skill content. Minority students may know the skill but may be unfamiliar with the contextual scenario. This limitation interferes with the effective demonstration of their knowledge of the skill. Most Anglo students do not have this problem. Both the context and the performance format are familiar to them, and if they know the skill, they have no problem demonstrating their mastery. Thus, ethnic minority students are placed at an unfair disadvantage, and their overall performance on achievement measures reflects this disadvantage.

This is not to say that minority students should not take achievement tests, that their school performance should not be evaluated, or that high levels of achievement should not be expected of them. Rather, it is to suggest that to avoid perpetuating educational inequality through assessment procedures, a wide variety of measures should be used so that no single one that is highly advantageous to one ethnic group over another is used consistently. It is also to suggest that the substance of education, including curriculum, teaching, and testing, should be revised to incorporate more fully the contributions and experiences of the full range of ethnic groups in the United States.

ACHIEVING EDUCATIONAL EQUALITY

The College Entrance Examination Board concluded its report on *Equality and Excellence* with the observation that "excellence for Black students will not become a reality until they receive enriched curricular opportunities in elementary and secondary schools, sufficient financial assistance to pursue higher education opportunities, and instruction from well-qualified teachers."[29] John-Steiner and Leacock state that "when the background of the teacher differs greatly from that of the children she works with, a setting results which is alien and tension-producing for the teacher or the student or both."[30]

To this observation we can add that alien and tension-filled environments substantially reduce the potential for educational equality for students who live and function in them. This is too often the fate of ethnic minorities in U.S. schools. Casso argues that "it is the educational system which needs to be changed and restructured rather than the Mexican-American child . . . lest it keep compounding the crime of attempting to remold every brown child into a cog for the white middle class machine."[31] Fantini proposes that efforts to bring about equality focus on providing equal access to quality education. This can be achieved through institutional reform aimed at creating school structures that respond positively to human diversity and through developing a policy of quality that views learners as educational consumers with some fundamental rights.[32] Two of these rights are educational equality and excellence.

Implicit in these suggestions and the issues of inequality discussed earlier in this chapter is that educational equality for ethnic minority students cannot be achieved without massive schoolwide, institutional reform. The reform efforts should begin with a redefinition of *equality* as equal access to the best-quality substance of schooling for all students. Quality should be determined by the degree to which learning experiences engage minority students' interest and involvement and empower them with personal development. Defining equality as access shifts attention away from evaluating quality and equality primarily in terms of dollar inputs, teacher certifications, test scores, and locations of school attendance to the intrinsic dynamics of the learning process itself. In operational terms, this redefinition of educational equality means affirming that problems or shortcomings in learning are located not so much in shortcomings in ethnic minority students as in inequalities in the schools they attend. It also means refocusing schools toward being more responsive to human variability, spending less time manipulating ethnic students to make them comply to institutional structures, and instituting programs and processes that empower students through access to high-quality knowledge and experiences.[33] This will be a significant departure from most current notions of equality as access to uniform school resources.

Such a concept of educational equality requires reform in all aspects of the schooling enterprise, including teacher training, curriculum design, classroom instruction, grouping of students for instruction, the climates in which students learn, and how students' needs are diagnosed and their achievement assessed. All of these issues cannot be discussed in detail here. Because of the crucial role teachers play in determining the quality of learning opportunities students receive in classrooms, more attention is given to teacher training.

All forms of tracking should be eliminated entirely. Even under the best of circumstances, tracking denies equal educational opportunities to minority students and also to other students who populate the lower levels. It closes rather than opens paths to social and academic advancement and commits some students early to an educational underclass. Tracking should be replaced with flexible and frequently changed groupings of students for specific instructional tasks or skill development purposes only. For example, students grouped together to learn geographical directions should remain together only until that skill is mastered.

All forms of norm-referenced tests for evaluating student achievement also should be eliminated. Instead, students should be evaluated against their own records, with range of improvement between different points of reference being the focus of attention, as opposed to performance at isolated points in time. This means that schools should use multiple techniques and procedures, including academic, social, psychological and emotional measures, as well as verbal, visual, observational, participatory, and kinetic means to assess students' school performance. These approaches should always serve diagnostic and developmental functions. That is, they should be used to determine how and why students are proceeding with specific learning tasks. They should be administered frequently, and instructional programming should be changed according to the results obtained. Thus, ethnic minority students should be put on self-referenced and self-paced programs to complete their schooling. Narrative reports, developmental profiles, student-teacher-parent conferences, and anecdotal records should replace letter and symbol grades for reporting student progress.

School curricula, too, must be reformed if equal educational opportunities are to be assured for all students. However, the emphases of the various commission studies and proposals for greater curriculum quantity as the measure of quality is not the answer. More of the same irrelevant school subjects will not improve the quality of schooling for any students, especially ethnic minorities. This more-of-the-same approach to quality increases the likelihood of school failure and educational inequality by broadening the gap between the kinds of learning opportunities minority and low-achieving students receive compared to Anglo and high-achieving students. If minority students are already failing science, taking more of it means they will have even greater opportunities to fail. If low-track students are already taking substantially different kinds of mathematics courses than high-track students, then the gap in the substantive content they are learning widens as the high-track students take even more advanced courses, and the low-track students take even more remedial math courses.

What schools consider to be essential knowledge and skills for all students to learn and how these are understood and taught—that is, the canons of U.S. education—need to be revised. These revisions should reflect the comprehensive realities of U.S. society and the world, not just the technological and economic sides of life in the United States. This means, first, that school curricula should demonstrate and emulate the interdisciplinary nature of human knowledge, values, and skills. Second, they should teach and model the interdependence of the world, a world in which Whites are a small numerical minority and in which the control of natural resources and social aspirations is gradually shifting from Western to non-Western, non-White nations. Third, a concerted effort should be made to achieve a greater balance between technological developments and humanistic concerns. These curricular reform emphases increase the possibility that the experiences, cultures, and contributions of ethnic minority groups in the United States will be included across the various subject matter content areas; that ethnic minority students will identify with and relate better to the substance of school curricula; that they will have a greater sense of ownership in the schooling enterprise; and that African Americans, Asians, Hispanics, and American Indians will have opportunities comparable to those of Anglo students to establish personally enabling connections with schools and thereby improve their overall academic achievement.

Because teachers play such a central role in the kinds of educational opportunities minority students receive in classrooms, their reeducation and training are fundamental to providing educational equality. This training should have four primary emphases. The first is self-knowledge. Teachers, counselors, and administrators need to become familiar with the attitudes and behaviors they have toward different ethnic groups and with how these are habitually exhibited in their school functions. They also need to understand the effects of these on students, relative to self-concepts, academic abilities, and educational opportunities available to students.

Merely telling teachers about the existence and effects of negative attitudes and low expectations on ethnic minority students' chances for educational equality will not suffice. Nor will reading the impressive body of research that documents these effects. These approaches seem too much like personal indictments and tend to cause teachers to become defensive and alienated. Teachers need to be shown how they behave toward minority students. This can be done by projecting mirror images of or replaying their classroom behaviors back to them, training teachers how to be participant observers of their own classroom dynamics and how to use different techniques systematically to analyze their instructional behaviors. Audio- and videotapes of individual teaching behaviors are invaluable for showing teachers what they actually do in classrooms. They are much better than outside observers, because recorders and cameras do not misrepresent what actually occurs. Training in ethnographic techniques, interactional analysis, questioning strategies, cultural decoding, frame analysis, and feedback mechanisms are very useful for these purposes.

While learning how to see their classroom attitudes and behaviors more clearly, teachers also need to be taught how to analyze these from different cultural perspectives. Without training, most educators cannot see the cultural biases and prejudices of their routine school behaviors. When suggestions are made to the effect that they are not treating ethnic minority and Anglo students equally, they associate these claims with blatant acts of discrimination. They do not understand the subtleties of negative ethnic attitudes and low expectations. For instance, educators need to know how and why treating all students the same can be an effective way to deny ethnic minority students equal educational opportunities.

A second emphasis in teacher reeducation for educational equality is understanding the differences in cultural values and behavioral codes between themselves as middle-class Anglos and ethnic minority students, how these values and codes operate in classrooms, and how instructional processes can be restructured to accommodate them better. Teachers cannot begin to treat African Americans, Hispanics, Indians, and Asians comparable to Anglos until they accept that these students have comparable human worth. This acceptance begins with acquiring knowledge about ethnic groups' cultural backgrounds, life experiences, and interactional styles to replace racial myths and stereotypes. Once they understand the organized structures and motivations behind these cultural behaviors, teachers can begin to design instructional options more compatible with them and thereby improve the quality of the learning experiences ethnic minority students receive.

The third focus of teacher reeducation should be the development of technical instructional skills that are more appropriate for use with ethnic minorities. The point of departure for this training should be understanding the specific traits of different teaching styles and ethnic learning styles. This knowledge should be combined with learning how to diversify teaching strategies ethnically; to create more supportive environments for learning and demonstrating achievement; to reduce stress, tension, and conflict in ethnically pluralistic classrooms; to select materials that have high-quality interest appeal for different ethnic groups; to develop and use learning activities that are meaningful, involving, enabling, and empowering for ethnic minority students; and to integrate ethnically diverse perspectives, aspirations, and experiences into curricula, program planning, and student evaluation. That is, teachers need to learn how to integrate ethnically their structural arrangements for teaching, culturally diversify their instructional strategies, multiculturalize the substance of learning, and democraticize the environments constructed for learning. These general skills can be operationalized by helping teachers learn how to use specific instructional skills with ethnic minority students such as questioning, feedback, and reinforcement, cooperative learning, inductive teaching, social context learning, and auditory and visual learning.

The approaches used in teacher training to develop these skills should be three-dimensional, including diagnosis, design and development, and debriefing, with teachers-in-training actively involved in each aspect. The training process should begin with a careful assessment of the value of and problems associated with using various instructional strategies with ethnic minority students. Examples of actual teaching behaviors should be used for this purpose. The training should then proceed to having teachers develop alternative instructional strategies and try them out in real or simulated teaching situations. Finally, these development efforts should be carefully examined to determine their strengths and weaknesses in terms of design and implementation criteria. That is, teachers should analyze them to assess the quality of the new teaching strategies relative to their ethnic sensitivity and ability to increase educational opportunities for ethnic minority students and to determine how effective they are in presenting the teaching tasks.

A fourth emphasis in the retraining of teachers, counselors, and school administrators for educational equality is public relations skill development. Major reform is needed in how educators are trained to communicate and interact with ethnic parents and to mobilize ethnic community resources to help in the educational process. There is a growing tendency to blame the school failure of ethnic minority students on the lack of involvement of their parents in school affairs. However, this buck-passing is counterproductive. It is another form of educators' blaming the victims and abdicating their responsibility for teaching minority youths.

Certainly minority parents should be more actively involved in their children's education, but it is understandable why they are reluctant or unable to do so. The schools that are failing their children are the same ones that failed them when they were students and that still treat them in paternalistic ways. Educators usually approach parents about their children only when the children get into trouble with the school system. This punitive, adversarial posture is not conducive to cooperation among educators and minority parents. Furthermore, many minority parents do not have the time, the personal resources, or the technical skills to assist in the education of their children in ways educators typically expect. How can parents effectively supervise their children's homework or come to the schools on demand when they are unfamiliar with the latest pedagogical strategies used in schools and when they are working at hourly wage or low-salaried jobs that do not permit them to take time off without significant cost? Teacher training programs should help educators develop different interactional skills that work well with minority parents and community organizations.

This retraining process should begin with the inclusion of ethnic minority community relations skill building in all levels of professional preparation, undergraduate and graduate, preservice and in-service. It should start with acquiring an accurate knowledge base about the cultural dynamics of different ethnic communities, who the power brokers are in these communities, and how interactions and relationships are negotiated. It should also include specific strategies and skills about how to approach ethnic communities and parents—for instance, identifying and tapping informal networks of influence within the communities, understanding different ethnic interactional decorums, establishing consultancy relations with ethnic minority parents and community organizations, and communicating effectively with ethnic parents.

Instead of always expecting parent-school interactions to take place in schools (which often are alien and hostile territory for ethnic minority parents and students), educators need to locate their efforts to increase parental involvement more within ethnic communities, or at least in neutral territory. Where school-parent interactions, discussions, conferences, and consultations occur is important as a symbolic statement of how committed schools are to involving parents in decisions about their children's education. When parents always have to go to the school at the educator's convenience, the implicit messages are that parents must defer to the school's position and that their inputs are not as valuable as those of the school personnel.

All of these are elements of the cultural diplomacy that classroom teachers, guidance counselors, and school administrators need to master in order to develop more constructive and cooperative relations with ethnic minority parents and communities. They, like the components of teacher self-knowledge, understanding ethnic minority cultures, and culturally specific instructional skills, are fundamental to establishing more culturally informed and ethnically sensitive foundations for changing how schools and teachers interact with ethnic minority students and to improving the educational opportunities these students receive.

CONCLUSION

Many researchers and scholars agree that the quality of student-teacher interactions in instructional situations is the ultimate test of educational equality, and that the central focus of both equality and excellence in education is maximum development of the personal talents of all students. The access of ethnic minority students to high-quality programs, materials, resources, and facilities is necessary for educational equality. But this is not sufficient. These students must also have access to quality knowledge and classroom interactions. As John Goodlad suggests, the central problem of both educational equality and excellence for today and tomorrow is "no longer access to school. It is access to knowledge for all."[34] This means that school reform toward improving educational equality for ethnic minority students needs to concentrate on equalizing the quality and comparability of the day-to-day learning experiences of ethnic minority and Anglo students within schools.

QUESTIONS AND ACTIVITIES

1. How do popular conceptions of educational equality differ from the view of this concept presented by Gay, the author of this chapter? What unfortunate assumptions, according to Gay, underlie these popular notions of educational equality?

2. In what ways did the educational status of ethnic minority students improve between the 1970s and the early 1980s? Why did the educational status of ethnic minority students improve during this period?

3. In what ways did the educational status of ethnic minorities decline during the 1980s? What is the reason for the decline?

4. How does the reference to Asian Americans as the "model minority" oversimplify their educational status? Give specific examples from this chapter to support your response.

5. How do school and curriculum practices such as tracking, vocational courses, and special education classes deny ethnic minority students equal educational opportunities?

6. The author argues that ethnic minority students are often placed in double jeopardy in school, in part because of differences between their cultures and the culture of the school. Explain what the author means by this concept. How can teachers help reduce the problems ethnic minority students experience in the schools?

7. How does testing, according to the author, promote educational inequality for lower-class and minority students? How can assessment programs be changed so they will contribute to educational equality for all students?

8. According to the author, how can curriculum reforms related to ethnic diversity contribute to educational equality?

9. Gay contends that educational equality for ethnic minority students cannot be achieved short of "massive schoolwide, institutional reform." What factors in the school environment and in teacher education does she think require reform? What specific recommendations does she make for attaining these reforms?

10. Observe for several days in an inner-city school that has a large percentage of students of color. In what ways do your observations support the conclusions by Gay about the problems students of color experience in the schools? What programs and efforts are being implemented in the school you observed to improve the educational status of students of color?

NOTES

1. Alexander A. Astin, *Achieving Educational Excellence: A Critical Assessment of Priorities and Practices in Higher Education* (San Francisco: Jossey-Bass, 1985).

2. Carl A. Grant and Christine E. Sleeter, *After the School Bell Rings* (Philadelphia: Falmer Press, 1986).

3. *Equality and Excellence: The Educational Status of Black Americans* (New York: College Entrance Examination Board, 1985), p. vii.

4. *Teachers' Views on Equity and Excellence* (Washington, D.C.: National Education Association, 1983), pp. 3–4; Lori S. Orum, *The Education of Hispanics: Status and Implications* (Washington, D.C.: National Council of La Raza, August 1986, ERIC Document, ED 274753); Evangelina Mangino, David Wilkinson, Richard Battaile, and Wanda Washington, "Student Achievement, 1984–85 in the Austin Independent School District," (ERIC Document, ED 264286).

5. *Teachers' Views on Equity and Excellence,* 4–5.

6. Michael A. Olivas, "Research on Latino College Students: A Theoretical Framework and Inquiry," in Michael A. Olivas, ed., *Latino College Students* (New York: Teachers College Press, 1986), pp. 1–25; Orum, *The Education of Hispanics; Education That Works: An Action Plan for the Education of Minorities* (Cambridge, Mass.: Massachusetts Institute of Technology, Quality Education for Minorities Project, January 1990).

7. *USA Today,* May 13, 1986, p. 1; Orum, *The Education of Hispanics; Education That Works.*

8. *Statistical Abstract of the United States, 1987,* 107th ed. (Washington, D.C.: U.S. Department of Commerce, Bureau of the Census, 1986); *Education That Works; Digest of Education Statistics,* 25th ed (Washington, D.C.: National Center for Education Statistics, U.S. Department of Education, Office of Educational Research and Information, 1989).

9. Isaura Santiago Santiago; "The Education of Hispanics in the United States: Inadequacies of the Melting Pot Theory," in Dietmar Rothermund and John Simon, eds., *Education and the Integration of Ethnic Minorities* (New York: St. Martin's Press, 1986), pp. 151–185; The College Entrance Examination Board, *Equality and Excellence;* Orum, *The Education of Hispanics;* Cheryl M. Fields, "Closing the Education Gap for Hispanics: State Aims to Forestall a Divided Society," *Chronicle of Higher Education* 34, No. 3 (September 16, 1987): A1, A36, A38. *Digest of Education Statistics, 1989.*

10. Francois Nielsen, "Hispanics in High School and Beyond," in Michael A. Olivas, ed., *Latino*

College Students (New York: Teachers College Press, 1986), p. 79.

11. *The Condition of Education,* Vol. 1, *Elementary and Secondary Education* (Washington, D.C.: National Center for Education Statistics, U.S. Department of Education, Office of Educational Research and Information, 1990).

12. *1980 Census of Population,* Vol. I, *Characteristics of the Population.* Chapter C, *Social and Economic Characteristics,* Part I, *United States Summary,* Rept. No. PC–80–1–C1 (Washington, D.C.: Bureau of the Census, U.S. Department of Commerce, December 1983).

13. Elena S. H. Yu, Mary Doi, and Ching-Fu Chang, *Asian American Education in Illinois: A Review of the Data* (Springfield: Illinois State Board of Education, November 1986).

14. Reginald A. Gougis, "The Effects of Prejudice and Stress on the Academic Performance of Black-Americans," in Ulric Neisser, ed., *The Achievement of Minority Children: New Perspectives* (Hillsdale, N.J.: Lawrence Erlbaum Associates, 1986), pp. 145–158.

15. Scott Heller, "17-Year-Olds Get 'Failing Marks' in Their Knowledge of Great Works of Literature and Historical Events," *Chronicle of Higher Education* 34, No. 3 (September 16, 1987): A35, A38; *American Memory: A Report on the Humanities in the Nation's Public Schools* (Washington, D.C.: National Endowment for the Humanities, 1987). *Condition of Education,* Vol. 1, 1990; *Digest of Education Statistics,* 1989.

16. Yu et al., *Asian American Education in Illinois;* Valerie O. Pang, Donald T. Mizokawa, James K. Morishima, and Roger G. Olstad, "Self-Concept of Japanese American Children," *Journal of Cross-Cultural Psychology* 16 (March 1985): 99–108. *Digest of Education Statistics,* 1989.

17. The College Entrance Examination Board, *Equality and Excellence; Digest of Education Statistics,* 1989.

18. Arthur N. Applebee, Judith A. Langer, and Ina V. S. Mullis, *The Writing Report Card: Writing Achievement in American Schools,* Rept. No. 15–W–02 (Princeton, N.J.: Educational Testing Service, 1986). *Condition of Education,* Vol. 1, 1990.

19. U.S. Civil Rights Commission, *Mexican-American Educational Study,* Reports I–VI (Washington, D.C.: Government Printing Service, 1971–1974); Geneva Gay, *Differential Dyadic Interactions of Black and White Teachers with Black and White Pupils in Recently Desegregated Social Studies Classrooms: A Function of Teacher and Pupil Ethnicity* (Washington, D.C.: Office of Education, National Institute of Education, January 1974); Carl A. Grant and Christine E, Sleeter, "Equality, Equity, and Excellence: A Critique," in Philip G. Altbach, Gail P. Kelly, and Lois Weis, eds. *Excellence in Education: Perspectives on Policy and Practice* (Buffalo, N.Y.: Prometheus Books, 1985), pp. 139–159.

20. Jeannie Oakes, *Keeping Track: How Schools Structure Inequality* (New Haven, Conn.: Yale University Press, 1985).

21. The College Entrance Examination Board, *Equality and Excellence;* John D. Winkler, Richard J. Stravelson, Cathleen Stasz, Abby Robyn, and Werner Fiebel, *How Effective Teachers Use Microcomputers in Instruction* (Santa Monica, Calif.: The Rand Corporation, 1984).

22. Oakes, *Keeping Track;* John I. Goodlad, *A Place Called School: Prospects for the Future* (New York: McGraw-Hill, 1984); James E. Rosenbaum, *Making Equality: The Hidden Curriculum in High School Tracking* (New York: John Wiley & Sons, 1976); Edward P. Morgan, *Inequality in Classroom Learning: Schooling and Democratic Citizenship* (New York: Praeger, 1977); Richard R. Verdugo, "Educational Stratification and Hispanics," in Michael A. Olivas, ed. *Latino College Students* (New York: Teachers College Press, 1986), pp. 325–347; Caroline Hodges Persell, *Education and Inequality: A Theoretical and Empirical Synthesis* (New York: Free Press, 1977).

23. Morgan, *Inequality in Classroom Learning.*

24. The College Entrance Examination Board, *Equality and Excellence; Astin, Achieving Educational Excellence; The Condition of Education,* Vol. 2, *Postsecondary Education* (Washington, D.C.: National Center for Education Statistics, U.S. Department of Education, Office of Educational Research and Information, 1990).

25. The College Entrance Examination Board, *Equality and Excellence,* 49.

25. Vera P. John-Steiner and Eleanor Leacock, "Transforming the Structure of Failure," in Doxey A. Wilkerson, ed. *Educating All of Our Children: An Imperative for Democracy* (Westport, Conn.: Mediax, 1979), p. 87.

27. Persell, *Education and Inequality,* 112.

28. Grant and Sleeter, "Equality, Equity, and Excellence, 139–159;" Morgan, *Inequality in Classroom Learning; Persell, Education and Inequality.*

29. The College Entrance Examination Board, *Equality and Excellence,* 4.

30. John-Steiner and Leacock, "Transforming the Structure of Failure," 87–88.

31. Henry J. Casso, "Educating the Linguistically and Culturally Different," in Doxey A. Wilkerson, ed., *Educating All of Our Children: An Imperative for Democracy* (Westport, Conn.: Mediax, 1979), p. 121.

32. Mario D. Fantini, "From School System to Educational System: Policy Considerations," in Doxey A. Wilkerson, ed., *Educating All of Our Children: An Imperative for Democracy.* (Westport, Conn.: Mediax, 1979), pp. 134–153.

33. Ibid., 147.

34. Goodlad, *A Place Called School,* 140.

CHAPTER 10

Approaches to Multicultural Curriculum Reform

■ JAMES A. BANKS

THE MAINSTREAM-CENTRIC CURRICULUM

The United States is made up of many different racial, ethnic, religious, and cultural groups. In many school curricula, textbooks, and other teaching materials, most of these groups are given scant attention. Rather, most curricula, textbooks, and teaching materials focus on White Anglo-Saxon Protestants. This dominant cultural group in U.S. society is often called mainstream Americans. A curriculum that focuses on the experiences of mainstream Americans and largely ignores the experiences, cultures, and histories of other ethnic, racial, cultural, and religious groups has negative consequences for both mainstream American students and students of color. A mainstream-centric curriculum is one major way in which racism and ethnocentrism are reinforced and perpetuated in the schools and in society at large.

A mainstream-centric curriculum has negative consequences for mainstream students because it reinforces their false sense of superiority, gives them a misleading conception of their relationship with other racial and ethnic groups, and denies them the opportunity to benefit from the knowledge, perspectives, and frames of reference that can be gained from studying and experiencing other cultures and groups. A mainstream-centric curriculum also denies mainstream American students the opportunity to view their culture from the perspectives of other cultures and groups. When people view their culture from the point of view of another culture, they are able to understand their own culture more fully, to see how it is unique and distinct from other cultures, and to understand better how it relates to and interacts with other cultures.

A mainstream-centric curriculum negatively influences students of color, such as African Americans, Hispanics, and Asian Americans. It marginalizes their experiences and cultures and does not reflect their dreams, hopes, and perspectives. Students learn best and are more highly motivated when the school curriculum reflects their cultures, experiences, and perspectives. Many students of color are alienated in the school in part because they experience cultural conflict and discontinuities that result from the cultural differences between their school and community. The school can help students of color mediate between their home and school cultures by implementing a curriculum that reflects the culture

195

of their ethnic groups and communities. The school can and should make effective use of the community cultures of students of color when teaching them such subjects as writing, language arts, science, and mathematics.[1]

In the mainstream-centric approach, events, themes, concepts, and issues are viewed primarily from the perspective of middle-class Anglo-Americans and Europeans. Events and cultural developments such as the European explorations in the Americas and the development of American music are viewed from Anglo and European perspectives and are evaluated using mainstream-centric criteria and points of view.

When the European explorations of the Americas are viewed from a Eurocentric perspective, the Americas are perceived as having been "discovered" by the European explorers such as Columbus and Cortés. The view that native peoples in the Americas were discovered by the Europeans subtly suggests that Indian cultures did not exist until they were "discovered" by the Europeans and that the lands occupied by the American Indians were rightfully owned by the Europeans after they settled on and claimed them. The Anglocentric view, below, of the settlement of Fort Townsend in the state of Washington appears on a marker in a federal park on the site where a U.S. Army post once stood. With the choice of words such as *settlers* (instead of *invaders*), *restive,* and *rebelled,* the author justifies the taking of the Indian's lands and depicts their resistance as unreasonable.

Fort Townsend
A U.S. Army Post was Established on this Site in 1856
In mid-nineteenth century the growth of Port Townsend caused the Indians to become restive. Settlers started a home guard, campaigned wherever called, and defeated the Indians in the Battle of Seattle. Indians rebelled as the government began enforcing the Indian Treaty of 1854, by which the Indians had ceded most of their territory. Port Townsend, a prosperous port of entry on Puget Sound, then asked protection of the U.S. army.

When the formation and nature of U.S. cultural developments, such as music and dance, are viewed from mainstream-centric perspectives, these art forms become important and significant only when they are recognized or legitimized by mainstream critics and artists. The music of African American musicians such as Chuck Berry and Little Richard were not viewed as significant by the mainstream society until White singers such as the Beatles and Rod Stewart publicly acknowledged the significant ways their own music had been deeply influenced by these African American musicians. It often takes White artists to legitimize ethnic cultural forms and innovations created by Asian Americans, African Americans, Hispanics, and Native Americans.

EFFORTS TO ESTABLISH A MULTICULTURAL CURRICULUM

Since the civil rights movement of the 1960s, educators have been trying, in various ways, to better integrate the school curriculum with ethnic content and to move away from a mainstream-centric and Eurocentric curriculum. These have proven to be difficult goals for schools to attain for many complex reasons. The strong assimilationist ideology embraced by most U.S. educators is one major reason.[2] The assimilationist ideology makes it difficult for educators to think differently about how U.S. society and culture developed and to acquire a commitment to make the curriculum multicultural. Individuals who have a strong assimilationist ideology believe that most important events and developments in U.S. society are related to the nation's British heritage and that the contributions of other ethnic and cultural groups are not very significant by comparison. When educators acquire a multicultural ideology and conception of U.S. culture, they are then able to view the experiences and contributions of a wide range of cultural, ethnic, and religious groups as significant to the development of the United States.

Ideological resistance is a major factor that has slowed and is still slowing the development of a multicultural curriculum, but other factors have also affected its growth and development. Political resistance to a multicultural curriculum is closely related to ideological resistance. Many people who resist a multicultural curriculum believe that knowledge is power and that a multicultural perspective on U.S. society challenges the existing power structure. They believe that the dominant mainstream-centric curriculum supports, reinforces, and justifies the existing social, economic, and political structure. Multicultural perspectives and points of view, in the opinion of many observers, legitimize and promote social change and social reconstruction.

In recent years a heated debate has occurred about the extent to which the curriculum should be Western and European-centric and to which it should reflect the cultural, ethnic, and racial diversity in the United States. At least three major positions in this debate can be identified. The Western traditionalists argue that the West, as defined and conceptualized in the past, should be the focus in school and college curricula because of the major influence of Western civilization and culture in the United States and throughout the world.[3] Afrocentric scholars contend that the contributions of Africa and of African peoples should receive major emphasis in the curriculum.[4] The multiculturalists argue that although the West should receive a major emphasis in the curriculum, the West should be reconceptualized so that it reflects the contributions that people of color have made to the West. In addition to teaching about Western ideals, the gap between the ideals of the West and its realities of racism, sexism, and discrimination should be taught.[5] Multiculturalists also believe that in addition to learning about the West, students should study other world cultures, such as those in Africa, Asia, the Middle East, and America, as they were before the Europeans arrived.

Other factors that have slowed the institutionalization of a multicultural curriculum include the low level of knowledge about ethnic cultures that most educators have and the heavy reliance on textbooks for teaching. Teachers must have an in-depth knowledge about ethnic cultures and experiences to integrate ethnic content, experiences, and points of view into the curriculum. Many teachers tell their students that Columbus discovered America and that America is a "new world" because they know little about the diverse Native American cultures that existed in the Americas more than 40,000 years before the Europeans began to settle in the Americas in significant numbers in the sixteenth century.

Many studies have revealed that the textbook is still the main source for teaching, especially in such subjects as the social studies, reading, and language arts.[6] Some significant changes have been made in textbooks since the civil rights movement of the 1960s. More ethnic groups and women appear in textbooks today than in those of yesteryear.[7] However, the content about ethnic groups in textbooks is usually presented from mainstream perspectives, contains information and heroes that are selected using mainstream criteria, and rarely incorporates information about ethnic groups throughout the text in a consistent and totally integrated way. Information about ethnic groups is usually discussed in special units, topics, and parts of the text. Because most teachers rely heavily on the textbook for teaching, they approach the teaching of ethnic content in a fragmented fashion.

LEVELS OF INTEGRATION OF MULTICULTURAL CONTENT

The Contributions Approach

Four approaches to the integration of ethnic and multicultural content into the curriculum that have evolved since the 1960s can be identified (see Figure 10.1). The *contributions approach* to integration (level 1) is one of the most frequently used and is often used extensively during the first phase of an ethnic revival movement. It is also frequently used when a school or district first attempts to integrate ethnic and multicultural content into the mainstream curriculum.

The contributions approach is characterized by the insertion of ethnic heroes and discrete cultural artifacts into the curriculum, selected using criteria similar to those used to select mainstream heroes and cultural artifacts. Thus, individuals such as Crispus Attucks, Benjamin Bannaker, Sacajawea, Booker T. Washington, and César Chávez are added to the curriculum. They are discussed when mainstream American heroes such as Patrick Henry, George Washington, Thomas Jefferson, and John F. Kennedy are studied in the core curriculum. Discrete cultural elements such as the foods, dances, music, and artifacts of ethnic groups are studied, but little attention is given to their meanings and importance within ethnic communities.

An important characteristic of the contributions approach is that the mainstream curriculum remains unchanged in its basic structure, goals, and salient characteristics. Prerequisites for the implementation of this approach are minimal. They include basic knowledge about U.S. society and knowledge about ethnic heroes and their roles and contributions to U.S. society and culture.

Individuals who challenged the dominant society's ideologies, values, and conceptions and advocated radical social, political, and economic reform are seldom included in the contributions approach. Thus, Booker T. Washington is more likely to be chosen for study than is W. E. B. Du Bois, and Sacajawea is more likely to be chosen than is Geronimo. The criteria used to select ethnic heroes for study and to judge them for success are derived from the mainstream society and not from the ethnic community. Consequently, use of the contributions approach usually results in the study of ethnic heroes who represent only one important perspective within ethnic communities. The more radical and less conformist individuals who are heroes only to the ethnic community tend to be ignored in textbooks, teaching materials, and activities used in the contributions approach.

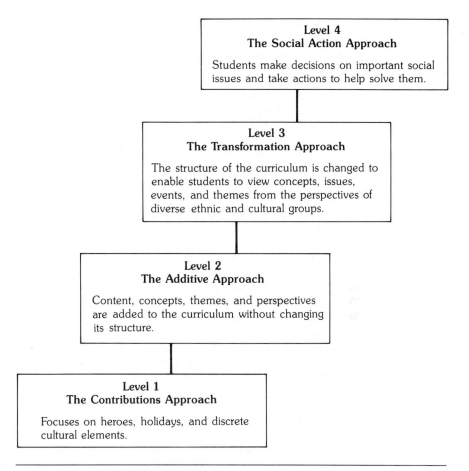

FIGURE 10.1
Levels of Integration of Multicultural Content

The heroes and holidays approach is a variant of the contributions approach. In this approach, ethnic content is limited primarily to special days, weeks, and months related to ethnic events and celebrations. Cinco de Mayo, Martin Luther King's Birthday, and African American History Week are examples of ethnic days and weeks celebrated in the schools. During these celebrations, teachers involve students in lessons, experiences, and pageants related to the ethnic group being commemorated. When this approach is used, the class studies little or nothing about the ethnic group before or after the special event or occasion.

The contributions approach (level 1 in Figure 10.1) provides teachers with a way to integrate ethnic content into the curriculum quickly, thus giving some recognition to ethnic contributions to U.S. society and culture. Many teachers who are committed to integrating their curricula with ethnic content have little knowledge about ethnic groups and curriculum revision. Consequently, they use the contributions approach when teaching about ethnic groups. These teachers should be encouraged, supported, and given the opportunity to acquire the knowledge and skills needed to reform their curricula by using one of the more effective approaches described later in this chapter.

There are often strong political demands from ethnic communities for the school to put their heroes, contributions, and cultures into the school curriculum. These political forces may take the form of demands for heroes and contributions because mainstream heroes, such as Washington, Jefferson, and Lincoln, are highly visible in the school curriculum. Ethnic communities of color want to see their own heroes and contributions alongside those of the mainstream society. Such contributions may help give them a sense of structural inclusion, validation, and equity. Curriculum inclusion also facilitates the quests of victimized ethnic and cultural groups for a sense of empowerment and efficacy. The school should help ethnic-group students acquire a sense of empowerment and efficacy. These factors are positively correlated with academic achievement.[8]

The contributions approach is also the easiest approach for teachers to use to integrate the curriculum with ethnic content. However, this approach has several serious limitations. When the integration of the curriculum is accomplished primarily through the infusion of ethnic heroes and contributions, students do not attain a global view of the role of ethnic and cultural groups in U.S. society. Rather, they see ethnic issues and events primarily as an addition to the curriculum and consequently as an appendage to the main story of the development of the nation and to the core curriculum in the language arts, the social studies, the arts, and other subject areas.

Teaching ethnic issues with the use of heroes and contributions also tends to gloss over important concepts and issues related to the victimization and oppression of ethnic groups and their struggles against racism and for power. Issues such as racism, poverty, and oppression tend to be avoided in the contributions approach to curriculum integration. The focus tends to be on success and the validation of the Horatio Alger myth that all Americans who are willing to work hard can go from rags to riches and "pull themselves up by their bootstraps."

The success stories of ethnic heroes such as Booker T. Washington, George Washington Carver, and Jackie Robinson are usually told with a focus on their success, with little attention to racism and other barriers they encountered and how they succeeded despite the hurdles they faced. Little attention is also devoted to the process by which they become heroes. Students should learn about the process by which people become heroes as well as about their status and role as heroes. Only when students learn the process by which individuals become heroes will they understand fully how individuals, particularly individuals of color, achieve and maintain hero status and what the process of becoming a hero means for their own lives.

The contributions approach often results in the trivialization of ethnic cultures, the study of their strange and exotic characteristics, and the reinforcement of stereotypes and misconceptions. When the focus is on the contributions and unique aspects of ethnic cultures, students are not helped to view them as complete and dynamic wholes. The contributions approach also tends to focus on the life-styles of ethnic groups rather than on the institutional structures, such as racism and discrimination, that strongly affect their life chances and keep them powerless and marginalized.

The contributions approach to content integration may provide students with a memorable one-time experience with an ethnic hero, but it often fails to help them understand the role and influence of the hero in the total context of U.S. history and society. When ethnic heroes are studied separate and apart from the social and political context in which they lived and worked, students attain only a partial understanding of their roles and significance in society. When Martin Luther King, Jr., is studied outside the social and political context of institutionalized racism in the U.S. South in the 1940s and 1950s, and without attention to the more subtle forms of institutionalized racism in the North during this period, his full significance as a social reformer is neither revealed nor understood by students.

The Additive Approach

Another important approach to the integration of ethnic content to the curriculum is the addition of content, concepts, themes, and perspectives to the curriculum without changing its basic structure, purposes, and characteristics. The *additive approach* (level 2 in Figure 10.1) is often accomplished by the addition of a book, a unit, or a course to the curriculum without changing it substantially. Examples of this approach include adding a book such as *The Color Purple* to a unit on the twentieth century in an English class; the use of the film *Miss Jane Pittman* during a unit on the 1960s; and the addition of a unit on the internment of the Japanese Americans during a study of World War II in a class on U.S. history.

The additive approach allows the teacher to put ethnic content into the curriculum without restructuring it, a process that would take substantial time, effort, training, and rethinking of the curriculum and its purposes, nature, and goals. The additive approach can be the first phase in a transformative curriculum reform effort designed to restructure the total curriculum and to integrate it with ethnic content, perspectives, and frames of reference.

However, this approach shares several disadvantages with the contributions approach. Its most important shortcoming is that it usually results in the viewing of ethnic content from the perspectives of mainstream historians, writers, artists, and scientists because it does not involve a restructuring of the curriculum. The events, concepts, issues, and problems selected for study are selected using mainstream-centric and Eurocentric criteria and perspectives. When teaching a unit such as The Westward Movement in a fifth-grade U.S. history class, the teacher may integrate the unit by adding content about the Oglala Sioux Indians. However, the unit remains mainstream-centric and focused because of its perspective and point of view. A unit called The Westward Movement is mainstream and Eurocentric because it focuses on the movement of European Americans from the Eastern to the Western part of the United States. The Oglala Sioux were already in the West and consequently were not moving westward. The unit might be called The Invasion from the East, from the point of view of the Oglala Sioux. Black Elk, an Oglala Sioux holy man, lamented the conquering of his people, which culminated in their defeat at Wounded Knee Creek on December 29,

1890. Approximately 200 Sioux men, women, and children were killed by U.S. troops. Black Elk said, "The [Sioux] nation's hoop is broken and scattered. There is no center any longer, and the sacred tree is dead."[9]

Black Elk did not consider his homeland "the West," but rather the center of the world. He viewed the cardinal directions metaphysically. The Great Spirit sent him the cup of living water and the sacred bow from the West. The daybreak star and the sacred pipe originated from the East. The Sioux nation's sacred hoop and the tree that was to bloom came from the South.[10] When teaching about the movement of the Europeans across North America, teachers should help students understand that different cultural, racial, and ethnic groups often have varying and conflicting conceptions and points of view about the same historical events, concepts, issues, and developments. The victors and the vanquished, especially, often have conflicting conceptions of the same historical event. However, it is usually the point of view of the victors that becomes institutionalized within the schools and the mainstream society. This happens because history and textbooks are usually written by people who won the wars and gained control of the society, and not by the losers—the victimized and the powerless. The perspectives of both groups are needed to help us fully understand our history, culture, and society.

The people who are conquered and the people who conquered them have histories and cultures that are intricately interwoven and interconnected. They have to learn each others' histories and cultures to understand their own fully. White Americans cannot fully understand their own history in the Western United States and in America without understanding the history of the American Indians and the ways their histories and the histories of the Indians are interconnected. James Baldwin insightfully pointed out that when White Americans distort African American history, they do not learn the truth about their own history because the history of Blacks and Whites in the United States is tightly bound together.[11] This is also true for African American history and Indian history. The history of African Americans and Indians in the United States is closely interconnected, as Katz documents in his book *Black Indians: A Hidden Heritage.*[12] The additive approach fails to help students view society from diverse cultural and ethnic perspectives and understand the ways that the histories and cultures of the nation's diverse ethnic, racial, cultural, and religious groups are interconnected.

Content, materials, and issues that are added to a curriculum as appendages instead of being integral parts of a unit of instruction can become problematic. Problems might result when a book such as *The Color Purple* or a film like *Miss Jane Pittman* is added to a unit when the students lack the concepts, content background, and emotional maturity to deal with the issues and problems in this material. The effective use of such emotion-laden and complex materials usually requires that the teacher help students acquire, in a sequential and developmental fashion, the content background and attitudinal maturity to deal with them effectively. The use of both of these materials in different classes and schools has resulted in major problems for the teachers using them. A community controversy arose in each case. The problems developed because the material was used with students who had neither the content background nor the attitudinal sophistication to respond to them appropriately. Adding ethnic content to the curriculum in a sporadic and segmented way can result in pedagogical problems, trouble for the teacher, student confusion, and community controversy.

The Transformation Approach

The *transformation approach* differs fundamentally from the contributions and additive approaches. In both approaches, ethnic content is added to the mainstream core curriculum without changing its basic assumptions, nature, and structure. The fundamental goals, structure, and perspectives of the curriculum are changed in the transformation approach.

The transformation approach (level 3 in Figure 10.1) changes the basic assumptions of the curriculum and enables students to view concepts, issues, themes, and problems from several ethnic perspectives and points of view. The mainstream-centric perspective is one of only several perspectives from which issues, problems, concepts, and issues are viewed. It is neither possible nor desirable to view every issue, concept, event, or problem from the point of view of every U.S. ethnic group. Rather, the goal should be to enable students to view concepts and issues from more than one perspective and from the point of view of the cultural, ethnic, and racial groups that were the most active participants in, or were most cogently influenced by, the event, issue, or concept being studied.

The key curriculum issues involved in multicultural curriculum reform is not the addition of a long list of ethnic groups, heroes, and contributions, but the infusion of various perspectives, frames of references, and content from various groups that will extend students' understandings of the nature, development, and complexity of U.S. society. When students are studying the revolution in the British colonies, the perspectives of the Anglo revolutionaries, the Anglo loyalists, African Americans, Indians, and the British are essential for them to attain a thorough understanding of this significant event in U.S. history (see Figure 10.2). Students must study the various and sometimes divergent meanings of the revolution to these diverse groups to understand it fully.[13]

In the language arts, when students are studying the nature of U.S. English and proper language use, they should be helped to understand the rich linguistic and language diversity in the United States and the ways that a wide range of regional, cultural, and ethnic groups have influenced the development of U.S. English. Students should also examine how normative language use varies within the social context, the region, and the situation. The use of Black English is appropriate in some social and cultural contexts and inappropriate in others. This is also true of standard U.S. English. The United States is rich in languages and dialects. The nation has more than 20 million Hispanic citizens; Spanish is the first language for most of them. Most of the nation's approximately 30 million African Americans speak both standard English as well as some form of Black English or Ebonics. The rich language diversity in the United States includes more than twenty-five European languages; Asian, African, and Middle-Eastern languages; and American Indian languages. Since the 1970s, languages from Indochina, spoken by groups such as the Hmong, Vietnamese, Laotians, and the Cambodians, have further enriched language diversity in the United States.

When subjects such as music, dance, and literature are studied, the teacher should acquaint students with the ways these art forms among U.S. ethnic groups have greatly influenced and enriched the nation's artistic and literary traditions. The ways that African American musicians such as Bessie Smith, W. C. Handy, and Leontyne Price have influenced the nature and development of U.S. music should be examined when the development of U.S. music is studied. African Americans and Puerto Ricans have significantly influenced the

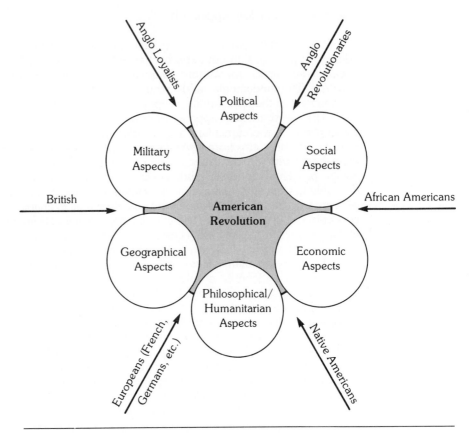

FIGURE 10.2
A Multicultural Interdisciplinary Model for Teaching the American Revolution
Source: Reprinted with permission from Geneva Gay and James A. Banks, "Teaching the American Revolution: A Multiethnic Approach," *Social Education,* 7 (November–December 1975): 462.

development of American dance. Writers of color, such as Langston Hughes, N. Scott Momaday, Carlos Bulosan, Maxine Hong Kingston, Rudolfo A. Anaya, and Piri Thomas, have not only significantly influenced the development of American literature, but have also provided unique and revealing perspectives on U.S. society and culture.[14]

When studying U.S. history, language, music, arts, science, and mathematics, the emphasis should not be on the ways that various ethnic and cultural groups have contributed to mainstream U.S. society and culture. *The emphasis, rather, should be on how the common U.S. culture and society emerged from a complex synthesis and interaction of the diverse cultural elements that originated within the various cultural, racial, ethnic, and religious groups that make up U.S. society.* I call this process *multiple acculturation* and argue that even though Anglo-Saxon Protestants are the dominant group in the United States—culturally, politically, and economically—it is misleading and inaccurate to describe U.S. culture and society as an Anglo-Saxon Protestant culture.[15] Other

U.S. ethnic and cultural groups have deeply influenced, shaped, and participated in the development and formation of U.S. society and culture. African Americans, for example, profoundly influenced the development of the U.S. Southern culture, even though they had very little political and economic power.[16] One irony of conquest is that those who are conquered often deeply influence the cultures of the conquerors.

A multiple acculturation conception of U.S. society and culture leads to a perspective that views ethnic events, literature, music, and art as integral parts of the common, shared U.S. culture. Anglo-Saxon Protestant culture is viewed as only a part of this larger cultural whole. Thus, to teach American literature without including significant writers of color, such as those named above, gives a partial and incomplete view of U.S. literature, culture, and society.

The Social Action Approach

The *social action approach* (level 4 in Figure 10.1) includes all the elements of the transformation approach but adds components that require students to make decisions and take actions related to the concept, issue, or problem studied in the unit. Major goals of instruction in this approach are to educate students for social criticism and social change and to teach them decision-making skills. To empower students and help them acquire political efficacy, the school must help them become reflective social critics and skilled participants in social change. The traditional goal of schooling has been to socialize students so they would accept unquestioningly the existing ideologies, institutions, and practices within society and the nation-state.[17]

Political education in the United States has traditionally fostered political passivity rather than political action. A major goal of the social action approach is to help students acquire the knowledge, values, and skills they need to participate in social change so that victimized and excluded ethnic and racial groups can become full participants in U.S. society and so the nation will move closer to attaining its democratic ideals. To participate effectively in democratic social change, students must be taught social criticism and must be helped to understand the inconsistency between our ideals and social realities, the work that must be done to close this gap, and how students can, as individuals and groups, influence the social and political systems in U.S. society. In this approach, teachers are agents of social change who promote democratic values and the empowerment of students. Teaching units organized using the social action approach have the components described below.

1. *A decision problem or question.* An example of a question is: What actions should we take to reduce prejudice and discrimination in our school?

2. *An inquiry that provides data related to the decision problem.* The inquiry might consist of these kinds of questions:
   a. What is prejudice?
   b. What is discrimination?
   c. What causes prejudice?
   d. What causes people to discriminate?
   e. What are examples of prejudice and discrimination in our nation, community, and school?

f. How do prejudice and discrimination affect the groups below? How does each group view prejudice? Discrimination? To what extent is each group a victim or a perpetuator of prejudice and discrimination?

g. How has each group dealt with prejudice and discrimination? (Groups: White mainstream Americans, African Americans, Asian Americans, Hispanic Americans, Native Americans.)

The inquiry into the nature of prejudice and discrimination would be interdisciplinary and would include readings and data sources in the various social sciences, biography, fiction, poetry, and drama. Scientific and statistical data would be used when students investigated how discrimination affects the income, occupations, frequency of diseases, and health care within these various groups.

3. *Value inquiry and moral analysis.* Students are given opportunities to examine, clarify, and reflect on their values, attitudes, beliefs, and feelings related to racial prejudice and discrimination. The teacher can provide the students with case studies from various sources, such as newspapers and magazines. The case studies can be used to involve the students in discussions and role-playing situations that enable them to express and to examine their attitudes, beliefs, and feelings about prejudice and discrimination.

Poetry, biography, and powerful fiction are excellent sources for case studies that can be used for both discussion and role playing. Countee Cullen's powerful poem "Incident" describes the painful memories of a child who was called "nigger" on a trip to Baltimore. Langston Hughes's poem "I, Too" poignantly tells how the "darker brother" is sent into the kitchen when company comes. The teacher and the students can describe verbally or write about incidents related to prejudice and discrimination they have observed or in which they have participated. The following case, based on a real-life situation, was written by the author for use with his students.[18] After reading the case, the students discuss the questions at the end of it.

Trying to Buy a Home in Lakewood Island

About a year ago, Joan and Henry Green, a young African American couple, moved from the West Coast to a large city in the Midwest. They moved because Henry finished his Ph.D. in chemistry and took a job at a big university in Midwestern City. Since they have been in Midwestern City, the Greens have rented an apartment in the central area of the city. However, they have decided that they want to buy a house. Their apartment has become too small for the many books and other things they have accumulated during the year. In addition to wanting more space, they also want a house so that they can receive breaks on their income tax, which they do not receive living in an apartment. The Greens also think that a house will be a good financial investment.

The Greens have decided to move into a suburban community. They want a new house and most of the houses within the city limits are rather old. They also feel that they can obtain a larger house for their money in the suburbs than in the city. They have looked at several suburban communities and decided that they like Lakewood Island better than any of the others. Lakewood Island is an all-White community, which is comprised primarily of lower-middle-class and middle-class residents. There are a few wealthy families in Lakewood Island, but they are exceptions rather than the rule.

Joan and Henry Green have become frustrated because of the problems they have experienced trying to buy a home in Lakewood Island. Before they go out to look at a house, they carefully study the newspaper ads. When they arrived at the first house in which they were interested, the owner told them that his house had just been sold. A week later they decided to work with a realtor. When they tried to close the deal on the next house they wanted, the realtor told them that the owner had raised the price $10,000 because he had the house appraised since he put it on the market and had discovered that his selling price was much too low. When the Greens tried to buy a third house in Lakewood Island, the owner told them that he had decided not to sell because he had not received the job in another city that he was almost sure he would receive when he had put his house up for sale. He explained that the realtor had not removed the ad about his house from the newspaper even though he had told him that he had decided not to sell a week earlier. The realtor the owner had been working with had left the real estate company a few days ago. Henry is bitter and feels that he and his wife are victims of racism and discrimination. Joan believes that Henry is paranoid and that they have been the victims of a series of events that could have happened to anyone, regardless of their race.

Questions: What should the Greens do? Why?

4. *Decision making and social action* (synthesis of knowledge and values). Students acquire knowledge about their decision problem from the activities in 2, above. This interdisciplinary knowledge provides them with the information they need to make reflective decisions about prejudice and discrimination in their communities and schools. The activities in 3 enable them to identify, clarify, and analyze their values, feelings, and beliefs about prejudice and discrimination: The decision-making process enables the students to synthesize their knowledge and values to determine what actions, if any, they should take to reduce prejudice and discrimination in their schools. They can develop a chart in which they list possible actions to take and their possible consequences. They can then decide on a course of action to take and implement it.

Mixing and Blending Approaches

The four approaches for the integration of multicultural content into the curriculum (see Table 10.1) are often mixed and blended in actual teaching situations. One approach, such as the contributions approach, can be used as a vehicle to move to other, more intellectually challenging approaches such as the transformation and social action approaches. It is unrealistic to expect a teacher to move directly from a highly mainstream-centric curriculum to one that focuses on decision making and social action. Rather, the move from the first to higher levels of multicultural content integration is likely to be gradual and cumulative.

A teacher who has a mainstream-centric curriculum might use the school's Martin Luther King's birthday celebration as an opportunity to integrate the curriculum with ethnic content about King, as well as to think seriously about how content about African Americans and other ethnic groups can be integrated into the curriculum in an ongoing fashion. The teacher could explore with the students these kinds of questions during the celebration: *(to p. 210)*

TABLE 10.1
Approaches for the Integration of Multicultural Content

Approach	Description	Examples	Strengths	Problems
Contributions	Heroes, cultural components, holidays, and other discrete elements related to ethnic groups are added to the curriculum on special days, occasions, and celebrations.	Famous Mexican Americans are studied only during the week of Cinco de Mayo (May 5). African Americans are studied during African American History Month in February but rarely during the rest of the year. Ethnic foods are studied in the first grade with little attention devoted to the cultures in which the foods are embedded.	Provides a quick and relatively easy way to put ethnic content into the curriculum. Gives ethnic heroes visibility in the curriculum alongside mainstream heroes. Is a popular approach among teachers and educators.	Results in a superficial understanding of ethnic cultures. Focuses on the life-styles and artifacts of ethnic groups and reinforces stereotypes and misconceptions. Mainstream criteria are used to select heroes and cultural elements for inclusion in the curriculum.
Additive	This approach consists of the addition of content, concepts, themes, and perspectives to the curriculum without changing its structure	Adding the book *The Color Purple* to a literature unit without reconceptualizing the unit or giving the students the background knowledge to understand the book. Adding a unit on the Japanese American internment to a U.S. history course without treating the Japanese in any other unit. Leaving the core curriculum intact but adding an ethnic studies course, as an elective, that focuses on a specific ethnic group.	Makes it possible to add ethnic content to the curriculum without changing its structure, which requires substantial curriculum changes and staff development. Can be implemented within the existing curriculum structure.	Reinforces the idea that ethnic history and culture are not integral parts of U.S. mainstream culture. Students view ethnic groups from Anglocentric and Eurocentric perspectives. Fails to help students understand how the dominant culture and ethnic cultures are interconnected and interrelated.
Transformation	The basic goals, structure, and nature of the curriculum are changed to enable	A unit on the American Revolution describes the meaning of the	Enables students to understrand the complex ways in which diverse racial and cultural groups	The implementation of this approach requires substantial curriculum revision,

TABLE 10.1
Continued

Approach	Description	Examples	Strengths	Problems
	students to view concepts, events, issues, problems, and themes from the perspectives of diverse cultural, ethnic, and racial groups.	revolution to Anglo revolutionaries, Anglo loyalists, African Americans, Indians, and the British. A unit on 20th-century U.S. literature includes works by William Faulkner, Joyce Carol Oates, Langston Hughes, N. Scott Momoday, Saul Bellow, Maxine Hong Kingston, Rudolfo A. Anaya, and Piri Thomas.	participated in the formation of U.S. society and culture. Helps reduce racial and ethnic encapsulation. Enables diverse ethnic, racial, and religious groups to see their cultures, ethos, and perspectives in the school curriculum. Gives students a balanced view of the nature and development of U.S. culture and society. Helps to empower victimized racial, ethnic, and cultural groups.	in-service training, and the identification and development of materials written from the perspectives of various racial and cultural groups. Staff development for the institutionalization of this approach must be continual and ongoing.
Social Action	In this approach, students identify important social problems and issues, gather pertinent data, clarify their values on the issues, make decisions, and take reflective actions to help resolve the issue or problem.	A class studies prejudice and discrimination in their school and decides to take actions to improve race relations in the school. A class studies the treatment of ethnic groups in a local newspaper and writes a letter to the newspaper publisher suggesting ways that the treatment of ethnic groups in the newspapers should be improved.	Enables students to improve their thinking, value analysis, decision-making, and social-action skills. Enables students to improve their data-gathering skills. Helps students develop a sense of political efficacy. Helps students improve their skills to work in groups	Requires a considerable amount of curriculum planning and materials identification. May be longer in duration than more traditional teaching units. May focus on problems and issues considered controversial by some members of the school staff and citizens of the community. Students may be able to take few meaningful actions that contribute to the resolution of the social issue or problem.

1. What were the conditions of African Americans before the emergence of Martin Luther King as a leader?

2. What has happened to the social, economic, and political condition of African Americans since the civil rights movement of the 1960s?

3. What is the social, economic, and political condition of African Americans today?

To bring in elements of the transformation and social action approaches, the teacher could explore these questions with the students:

1. What were the conditions of other ethnic groups during the time that King was a civil rights leader?

2. How did other ethnic groups participate in and respond to the civil rights movement?

3. How did these groups respond to Martin Luther King, Jr.?

4. What can we do today to improve the civil rights of groups of color?

5. What can we do to develop more positive racial and ethnic attitudes?

The students will be unable to answer all the questions they have raised about ethnic groups during the celebration of Martin Luther King's birthday. Rather, the questions will enable the students to integrate content about ethnic groups throughout the year as they study such topics as the family, the school, the neighborhood, and the city. As the students study these topics, they can use the questions they have formulated to investigate ethnic families, the ethnic groups in their school and in schools in other parts of the city, ethnic neighborhoods, and various ethnic institutions in the city such as churches, temples, synagogues, schools, restaurants, and community centers. As a culminating activity for the year, the teacher can take the students on a tour of an ethnic community in the city. However, such a tour should be both preceded and followed by activities that enable the students to develop perceptive and compassionate lenses for seeing ethnic and cultural differences and for responding to them with sensitivity. A field trip to an ethnic community or neighborhood might reinforce stereotypes and misconceptions if students lack the knowledge and insights needed to view ethnic cultures in an understanding and caring way. Theory and research indicate that contact with an ethnic group does not necessarily lead to more positive racial and ethnic attitudes.[19] Rather, the conditions under which the contact occurs and the quality of the interaction in the contact situation are the important variables.

GUIDELINES FOR TEACHING MULTICULTURAL CONTENT

The following fourteen guidelines are designed to help you better integrate content about ethnic groups into the school curriculum and to teach effectively in multicultural environments.

1. You, the teacher, are an extremely important variable in the teaching of ethnic content. If you have the necessary knowledge, attitudes, and skills, when you encounter racist content in materials or observe racism in the statements and behavior of students you can use these situations to teach important lessons about the experiences of ethnic groups in the United States.

2. Knowledge about ethnic groups is needed to teach ethnic content effectively. Read at least one major book that surveys the histories and cultures of U.S. ethnic groups. One book that includes historical overviews of U.S. ethnic groups is James A. Banks, *Teaching Strategies for Ethnic Studies,* 5th ed. (Boston: Allyn and Bacon, 1991).

3. Be sensitive to your own racial attitudes, behavior, and the statements you make about ethnic groups in the classroom. A statement such as "Sit like an Indian" stereotypes Native Americans.

4. Make sure that your classroom conveys positive images of various ethnic groups. You can do this by displaying bulletin boards, posters, and calendars that show the racial and ethnic diversity within U.S. society.

5. Be sensitive to the racial and ethnic attitudes of your students and do not accept the belief, which has been refuted by research, that "kids do not see colors." Since the pioneering research by Lasker in 1929, researchers have known that very young children are aware of racial differences and that they tend to accept the evaluations of various racial groups that are normative within the wider society.[20] Do not try to ignore the racial and ethnic differences that you see; try to respond to these differences positively and sensitively.

6. Be judicious in your choice and use of teaching materials. Some materials contain both subtle and blatant sterotypes of ethnic groups. Point out to the students when an ethnic group is stereotyped, omitted from, or described in materials from Anglocentric and Eurocentric points of view. A helpful guide is *Guidelines for Selecting Bias-Free Textbooks and Storybooks* (New York: Council on Interracial Books for Children, n.d.).

7. Use trade books, films, videotapes, and recordings to supplement the textbook treatment of ethnic groups and to present the perspectives of ethnic groups to your students. Many of these sources contain rich and powerful images of the experience of being a person of color in the United States.

8. Get in touch with your own cultural and ethnic heritage. Sharing your ethnic and cultural story with your students will create a climate for sharing in the classroom, will help motivate students to dig into their ethnic and cultural roots, and will result in powerful learning for your students.

9. Be sensitive to the possible controversial nature of some ethnic studies materials. If you are clear about the teaching objectives you have in mind, you can often use a less controversial book or reading to attain the same objectives. *The Color Purple* by Alice Walker, for example, is a controversial book. A teacher, however, who wants her students to gain insights about African Americans in the South can use *Roll of Thunder, Hear My Cry* by Mildred D. Taylor instead of *The Color Purple.*[21]

10. Be sensitive to the developmental levels of your students when you select concepts, content, and activities related to ethnic groups. Concepts and learning activities for students in kindergarten and the primary grades should be specific and concrete. Students in these grades should study such concepts as *similarities, differences, prejudice,* and *discrimination* rather than higher-level concepts such as *racism* and *oppression.* Fiction and biographies are excellent vehicles for introducing these concepts to students in kindergarten and the primary grades. As students progress through the grades, they can be introduced to more complex concepts, examples, and activities.

If you teach in a racially or ethnically integrated classroom or school you should keep the following guidelines in mind.

11. View your students of color as winners. Many students of color have high academic and career goals. They need teachers who believe they can be successful and are willing to help them succeed. Both research and theory indicate that students are more likely to achieve highly when their teachers have high academic expectations for them.

12. Keep in mind that most parents of color are very interested in education and want their children to be successful academically even though the parents may be alienated from the school.[22] Do not equate education with schooling. Many parents who want their children to succeed have mixed feelings about the schools. Try to gain the support of these parents and make them partners in the education of their children.

13. Use cooperative learning techniques and group work to promote racial and ethnic integration in the school and classroom. Research indicates that when learning groups are racially integrated, students develop more friends from other racial groups, and race relations in the school improve. A helpful guide is Elizabeth G. Cohen's *Designing Groupwork: Strategies for the Heterogenous Classroom* (New York: Teachers College Press, 1986).

14. Make sure that school plays, pageants, cheerleading squads, school publications, and other formal and informal groups are racially integrated. Also make sure that various ethnic and racial groups have equal status in school performances and presentations. In a multiracial school, if all of the leading roles in a school play are filled by White characters, an important message is sent to students and parents of color whether such a message was intended or not.

SUMMARY

In this chapter, I describe the nature of the mainstream-centric curriculum and the negative consequences it has for both mainstream students and students of color. This curriculum reinforces the false sense of superiority of mainstream students and fails to reflect, validate, and celebrate the cultures of students of color. Many factors have slowed the institutionalization of a multicultural curriculum in the schools, including ideological resistance, lack of teacher knowledge of ethnic groups, and the heavy reliance of teachers on textbooks.

Four approaches to the integration of ethnic content into the curriculum are identified in this chapter. In the *contributions approach,* heroes, cultural components, holidays, and other discrete elements related to ethnic groups are added to the curriculum without changing its structure. The *additive approach* consists of the addition of content, concepts, themes, and perspectives to the curriculum, with its structure remaining unchanged. In the *transformation approach,* the structure, goals, and nature of the curriculum are changed to enable students to view concepts, issues, and problems from diverse ethnic perspectives. The *social action approach* includes all elements of the transformation approach, as well as elements that enable students to identify important social issues, gather data related to them, clarify their values, make reflective decisions, and take actions to implement their decisions. This approach seeks to make students social critics and reflective agents of change. The final part of this chapter presents guidelines to help you teach ethnic content and to function more effectively in multiethnic classrooms and schools.

QUESTIONS AND ACTIVITIES

1. What is a mainstream-centric curriculum? What are its major assumptions and goals?

2. Examine several textbooks and find examples of the mainstream-centric approach. Share these examples with colleagues in your class or workshop.

3. How does a mainstream-centric curriculum influence mainstream students and students of color?

4. According to Banks, what factors have slowed the development of a multicultural curriculum in the schools? What is the best way to overcome these factors?

5. What are the major characteristics of the following approaches to curriculum reform: the contributions approach; the additive approach; the transformation approach; the social action approach?

6. Why do you think the contributions approach to curriculum reform is so popular and widespread within schools, especially in the primary and elementary grades?

7. In what fundamental way do the transformation and social action approaches differ from the other two approaches identified above?

8. What are the problems and promises of each of the four approaches?

9. What does the author mean by "multiple acculturation"? Do you think this concept is valid? Why or why not?

10. What problems might a teacher encounter when trying to implement the transformation and social action approaches? How might these problems be overcome?

11. Assume that you are teaching a social studies lesson about the westward movement in U.S. history and a student makes a racist, sterotypic, or misleading statement about Native Americans, such as, "The Indians were hostile to the White settlers." How would you handle this situation? Give reasons to explain why you would handle it in a particular way.

12. Develop a teaching plan in which you illustrate how you would teach a unit incorporating elements of the transformation and social action approaches to curriculum reform.

NOTES

1. Stephen Diaz, "Learning Styles and Teaching Styles." Paper presented at the institute *Increasing the Academic Achievement of Minority Students,* sponsored by the Educational Materials and Services Center, Bellevue, Wash., July 1987.

2. James A. Banks, *Multiethnic Education: Theory and Practice,* 2d ed. (Boston: Allyn and Bacon, 1988).

3. Diane Ravitch, "Diversity and Democracy: Multicultural Education in America," *American Educator* (Spring 1990): 16–48; Arthur M. Schlesinger, Jr., *The Disuniting of America: Reflections on a Multicultural Society* (Knoxville, Tenn.: Whittle Direct Books, 1991).

4. Molefi Kete Asante, "The Afrocentric Idea in Education," *Journal of Negro Education* 60, 2 (1991): 170–180; Molefi Kete Asante and Diane Ravitch, "Multiculturalism: An Exchange," *The American Scholar* 60, 2 (Spring 1991): 267–276.

5. Bhikhu Parekh, "The Concept of Multicultural Education," in Sohan Modgil, Gajendra K. Verma, Kanka Mallick, and Celia Modgil, eds., *Multicultural Education: The Interminable Debate* (London: Falmer Press, 1986), pp. 19–31; James A. Banks, "Multicultural Literacy and Curriculum Reform," *Educational Horizons* 69, 3 (Spring 1991): 135–140.

6. John I. Goodlad, *A Place Called School* (New York: McGraw-Hill, 1984); *The Current State of Social Studies: A Report of Project SPAN* (Boulder, Colo.: Social Science Education Consortium, 1982).

7. Jesus Garcia and Julie Goebel, "A Comparative Study of the Portrayal of Black Americans in Selected U.S. History Books," *Negro Educational Review* 36 (1985): 118–127.

8. James S. Coleman, Ernest Q. Campbell, Carol J. Hobson, James McPartland, Alexander M. Mood, Frederic D. Weinfeld, and Robert L. York, *Equality of Educational Opportunity* (Washington, D.C.: U.S. Government Printing Office, 1966).

9. John G. Neihardt, *Black Elk Speaks* (New York: Pocket Books, 1972), p. 230.

10. "Black Elk's Prayer from a Mountaintop in the Black Hills, 1931," in Jack D. Forbes, ed., *The Indian in America's Past* (Englewood Cliffs, N.J.: Prentice-Hall, 1964), p. 69.

11. James Baldwin, *The Price of the Ticket: Collected Nonfiction 1948–1985* (New York: St. Martin's Press, 1985).

12. William Loren Katz, *Black Indians: A Hidden Heritage* (New York: Atheneum, 1986).

13. Geneva Gay and James A. Banks, "Teaching the American Revolution: A Multiethnic Approach," *Social Education* 39 (November–December 1975): 461–465.

14. Selections by most of these writers are reprinted in Henry Knepler and Myrna Knepler, eds., *Crossing Cultures: Readings for Composition* (New York: Macmillan, 1983); see also Paul Lauter et al., eds., *The Heath Anthology of American Literature,* Vol. 2 (Lexington, Mass.: D.C. Heath and Company, 1990).

15. Banks, *Multiethnic Education,* 128–130.

16. See, for example, Dorothy Abbott, ed., *Mississippi Writers: Reflections on Childhood and Youth,* II: *Nonfiction* (Jackson: University Press of Mississippi, 1986).

17. Fred N. Newmann, "Discussion: Political Socialization in the Schools," *Harvard Educational Review* 38 (1968): 536–545.

18. Reprinted with permission from James A. Banks, *Teaching Strategies for Ethnic Studies,* 5th ed. (Boston: Allyn and Bacon, 1987), p. 220.

19. Gordon W. Allport, *The Nature of Prejudice,* 25th anniversary ed. (Reading, Mass.: Addison-Wesley, 1979).

20. James A. Banks, "Multicultural Education: Its Effects on Students' Racial and Gender Role Attitudes," in James P. Shaver, ed., *Handbook on Research on Social Studies Teaching and Learning* (New York: Macmillan, 1991), pp. 459–469.

21. Alice Walker, *The Color Purple* (New York: Harcourt Brace, 1982); Mildred Taylor, *Roll of Thunder, Hear My Cry* (New York: Dial, 1976).

22. Reginald M. Clark, *Family Life and School Achievement: Why Poor Black Children Succeed or Fail* (Chicago: University of Chicago Press, 1983).

CHAPTER 11

Language Diversity and Education

■ CARLOS J. OVANDO

"Language is a shared and sharing part of culture that cares little about formal classifications and much about vitality and connection, for culture itself perishes in purity or isolation."
                                                      Carlos Fuentes[1]

Language diversity has a strong influence on the content and process of schooling practices for both language minority and majority students in the United States. Language, as a system of communication linking sound, written or visual symbols, and meaning, is an indispensable bridge for accessing knowledge, skills, values, and attitudes within and across cultures. It has tremendous power as the paramount instrument of cognitive development, and it can open or close the door to academic achievement. How, then, is the educational inequality experienced by language minority students related to their inability to understand, speak, read, and write standard English in the curriculum?

To present an overview of how language diversity is related to educational outcomes, this chapter is organized in three sections. In the first section we consider what language is and how children and adults acquire their first and second languages. In the second section we survey varieties of nonstandard English as well as non–English-language diversity in the United States. In the third section we address classroom adaptations to meet the needs of language minority students.

THE SOCIOCULTURAL NATURE OF LANGUAGE AND LANGUAGE ACQUISITION

Language is an important part of culture. As with culture, language is learned, it is shared, and it evolves and changes over time. Language can be analyzed from many different points of view. For instance, at the physical level, it is a system of sounds and movements made by the human body and decoded by the listener's auditory system. From the psychological or cognitive point of view, it is a tool for the expression of thought. From the anthropological point of view, it is an intricate and pervasive component of culture. Language can also be studied as a system of signs and symbols that have socially determined meanings.[2]

Language is much more than a set of words and grammar rules. It is a forceful instrument for giving individuals, groups, institutions, and cultures their identity. Through language we share and exchange our values, attitudes, skills, and aspirations as bearers of culture and as makers of future culture.

From the pedagogical point of view, what has an individual learned when he or she is said to have gained communicative competence in a particular language? To begin with, there are the more familiar domains of language:

1. Phonetics and phonology—learning how to pronounce the language
2. Morphology—the study and description of word formation
3. Syntax—the grammar of sentence formation
4. Lexicon (the vocabulary)

Beyond these, however, are the five culture-related domains to be mastered for communicative competence. These domains illustrate the subtleties and cultural components of the process of learning a language.

1. Discourse: How the language is organized in speech and writing beyond the sentence level (for example, topic sentence and supporting details).

2. Appropriateness: The kind of language use according to the social situation (for example, "Hit the lights, will ya?" versus "Would you mind turning the lights off, please?").

3. Paralinguistics: Gestures, facial expressions, distance between speakers, intonation, and volume and pitch of speech.

4. Pragmatics: Brings together discourse, appropriateness, and paralinguistics. For example, pragmatics have to do with implicit cultural norms for when it is and is not appropriate to talk, how speech is paced, the correct way to listen, when to be direct and when to be indirect, how to take turns in conversation, and how to adapt language according to roles, social status, attitudes, settings, and topics.

5. Cognitive-academic language proficiency: Mastery of the language skills needed to learn and develop abstract concepts in such areas as mathematics, science, and social studies.[3]

Even such a cursory listing of these skills and domains clearly suggests that language acquisition is a complicated, subtle, and culture-specific process. Educators thus need to realize that the difference between English and Spanish, for example, or even between standard English and Black English, is much more than a difference in pronunciation, grammar, and vocabulary. We could also argue that learning basic communication in one's first language is a simple process—child's play, so to speak. However, when examined carefully, even one's full development of the first language—including literacy skills and knowledge about the structure and function of the language—is a sophisticated endeavor that takes years to master. Knowing this, teachers are more likely to develop respect for and sensitivity to students who arrive in the classroom speaking anything other than standard English. For non-English speakers in particular, teachers should be realistic as to the years of exposure it takes speakers to move from basic communication in English to full communicative competence.

Languages grow and develop as tools of communication within a given environment. In this sense, there is no such thing as "right" or "wrong" language, only language that is appropriate or inappropriate in a given context. Languages and language varieties develop and thrive because they meet the needs of communities. If a given community of speakers finds it necessary to maintain a language because it satisfies spiritual, social, intellectual, technical, scientific, economic, or political needs, then the chances that that particular linguistic community will survive are greatly enhanced. Thus, for example, Yupik (an Eskimo Aleut language spoken by the Yupik, a group of Eskimos) is alive in Akiachak, Alaska, despite the powerful influence of English, because it fulfills the people's need for continuity with their heritage. Within the domain of English itself, the United States teems with a variety of linguistic microcultures representing a diversity of experiences: American Indian varieties of English, Creoles, Black English, and a broad array of regional accents, vocabularies, and styles.

Because multicultural education seeks to promote equity and excellence across such variables as race, ethnicity, nationality, gender, social class, regional groups, religion, exceptionality, literacy background, age, and language background, educators must understand the function language can play in either helping or inhibiting the educational fulfillment of individuals. As Dell Hymes states,

> The law of the land demands that equal educational opportunity not be denied because of language. "Language" has been understood most readily in terms of "languages," such as Spanish, and structurally definable varieties of a language, such as Black English Vernacular. If one defines "language," as I do, in terms of ways of speaking, as involving both structure and ways of using structure, there are even deeper implications, implications not yet legally explored. One's language affects one's chances in life, not only through accent, but also through action. Access to opportunities in the form of access to schools, jobs, positions, memberships, clubs, homes, may depend on ways of using language that one has no chance to master, or chooses not to master.[4]

Within and outside the school setting, it becomes important to consider how persons come to acquire and value the particular types of first and second languages they prefer to use in formal and informal situations. Therefore, we now turn to research on first and second language acquisition and its application in classrooms. We focus here on the process by which non-English speakers acquire English language skills.

For the past twenty years, linguists and cognitive psychologists have made considerable progress in understanding first and second language acquisition. The research indicates that language learning is a developmental process that goes through predictable stages. We acquire our first language as children, in the context of a natural, interesting, and meaningful interaction with the social and physical environment. In such an environment, the child is exposed day after day to peer and adult language models in a context that gives meaning to language. Because of this strongly contextualized environment, speakers tend to learn communication shortcuts such as incomplete responses, a limited vocabulary, and many nonverbal cues.

Cummins refers to this type of language as basic interpersonal communicative skills (BICS) and suggests that an average non–English-speaking student can learn to communicate at this level in English after about two years of instruction in an acquisition-rich environment similar to that of a child learning a first language.[5] This ability to get along in the world conversationally enables students limited in English proficiency to make everyday conversational contact with their English-speaking peers. Such contact, in turn, provides a pivotal function in the acculturation of such students, especially to the school culture. In addition, such face-to-face communication serves as an initial platform for building a self-concept in social relationships. In other words, the acquisition of BICS serves a powerful and important sociolinguistic function in the lives of persons learning their second languages.

However, even though a student of limited English proficiency may seem to be making rapid progress in the acquisition of English judging from the informal observations in the social environment of the school setting, such control of BICS does not necessarily equip the student for the curriculum's more cognitively demanding tasks. Cognitive tasks require a second developmental level beyond BICS that consists of the language used in school and many facets of adult life. Here, the context is less clear; instead, communication depends on a speaker's (or writer's) ability to manipulate the vocabulary and syntax with precision.[6] Again, research by Cummins indicates that, as measured in standardized tests, children with little or no prior schooling experience attain nativelike control of English in cognitive-academic language proficiency (CALP) in about five to seven years.[7]

Just as speakers of nonstandard varieties of English come to school with a wealth of home experience that can be tapped by the teacher, non-English speakers also come to school not as a blank tablet but with a vast array of skills that can be drawn on. Again, Cummins's research[8] concludes that prior acquired knowledge and skills in the home language transfer automatically to the new language. This is known as the common underlying proficiency (CUP) for both languages. Of importance to language minority educators is Cummins's conclusion on the instructional use of both the home language (L1) and English (L2):

> The results of research on bilingual programs show that minority children's L1 can be promoted in school at no cost to the development of proficiency in the majority language. . . .
> The data clearly show that well-implemented bilingual programs have had remarkable success in developing English academic skills and have proved superior to ESL-only programs in situations where direct comparisons have been carried out.[9]

Thus, native language support can provide a base for skills development that is comprehensible to students. This development can then be applied to their academic and language growth in English. A highly significant longitudinal study conducted by Ramírez[10] for the United States Department of Education compared the relative effectiveness of structured English immersion strategy and late-exit transitional bilingual education with early-exit transitional bilingual education. The results of this study clearly support the advantages of sustained native language instruction. As Ramírez notes, *providing limited English proficient (LEP) students with substantial amounts (i.e., greater than or equal to 40%) of native language instruction not only does not impede their acquisition of English language and reading skills, but there is some support to the hypothesis that primary language instruction may facilitate the acquisition of content area skills such as mathematics.[11]*

LANGUAGE VARIETY IN THE UNITED STATES

As a language laboratory, the United States is truly remarkable. To date, about 206 Native American languages have survived the overwhelming assimilative powers of the English language.[12] Languages other than English used by the colonizers of the United States—such as Spanish and French—continue not only to survive but also to serve as lively communicative and cultural instruments in various regions of the country. The successive waves of immigrants to the United States made the nation linguistically rich. The language assets range from such languages as Navajo—still spoken today in the same communities in which it was spoken hundreds of years ago—to Hmong, spoken by recent refugees from the highlands of Laos and Cambodia.

In addition to the varied mix of languages, language contact in the United States has produced many indigenous language varieties known as creole, pidgin, and dialect. Creole is the adoption of a pidgin as the accepted language of a community. As Anttila puts it, "this happened often on the plantations of the New World, where slaves from different language backgrounds were forced to use a pidgin among themselves, and between themselves and the masters. After escape, freedom, or revolution the pidgin was all they had, and it had to become the first language of the community."[13] Three examples of creole varieties in the United States are (1) Gullah, an English- and West African–based creole spoken on the Sea Islands, from the Carolinas to northern Florida; (2) Louisiana French Creole, which coexists with two local varieties of French and another local variety of English; and (3) Hawaiian Creole, which has been influenced by Hawaiian, Japanese, Chinese, Portuguese, English, and Ilocano. Complementing the rich indigenous creole traditions of the United States is Black English, spoken by a large segment of the African American population.

As noted earlier, Gullah is geographically associated with African Americans who initially settled in South Carolina in the 1700s. Nichols estimates that there are now about 300,000 African Americans who speak Gullah in an area including South Carolina, Georgia, and parts of lower North Carolina and Northern Florida.[14] Ties between Gullah and its West African language ancestors include similar vowel sounds and some vocabulary items, such as *goober* for "peanut," *cooter* for "turtle," and *buckra* for "White man."[15] Structurally, Gullah also differs from standard English. For example, instead of using *he* and *she,* the neuter pronoun *ee* is used for both male and female. *Fuh* is used to indicate an infinitive clause, as in "I came *fuh* get my coat." Progressive action can be indicated by *duh* plus the verb: "Greg duh hide" instead of "Greg is hiding."[16]

Most members of the Gullah-speaking community are not strictly creole speakers. What is found instead are individuals "who show greater or lesser use of creole features along a continuum of language use ranging from creole to a dialect of English."[17] Not surprisingly, there is a strong association of Gullah use with age and amount of formal schooling. For example, the very old and the very young tend to use Gullah more extensively. Young school-age children tend to switch back and forth between Gullah—referred to as "country talk"—and the prestige variety of standard English, especially for the benefit of teachers, who usually do not understand Gullah.

Gullah has been analyzed extensively by linguists, and much is known about its phonology, grammar, vocabulary, and sociolinguistic usage. Gullah has also been popularized through literature such as the stories of Ambrose Gonzalez[18] and the novels and Gullah sketches of Pulitzer Prize winner Julia Peterkin.[19] Yet the children who speak Gullah have been stigmatized in the schools, and there has not been a vigorous effort to incorporate their language into the curriculum to create bridges to standard English. To date, no curricular materials have been written in Gullah. Although some teachers are addressing literacy development for such children by using the language-experience approach, by and large such creole-speaking children may not be receiving equal educational opportunities in classrooms in which standard English is the accepted medium of instruction.

Like Gullah, Louisiana French Creole reflects a linguistic structure that sets it apart from English. Louisiana Creole speakers may have difficulty understanding English, and vice versa. Louisiana French Creole, a contemporary of Gullah, supposedly evolved via West African slaves who were introduced by French colonists to Southern Louisiana and needed a common language to communicate with each other. Louisiana French Creole has structural similarities with English-related creoles such as Gullah. For example, the pronoun *li* is used for both *he* and *she*. Also, like Gullah, no verb "to be" is used in equative clauses. However, unlike Gullah, most of the Louisiana French Creole vocabulary is derived from French rather than from English, with some use of African vocabulary items.[20]

Although Acadian and standard French are officially affirmed in the school curriculum, Louisiana French Creole does not seem to have the same status. As with Gullah, children who speak Louisiana French Creole therefore run the risk of not receiving equal educational opportunities. Furthermore, they and their parents may interpret the neglect of their primary language as a devaluation of their sociolinguistic background in the eyes of school personnel and society at large.

A recent newcomer into the family of indigenous creoles in U.S. society is Hawaiian Creole, the use of which dates back to the late nineteenth or early twentieth century. Unlike Louisiana Creole, there is considerably more careful scholarly documentation about its origin, structure, and function.[21] Hawaiian Creole evolved as a pidgin during the late nineteenth century, when plantations were developed and the Hawaiian Islands came under the influence of English speakers from the United States mainland. Similar to Gullah, Hawaiian Creole is English-related, and its lexicon is predominantly English, with the aforementioned influence from Hawaiian, Japanese, Chinese, Portugese, and Ilocano. This rich linguistic mixture in the Hawaiian Islands has led language scholars to view Hawaiian English "in terms of three coexistent systems—a pidgin, Creole, and dialect of English—none of which occurs in unadulterated forms but only in combinations of different proportions."[22]

Whether Hawaiian English is a dialect of English or a creole language is a complex issue. Somewhat like Gullah, its degree of similarity to English ranges on a continuum depending on the community and the context. For example, linguists note a highly decreolized language variety in the more urbanized population centers like Oahu and more creolized traditional patterns in the more remote islands of Kauai and Hawaii.[23]

In any event, Hawaiian Creole is a lively language that plays a key role in the lives of many Hawaiian children both socially and academically. As with Gullah and Louisiana French Creole, Hawaiian Creole, or Pidgin English, as it is known by island residents, is a highly stigmatized language variety that until the 1970s had been singled out by educational policymakers as a cause of the many academic problems experienced by Hawaiian students. According to Nichols, the policy was to decreolize the students' language. Because such a posture toward Hawaiian Creole did not produce the desired result of eliminating it from the lives of students, education policies since then have tended toward acceptance of the language in the lives of the students. However, there is still a sense that it is a "deficient language" and thus in need of correction.[24] The attempt in Hawaii to eradicate Hawaiian Creole confirms once more that when something as important as a language is threatened, its users tend to protect and defend it. This is what happened in the islands, where Hawaiian Creole speakers began to see their use of creole as an important symbol of solidarity in their community.

Black English, although a dialect of English rather than a creole language, shows parallels in historical development with creole languages. Black English reflects influence from British and American English as well as English-based pidgin from sixteenth-century West Africa. In situations involving language contact, one has to understand the nature of the social relationships within and outside the involved communities. Slave-master relationships were not generally conducive to a trusting and caring communicative process. But it is in this type of socially strained context that Black English and White English coexisted and influenced each other. From the late 1700s until the early 1900s, approximately 90 percent of the United States' African American population lived in the Southern states.[25] With such a high concentration of speakers, Black English was able to mature into a highly sophisticated and rule-governed "subsystem within the larger grammar of English."[26]

Unlike Gullah, Louisiana French Creole, and Hawaiian Creole, Black English spread throughout the United States. In the twentieth century, many African Americans began to migrate to the large urban centers of the North. Through this two-way connection between Black communities in the rural South and the industrial North, Black English emerged. As Whatley observes, "Funerals, homecoming celebrations at churches, and family reunions took northerners 'down home' at least annually."[27] Strong regional and familial ties between the rural South and the industrial North generated much cross-fertilization of old and new communication patterns.

On the other hand, de facto segregation in the large urban centers of the North tended to insulate African American and White communities from each other. That meant that, given the social distance created between the speakers of Black English and White English, both languages had minimal influence on one another. Thus, Black English tended to continue developing its own set of structures, functional patterns, and styles.

Despite the presence of Black English throughout the United States, the perception of Whites and others as to what Black English is may be highly distorted. As Whatley points out, much of what the nation has come to understand as Black English has come about through Hollywood and the electronic media, with all their distortions and stereotypic tendencies. Thus, the world of entertainment has given White society an opportunity to observe highly stylized Black speech—*jiving, copping, playing the dozens, boasting, preaching,* and *fussing*—within a family entertainment format. However, the impression television, radio, theater, and musicals have given White audiences regarding Black communities is just the tip of the linguistic iceberg. As Whatley indicates, there are many uses of Black English other than those portrayed in the media.[28]

As with any other language, there is great speech variation among speakers of Black English. Also, speech behavior is highly contextualized. That is, individuals tend to assess the communicative situation and respond accordingly. Most people speak a variety of English in their daily lives, ranging on continua of degrees of formality and social status. Within the African American experience, praising, fussing, teasing, lying, preaching, jiving, boasting, or joking are carefully determined by the age, gender, and status of speakers. For example, the eldest members of the African American community tend to have greater latitude and prestige in language use, and children are the lowest-ranking members of the speech community. This, of course, does not mean that African American children are not allowed to interact with adults in creative and expressive ways. What it does mean, however, is that there is a certain speech protocol that is sensitive to such variables as age, social status, gender, and formal and informal settings.

Because of African Americans' historical status as an oppressed minority, Whites have tended to perceive Black English not as a valid linguistic system, but rather as "a mass of random errors committed by Blacks trying to speak English."[29] The language variety used by African Americans, however, has an internal linguistic infrastructure and a set of grammar rules just as any other language does. For example, the use of the verb "to be" follows different rules in Black English than in standard English. Speakers of standard English tend to contract forms of the verb "to be," as in the sentence, "She's tall" instead of "She is tall." Black English deletes "is" entirely so that the sentence becomes "She tall." Black English also has a use for "be" that standard English does not. The sentences "He always be walkin' on a desert on TV" and "He jus' be walkin' dere sometime" use what linguists call the "invariant be." This use of the verb refers to action that takes place habitually over a period of time, and for this there is no exact standard English equivalent.[30]

Multiple negation is perhaps one of the most stigmatized aspects of Black English when speakers enter the formal school system. Yet there are no logical bases for such stigmatization. Acceptance or nonacceptance of the double negative as a socially correct form is essentially a historical accident. According to language scholars, multiple negation was an integral part of the English language up to the time of Shakespeare. Also, it is useful to know that although Latin is credited for having influenced the single negation in English, other Romance

(a) Content is based on the students' communicative needs; (b) instruction makes extensive use of contextual clues; (c) the teacher uses only English, but modifies speech to students' level and confirms student comprehension; (d) students are permitted to respond in their native language when necessary; (e) the focus is on language function or content, rather than grammatical form; (f) grammatical accuracy is promoted, not by correcting errors overtly, but by providing more comprehensible instruction; and (g) students are encouraged to respond spontaneously and creatively.[54]

5. The social status implicitly ascribed to students and their languages affects student performance. Therefore, majority and minority students should be in classes together in which cooperative learning strategies are used. English speakers should be provided with opportunities to learn the minority languages, and teachers and administrators should model using the minority languages for some noninstructional as well as instructional purposes.[55]

As noted earlier, there are no instructional panaceas for addressing the cognitive, linguistic, and cultural needs of stigmatized language minority students. But these five principles and their practical implications can help educators who are genuinely interested in putting into practice in their classrooms what we have learned over the past twenty years or so about how people acquire their first and second languages, learn in their primary and secondary languages, and adjust socioculturally to the dominant culture.

Language diversity, as a powerful and ubiquitous ingredient of the U.S. multicultural mosaic, enriches the lives of those who use such languages and the lives of those privileged to come into contact with them. As educators we need to assure that the rich and varied sociolinguistic experiences of language minorities do not continue to be translated into negative cognitive, cultural, and linguistic outcomes. As suggested in this chapter, we now have some of the conceptual, programmatic, and curricular tools with which to begin the job.

SUMMARY

Throughout this chapter I stress the power that language issues have to affect schooling outcomes for language minority students. In the first section I discuss how language is interwoven with cultural styles and values. As such, language comprises more than grammar rules, vocabulary, and a sound system. To have communicative competence in a language requires not only these things but also the appropriate facial and body gestures, use of varying levels of formality in the appropriate contexts, correct styles of conversation, and the ability to express abstract concepts.

By studying how children learn language, linguists and cognitive psychologists have determined that language learning is a developmental process that goes through predictable stages. Cummins has identified two levels of language proficiency that are particularly important when designing educational programs for limited-English-proficient (LEP) students: basic interpersonal communicative skills (BICS), which take approximately two years to obtain; and cognitive-academic language proficiency (CALP), which may take five to seven years to achieve. Equally important is the common underlying proficiency (CUP), the concept that skills learned in the first language will automatically transfer to the second language.

The second section of the chapter surveys the extensive nature of language variety in the United States. An examination of nonstandard English and creole languages emphasizes that language changes fulfill sociohistorical needs. Likewise, the language varieties resulting from these changes have their own grammatical and phonological rules and appropriate cultural styles. The number of students from non-English-speaking backgrounds continues to increase in the United States, and these students are present in significant numbers in every state.

In the final section of the chapter I describe some principles and methods for instruction of language minority students. In nonstandard English varieties, the home language cannot be blamed for school failure. The more likely cause for language-related school failure is the educator's negating approach toward the home language. Through an additive process, the value of the home language can be affirmed while models are also provided for use of the standard language in appropriate contexts.

For students who come from non-English-speaking backgrounds, an active teaching style rather than a lecture style is needed, with frequent checking for understanding. Skills should continue to be developed in the home language while the students are also studying English as a second language (ESL). Regarding ESL instruction, basic interpersonal communicative skills are not sufficient for academic success. Schools must continue to provide support for limited-English-proficient students to achieve cognitive-academic language proficiency.

Finally, there is a need for the continued development and maintenance of social and cultural bridges between the language minority student's home life and school life. An awareness of how language is used in the home community will enable educators to be sensitive to school genres that are different. Efforts to equalize the social and language status of majority and minority students within the school setting will also produce positive results for all students in the classroom, and ultimately, in society.

QUESTIONS AND ACTIVITIES

1. What are some of the major characteristics of a language? What role does language play in the maintenance of a culture?

2. How can teachers draw on the home experiences of non-English speakers and speakers of nonstandard varieties of English to help these students develop competence in standard English?

3. What is creolization? Name three creole varieties in the United States.

4. What is Black English? What are some of its major characteristics? What common misconceptions about Black English are held by some educators?

To what extent is Black English spoken by African Americans? How can a knowledge of the nature of Black English be helpful to teachers of African American students?

5. What are Gullah and Hawaiian Creole? What problems do the speakers of these creole languages experience in schools? Why?

6. Prepare a report on the 1974 *Lau v. Nichols* Supreme Court Decision for presentation in your class or workshop. How has this court decision influenced bilingual education programs in the United States? Why is this decision controversial?

7. Visit an inner-city or suburban school in a nearby school district. Find out how many different languages are spoken by the students in the district when they first come to school and what programs are being implemented to deal with the language diversity of the students.

8. What special problems do limited-English-proficient students experience in schools? What programs and practices can schools implement to help these students experience educational success?

9. Identify some principles the author describes for working effectively with dialect and language minority students. What support and training might teachers need to implement these principles in the classroom?

NOTES

1. Carlos Fuentes, *Myself with Others: Selected Essays* (New York: Farrar, Straus & Giroux, 1988), p. 27.

2. Sebastian Shaumyan, *A Semiotic Theory of Language* (Bloomington and Indianapolis: Indiana University Press, 1987), pp. 1–2.

3. Carlos J. Ovando and Virginia P. Collier, *Bilingual and ESL Classrooms: Teaching in Multicultural Contexts* (New York: McGraw-Hill, 1985), pp. 229–230.

4. Dell H. Hymes, "Foreword," in Charles A. Ferguson and Shirley Brice Heath, eds., *Language in the USA* (Cambridge, Mass.: Cambridge University Press, 1981), pp. vii–viii.

5. Jim Cummins, "The Role of Primary Language Development in Promoting Educational Success for Language Minority Students," in California State Department of Education, *Schooling and Language Minority Students: A Theoretical Framework* (Los Angeles: National Evaluation, Dissemination, and Assessment Center, California State University, 1981), p. 16.

6. Carlos J. Ovando, "Bilingual/Bicultural Education: Its Legacy and Its Future," *Phi Delta Kappan* 64, No. 8 (April 1983): 566.

7. Cummins, *Schooling and Language Minority Students*, 16.

8. Ibid., 23–25.

9. Ibid., 28.

10. J. David Ramírez, Sandra D. Yuen, and Dena R. Ramey, *Executive Summary Final Report: Longitudinal Study of Structured English Immersion Strategy, Early-Exit and Late-Exit Transitional Bilingual Education Programs for Language-Minority Children*, Contract No. 300–87–0156 (Washington, D.C.: U.S. Department of Education, February 1991).

11. David Ramírez, "Study Finds Native Language Instruction Is a Plus," *NABE News* 14, No. 5 (March 15, 1991): 1.

12. William L. Leap, "American Indian Languages," in Charles A. Ferguson and Shirley Brice Heath, eds., *Language in the USA* (Cambridge, Mass.: Cambridge University Press, 1981), p. 116.

13. Raimo Anttila, *An Introduction to Historical and Comparative Linguistics* (New York: Macmillan, 1972), p. 176.

14. Patricia Nichols, "Creoles of the USA," in Charles A. Ferguson and Shirley Brice Heath, eds., *Language in the USA* (Cambridge, Mass.: Cambridge University Press, 1981), p. 73.

15. Ibid., 75.

16. Ibid., 73–75.

17. Ibid., 73.

18. Ibid., 75.

19. Ibid.

20. Ibid., 79.

21. Ibid., 83.

22. Ibid.

23. Ibid.

24. Ibid., 86.

25. Elizabeth Whatley, "Language among Black Americans," in Charles A. Ferguson and Shirley Brice Heath, eds., *Language in the USA* (Cambridge, Mass.: Cambridge University Press, 1981), p. 104.

26. William Labov, *Language in the Inner City: Studies in the Black English Vernacular* (Philadelphia: University of Pennsylvania Press, 1972), p. 64.

27. Whatley, *Language in the USA,* 94.

28. Ibid., 95.

29. William Labov, Paul Cohen, Clarence Robins, and John Lewis, *A Study of the Non-Standard English of Negro and Puerto Rican Speakers in New York City,* Rept. on Cooperative Research Project 3288 (New York: Columbia University, 1968).

30. Whatley, *Language in the USA,* 102.

31. Ibid., 103.

32. Ibid., 99.

33. Ibid., 30.

34. James V. Wertsch, *Vygotsky and the Social Formation of Mind* (Cambridge, Mass.: Harvard University Press, 1985).

35. Ferguson and Brice Heath, *Language in the USA,* xxxi.

36. Carlos E. Cortes, "The Education of Language Minority Students: A Contextual Interaction Model," in California State Department of Education, *Beyond Language: Social and Cultural Factors in Schooling Language Minority Students* (Los Angeles: Evaluation, Dissemination, and Assessment Center, California State University, 1986), pp. 8–9.

37. James A. Banks, *Teaching Strategies for Ethnic Studies,* 5th ed. (Boston: Allyn and Bacon, 1987).

38. Cortes, *Beyond Language,* 9.

39. Ibid., 10.

40. Dorothy Waggoner, "Basic Questions Spur Controversy," *Education Week* 6, 27 (April 1, 1987): 25.

41. Louis G. Pol, Rebecca Oxford-Carpenter, and Samuel Peng, "Limited English-Proficiency: Analytical Techniques and Projections," in Eugene C. Garcia and Raymond V. Padilla, eds., *Advances in Bilingual Education Research* (Tucson: The University of Arizona Press, 1985), p. 259.

42. Daniel M. Ulibarri, "Issues in Estimates of the Number of Limited English Proficient Students," in *A Report of the Compendium of Papers on the Topic of Bilingual Education of the Committee on Education and Labor House of Representatives,* 99th Congress, 2D Session (Washington, D.C.: U.S. Government Printing Office, 1986), p. 57.

43. Gary A. Griffin and Susan Barnes, "Using Research Findings to Change School and Classroom Practices: Results of an Experimental Study," *American Educational Research Journal* 23, No. 4 (Winter 1986): 573–574.

44. Ovando and Collier, *Bilingual and ESL Classrooms,* 69.

45. Jane W. Torrey, "Black Children's Knowledge of Standard English," *American Educational Research Journal* 20, No. 4 (Winter 1983), p. 627.

46. Reynaldo F. Macias, *"Teacher Preparation for Bilingual Education,"* in *A Report of the Copendium of Papers on the Topic of Bilingual Education of the Committee on Education and Labor House of Representatives,* 99th Congress, 2D Session (Washington, D.C.: U.S. Government Printing Office, 1986), pp. 43–44.

47. Ibid.

48. Rudolph C. Troike, "Improving Conditions for Success in Bilingual Education Programs," in *A Report of the Compendium,* 2.

49. Marianne Celce-Murcia and Diane Larsen-Freeman, *The Grammar Book: An ESL/EFL Teacher's Course* (Rowley, Mass.: Newbury House, 1983), p. 1.

50. Shirley Brice Heath, "Sociocultural Contexts of Language Development," in California State Department of Education, *Beyond Language:*

Social & Cultural Factors in Schooling Language Minority Students (Los Angeles: National Evaluation, Dissemination, and Assessment Center, California State University, 1986), p. 145.

51. Virginia P. Collier, "Age and Rate of Acquisition of Cognitive-Academic Second Language Proficiency." Paper presented at the American Educational Research Association Meeting, April 23, 1987), p. 12.

52. Brice Heath, "Sociocultural Contexts of Language Development," p. 166.

53. Ibid., 168–170.

54. James Crawford, "Bilingual Education: Language, Learning, and Politics," *Education Week: A Special Report* (April 1, 1987): 43.

55. Ibid., 43.

Students with disabilities as well as those with special gifts and talents have unique gifts and talents that educators need to recognize and respond to.

PART FIVE

Exceptionality

Expanded rights for students with disabilities was one major consequence of the civil rights movement of the 1960s and 1970s. The Supreme Court's *Brown* decision, issued in 1954, established the principle that to segregate students solely because of their race is inherently unequal and unconstitutional. This decision, as well as other legal and social reforms of the 1960s, encouraged advocates for the rights of students with disabilities to push for expanded rights for them. If it were unconstitutional to segregate students because of their race, it was reasoned, segregating students because they were disabled could also be challenged.

The advocates for the rights of students with disabilities experienced a major victory in 1975 when Congress enacted Public Law 94-142, The Education for All Handicapped Children Act. This act was unprecedented and revolutionary in its implications. It requires free public education for all children with disabilities, nondiscriminatory evaluation, and an individualized education program (IEP) for each student with a disability, and it stipulates that each student with a disability should be educated in the least restricted environment. This last requirement has been one of the most controversial provisions of Public Law 94-142. Most students who are classified as disabled—about 90 percent—are mildly disabled. Consequently, most students with disabilities—about two-thirds—spend at least part of the school day in regular classrooms. Students with disabilities who are taught in the regular classroom are *mainstreamed;* this process is called *mainstreaming.*

Exceptionality intersects with factors such as gender and race or ethnicity in interesting and complex ways. Males and students of color are more frequently classified as special education students than are females and White mainstream students. Nearly twice as many males as females are classified as special education students. Consequently, males of color are the most likely group to be classified as mentally retarded or learning disabled. The higher proportion of males and students of color in special education programs is related to the fact that mental retardation is a socially constructed category (see Chapter 1).

Disabled as well as gifted students are considered *exceptional.* Exceptional students are those who have learning or behavioral characteristics that differ substantially from most other students and that require special attention in instruction. Concern for American students who are gifted and talented increased after the Soviet Union successfully launched Sputnik in 1957. A Gifted and Talented Children's Education Act was passed by Congress in 1978. However, the nation's concern for the gifted is ambivalent and controversial. In 1982, special funding for gifted education was consolidated with twenty-nine other educational programs. The controversy over gifted education stems in part from the belief by many people that it is elitist. Others argue that gifted education is a way for powerful mainstream parents to acquire a special education for their children in the public schools. The fact that few students of color are classified as gifted is another source of controversy. Despite the controversies that surround programs for gifted and talented youths, schools need to find creative and democratic ways to satisfy the needs of these students.

The chapters in this section describe the major issues, challenges, and promises involved in creating equal educational opportunities for students who are exceptional—those with mental retardation as well as those who are intellectually gifted and talented.

CHAPTER 12

Educational Equality for Students with Disabilities

■ **WILLIAM L. HEWARD and
RODNEY A. CAVANAUGH**

All children differ from one another in their physical attributes and in their ability to learn. Some are taller, some are stronger, some can run fast, and some cannot run at all. Some children learn quickly and can use what they have learned in new situations. Other children must be given repeated practice to master a simple task, and then they may have difficulty successfully completing the same task the next day. The differences among most children are relatively small, and most children can benefit from the general education program offered by their school. The physical attributes or learning abilities of some children, however, differ from the norm to such an extent that typical school curricula or teaching methods are not appropriate or effective. Individualized programs of special education are required to meet the needs of these children.

In this chapter, we briefly outline the history of exclusion and educational inequality experienced by many students with disabilities in U.S. schools. We also examine the progress during the past two decades that has led to federal legislation requiring that all children, regardless of the type or severity of their disability, be provided with appropriate educational opportunity. We look at the key features of this landmark law, the outcomes of its implementation, and the major barriers that still stand in the way of true educational equality for students with disabilities. But first, let us take a closer look at the concept of disability and find out how many students with disabilities there are.

WHO ARE STUDENTS WITH DISABILITIES?

The term *exceptional students* (or *exceptional children*) includes both children who have difficulty learning and children whose performance is so advanced that an individualized educational program is necessary to meet their needs.[1] Thus, *exceptional* is an inclusive term that includes both students who are severely disabled and students who are gifted and talented. Technically, the terms *disability* and *handicap* have different meanings. In practice, however, most professionals use the two words interchangeably. The term *disability* refers to the loss or

reduced function of a certain body part or organ; *impairment,* although technically referring to defective or diseased tissue, is often used synonymously with
disability. A child with a disability cannot perform certain tasks (e.g., walking,
speaking, seeing) in the same way in which most nondisabled children do. A
disability is not considered a handicap unless the disability results in educational,
personal, social, or other problems. For example, a child with one arm who can
function in and out of school without problems is not considered handicapped
for educational purposes.

Handicap refers to the difficulties a person with a disability experiences
when interacting with the environment. Some disabilities pose a handicap in
some environments but not in others. The child with only one arm may be
handicapped when playing with nondisabled classmates on the playground, but
having the use of only one arm might not pose a handicap in the classroom.
Unlike the term *exceptional children,* the term *handicapped children* does not
include students who are gifted and talented.

One more term is important to understanding educational equality for
students who are exceptional. Children not currently identified as handicapped
but who are considered to have a higher-than-normal chance of developing a
handicap are referred to as *at risk* or *high risk.* This term is used with infants and
preschoolers who, because of difficulties experienced at birth or conditions in the
home environment, may be expected to have developmental problems as they
grow older. Some educators also use the term to refer to students who are having
learning problems in the regular classroom and are therefore "at risk" of being
identified as handicapped and in need of special education services. Physicians
also use the terms *at risk* or *high risk* to identify pregnancies in which there is a
higher-than-usual probability of the baby's being born with a physical or developmental disability.

The physical and behavioral disabilities that adversely affect the learning
and development of students can be roughly classified into the following categories.

- Mental retardation or developmental disabilities[2]
- Learning disabilities[3,4]
- Behavior disorders or emotional disturbance[5]
- Communication (speech and language) disorders[6,7]
- Hearing impairments[8,9]
- Visual impairments[10]
- Physical and other health impairments[11]
- Severe and multiple disabilities[12,13]
- Autism[14]
- Traumatic brain injury[15]

It is beyond the purpose and scope of this chapter to describe the defining
characteristics and educational implications of each type of exceptionality. Interested readers can refer to the sources identified in the Notes to obtain sound and
current information about each area.

Regardless of the terms used to refer to students who experience differences in learning and development, it is incorrect to believe that there are two
kinds of students—those who are exceptional and those who are normal. All
children differ from one another to some extent; exceptional students are those
whose differences are significant enough to require a specially designed program

of instruction in order to achieve educational equality. We cannot state too strongly that students who are exceptional are more like other students than they are different from them. All students, whether considered exceptional or not, are unique individuals who deserve individual attention and nurturing. Yet *all* students are more like one another than they are different in that *all* students benefit from an education in which carefully selected curriculum content is taught through direct, systematic instruction.

Classification of Exceptional Students

The classification of students according to the various categories of exceptionality is done largely under the presumption that students in each category share certain physical, behavioral, and learning characteristics that hold important implications for planning and delivering educational services. It is a mistake, however, to believe that once a child has been identified as belonging to a certain disability category, his or her educational needs and how those needs should be met have also been identified.

The classification and labeling of exceptional students have been widely debated for many years. Some educators believe that a workable system of classification is necessary to obtain the special educational services and programs that are prerequisite to educational equality for exceptional students. Others argue that the classification and labeling of exceptional students serve only to exclude them from the mainstream of educational opportunity. The classification of exceptional students is a complex issue affected not only by educational considerations, but by social, political, and emotional concerns as well. Research conducted to assess the effects of labeling has been of little help, with most of the studies contributing inconclusive and contradictory evidence.[16] Here are the most common arguments given for and against the labeling of students who are exceptional.[17]

Possible Advantages of Labeling
- Categories can relate diagnosis to specific treatment.
- Labeling may lead to a protective response in which nonlabeled children accept certain behaviors of their peers with disabilities more fully than they would accept those same behaviors in normal children.
- Labeling helps professionals communicate with one another and to classify and assess research findings.
- Funding of special education programs is often based on specific categories of exceptionality.
- Labels allow special-interest groups to promote specific programs and to spur legislative action.
- Labeling helps make the special needs of exceptional children more visible in the public eye.

Possible Disadvantages of Labeling
- Labels usually focus on negative aspects of the child, causing other people to think about the child only in terms of inadequacies or defects.
- Labels may cause other people to react to and hold low expectations of a child based on the label, resulting in a self-fulfilling prophecy.

■ Labels may cause other people to react to and hold low expectations of a child based on the label, resulting in a self-fulfilling prophecy.

■ Labels that describe a child's performance deficit often mistakenly acquire the role of explanatory constructs (e.g., "Sherry acts that way because she is emotionally disturbed.").

■ Labels used to classify children in special education emphasize that learning problems are primarily the result of something wrong within the child, thereby reducing the likelihood of examining instructional variables as the cause of performance deficits.

■ A label may help cause a child to develop a poor self-concept.

■ Labels may lead peers to reject or ridicule the labeled child.

■ Labels have a certain permanence about them. Once labeled as *retarded* or *learning disabled,* a child has difficulty ever achieving the status of being just like the other kids.

■ Labels often provide a basis for keeping students out of the regular classroom.

■ A disproportionate number of students from culturally diverse groups have been inaccurately labeled *disabled.*

■ The classification of exceptional children requires the expenditure of much professional and student time that could be better spent in planning and delivering instruction.

As can be seen, there are strong reasons both for and against the classification and labeling of students who are exceptional. At one level, classification can be seen as a way to organize the funding and administration of special education programs in the schools. In fact, the federal government and most states and school districts allocate money and resources according to the number of students in each category of exceptionality. To receive an individualized program of educational services to meet his or her needs, a student must first be identified as having a disability and then, with few exceptions, be further classified into one of the categories, such as for learning disabilities or visual impairment. So, in practice, being labeled as belonging to a given category, and therefore being exposed to all of the potential disadvantages that label carries with it, is prerequisite to receiving the special education services necessary to achieve educational equality. Many educators are aware of this problem and argue that the classification and labeling of exceptional students by category of condition actually interfere with the kind of assessment and instruction most needed by the student. Stainback and Stainback,[18] for example, contend that

> these categories often do not reflect the specific educational needs and interests of students in relation to such services. For example, some students categorized as visually handicapped may not need large print books, while others who are not labeled visually impaired and thus are ineligible for large print books could benefit from their use. Similarly, not all students labeled behaviorally disordered may need self-control training, while some students not so labeled may need self-control training as a part of their educational experience. Such categories . . . actually interfere with providing some students with the services they require to progress toward their individual educational goals. Eligibility for educational and related services should be based on the abilities, interests, and needs of each student as they relate to instructional options and services, rather than on the student's inclusion in a categorical group.

One major challenge facing education today lies in determining how to meet the individualized needs of exceptional students without subjecting them to the potentially negative outcomes of classification and labeling as it is currently practiced.

How Many Exceptional Students Are There?

It is impossible to know for certain how many exceptional students there are in U.S. schools. Six reasons for this uncertainty are:

1. State and local school systems use different criteria for identifying exceptional students.

2. The identification of students who are exceptional is not completely systematic because of the less-than-exact nature of screening and assessment procedures.

3. The significant role played by subjective judgment in interpreting the results of referral and assessment data makes identification inconsistent from case to case.

4. The number of exceptional students identified by a given school is affected by the school's relative success in providing instructional support to the regular classroom teacher so that an at-risk student does not become a student with a disability.

5. The relative ability of a school system to provide special education services for *every* student identified as having a disability (a requirement of federal legislation) may affect how hard the school system works to identify students with exceptional needs.

6. A student might be identified as exceptional at one time and as not exceptional (or included in another exceptional category) at another time.

In spite of the difficulty these and other factors pose in determining the actual number of exceptional students, data are available showing how many students with disabilities receive special education services in the United States. Each year, the U.S. Department of Education, Office of Special Education and Rehabilitation Services (OSERS), submits a report to Congress on the education of children with disabilities. The most recent information available is for the 1988–1989 school year.[19]

Consider these nine facts about exceptional students in the United States:

1. More than 4.5 million students with disabilities, aged three to twenty-one, received special educational services during the 1988–1989 school year. Children with disabilities in special education represent approximately 9.4 percent of the school-age population.

2. The number of children and youths receiving special education services has increased 24 percent since a national count was begun in 1976. A major contributor to these increases since 1986 has been the widespread initiation of early intervention programs for children at birth to age five.

3. The number of children receiving special education services varies with the age of the child. From age three through nine, the number of children in special education increases. This trend is reversed with a gradual decrease in each successive year after age nine through age seventeen. After age seventeen, there is a dramatic decrease in the number of students receiving special education services.

4. Learning disabilities (48 percent), speech and language impairment (23 percent), mental retardation (16 percent), and emotional disturbance (9 percent) account for 96 percent of all school-age children receiving special education. Of these groups, the number of children identified as learning disabled is up 152 percent since 1976, while the number of children identified as mentally retarded is down 36 percent.

5. There are approximately twice as many males as females receiving special education services.

6. During the 1987–1988 school year, two-thirds of all children with disabilities received at least part of their school-based instruction with their non-disabled peers in regular classrooms.

7. One-fourth of children with disabilities received all of their instruction in special classrooms. Approximately one in twenty school-age children have disabilities that are so severe that they require special schools for their education. Residential schools and nonschool settings such as hospitals or homebound programs serve less than 1 percent of all children with disabilities.

8. Of all the school-aged children receiving special education services, the overwhelming majority (approximately 90 percent) have mild disabilities.

9. A look at the numbers of and sites in which educational services are delivered reveals that in the United States, the typical child receiving special education is a nine-year-old boy with learning disabilities who spends part of each school day in the regular classroom and part in a resource room.

HISTORY OF EDUCATIONAL EQUALITY FOR EXCEPTIONAL STUDENTS

If our society and its institutions were to be judged by how they treat people who are different, our educational system would not be judged very favorably.[20] Students who are different, whether because of race, culture, language, gender, or exceptionality, have often been denied equal access to educational opportunities. For many years, educational opportunity of any kind did not exist for many students with disabilities. Students with severe disabilities were completely excluded from public schools. Before 1970, many states had laws permitting local school districts to deny access to children whose physical or intellectual disability caused them, in the opinion of school officials, to be unable to benefit from typical instruction.

Most students with disabilities were enrolled in school, but perhaps half of the nation's children with disabilities were denied an appropriate education through what Turnbull[21] calls "functional exclusion." The students were allowed to come to school but were not participating in an educational program designed to meet their special needs. Students with mild learning and behavior problems remained in the regular classroom but were given no special help. If they failed to make satisfactory progress in the curriculum, they were called "slow learners"; if they acted-out in class, they were called "disciplinary problems" and were suspended from school.

For students who did receive a program of differentiated curriculum or instruction, special education usually meant a separate education in segregated classrooms and special schools isolated from the mainstream of education. These children were labeled *mentally retarded, crippled,* or *emotionally disturbed.* Special education often meant a classroom specially reserved for students who could not measure up in the regular classroom. The following passage exemplified what was too often a common occurrence:

> *I accepted my first teaching position, in a special education class in a basement room next door to the furnace. Of the 15 "educable mentally retarded" children assigned to work with me, most were simply nonreaders from poor families. One child had been banished to my room because she posed a behavior problem to her fourth-grade teacher.*
>
> *My class and I were assigned a recess spot on the opposite side of the play yard, far away from the "normal" children. I was the only teacher who did not have a lunch break. I was required to eat with my "retarded" children while the other teachers were permitted to leave their students.*[22]

Students who are gifted and talented seldom received any special attention in the schools. Many educators believed (as some still do today) that these students can make it on their own without any special programming.

Education's response to exceptional students has changed considerably over the past several decades, from a pattern of exclusion and isolation to one of integration and participation. But this change did not come easily, nor did it come by chance. Judiciary authority was necessary to correct these educational inequities for children with disabilities. Today's efforts to ensure educational equality for exceptional students can be viewed as an outgrowth of the civil rights movement. All of the issues and events that helped shape society's attitudes during the 1950s and 1960s affected the development of special education for exceptional students, particularly the 1954 landmark case of *Brown* v. *Board of Education of Topeka.*[23] This case challenged the practice, common in 1954, of segregating schools according to the race of the children. The U.S. Supreme Court ruled that education must be available to all children on equal terms, and that it is unconstitutional to operate segregated schools under the premise that they are separate but equal.

The *Brown* decision initiated a period of intense questioning by parents of children with disabilities who wondered why the same principles of equal access to education did not also apply to their children. Numerous cases challenging the exclusion and isolation of children with disabilities by the schools were brought to court by parents and advocacy groups. At issue in these cases were numerous questions, including (1) the fairness of intelligence testing and the legitimacy of placing children in special education classes solely on the basis of those tests, (2) intelligence tests that were not administered in a child's native language, and (3) arguments by schools that they could not afford to educate exceptional students. One of the most influential court cases in the development of educational equality for exceptional students was the 1972 *Pennsylvania Association for Retarded Children* v. *Commonwealth of Pennsylvania.*[24] The association (PARC) brought the class-action suit to challenge a state law that enabled public schools to deny education to children they considered "unable to profit from public school attendance."

The attorneys and parents who represented PARC argued that it was neither rational nor necessary to assume that the children were uneducable. Because the state could neither prove that the children were uneducable nor demonstrate a rational basis for excluding them from public school programs, the court decided that the children were entitled to a free public education. Other court cases followed with similar rulings—children with disabilities, like all other people in the United States, are entitled to the same rights and protection under the law as guaranteed in the Fourteenth Amendment, which declares that people may not be deprived of their equality or liberty on the basis of any classification such as race, nationality, or religion.

The phrase *progressive integration*[25] has been used to describe the history of special education and the gradual but unrelenting progress of ensuring equal educational opportunity for all children. Of the many court cases involving education for exceptional learners, no case resulted in sweeping educational reform. With each instance of litigation, however, the assembly of what was to become P.L. 94-142 became more complete. Together, all of these developments contributed to the passage of a federal law concerning educational equality for students with disabilities.

PUBLIC LAW 94-142: A LEGISLATIVE MANDATE FOR EDUCATIONAL EQUALITY FOR EXCEPTIONAL STUDENTS

In 1975, Public Law 94-142, originally titled the Education for All Handicapped Children Act, was reluctantly signed by President Gerald Ford, who expressed concern that the federal government was promising more than it could deliver. This landmark bill represented the culmination of the efforts of a great many parents, educators, and legislators to bring together under one comprehensive law the requirements and safeguards deemed necessary if students with disabilities were to experience educational equality. P.L. 94-142 forever changed how children with disabilities are educated and the roles that teachers, administrators, and parents play in that educational process.

Legislative Changes to P.L. 94-142

As it does with other comprehensive federal laws, Congress periodically reauthorizes and amends P.L. 94-142. Since its passage, the law has been amended three times. In 1982, the administration attempted to revise some of the rules and regulations governing the law's implementation. Had these changes been successful, the law would have been weakened in several respects. Advocacy groups composed of parents and professionals rallied to voice their opposition to these proposed changes. As a result, in 1983, when the law was amended for the first time (P.L. 98-199), Congress reaffirmed all of the major provisions of the law and included language that would expand research and services aimed at easing the transition from school to work for high school students. This initial amendment also provided for increases in funding for a number of programs.

Three years later, Congress passed the Education Amendments of 1986. This legislation was aimed at expanding special educational services to three- to five-year-old children. These amendments required school districts to provide full educational services to this population of young children by the beginning of the 1990–1991 school year. In addition, financial incentives were established to encourage schools to initiate programs for children from birth through age two.

In 1990, Congress changed the law's title to the Individual with Disabilities Education Act (P.L. 101-476). This law retained all of the basic provisions of P.L. 94-142. It also made several important additions, including "autism" and "traumatic brain injury" to the categories of exceptionality covered by the original legislation, and specific requirements for helping secondary students make the transition from school to adult life.

There have also been numerous legal challenges to P.L. 94-142. These challenges have focused primarily on what constitutes a free, appropriate education in the least restrictive environment. In spite of these challenges, the basic rules it originally outlined today still govern the education of students with disabilities.

Major Components of P.L. 94-142

To receive any federal tax dollars to support the cost of educating students with disabilities, each state must show evidence that its local school districts comply with each of the following six major components of P.L. 94-142.[26]

Free, Public Education for All Children with Disabilities

P.L. 94-142 requires that children aged three to twenty-one with disabilities, regardless of the type or severity of their disabilities, must be provided with a "free, appropriate public education which emphasizes special education and related services designed to meet their unique needs." In addition, incentive funds were made available to states that provided early intervention programs to children who are at risk and who have disabilities from birth through age two. The law clearly mandates a "zero reject" policy, prohibiting schools from excluding any child solely because the child has a disability. This fundamental requirement of the law is based on the proposition that all children with disabilities can learn and benefit from an appropriate education, and that schools therefore do not have the right to deny any child access to educational opportunity.

The principle of "zero reject" means more than schools *not denying* children *educational opportunities*. The principal requires that schools *provide an appropriate education* that is free of cost, takes place in the least restrictive environment, and includes those related services needed for the child to benefit from the educational program (e.g., special transportation services, physical therapy) regardless of the nature or severity of the child's disability. When designing educational programs for children with disabilities, the intent of the term *equality* is not limited to equal access to the same educational opportunities as other children. The definition is broader in that these children are also entitled to different types of services because their disabilities justify special educational approaches.[27]

Nondiscriminatory Evaluation

The law requires that exceptional students be evaluated fairly. Assessment must be nondiscriminatory so that it does not wrongly identify as disabled students who are not. This requirement of P.L. 94-142 is particularly important because of the disproportionate number of children from non-White and non-English-speaking cultural groups who were being identified as having disabilities, often solely on the basis of a score from standardized intelligence tests. Both of the intelligence tests that have been used most often in the identification of students with learning problems had been developed based on the performance of White, middle-class children. Because of their Anglocentric nature, the tests are often considered to be unfairly biased against children from diverse cultural groups who have had less of an opportunity to learn the knowledge sampled by the test items.[28] P.L. 94-142 states clearly that the results of one test cannot be used as the sole criterion for placement into a special education program.

In addition to the concern for fair identification of students who are exceptional, in order to determine the extent of all of a child's special needs so that an appropriate program of individualized education can be developed, multifactored assessment that includes several tests and observational techniques is necessary. The law requires that a child be assessed by a multidisciplinary team in all areas of functioning.

A child who has been referred for a multifactored assessment for a learning disability, for example, must be evaluated by several individuals across several different social and academic areas. The school psychologist may administer several different tests in order to obtain reliable data about the child's ability and achievement levels. The school counselor may observe the child in various academic settings as well as nonacademic settings such as the playground and lunchroom. Observational data from the child's teachers and samples of the child's work should be compiled. A speech and language therapist, occupational therapist, rehabilitation counselor, or social worker may also be included in the assessment process. Finally, parental input and the child's own perceptions of his or her needs should be obtained and documented. The result of these efforts should be an accurate picture of the child's current levels of performance, with clear indications as to what type of educational program will be most appropriate.

Individualized Education Program

Perhaps the most significant aspect of P.L. 94-142 is the requirement that an *individualized education program,* or IEP, be developed and implemented for each child with a disability. The law is very specific in identifying the kind of information an IEP must include and who is to be involved in its development. Each IEP must be created by a child-study team consisting of (at least) the child's teacher(s), a representative of the local school district, the child's parents or guardians, and, whenever appropriate, the child.

Although the law states that the student can be a member of the IEP team, in practice, the student has been called an overlooked participant. Exceptional students can and do make valuable contributions to their own educational programs if provided with an appropriate forum in which to do so.[29] Many child-study teams include professionals from various disciplines such as school psychology, physical therapy, and medicine. Special education experts believe that an interdisciplinary team whose members represent varied training, experience, and points of view is best able to determine the special educational and related services that many students with disabilities need.

Although the particular formats vary from school district to school district, all IEPs must include the following items:

- A statement of the child's present level of educational performance.
- A statement of the annual goals to be achieved by the end of the school year in each area requiring specially designed instruction.
- Short-term objectives stated in measurable, intermediate steps between the present level of performance and the annual goals.
- The specific educational and related services (e.g., physical therapy) needed by the child, including the physical education program and any special instructional media and materials that are needed.
- The date by which those services will begin and the anticipated length of time the services will be provided.
- A description of the extent to which the child will participate in the regular education program of the school.
- A statement of the needed transition services for students, beginning no later than age sixteen and annually thereafter (when determined appropriate for the individual, beginning at age fourteen or younger), including, when appropriate, a statement of the interagency responsible or linkages (or both) before the student leaves the school setting.
- Objective criteria, procedures, and schedules for determining, at least annually, whether the short-term objectives are being achieved.
- A justification for the type of educational placement being recommended for the child.
- A list of the individuals responsible for implementing the IEP.

Although the IEP is a written document signed by both school personnel and the child's parents, it is not a legally binding contract. That is, parents cannot take their child's teachers or the school to court if all goals and objectives stated in the IEP are not met. However, schools should be able to document that the services described in the IEP have been provided in a systematic effort to meet those goals. IEPs must be reviewed by the child-study team at least annually.

A carefully planned and written IEP should specify the child's present level of performance, the skills the child needs to learn in the future, the procedures that will be used to occasion that learning, and the means of determining to what extent learning has taken place.[30] The IEP itself, however, does not teach. Too often there is a discrepancy between what is written on the IEP and the instructional programs students actually receive.[31,32] The teachers responsible for the IEP's implementation must ensure that the goals and objectives specified are, in fact, systematically taught and routinely evaluated.

Least Restrictive Environment

As described earlier, the 1972 PARC class-action case was settled by a ruling that it was neither rational nor necessary to exclude or segregate students from regular education programs solely because of a disability. P.L. 94-142 made this finding of the PARC case the law by mandating that students with disabilities must be educated in the least restrictive environment (LRE). Specifically, the law states that *to the maximum extent appropriate, handicapped children, including children in public or private institutions or other care facilities, are educated with children who are not handicapped, and that special classes, separate schooling, or other removal of handicapped children from the regular educational environment occurs only when the nature or severity of the handicap is such that education in regular classes with the use of supplementary aids and services cannot be achieved satisfactorily.*[33]

The LRE requirement has been one of the most controversial and least understood aspects of P.L. 94-142. During the first few years after its passage, some professionals and parents erroneously interpreted the law to mean that all children with disabilities, regardless of type or severity of their disabilities, had to be placed in regular classrooms. Instead, the LRE principle requires that each child with a disability be educated in a setting that most closely resembles a regular class placement and in which his or her individual educational needs can be met. Although some people argue that any decision to place a child with a disability in a special class or school is inappropriate, most educators and parents realize that a regular classroom placement can be overly restrictive if the child's academic and social needs are not met. Two students who have the same disability should not necessarily be placed in the same setting. LRE is a relative concept; the least restrictive environment for one student with a disability would not necessarily be appropriate for another.

A number of factors should be considered when determining the restrictiveness of a particular educational environment. These factors include the extent to which the child has opportunities to acquire new skills, the availability of the regular education teacher to all students, and the opportunity a child with a disability has to establish relationships with other students.[34]

To provide an appropriate LRE for each child with a disability, most schools must offer a *continuum of services* made up of a range of placement and instructional options. Figure 12.1 shows a continuum of placement options as it is most often depicted. The regular classroom is at the bottom of the pyramid and is widest to show that the greatest number of exceptional students should be placed there. Moving up from the bottom of the pyramid, each successive placement option represents an environment in which increasingly more restrictive, specialized, and intensive instructional and related services can be offered. The more severe a child's disability, the greater the need for specialized services. As we have noted, however, the majority of exceptional students experience mild disabilities; hence, the pyramid grows smaller at the top to show that more restrictive settings are required for fewer students.

The continuum-of-services concept is meant to be flexible. That is, decisions regarding the placement of students who are exceptional should not be considered permanent, but should be reviewed periodically. A student may be moved to a more restrictive setting for a limited time, but when certain performance objectives have been met, the student should be returned to the more integrated setting as soon as possible.

Although the continuum-of-services model represents well-established practice in special education, it is not without controversy. A number of specific criticisms have been leveled at this tradition of providing services to exceptional students.[35] It has been argued that the continuum overly legitimizes the use of restrictive placements, implies that integration of persons with disabilities can take place only in least-restrictive settings, and may infringe on the rights of people with disabilities to participate in their communities. In addition, the model suggests that

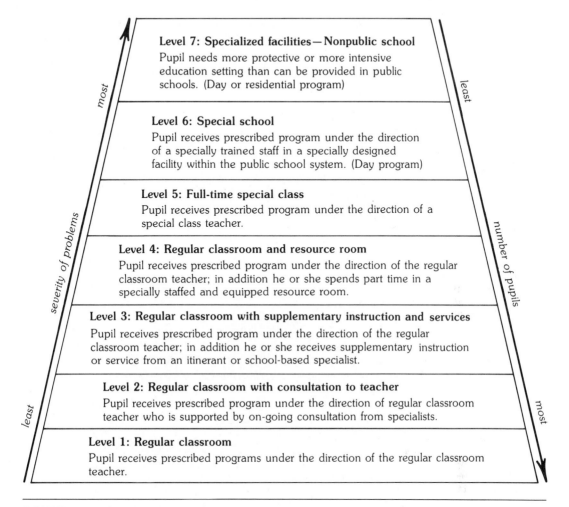

FIGURE 12.1
Continuum of Educational Services for Students with Disabilities
Source: Used with permission of Montgomery County Public Schools, Rockville, Md., and Maynard D. Reynolds.

people move through the continuum in a developmental, step-wise fashion, ignoring transitional states between steps. Perhaps the feature of the continuum that is least useful is its preoccupation with the physical setting in which education takes place, rather than with the quality of services provided. As special education continues to improve the effectiveness of its instructional methods, it is likely that the most restrictive options of the continuum will rarely be considered as proper placements.[36]

Note that in the first three placement options, students with disabilities spend the entire school day in regular classes with their nondisabled peers. In fact, two-thirds of all students with disabilities receive at least part of their education in regular classrooms with their nondisabled peers (see Figure 12.2). Many of these students, however, spend a portion of each school day in a resource room (Level 4 in Figure 12.1), where they receive individualized instruction from a specially trained teacher. Approximately one of every four students with a disability is educated in a separate classroom in a regular public school. Special schools provide the education for about one in twenty children with disabilities, usually students with the most severe disabilities.

Due Process Safeguards

P.L. 94-142 acknowledges that students with disabilities are people with important legal rights. The law makes it clear that school districts do not have absolute authority over exceptional students: schools may not make decisions about the educational programs of children with disabilities in a unilateral or arbitrary manner. Due process is a legal concept that is implemented through a series of procedural steps designed to assure fairness of treatment among school systems,

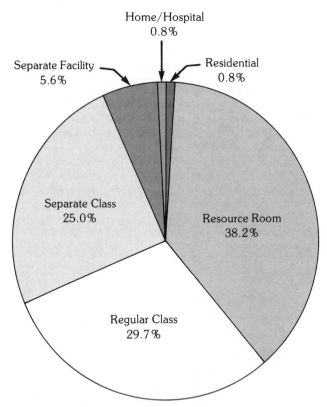

Note: Includes data from 50 States and Puerto Rico

FIGURE 12.2
Percentage of All Students with Disabilities Ages 3 to 21 Served in Six Educational Placements   (includes data from 50 states and Puerto Rico)

Source: Twelfth Annual Report to Congress on the Implementation of the Education of the Handicapped Act, (Washington, D.C.: U.S. Government Printing Office, 1990), p. 20. U.S. Department of Education

parents, and students. Specific due process safeguards have been incorporated into P.L. 94-142 because of past educational abuses of children with disabilities.[37] In the past, special education placements were often permanent, void of periodic reviews, and made solely on the basis of teacher recommendations. Further, students with severe and profound disabilities were automatically excluded from public school programs and placed in residential programs where the quality of instructional programs often was very poor. The fact that children from minority cultural groups were disproportionately placed into special education programs was another factor in mandating the due process procedures.

Due process requires that parents (1) must be notified whenever the school system wishes to initiate a change in educational placement of services, (2) have access to all records about their child, (3) can protest the school's decision by presenting their case in front of an impartial party, and (4) can appeal a ruling they consider unfavorable.

Turnbull and Turnbull, who are both special educators and the parents of a child with severe disabilities, describe due process in these terms:

> *Due process is a way to help families and students make schools accountable. The first four principles of the law—zero reject, nondiscriminatory evaluation, appropriate education, and least restrictive placement—are the "inputs" from the school to the student. Due process is a way to ensure the school has done its job under those principles. . . . Due process is a way of changing the balance of power between professionals, who have traditionally wielded power, and families, who have felt they could not affect their children's education.[38]*

The due process requirements of P.L. 94-142 do more than just protect the rights of students and their parents. Schools may bring a due process hearing against parents who object to the school's proposed plan for a given child.

Parent Participation

P.L. 94-142 recognizes the benefits of active parent participation. The authors believed that parents not only have a right to be involved in their child's education, but that parents of exceptional students also can help professionals select appropriate instructional goals and can provide information that will help teachers be more effective in working with their children. As noted, parents are to take an active role as full members of the child-study team that develops the IEP for their child. Of course, parents cannot be forced to do so and may waive their right to participate. In addition to involving parents in IEP development, P.L. 94-142 requires each state to include parents of students who are exceptional on their special education advisory panel that is responsible for helping the state education agency develop its overall plan and policies for meeting the needs of students with disabilities.

LEGISLATION AFFECTING THE EDUCATION OF GIFTED STUDENTS

P.L. 94-142 mandates that special education and related services be provided to meet the individual needs of all students with disabilities; it does not speak to the educational needs of students who are gifted and talented. Nor is there a comparable federal law that requires states to provide special-education services to gifted students. In 1978, Congress passed P.L. 95-561, the Gifted and Talented Children's Education Act, which provided financial incentives to states and local education agencies for developing special programs for such students. The law included special procedures to ensure that gifted and talented students from disadvantaged backgrounds would be identified and served. Money was also appropriated for the funding of in-service teacher training and research.

However, in 1982 the Education Consolidation Act phased out the federal Office of Gifted and Talented created by P.L. 95-561 and merged funding for gifted education with twenty-nine other education programs. States now receive federal dollars to support these thirty wide-ranging K–12 education programs in the form of block grants. Each state must decide what amount of the block grant funding, if any, will be used to develop and support special education programs and services for gifted students. Nevertheless, a national survey reported in 1984 found that forty-seven state departments of education had appointed state directors or consultants in change of gifted education.[39] This is a significant improvement over a 1972 report that only ten state education agencies had members of their staff whose primary responsibilities were gifted education.

In 1988, the Jacob K. Javits Gifted and Talented Student Education Act was passed as part of the Elementary and Secondary Education Act. This legislation allocated $8 million for teacher education and services for and identification of gifted children. The National Center for the Education of the Gifted was also created as part of federal initiative.

AMERICANS WITH DISABILITIES ACT

The Americans with Disabilities Act (ADA, P.L. 101-336) was passed in 1990. The law contains a number of important provisions that go into effect between 1992 and 1994. ADA requires that employers with more than fifteen workers may not refuse to hire or promote a person because of a disability. The law stipulates that new purchases by public transit authorities be accessible to people with disabilities. It will be illegal for persons with disabilities to be excluded from public accommodations such as hotels, restaurants, and parks. In addition, persons with hearing impairments who use specialized telecommunication devices must be provided with relay services by telephone-service providers. Although it does not speak to education directly, passage of the ADA gives positive evidence that the attitudes of society are changing to accommodate the needs of exceptional persons.

EDUCATIONAL EQUALITY FOR STUDENTS WITH DISABILITIES: SOME PROGRESS AND REMAINING CHALLENGES

What effect has P.L. 94-142 had? The most obvious effect is that many more exceptional students are receiving special education and related services than before the law's passage. But this is what the law requires and is only one aspect of its impact. Educational equality for exceptional students is also evidenced in the ways that today's schools function as complex human services agencies. Since the passage of P.L. 94-142, there has been a dramatic increase in the number of both special education teachers and support staff. Providing the related services necessary to meet the diverse needs of students with disabilities requires that the number of nonclassroom professionals be nearly equal to that of special education teachers. School psychologists, social workers, speech and language therapists, occupational therapists, physical therapists, audiologists, recreational therapists, adaptive physical educators, vocational specialists, and mental health professionals all lend support and expertise to the education of exceptional learners.

Perhaps the law has had its most dramatic effect on students with severe disabilities, many of whom had been completely denied the opportunity to benefit from an appropriate education. No longer can schools exclude students with disabilities on the premise that they are ineducable. Indeed, P.L. 94-142 states clearly that all students can benefit from an appropriate education, and that it is the local school's responsibility to make the modifications in curriculum content and teaching method dictated by the unique needs of each handicapped student. In essence, the law requires schools to adapt themselves to the needs of students rather than allowing schools to deny educational equality to students who do not fit the school.

Most people would agree that P.L. 94-142 has contributed positively to the education of students with disabilities, but significant barriers remain to full educational equality for exceptional students in the United States. We briefly examine four of these impediments. If a truly appropriate educational opportunity is to be a reality for students with disabilities, U.S. schools must work hard to (1) encourage cooperation and collaboration between special and regular educators, (2) move beyond simple compliance with the law to effective instruction, (3) provide more and better early intervention programs for young children with disabilities, and (4) increase the success of young adults with disabilities as they make the transition from school to community.

Toward a Regular/Special Education Partnership

The Individuals with Disabilities Education Act has had a tremendous impact on education. The law requires that all students with disabilities be provided an appropriate education in the least restrictive environment. As noted, most children with disabilities spend at least part of each school day in regular classrooms. Traditionally, regular and special education have been viewed as separate disciplines, each serving different student populations. With the passage of P.L. 94-142, regular classroom teachers became major contributors to the education of children they previously had not been required to teach.

Mainstreaming is the process of integrating students who are exceptional into regular schools and classes. Mainstreaming can be successful only when there is cooperation and collaboration among those responsible for the educational programs of exceptional students. P.L. 94-142 does not specifically mention mainstreaming, but it does require that educational services be provided in the least restrictive environment and that cooperation between regular and special education facilitates those placements.

The role of special and regular education is an issue receiving a great deal of discussion among parents and educators. Many argue that special and regular education should merge their respective talents and methods to create an approach more efficient than the dual system commonly practiced. Creating a general education system that services the needs of all students by combining the most effective practices of regular and special education is commonly referred to as the "regular education initiative."[40,41,42]

Others argue that such a merger would not be in the best interests of exceptional students until teacher training and professional practice improve and child-centered curricula become more common.[43,44,45]

The effects of P.L. 94-142 on regular education are neither entirely clear nor without controversy. What is clear, however, is that it is the responsibility of the educational community as a whole to do the best job it can in meeting the needs of children who have difficulty learning. In the final analysis, issues of labeling, classification, placement, and who does the teaching are secondary to the quality of instruction that takes place in the classroom.[46]

Effective Instruction

Educational equality for students who are exceptional is required by P.L. 94-142. The *letter* of the law can be met by following the mandates for multifactored evaluations, IEPs, due process, and placements in the least restrictive environment. None of these mandated processes, however, teach. Educational equality can be achieved only through effective instruction.

In practice, the *spirit* of the law sets the stage for educational equality. The procedures and results of multifactored assessments must be scrutinized. Members of the child-study teams must ask, Do these results provide the means of making placement decisions that will truly benefit the child? The spirit of the law requires that IEPs be more than correctly completed forms that get filed away and never consulted. The IEP must be a collective effort by teachers, parents, administrators, and other professionals that guides the education of exceptional children. The spirit of the law requires that due process safeguards be more than a formality. They must protect the wishes of parents and the needs of children throughout the process of securing special education services.

Equally important is the law's intent concerning least restrictive environments. Children's academic and social needs must both be accommodated through opportunities to interact with nondisabled students to the greatest extent possible.

Teachers, of course, are ultimately responsible for providing effective instruction to exceptional students. With this responsibility comes several obligations. With the support of the school administration, teachers must (1) use direct assessment and observation of students' performance as a means of designing instruction and evaluating its effectiveness,[47] (2) use empirically validated methods of instruction,[48,49] (3) teach so that newly learned skills are useful outside of the classroom,[50] (4) change an instructional program when it does not promote achievement and success,[51] (5) consult with their regular education colleagues and their student's parents,[52] and (6) be an advocate for the needs of exceptional learners in the school as a whole.[53]

Although P.L. 94-142 does not state that the job of a teacher is to change behavior, that is what a teacher does. When a teacher helps children who previously could not add, spell, compose, tie their shoes, apply for a job, or make a friend, and they learn to do so, behavior has been changed. Effective instruction changes behavior deliberately so that children have an equal opportunity to lead productive, independent lives.

Early Intervention

The years from birth to school age are very important to a child's learning and development. The typical child enters school with a large repertoire of intellectual, language, social, and physical skills on which to build. Unfortunately, for many children with disabilities, the preschool years represent a long period of missed opportunities. Without systematic instruction, most young children with disabilities do not acquire many of the basic skills their nondisabled peers seemingly learn without effort. Parents concerned about their child's inability to reach important developmental milestones have often been told by professionals, "Don't worry. He'll probably grow out of it before too long." Many children with disabilities, as a result, fall further and further behind their nondisabled peers, and minor delays in development often become major delays by the time the child reaches school age.

Although there were virtually no early intervention programs two decades ago for children with disabilities from birth to school age, early childhood special education is today perhaps the fastest-growing area in the field of education. As with special education of school-age exceptional students, federal legislation has played a major role in the development of early intervention programs. By passing Public Law 99-457, the Education of the Handicapped Act Amendments of 1986, Congress reaffirmed the basic principles of P.L. 94-142 and added two major sections concerning early intervention services.

It was estimated that only about 70 percent of the preschoolers aged three to five with disabilities were being served under the incentive provisions of P.L. 94-142 (which did not require states to provide a free, public education to children with disabilities under the age of six years). P.L. 99-457 requires each state to show evidence of serving all three- to five-year-old children with disabilities in order to receive any preschool funds.

The second major change brought about by P.L. 99-457 is that incentive grants are available to states for developing systems of early identification and intervention for infants and toddlers with disabilities from birth to age two. The services must be planned by a multidisciplinary team that includes the child's parents and must be implemented according to an individualized family services plan that is similar in concept to the IEP for school-aged students with disabilities.

Nearly every special educator today now realizes the critical importance of early intervention for both children who are at risk and who have disabilities, and most also agree that the earlier intervention is begun, the better. Fortunately, many educators are working to develop the programs and services so desperately needed by the increasing numbers of babies and preschoolers, especially as a result of prenatal exposure to drugs and alcohol.[54] These programs are necessary to give these children a fighting chance of experiencing educational equality when they enter school.

Transition from School to Adult Life

If the degree of educational equality afforded to students who are exceptional is to be judged, as we think it should, by the extent to which students with disabilities can function independently in everyday environments, then we still have a long way to go. Follow-up studies of young adults who have graduated or left public school secondary special education programs have produced disquieting results. Only about 60 percent find work, and much of the work is part time and at or below minimum wage.[55] The probability of a person with moderate or severe disabilities finding real work in the community is much lower. One study of 117 young adults with moderate, severe, or profound mental retardation found an *un*employment rate of 78.6 percent.[56] Of the 25 who had jobs, only 14 were in the community; 11 were working in sheltered workshops. Only 8 of those working earned more than $100 per month.

Employment problems are not the only difficulties faced by adults with disabilities. One recent national survey found that 56 percent of Americans with disabilities indicated that their disabilities prevented them from doing many everyday activities taken for granted by nondisabled people, such as getting around the community, attending cultural or sporting events, and socializing with friends outside their homes.[57]

Education cannot be held responsible for all of the difficulties faced by adults with disabilities, but the results of these and other studies make it evident that many young people leave public school special education programs without the skills necessary to function in the community. Many educators today see the development of special-education programs that will effectively prepare exceptional students for adjustment and successful integration in the adult community as the ultimate measure of educational equality for students with disabilities.

SUMMARY

The task of providing educational equality for exceptional students is enormous. By embracing the challenge, U.S. schools have made a promise to exceptional students, to their parents, and to society. Progress has been made, but, as we have seen, significant challenges must still be overcome if the promise is to be kept. The views of our society are changing and continue to be changed by people who believe that our past practice of excluding people with disabilities was primitive and unfair. As an institution, education reflects the attitudes of society.

Providing educational equality to students with disabilities does not mean either ignoring a child's disability or pretending that it does not exist. Children with disabilities do have differences from children who do not have disabilities. But, as we state at the beginning of this chapter, students who are exceptional are more like than unlike other students. Every exceptional student must be treated first as an individual, not as a member of a labeled group or category.

There is a limit to how much educational equality can be legislated, for in many cases it is possible to meet the letter of the law but not necessarily the spirit of the law. Treating *every* student with a disability as a student first and as an individual with a disability second may be the most important factor in providing true educational equality. This approach does not diminish the student's exceptionality, but instead it might give us a more objective and positive perspective that allows us to see a disability as a set of special needs. Viewing exceptional students as individuals with special needs tells us a great deal about how to help them achieve the educational equality they deserve.

QUESTIONS AND ACTIVITIES

1. Why are both children who are learning disabled and who are gifted considered exceptional?

2. In what ways are exceptional students similar to and different from other students?

3. Name ten categories of disability. Identify community and school resources from which teachers can receive help when working with students who are exceptional.

4. What are the advantages and disadvantages of labeling exceptional students? Be sure to consider the views of educators, parents, and students.

5. Interview a local special education school administrator to determine (a) how many students in the district receive special education services; (b) how many of these students are bilingual, males, females, or are students of color; (c) how many students are in each of the ten categories of exceptionality; (d) how many special education students are mainstreamed, the portion of the school day in which they are mainstreamed, and the classes in which mainstreamed students participate.

6. How did the civil rights movement influence the movement for educational equality for students who are exceptional?

7. What is an IEP and how can it benefit students with disabling conditions? Visit a special education classroom and ask to review some of the student IEPs. Talk with the special education teacher about how an IEP may influence regular classroom teachers when students are mainstreamed.

8. Are all students with disabling conditions mainstreamed? Why or why not? How does the concept of least restrictive environment (LRE) influence alternative placements for students with disabling conditions?

9. How does your state support special programs and services for students who are gifted? Are state funds provided for gifted education?

10. In your view, which of the challenges facing the education of exceptional students is the most critical? What suggestions would you make for meeting that challenge?

NOTES

1. William L. Heward and Michael D. Orlansky, *Exceptional Children: An Introductory Survey of Special Education,* 4th ed. (Columbus, Ohio: Merrill, 1992).

2. J. R. Patton, M. Beirne-Smith, and J. S. Payne, *Mental Retardation,* 3rd ed. (Columbus, Ohio: Merrill, 1990).

3. Cecil D. Mercer, *Students with Learning Disabilities,* 3rd ed. (Columbus, Ohio: Merrill, 1987).

4. P. I. Myers and D. D. Hammill, *Learning Disabilities: Basic Concepts, Assessment Practices, and Instructional Strategies,* 4th ed. (Austin, Texas: Pro-Ed, 1990).

5. J. M. Kauffman, *Characteristics of Behavior Disorders of Children and Youth,* 4th ed. (Columbus, Ohio: Merrill, 1989).

6. L. McCormick and R. L. Schiefelbusch, *Early Language Intervention: An Introduction,* 2nd ed. (Columbus, Ohio: Merrill, 1990).

7. G. H. Shames and E. H. Wiig, *Human Communication Disorders,* 3rd ed. (Columbus, Ohio: Merrill, 1990).

8. Donald F. Moores, *Educating the Deaf: Psychology, Principles, and Practices,* 3rd ed. (Boston: Houghton Mifflin, 1987).

9. P. V. Paul and S. P. Quigley, *Education and Deafness* (New York: Longman, 1990).

10. G. T. Scholl, ed., *Foundations of Education for Blind and Visually Handicapped Children and Youth: Theory and Practice* (New York: American Foundation for the Blind, 1986).

11. June L. Bigge, *Teaching Individuals with Physical and Multiple Disabilities,* 3rd ed. (Columbus, Ohio: Merrill, 1991).

12. Marti E. Snell, ed., *Systematic Instruction of Persons with Severe Handicaps,* 4th ed. (Columbus, Ohio: Merrill, in press).

13. L. Meyer, C. Peck, and L. Brown, eds., *Critical Issues in the Lives of People with Severe Disabilities* (Baltimore: Paul H. Brooks, 1990).

14. R. L. Koegel and A. Rincover, eds., *Educating and Understanding Autistic Children* (San Diego, California: College Hill, 1982).

15. *Journal of Learning Disabilities* 20, 8–10 (1987).

16. Donald L. MacMillan, *Mental Retardation in School and Society,* 3rd ed. (Boston: Little, Brown, 1988).

17. Heward and Orlansky, *Exceptional Children.*

18. William Stainback and Susan Stainback, "A Rationale for the Merger of Special and Regular Education," *Exceptional Children* 51 (October 1984): 105.

19. Twelfth Annual Report to Congress on the Implementation of the Education of All Handicapped Children Act (Washington, D.C.: U.S. Department of Education, 1990).

20. E. B. Fiske, "Special Education Is Now a Matter of Civil Rights," *The New York Times* (April 25, 1967): 14.

21. H. Rutherford Turnbull III, *Free Appropriate Education: The Law and Children with Disabilities* (Denver, Colo.: Love, 1986).

22. B. Aiello, "Up from the Basement: A Teacher's Story," *The New York Times* (April 25, 1976): 14.

23. *Brown v. Board of Education of Topeka,* 347 U.S. 483, 1954.

24. *Pennsylvania Association for Retarded Children v. Commonwealth of Pennsylvania,* 343 F., Supp. 279, 1972.

25. M. C. Reynolds, "An Historical Perspective: The Delivery of Special Education to Mildly Disabled and At-Risk Students," *Remedial and Special Education* 10, 6 (1989): 7–11.

26. H. Rutherford Turnbull III and Ann P. Turnbull, *Free Appropriate Public Education: Law and Implementation* (Denver, Colo.: Love, 1978).

27. Turnbull, *Free Appropriate Education: The Law and Children with Disabilities,* 60.

28. Jane R. Mercer, *Labelling the Mentally Retarded* (Berkeley: University of California Press, 1973).

29. Mary T. Peters, "Someone's Missing: "The Student as an Overlooked Participant in the IEP Process," *Preventing School Failure* 34 (Summer 1990): 32–36.

30. K. Bierly, "Public Law 94-142: Answers to the Questions You're Asking," *Instructor* 87 (September 1978): 63–67.

31. A. Nevin, S. McCann, and M. I. Semmel, "An Empirical Analysis of the Regular Classroom Teacher's Role in Implementing IEP's," *Teacher Education and Special Education* 6 (1983): 235–246.

32. S. W. Smith, "Individualized Education Programs (IEP'S) in Special Education—From Intent to Acquiescence," *Exceptional Children* 57 (1990): 6–14.

33. *Public Law 94-192: The Education of All Handicapped Children Act,* 1975, Section 612(5)B.

34. T. E. Heron and M. E. Skinner, "Criteria for Defining the Regular Classroom as the Least

Restrictive Environment for LD Students," *Learning Disability Quarterly* 4 (1981): 115–121.

35. S. J. Taylor, "Caught in the Continuum: A Critical Analysis of the Principle of Least Restrictive Environment," *The Journal of the Association for Persons with Severe Handicaps* 13 (1988): 41–53.

36. M. C. Reynolds, "An Historical Perspective: The Delivery of Special Education to Mildly Disabled and At-Risk Students," *Remedial and Special Education* 10 (1989): 7–11.

37. E. L. Meyen, ed., *Exceptional Children and Youth: An Introduction* (Denver, Colo.: Love, 1978).

38. Ann P. Turnbull and H. Rutherford Turnbull III, *Families, Professionals, and Exceptionality: A Special Partnership* (Columbus, Ohio: Merrill, 1986), p.254.

39. Dorothy Sisk, "A National Survey of Gifted Programs," Presentation to the National Business Consortium for Gifted and Talented (Washington, D.C.: October 1984).

40. M. C. Reynolds, M. C. Wang, and H. J. Walberg, "The Necessary Restructuring of Special and Regular Education," *Exceptional Children* 53 (1987): 391–398.

41. S. Stainback and W. Stainback, "Integration versus Cooperation: A Commentary on 'Educating Children with Learning Problems: A Shared Responsibility,'" *Exceptional Children* 54 (1987): 66–68.

42. M. C. Wang and H. J. Walberg, "Four Fallacies of Segregationism," *Exceptional Children* 55 (1988): 497–502.

43. J. F. Mesinger, "Commentary on 'A Rationale for the Merger of Special and Regular Education' or, Is It Time for the Lamb to Lie Down with the Lion?" *Exceptional Children* 51 (1985): 510–512.

44. L. M. Lieberman, "Special Education and Regular Education: A Merger Made in Heaven?" *Exceptional Children* 51 (1985): 513–516.

45. J. M. Kauffman, M. M. Gerber, and M. I. Semmel, "Arguable Assumptions Underlying the Regular Education Initiative," *Journal of Learning Disabilities,* 21 (1988): 6–11.

46. B. K. Keogh, "Narrowing the Gap between Policy and Practice," *Exceptional Children* 57 (1990): 186–190.

47. J. A. McLoughlin and R. B. Lewis, *Assessing Special Students,* 3rd ed. (Columbus, Ohio: Merrill, 1990).

48. "In Search of Excellence: Instruction That Works in Special Education Classrooms" (special issue), *Exceptional Children* 52 (April 1986).

49. E. J. Kameenui and D. C. Simmons, *Designing Instructional Strategies: The Prevention of Academic Learning Problems* (Columbus, Ohio: Merrill, 1990).

50. R. H. Horner, G. Dunlap, and R. L. Koegel, *Generalization and Maintenance: Life-Style Changes in Applied Settings* (Baltimore: Paul H. Brooks, 1988).

51. K. Howell and M. K. Morehead, *Curriculum Based Evaluation in Special and Remedial Education* (Columbus, Ohio: Merrill, 1987).

52. T. E. Heron and K. C. Harris, *The Educational Consultant: Helping Professionals, Parents, and Mainstreamed Students,* 2nd ed. (Austin, Tx.: Pro-Ed, 1987).

53. Jeptha V. Greer, "The Special Education Professional," *Exceptional Children* 55 (October 1988): 103–105.

54. Michael Dorris, "A Desperate Crack Legacy," *Newsweek* (June 25, 1990): 8.

55. Eugene Edgar, "How Do Special Education Students Fare after They Leave School? A Response to Hasazi, Gordon, and Roe," *Exceptional Children* 51 (April 1985): 470–473.

56. Paul Wehman, J. Kregel, and J. Seyfarth, "Employment Outlook for Young Adults with Mental Retardation," *Rehabilitation Counseling Bulletin* 5 (1985): 343–354.

57. *Eighth Annual Report to Congress on the Implementation of The Education of All Handicapped Children Act* (Washington, D.C.: U.S. Department of Education, 1986), p. xiv.

CHAPTER 13

Teaching Students with Disabilities in the Regular Classroom

■ JANE B. SCHULZ

All classrooms are characterized by diversity because society is characterized by diversity. Differences among children may be more obvious in school settings because of the nature of the tasks required of students. Thus, students who are not disabled in other situations may have difficulty in settings requiring attending skills, reading skills, and problem-solving skills. They may, however, be similar to other students in many ways. For this reason, "students who have a disability" is a better description than "disabled students."

A *disability* may be defined as "a disadvantage that makes achievement unusually difficult." This chapter focuses on the educational implications of disabling conditions and also on strategies to be used in facilitating achievement.

It is important to realize that children who are severely disabled are not usually placed in regular classes. Their needs are generally different from those of most other students, and therefore their learning environment must be different. It is also important to note that students with sensory difficulties, such as visual or auditory impairment, comprise a small segment of the school population. Students who are physically impaired are generally more easily integrated into classroom situations than are students who have learning and behavior problems.

The categories of disabilities most prevalent are communication disorders, mental retardation, learning disabilities, and emotional or behavior disorders. Students exhibiting problems in these areas are likely to be integrated into regular classes. Because their problems make it difficult for them to acquire and maintain academic skills and information, teachers often find that these students add to the ability levels in their classrooms. For example, in a traditional sixth-grade classroom, reading ability may vary from fourth- to seventh-grade levels. With the addition of students with disabilities, the level may drop to second grade or lower. Teachers may also notice discrepancies in their students' learning; a student may be at an extremely low level in math but be at grade level or above in other subject areas. It is also possible that students will exhibit unusual behavior and emotional immaturity that challenge even the best teachers.

One major component of the Education for All Handicapped Children Act (Public Law 94-142) is the requirement that children and young people identified as disabled be educated in the least restrictive environment. The concept of least restrictive environment (frequently referred to as *mainstreaming*) provides multiple programming options. The options include enrollment in a regular class for none, part, or all of the day, and enrollment in a special class or resource room for all, part, or none of the day. The many settings available require a different kind of school environment in which all personnel are comfortable with and skilled in working with students who are disabled. An effective working relationship depends on the development of positive attitudes and professional skills.

TEACHERS' ATTITUDES

In a measure of regular classroom teachers' attitudes toward teaching disabled children, Stephens and Braun[1] identified four variables related to teachers' willingness to accept students with disabilities into their classrooms:

1. Teachers who had taken courses in special education were more willing to integrate students with disabilities into their classes than were teachers who had not had such courses.

2. Teachers who believed that students with disabilities can become useful members of society were more willing to integrate them than were teachers who did not share this belief.

3. Teachers who believed that public schools should educate exceptional students were more willing to integrate them than were teachers who did not endorse this position.

4. Teachers confident of their abilities to teach exceptional children were more willing to integrate them than were teachers who were not confident.

Although willingness is not always equated with success, it seems to be a trait of teachers who are more successful in teaching students who are disabled. An examination of these four traits serves to pinpoint attitudes for success.

Special Education Courses

Many states now require that all preservice teachers take at least one course in special education. Usually such courses give an overview of different areas of exceptionality and are designed to help teachers develop appropriate teaching strategies. The main purposes of an introductory course are to create an awareness of different disabling conditions and to develop an attitude of acceptance toward students who exhibit those conditions and characteristics. Certainly it is helpful to have this knowledge; it is not essential. It is essential that teachers recognize that there is a problem, that they know the process of referral, and that they are aware of whom they can call on for help. The most knowledgeable teachers are not familiar with all disabling conditions. An experienced special education teacher once stated:

Although I have taught special education for many years, last year was the first time I had ever had a blind student. My first reaction was panic: Would I have to learn braille? How could I teach him math? To my surprise, I found that there were many resources available to me and to Josh. I found that there was a teacher of braille from Social Services; that the State Division for the Blind would send tapes, talking books, and the necessary equipment; and I even had an offer one day from a retired teacher who was willing to braille any textbook material I needed. Josh taught me how to use an abacus effectively, and together we worked out his mobility problems. I learned to think through problems with him. This was good for both of us.

Although formal coursework helps, many other avenues are open to teachers who want to learn about their students who have disabilities. In every school system, there are special education teachers, coordinators of special education programs, parents, and volunteers who can furnish valuable information. Once teachers encounter students who have disabilities they can ask the appropriate questions.

Acceptance of Students

An attitude of openness helps teachers recognize that students who have disabilities are useful members of society. The attitude of acceptance that pervades multicultural education is the same attitude that views all people as worthy citizens. Most students who are mainstreamed into the regular classroom have mild disabilities. This means that they are more like other students than they are different from them. Most of them will finish school, find jobs, and become part of the communities in which they live.

School Responsibility

It is the legal obligation of the school to provide an appropriate education for each student who is disabled. P.L. 94-142 clearly established the rights of students who are disabled to be placed in as normal a situation as possible, to have an individualized education program, to be evaluated with nondiscriminatory measures, to have their parents involved in educational decisions, and to receive all the benefits of due process.

Beyond the letter of the law is the belief held by many teachers that students with disabilities are entitled to an excellent education. This belief is necessary if teachers are to develop the appropriate skills for teaching exceptional children and young people.

Teachers' Confidence

Teachers who are confident of their abilities to teach students with disabilities are more willing to accept those students and are certainly more successful in meeting their needs. There has been a myth for some time that special-education teachers have some sort of magic that enables them to teach children who have learning problems. The truth is that the same skills are required for teaching all children. A college professor in special education expressed this philosophy in relating the following incident:

> *I had been asked to work with a teacher who was seeking certification in special education. She had an initial certification in business education and had been given a position teaching children who were moderately mentally retarded. I decided to visit her class and was amazed to see a class that was totally reading oriented, with phonics charts on the wall and books on every desk. I realized at that point that she didn't know much about the children she was teaching. However, I was amazed to find that the children were reading. I was reluctant to suggest that she take courses in which she would learn that they could not read!*

In the same way that good teaching generalizes to many situations, good traditional strategies can be adapted to meet diverse needs of students.

PROFESSIONAL SKILLS

Attitudinal changes must be accompanied by appropriate changes in instructional strategies. The same principles apply that have been applied to multicultural education: Teachers must become aware that they have to adapt instruction to the students' backgrounds and ability levels.

Adapting instruction is particularly difficult when one realizes that teachers have responsibilities to all of their students and may have limited time and resources to deal with individual needs. The concept of "reasonableness of accommodations" has been introduced as a process by which the regular classroom teacher determines which techniques are time, workload, and cost effective.[2] Thus, accommodations that require little extra time, little change in usual teaching practices, and little additional help are more useful to the classroom teacher than are techniques deemed less reasonable.

The appropriate selection of materials and techniques is also based on the understanding and use of three principles: readiness, relevance, and reinforcement.

Academic Readiness

One of the most difficult concepts to grasp is that academic readiness is not age oriented. Educators have tended to equate readiness with early grade activities and with young children. Readiness, at any age, is a concern of the classroom teacher. Many students with learning problems do not have the basic underlying skills and concepts on which more advanced learning is based. Examples are clear in the areas of reading and math.

Reading Readiness
Poor reading skills are apparent in every school experience. Teachers of social studies, science, and all other content areas frequently see the inability to read as the greatest problem they face in teaching students who have disabilities. Students who are mentally retarded, emotionally disabled, learning disabled,

visually impaired, and hearing impaired may exhibit reading levels far below those expected for their grade placement. The problem is compounded by the fact that textbooks, particularly in social studies and science, vary a great deal in readability range. Matching the content material to the student's reading level is difficult. In art, music, physical education, and vocational education, reading and following directions are essential to mastery of skills. Thus, reading becomes a major factor in all subject areas.

Reading is based on life experiences, skills in listening, and oral language facility. Many students who are disadvantaged because of cultural or learning differences have not had the experiences on which to build communication. Children with physical disabilities, for example, may have had limited opportunities to travel in the community as well as outside the community. A teacher reported that a student in a wheelchair had never been in a grocery store until the class went on a field trip. It is easy to understand his difficulty in relating to some of the stories he encountered in school. Providing a number of experiences may build toward readiness to read.

Listening skills are also an important aspect of reading. Children spend a great proportion of their school day listening, and teachers frequently assume that listening skills are developing. However, they may not be developing for all students. Assessment of listening skills may indicate that a deficiency exists and that specific activities should be developed to build listening skills. Listening behavior can be assessed informally by noting whether the student consistently asks to have directions repeated, appears to be easily distracted during class presentations, frequently completes the wrong pages in assignments, or does not participate in class discussions. Activities designed to improve listening skills are available in a number of language arts books. In addition, teachers should be aware of the following six procedures that promote good listening:

1. Provide a classroom environment that encourages good listening.
2. Listen to the students; model good listening.
3. Use appropriate tone, pitch, volume, and speed in speaking.
4. Vary the classroom program to provide listening experiences, such as films, discussions, debates, and reports.
5. Help students see the purpose for listening in various activities.
6. Build a program in which listening skills are consistently taught and practiced.

Listening is a basic skill; it can be improved through training.

Oral language production and comprehension are essential to the development of successful reading skills. Reading is communication; it begins with talking, listening to others, and understanding the message. Because reading is, as one child put it, "wrote-down talk," if the material is not within the student's language comprehension, it will not be meaningful. Children who have disabilities are frequently lacking in oral language ability. For children who are culturally different, the language patterns learned in the home may be different from those taught in school. For children who are disabled, this fact may be complicated by physical, mental, and emotional problems that directly relate to speech and language acquisition. One technique in teaching reading that overcomes this problem is the language experience approach. Although this technique is used for young children in traditional reading programs, it is quite appropriate for older students who are at a readiness level.

The language experience approach is based on the ideas that a person's oral language is important, that what is said can be written, and that what is written can be read. Stories can be dictated to the teacher or taped on a cassette recorder, and then written for the student. The story is in the student's language and therefore is a good start toward reading. One of the greatest challenges in teaching older students who are at the readiness level is finding appropriate materials. The language experience approach helps overcome this problem and can be used in any subject area. Other techniques are presented in the section on *relevance*.

Math Readiness

Math presents many examples of the importance of readiness and of building on basic concepts. Students struggling with the processes of multiplication and division can be found in many classrooms. Frequently, close examination reveals that such students may not know addition facts and may not understand that multiplication is a form of addition. If they do not exhibit skill in addition, they are not ready for more advanced concepts. It may be assumed that students have mastered the Piagetian concepts of classification, reversibility, and number concepts associated with numerals. Formal and informal assessment, including error analysis, may reveal some gaps in this learning.

There may also be gaps in math content. The following experience of a special education resource room teacher serves as an example:

> The fifth-grade teacher sent three students to my resource room, asking me to work with them on multiplication and division. As is my custom, I administered the Key Math test to each of the students. I found that although they were good in addition and subtraction, they had no knowledge of money values and did not even recognize different coins. Since money usage was not part of the fifth-grade curriculum, the teacher was not aware of this deficiency.

The same sort of problem may be demonstrated in math language. Children with learning disabilities, in particular, may have trouble with such concepts as *before* and *after* (related to telling time), and *first* and *last* (related to seriation). In these instances, teachers should use shorter, simpler sentences when giving directions and should determine whether the difficulty lies in math skills, math concepts, or language comprehension.

Readiness for math should be presented in concrete, exploratory activities. For example, reversibility can be demonstrated and discovered by depicting equations with poker chips ($4 + 2 = 6$; $6 - 4 = 2$) and with pictorial representation ($\cdots\cdot + \cdot\cdot = \cdots\cdots$; $\cdots\cdots - \cdots\cdot = \cdot\cdot$). Math readiness activities should proceed from concrete (poker chips) to semiconcrete (dots on cards) to abstract (numerals).

Motoric and sensory readiness are as important as conceptual readiness. Physical education, music, and art require basic abilities related to motor and sensory development. Children who are limited in these areas will need to start at a level below that of their nondisabled peers.

Relevance

There are two considerations in assuring that instruction is relevant for students who have disabilities. The first is based on the learning principle that meaningful material is more easily assimilated than is nonmeaningful material. The second relates to priorities. For students limited in the amount and quality of their learning, instructional time is critical. One mother of a child who is mentally retarded stated, "When I visited Mark's classroom and saw that he was learning his colors, I was sick. He had known his colors for years, and there were so *many* things he needed to learn."

Time can be used to greater advantage when the materials, curriculum, and techniques are relevant to students' ability, interests, and needs.

Ability

Assessment is important in determining the ability levels of all students; it is critical for students who have disabilities. Because students' levels of ability may differ across subject areas, assessment should go beyond the survey level, such as group achievement tests. Because this is a time-consuming task, it is logical for teachers to enlist the aid of the special education teacher in administering diagnostic tests. Subject area teachers can use their observational skills to find additional information. All tests, formal and informal, should lead to remediation and learning. Many diagnostic tests in use are criterion-referenced and provide objectives related to the student's ability.

Once the ability level is determined, adaptations need to be made. Although adaptations are challenging, demanding, and sometimes frustrating, there are some rather simple techniques that can be used.

In the elementary grades, materials developed at different reading levels can be used. In the upper elementary grades, there may be some stigma attached to materials, particularly reading books, graded at lower levels. One resourceful teacher, who observed the social implications of this problem, found book covers with motorcycles emblazened on them. With these covers on the primary books, his students were not embarrassed to carry their books on the bus. Language experience stories, referred to in the previous section, can also be used to develop topics at the reading and language levels of the student. Other areas of expression may be found for students who do not read at all. One student who did not speak and did not read was provided with an easel on which he could paint at any time. As he began to express himself in art, his abilities in other areas developed.

Difficulty in reading continues to be a problem at the secondary level. Even though several companies have published material on different grade levels dealing with the same topic, there is a paucity of such books in various subject areas. Teachers who have the time and help may decide to rewrite pertinent material themselves, using synonyms for difficult words and teaching specialized vocabulary words. Although this is a good technique, it may not be a reasonable accommodation in terms of time required.

Another strategy in adapting material for different ability levels and learning styles is to change the format. The change may be as simple as reducing the number of math problems on a page or reducing the reading assignment to a few paragraphs. Sometimes the style of presentation is a problem for the student with learning difficulties. In a home economics class, for instance, sewing directions were written in longhand by the teacher, with instructions and diagrams for two hand stitches on a single page (see Figure 13.1).

One student who had problems with space orientation could not follow the instructions. The perceptive teacher examined her directions and made a simpler presentation, as demonstrated in Figure 13.2. After noting the difference in student comprehension, the teacher decided that this format would be better for all of her students.

Running stitch – Basic sewing stitch used for gathering, mending, and tucking. Take several small stitches at a time, draw thread through the fabric, and repeat.

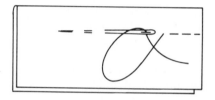

Backstitch — Used to reinforce seams, and make them stronger. Bring needle through the fabric and take a small back stitch, bringing the needle out ahead of the preceding stitch. Take another back stitch, putting the needle in at the end of the preceding stitch.

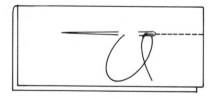

FIGURE 13.1
Sewing Instructions

RUNNING STITCH

A BASIC HAND SEWING STITCH.

USED FOR GATHERING, MENDING, AND TUCKING.

TO DO: PUT NEEDLE IN FABRIC AND TAKE A FEW SMALL STITCHES.

PULL THE THREAD UP TIGHT.

DO THIS AGAIN UNTIL YOU HAVE GONE ALL THE WAY ACROSS YOUR
    FABRIC.

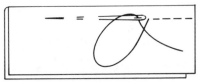

FIGURE 13.2
Adapted Sewing Instructions

In some cases, the reading problem can be circumvented. The use of films, audio programs, filmstrips, and hands-on experiments can replace reading assignments. In social studies, a great deal of information on current events can be learned from television and can enable all students to take part in group discussions.

At the secondary level, instructional adaptation is difficult. Teachers who work with large numbers of students may not have time to devote to individuals with disabilities. In such cases, peer assistance may prove to be invaluable. Such assistance cannot be haphazard; it must be carefully planned to be successful. However, an investment of time initially may prove to be efficient in the long run. A successful program was demonstrated in a high school resource room by a teacher who had taught English before working with students with disabilities. She explained her procedure:

> In the spring of each year, I visit the junior-level English classes. I ask for volunteers for my peer teaching program, explaining that the volunteers will be trained and that they will receive elective credit. During the summer, we have sessions in which I explain the program and demonstrate how it works. I teach them the techniques to be used and help them develop materials we will use.
>
> In the fall, I pair a volunteer with a student in the resource room. The volunteer assists the student in writing paragraphs, developing science projects, learning to use the telephone book, or whatever has been determined to be the student's need. Frequently the volunteers prepare instructional material that is usable in the regular classroom and can extend the learning that has taken place.
>
> Sometimes the volunteers and students ask if they can exchange partners. I ask them to wait for three weeks. Without exception, I find that after three weeks of working together, the pair is inseparable.
>
> This system extends my time and skills. It facilitates skill building for the volunteers and for the resource room students; it also promotes social integration. I could not run my program without it.

Peer helpers can also help teachers in regular classes in the same manner. The key to success is to remember that volunteers should be trained and should be reinforced in some way, either with school credit or with special privileges.

The use of peer assistants is not limited to students who are not disabled working with those who are. Sometimes students who have disabilities have developed special skills and strategies. The following example demonstrates this principle:

> David, who is blind, is particularly good in math. He has developed his skills through the use of an abacus and other manipulatives. In a discussion of class-room techniques, a fourth-grade teacher was heard to exclaim, "I'm having a real problem getting across the concept of place value to my children. Any suggestions?" David's special education teacher immediately suggested that he visit the fourth-grade class and demonstrate place value with his abacus. The teacher was delighted. David met with the class, related to them at their level, and simplified the process in a way that was totally understandable. The fourth-grade students were enthusiastic, asked a number of questions, and asked him to return one day and show them braille. The experience was successful for everyone.

Cross-age tutoring is another example of students with disabilities assisting nondisabled students. Students at an intermediate level in a special class were encouraged to read to kindergarten children. In preparation for this experience, they practiced until they could do it well. Another way to develop such a strategy is to have the older students read into a cassette recorder, improving their performance until they are satisfied with it. Both processes benefit everyone.

Interests

Instruction and materials should be relevant to the students' interests. As a start, interest inventories can be developed and used, teachers can observe what students do in their free time, and conversation can reveal major interests. In working with students with disabilities, teachers may find that interests have to be developed. This can be accomplished by placing the disabled student into a group of students who are working on projects of interest or with a peer who has status in the eyes of the disabled student.

When interests are revealed, implications for instruction may follow. For example, a student who is mentally retarded demonstrated an interest in working with wood and wanted to make a table for his family. His shop teacher worked with him and discussed the interest with other teachers. The outcome was that the math teacher worked with the student on using the ruler, and other teachers worked with him on reading and interpreting diagrams and instructions. The resulting table was only part of the learning that took place.

Needs

Skills for living are the ultimate goals of education for students with disabilities. Although some students who are mildly disabled will go to college, many will not. Most students who are mildly mentally retarded leave high school and go directly into the work world. If this probability can be ascertained during the early school years, it helps parents and teachers determine curriculum priorities. Every subject area can be used to prepare students for independent living.

Science teaches students to be aware of their surroundings, to interact with and respect their environment, and to become citizens in a world that depends on science and technology. It is also a valuable vehicle to teach students to solve problems and to make decisions based on facts and consequences. When science includes approaches to everyday problems and situations, it speaks to the future needs of students who have disabilities.

Social studies help students develop positive attitudes toward themselves and others, to develop value systems, and to acquire skills for working in groups. Social studies also provide a unique opportunity to discuss handicapism as a social phenomenon. For students who are disabled and for those who are not, the history of bias and prejudice includes all disenfranchised people, including those who are disabled. Understanding the issues raised by exceptionalism is as important as understanding the issues concerning racism and sexism.

Physical education speaks to the need that disabled students have for maximum development of their physical potential as well as the acquisition of healthy recreational outlets. Many of the jobs to be filled by students who have disabilities are in the unskilled and semiskilled labor force. These jobs demand physical stamina; physical education can teach proper care and use of the body.

Certainly the aesthetic aspects of life are important. Art and music provide outlets for emotional expression, the development of creativity, interaction with others, and tools for leisure activities. They also provide opportunities for students who have disabilities in academic areas to initiate their own ideas and projects rather than to assume passive roles.

Although it is assumed that vocational education will provide working skills for students who will not pursue advanced education programs, it becomes the responsibility of every teacher to incorporate living skills into the curriculum. This can be accomplished in a number of ways.

When selecting sight vocabulary and spelling words, teachers can substitute career and vocational words instead of using the traditional lists. Such words as *boss, emergency, danger, tools, late, and foreman* are more relevant to the needs of students who have disabilities than are the words presented in many textbooks.

Many ordinary materials respond to the needs of young people with disabilities. The newspaper, for example, is an ideal instructional device. It is written at a relatively low reading level, it is mature in format and acceptable in an adult world, and it provides for skill building in every area. The importance of reading newspapers is obvious; math skills can be gained from shopping lists, sporting events, and weather reports; scientific information is readily available; and social learning can be acquired not only from the news, but even from the advice columns. Specific vocational information is available from want ads, and guides for living from real estate ads. Other materials relevant to the needs of young people are driver's license manuals, cookbooks, vacation folders, maps, and magazines. Every teacher will find appropriate materials once the need is recognized.

Reinforcement

Although the term *reinforcement* has been used to denote a "payoff" in many cases, a more accurate interpretation would be to think of it in terms of encouragement. Because learning is the strongest reinforcer, encouraging the student to learn is the goal for all teachers. Reinforcement means to encourage, to strengthen, and to support. It applies to students, to teachers, and to parents.

Students

Students are encouraged to learn when the environment is conducive to their learning. If the teacher recognizes that there are different learning styles, for example, learning is strengthened. Students respond differently to various stimuli—visual materials, sound recording, printed media, manipulative materials, or combinations. Some students work best alone, some work best in small task groups, and some do their best work in large teams. Some prefer structured, teacher-directed learning; others work best with open-ended, self-directed assignments.

Students who have attention, behavior, or motivational problems may learn better in a controlled environment in which behavior management techniques and systems are implemented. Students who perform at a low level usually respond to immediate or short-term reinforcement schedules while learning to delay their gratification. For such students, games, music, art activities, and peer interaction serve this function. It is important to remember that the student should be involved in the selection of reinforcing activities, and that the rules for acquiring them should be clear and fair. Teachers who have students with emotional disabilities in their classes will need to work closely with special educators and school counselors to determine the best reinforcement system.

Disabled students are strongly supported when they are provided with materials and devices to help them learn. In addition to the previous suggestions, specific aids are available for students who need extra help. One obvious device is the calculator. In addition to traditional calculators, talking calculators are also available. Originally designed for visually impaired students, they are also helpful for those with learning disabilities who may need auditory as well as visual input. Certainly, computers have opened doors for many students who have not learned in other ways. They are strong motivators.

Teacher-made materials are also effective motivators. The reference dictionary has been used for a number of years for students of all ages. It can take any form, from a notebook of normal size to a pocket-sized booklet. Any information the student needs to refer to from time to time can be entered in the reference dictionary. It could include the student's name, address, telephone number, and Social Security number; it could contain the multiplication tables; it could list words the student finds difficult to spell; it can be changed as the student's needs change.

Teachers facilitate learning when they help students read. When a student has not learned to read, several techniques can minimize problems in all subject areas. In addition to alternate materials and rewriting techniques discussed previously, the teacher could use some of the following suggestions:

■ Have another student read the assignment, allowing for better comprehension of the material without penalizing the disabled student for poor reading ability.

■ Tape-record passages from the text and have the student listen or follow along in the text.

■ Underline words and ideas essential to the reading passage. Key sentences can be highlighted in text material, teacher-made selections, or newspapers.

■ Permit the student to have additional time to read, with the opportunity to take the assignment home or to a study hall.

■ Separate the reading assignment into parts, having the student concentrate on reading each small section.

■ Provide the student with questions to be answered during the reading process. This helps the student know what to look for and to stay on task.

Many students with learning problems encounter a great deal of difficulty in solving math problems. The most obvious problem is identifying the process to be used. One tangible way of assisting is to identify, with the students, different words that relate to different processes and then to list these words in color. For example, such words as *plus, and, sum,* and *together* could be listed in red under the word *add.* As a bridge to understanding the process, the teacher could underline words in the problem in the appropriate color. Color cues can gradually be reduced as students acquire the verbal skills associated.

In addition to instructional reinforcement, students need social reinforcement. Although they need acceptance and approval from the teacher, peer acceptance is even more important. Studies conducted since the implementation of mainstreaming indicate that social integration does not occur spontaneously; it must be planned. The three aspects of socialization that need to be addressed are attitudes toward people with disabilities; knowledge about disabling conditions, and behavior of and toward people who have disabilities.

Attitudes toward people with disabilities have been greatly facilitated by the media, especially television. Situation comedies, adventure series, and news stories frequently highlight people who are disabled and deal with their differences in a positive way. It is quite different, however, to have a disabled student enter the classroom, particularly if there has not been any prior preparation.

There are a number of social integration activities that help prepare teachers and students for successful integration. One simple activity aimed at dealing with bias in general is to point out similarities and differences among the class members. Encourage discussion about which differences are important and which are not. Some students may reveal instances in which their differences have proved embarrassing. In classrooms in which openness is encouraged, awareness of bias will become apparent.

Movies and videotapes provide visible stimuli to assist in the acquisition of knowledge and awareness concerning people who have disabilities. An even more powerful tool is the use of simulated disabilities. Teachers who are concerned about social acceptance and integration of students with disabilities will find that the time and effort involved in a simulation workshop prove to be a good investment.

A number of situations lend themselves to simulation. In every community there are companies that rent or sell prosthetic devices. Usually they are cooperative in providing wheelchairs, crutches, walkers, and other devices to aid persons with physical disabilities. Visual and auditory impairments can be simulated with the use of blindfolds and earplugs; learning problems can be experienced through test materials presented in unusual formats and at difficult levels. It is important to talk about the frustrations and difficulties experienced and to remind the students of the difference between simulated, temporary disabilities and permanent disabilities.

Ultimately, a student's attitude toward people who have disabilities is a reflection of the teacher's attitude. Teachers' attitudes provide powerful models of acceptance or rejection.

Knowledge about disabling conditions is important for students who have disabilities and for those who interact with them. Sometimes people are at a loss to know whether to ask questions about a condition or to ignore the problem. In classrooms in which communication is free and invited, there are many opportunities for knowledge and understanding to develop. It is natural for children to ask questions; such questions need to be answered.

Accurate information about disabilities is necessary to the complete acceptance of them. Guest speakers—both children and adults—are excellent providers of information. Children are frank in asking questions and thus become better informed at their own levels.

Understanding is a gradual process that may never be reached by some children (or adults). It is difficult to understand why some children are disabled and some are not, as well as why some children receive special consideration because they have disabilities. It has been observed, however, that as children and young people become more aware of differences and the origin of those differences, they grow in empathy.

Behavior of all students is an important aspect of social integration. Some students who are disabled may exhibit poor social skills and should learn appropriate, socially acceptable behavior. Some of these skills are very elementary, such as smiling, greeting, sharing and cooperating, and complimenting others. Classroom teachers should ask special educators and parents to assist in the teaching of social skills.

Some students will laugh, point, and label other students who have disabilities. Such behaviors should be discouraged by teachers as attempts are made to develop positive attitudes. It may be necessary to teach students who are disabled some short rebuttals to negative comments. One student, who was called "stupid," learned to respond, "But I'm not rude." The name-calling soon ceased.

Teachers

Classroom teachers are in a difficult position regarding students who have disabilities. For years, they have been told that special educators teach such children and that other teachers need only to be experts in their respective fields. Since the implementation of P.L. 94-142, the situation has changed drastically. Teachers are being asked to individualize instruction, to teach basic skills, and to model attitudes of acceptance.

Parents, administrators, and students should be aware that most teachers are trying to meet the needs of all of their students, including those with disabilities. A first-grade teacher was asked, "How can you accommodate Tommy in your class? He's severely retarded." The teacher replied, "It's no problem; all my children have folders for their work and Tommy has one that suits his ability." There are many caring, capable teachers who are meeting the needs of their students who have disabilities.

A survey of elementary and secondary teachers identified as effective instructors of students with disabilities in the regular classroom revealed several interesting practices. Elementary teachers reported using individualized instruction more frequently and also receiving more support from special education teachers than did secondary teachers. Both groups indicated their use of a number of practices that worked for them. The instructional modifications used most frequently were shortened assignments, oral tests, study buddies, lower-level worksheets, and preferential seating.[3] It is important to recognize the efforts that good teachers have made and to ensure that the support they need is available.

Teachers need to reinforce each other. One positive outcome of mainstreaming has been the opportunity for teachers and other professionals to work together. Through understanding the unique problems of each teaching situation, classroom teachers and specialists have gained empathy and respect for each other. Teachers who are experts in biology are not expected to be experts in special education; special educators are not necessarily experts in biology. Respect for each other promotes honesty about skills, responsibilities, and concerns. A harmonious working situation is reinforcing.

Certainly the strongest reinforcer for teachers occurs when their students learn. There is no feeling more rewarding than the knowledge that "this child learned in my class."

Parents

Parents are reinforced through communication and participation. Frequently, parents of children with disabilities have not had good experiences in school. They may have been unsuccessful in their own school careers, or they may have had a number of embarrassing and upsetting experiences with their disabled child. There are many reasons parents may be reluctant to come to school for conferences or meetings of any sort: The time may not fit into their work schedule, they may be reluctant to hear any problems about their child, or they may fear that they will be blamed for those problems.

The best way to build a good relationship with parents is to ensure that the first contact is a positive one. A letter of introduction at the beginning of the year or a note commenting on their child's progress is a good beginning. When the first contact concerns a problem, communication is difficult.

Parent participation is a main component of P.L. 94-142. This principle acknowledges the facts that parents are their child's first teachers, and that their knowledge and experience are valuable to the child's growth and development throughout the school years. Not all parents want or are capable of full participation, and different levels of involvement should be expected. However, all parents should be made to feel welcome and comfortable in the school and should be informed about their child's progress.

Parents, too, are reinforced when their child makes progress. Work samples, criterion-referenced assessment and advancement, and honest compliments let parents know that teachers care about their child and about them. Suggestions for helping their child do better in school are usually welcome. Parents' suggestions may also be sought and used to advantage.

CONCLUSION

Shortly after the passage of the law for the education of handicapped children, the president of the National Education Association declared that "P.L. 94-142's challenge for the education profession is incalculable, as is its promise for those handicapped students whose educational needs have been neglected or ignored by the public school."[4] Since that time, the challenge has permeated every level of education.

Schools and universities concerned with teacher education have been required to examine their purpose, strategies, and programs. The field of special educations has changed drastically to accommodate the changing population of exceptional children and young people and therefore the changing role and environment of the educator.

Perhaps more challenging has been the changing role of general educators. Teachers and other personnel have been required to change their attitudes and to increase their repertoire of competencies to enable them to understand and teach children whom they may not have expected to teach.

Although the role of the teacher appears to be overwhelming at times, there are also positive changes. Technological advances promise to alleviate some of the paperwork and to expedite communication between home and school. Community resources are becoming involved in schools and providing opportunities to students and teachers for extended experiences. Administrators are discovering the advantages of volunteer programs and the unlimited possibilities that develop through school-community-home interaction.[5]

There are still many unanswered questions: Are teachers and parents fully prepared for the responsibilities they have in educating children and young people who have disabilities? Is the present system working? Are students with disabilities leaving school with the skills they need? Concerned, capable teachers will help find answers to these and other questions as they learn to know and to work with students who have disabilities, their parents, and other teachers.

QUESTIONS AND ACTIVITIES

1. Why is it more appropriate to call a student with a learning disability a "student with a disability" rather than a "disabled student"?

2. Form a discussion group with other members of your class. Use Stephens and Braun's four variables related to teacher's willingness to accept students with disabilities into their classrooms as a departure point to discuss your attitudes toward teaching students with disabilities.

3. Select a chapter in the textbook you are currently using in your class. Devise three ways that you can help a poor reader understand the material.

4. Give three examples of "teacher-made" materials and tell why they can be effective motivators for students.

5. Make a chart giving examples of how you can help students with learning disabilities build listening, reading, and math skills.

6. Use a children's book such as *Yellow Bird and Me* by Joyce Hansen (New York: Houghton Mifflin, 1986) to develop a role-playing activity that can give students an opportunity to explore their feelings about people with disabilities.

7. Review several textbooks currently in use to determine how people with disabilities are portrayed. How many times are they mentioned or pictured in illustrations? In what context are they portrayed? What are their ethnic groups and gender? In what ways can you add materials on people with disabilities to supplement textbooks?

NOTES

1. T. M. Stephens and B. L. Braun, "Measures of Regular Classroom Teachers' Attitudes toward Handicapped Children," *Exceptional Children* 4 (1980): 292–294.

2. S. Fagen, D. Graves, S. Healy, and D. Tessier-Switlick, "Reasonable Mainstreaming Accommodations for the Classroom Teacher," *The Pointer* 1(1986): 4–7.

3. E. H. Bacon and J. B. Schulz, "A Survey of Mainstreaming Practices," *Teacher Education and Special Education* 2 (1991): 144–149.

4. J. Ryor, "Integrating the Handicapped," *Today's Education* 24 (1977): 24.

5. J. B. Schulz, *Parents and Professionals in Special Education* (Boston: Allyn and Bacon, 1987), p. 333.

CHAPTER 14

Educating Gifted Students in a Multicultural Society

■ BARBARA CLARK

Learners who are gifted present unique needs in education. When these needs are combined with the diverse values and practices of a variety of cultures, the educator must be aware of the results such an interaction can create. This chapter discusses who the gifted are, how giftedness develops, and how schools can meet the needs of gifted students. Research on culturally diverse gifted learners is discussed. This research will enhance the reader's understanding of the interaction between the needs of culturally diverse gifted students and their cultures so that their educational needs may be better met.

WHO ARE THE GIFTED LEARNERS?

Intelligence and Giftedness: Definitions

Intelligence and the label for the development of high intelligence, *giftedness,* have been defined in many ways. Some people refer to intelligence as what is measured by intelligence tests and giftedness as the upper 2 percent of those measures.[1] Some people insist that intelligence is many separate abilities and that a person can be gifted in any one of them.[2] Others define giftedness without reference to intelligence, insisting that giftedness is remarkable performance in any potentially valuable area.[3] One popular definition of giftedness denies the notion of a gifted learner and suggests that only gifted behavior can be discussed.[4] This definition requires above-average ability, creativity, and task-commitment to identify those who will be capable of gifted behavior. In Public Law 97-35, the Education Consolidation and Improvement Act, passed by Congress in 1981, (sec. 582) children who are gifted and talented are referred to as

> children who give evidence of high performance capability in areas such as intellectual, creative, artistic, leadership capacity, or specific academic fields, and who require services or activities not ordinarily provided by the school in order to fully develop such capabilities.

These definitions focus on performance as the defining feature of giftedness. While observable behavior is necessary for identifying high levels of intelligence, whether assessed by a test, a performance of skill, anecdotal reports, or other measures, such a basis for understanding giftedness is limited. New research in brain/mind function makes possible a different basis for defining and understanding intelligence, giftedness, and their development, including some processes not readily observable.

How giftedness is expressed depends on the individual's genetic patterns and anatomical structure and also on the support and opportunities provided by that individual's environment. At their brain research laboratories at the University of California at Berkeley, Krech,[5] Rosenzweig,[6] and their colleagues sought to discover the effect of learning on experience. Specifically, they questioned whether differential experience could modify the brain in measurable anatomical and chemical terms. Their findings revolutionized beliefs about the nurture and nature of intelligence. They discovered that stimulating environments significantly change the brain, allowing accelerated and more complex function. It is not only genetic endowment that results in intelligence or giftedness; the opportunities the environment provides to develop these genetic programs allow some children to enhance their abilities to the point of giftedness, while the lack of such opportunities inhibit others in their development.

Brain research has shown that very intelligent or gifted learners are biologically different. Their genetic patterns and environmental opportunities interact to produce cellular changes in the brain. These changes include an increase in neuroglial cell production, allowing more support for the neurons and a more effective and efficient neural system;[7,8] a biochemical enhancement of neurons after appropriate stimulation, allowing for more advanced and complex patterns of thought;[9,10] an increase in the amount of dendritic branching, thus increasing the potential for interconnections between neurons;[11] and an increase in the number of synapses and the size of the synaptic contact, allowing more accelerated and complex thought processes within the system.[8,9]

Brain research also shows that the most brain activity is associative and integrative. The major functions of cognition, emotion, physical sensing, and intuition work together to support mind/brain activity. Therefore, the concepts of intelligence and giftedness can no longer be confined to cognitive function but must include all brain functions and their efficient and integrated use.

Thus, *intelligence* is defined here as the aggregate of an individual's major brain functions; it can be enhanced or inhibited by the interaction between the genetic pattern and the environmental opportunities. *Giftedness* is the biologically rooted concept that labels a high level of intelligence showing advanced and accelerated function. It may be expressed through abilities such as those involved in cognition, creativity, academic aptitude, leadership, or the visual and performing arts. *Gifted individuals* perform, or show promise of performing, at high levels in any of these areas. Because of such advanced and accelerated development, they require services or activities not ordinarily provided by the schools in order to develop their capability more fully.

Most of our discussion relates to learners who are typically gifted. There also are *highly gifted* individuals who are as different from the typically gifted learners as they are from average learners. Individuals who are highly gifted seem to have different value structures, which usually allow them to cope with the dissonance they find between their perception of life and the average person's. They tend to be more isolated by choice, more invested in concerns of a metanature, and seldom seek popularity or social acclaim. Typically, schools offer these children little; some educators suggest that tutoring with accomplished authorities would be more productive.[14,15,16]

Characteristics of Gifted Learners

As individuals develop higher levels of functioning, unique patterns and traits emerge. This is not a homogeneous group. The more gifted a person becomes, the more unique that person may appear. Some characteristics, however, are commonly found within a population of gifted learners; no one individual has all of the characteristics, but the list can help educators understand and serve this population.

Learners who are gifted show differential characteristics in all areas of major brain function. Some possible characteristics in each area and the resulting needs and possible problems if these characteristics go unattended are described in Table 14.1.

Identifying Gifted Learners

As seen in the characteristics in Table 14.1, many needs of gifted students are not met in the regular classroom. Providing for these needs allows the gifted learner to grow and develop, preventing the regression and frustration commonly found with students who are not appropriately challenged. Because intelligence is a dynamic process depending on a constant and stimulating interaction with the environment, appropriate learning experiences should be planned and services delivered. The alternative is loss of ability and talent; as the brain researchers tell us, we must use what we have or lose what we had.

Knowing some characteristics typically found in populations of gifted learners can help identify such learners. The three steps to finding gifted learners are search, screening, and identification. After placement, the data collected for these processes are used to help assess the student so that an appropriate program can be developed.

The Search

The function of the search is to generate a list of possible gifted students from all school sites, making sure that all students have an equal opportunity to be selected. Nominations should be obtained from teachers, principals, psychologists, parents, peers, and the students themselves. Patterns of achievement on standardized tests should be analyzed, and student behavior and production observed. A list of possible characteristics should be given to the people involved in the search process to help them find students who are gifted.

Screening

The identification process continues by screening for students who show they need a different kind of educational experience. Some screens that can be used for all areas of ability are (to p. 284)

TABLE 14.1
Examples of Characteristics of Gifted Learners

Differentiating Characteristics	Examples of Related Needs	Possible Concomitant Problems
Cognitive Domain		
Extraordinary quantity of information, unusual retentiveness	To be exposed to new and challenging information of the environment and the culture, including aesthetic, economic, political, educational, and social aspects; to acquire early mastery of foundation skills	Boredom with regular curriculum; impatience with "waiting for the group"
Advanced comprehension	Access to challenging curriculum and intellectual peers	Poor interpersonal relationships with less able children of the same age; adults considering children "sassy" or "smart aleck"; a dislike of repetition of already understood concepts
Unusually varied interests and curiosity	To be exposed to varied subjects and concerns; to be allowed to pursue individual ideas as far as interest takes them	Difficulty in conforming to group tasks; overextending energy levels, taking on too many projects at one time.
High level of verbal ability	To share ideas verbally in depth	Dominates discussions with information and questions deemed negative by teachers and fellow students; use of verbalism to avoid difficult thinking tasks
Heightened capacity for seeing unusual and diverse relationships, integration of ideas and disciplines	To mess around with varieties of materials, ideas, opportunities for multidisciplinary learning	Frustration at being considered "off the subject" or irrelevant in pursuing inquiry in areas other than subject being considered; considered odd or weird by others
Affective Domain		
Idealism and sense of justice, which appear at an early age	To transcend negative reactions by finding values to which he or she can be committed	Attempts unrealistic reforms and goals with resulting intense frustration (suicide result from intense depression over issues of this nature)
Earlier development of an inner locus of control and satisfaction	To clarify personal priorities among conflicting values; to confront and interact with the value system of others	Has difficulty conforming; rejects external validation and chooses to live by personal values that may be seen as a challenge to authority or tradition
Unusual emotional depth and intensity	To find purpose and direction from personal value system; to translate commitment into action in daily life	Unusual vulnerability; has problems focusing on realistic goals for life's work
High expectations of self and others, often leading to high	To learn to set realistic goals and to accept setbacks as part	Discouragement and frustration from high levels of self-criticism;

282

TABLE 14.1
Continued

Differentiating Characteristics	Examples of Related Needs	Possible Concomitant Problems
Cognitive Domain		
levels of frustration with self, others, and situations; perfectionism	of the learning process; to hear others express their growth in acceptance of self	has problems maintaining good interpersonal relations as others fail to maintain high standards imposed by gifted individual; immobilization of action due to high levels of frustration resulting from situations that do not meet expectations of excellence
Unusual sensitivity to the expectations and feelings of others	To learn to clarify the feelings and expectations of others	Unusually vulnerable of criticism of others; high level of need for success and recognition
Physical Domain		
Unusual quantity of input from the environment through a heightened sensory awareness	To engage in activities that will allow integration and assimilation of sensory data	Attention moving diffusely toward many areas of interest; overexpenditure of energy due to lack of integration; seeming disconnectedness
Unusual discrepancy between physical and intellectual development	To appreciate their physical capacities	Results in gifted adults who function with a mind/body dichotomy; gifted children who are only comfortable expressing themselves in mental activity, resulting in limited development both physically and mentally
Low tolerance for the lag between their standards and their athletic skills	To discover physical activities as a source of pleasure; to find satisfaction in small increments of improvement; to engage in noncompetitive physical activities	Refuse to take part in any activities where they do not excel; limiting their experience with otherwise pleasurable, constructive physical activities
"Cartesian split"—can include neglect of physical well-being and avoidance of physical activity	To engage in activities leading to mind/body integration; to develop a commitment to own physical well-being; to extend this concern to the social and political realm	Detrimental to full mental and physical health; inhibiting to the development of potential for the individual
Intuitive Domain		
Early involvement and concern for intuitive knowing and metaphysical ideas and phenomena	Opportunities to engage in meaningful dialogue with philosophers and others concerned with these ideas, to	Ridiculed by peers; not taken seriously by elders; considered weird or strange

(continued)

TABLE 14.1
Continued

Differentiating Characteristics	Examples of Related Needs	Possible Concomitant Problems
Intuitive Domain		
	become aware of own intuitive energy and ability; guidance in developing and using intuitive energy and ability	
Open to experiences in this area; will experiment with psychic and metaphysical phenomena	Guidance in becoming familiar with, analyzing, and evaluating such phenomena; should be provided a historical approach	Can become narrowly focused toward ungrounded belief systems
Creativity apparent in all areas of endeavor	Guidance in evaluating appropriate uses of creative efforts; encouragement for continued development of creative abilities	Seen as deviant; becomes bored with more mundane tasks; may be viewed as troublemaker
Ability to predict; interest in future	Opportunities for exploration of "what if" questions, activities of probability and prediction	Loss of highly valuable human ability

Source: Reprinted with permission from Barbara Clark, *Growing Up Gifted,* 4th ed. Columbus, Ohio: Merrill-Macmillan, 1992, pp. 38–44.

   1. Nomination forms from teachers, principals, counselors, psychologists, and other people in the school.
   2. Teacher reports of student functioning including intellectual, physical, social, and emotional; learning styles; and motivation.
   3. Family history and student background, provided by parents, including historical and developmental data on the student, anecdotes of the student in the home that indicate unusual capacity and early development, family activities and interests, and the child's out-of-school activities and interests.
   4. Peer identification.
   5. Student inventory of self.
   6. Student work and achievements.
   7. Multidimensional screen tests.

For best results, these screens should be used in combination for screening and later as part of the data in the identification process.

Identification

The actual identification for the purposes of placement in a gifted program is best done by professionals representing various areas of expertise, such as a teacher, the principal, a counselor or psychologist, and the program coordinator. The group should develop a case study or profile to aid in the identification and also later in program planning for the individual. The report should provide enough information to make good educational planning and placement possible.

Guidelines for identification are generally developed with each area of giftedness suggested by the public law. Many state's definitions of giftedness include all of the federal areas:

Intellectual Ability: *May include evidence of or potential for high levels of abstract reasoning ability, advanced vocabulary, advanced academic performance, an accelerated rate of learning, and/or honors or recognition for outstanding accomplishments. Such evidence may be obtained from an analysis of group or individually given intelligence tests, group or individually given achievement tests, and/or the pattern of advanced academic ability.*

The most common tests of intellectual ability are the Revised Stanford-Binet Tests of Intelligence and the Wechsler Intelligence Scales for Children (WISC). A person's score on an intelligence test is given as the Intelligence Quotient (IQ). This score is computed by dividing the mental age by the chronological age, multiplied by 100. Standardized on the general population, the tests evolved to set the average IQ at any age at 100. The middle 50 percent of the population falls between 90 and 110 IQ. On the Stanford-Binet an IQ of 132 reflects placement in the upper 2 percent of the population.

Despite the many criticisms of using intelligence tests for identification, such tests can predict how the student will respond to school-related tasks if they are used to supply only one piece of the data on which the placement decision is made. Intelligence tests do not indicate the capacity or the potential of the student, but they do generally predict how well a student will perform on the skills taught in school.

General and Specific Academic Ability: *The best single indicator of future academic achievement is the present level of achievement in the area of interest. Some sources for obtaining evidence in this category are the California Test of Basic Skills, the Stanford Achievement Test, the Iowa Tests of Basic Skills, the Peabody Individual Achievement Test, a representative collection of student school work, tests in content areas, teacher observation, and pupil self-inventories.*

Creativity: *Measures of creativity emphasize divergent thinking and correlate modestly with tests of intelligence. Some sources for obtaining evidence of creativity are the Creativity Tests for Children, Torrance Tests of Creative Thinking, analysis of personality inventories and checklists of creative behaviors, and analysis of student projects and work samples.*

Leadership: *A combination of nominations from self, peers, and teachers can be used as a predictor of leadership ability.*

Visual and Performing Arts: *The best indicator of giftedness is the ability to perform in the specific area. A panel of experts can judge such performances. Many experts believed that the general level of cognitive skills and achievement in the academic areas should receive no weight in these decisions, as there is no evidence that such measures are predictive of artistic achievement. When used with other data, the Seashore's Measures of Musical Talents, the Horn Art Aptitude Inventory, and the Meier Art Tests have been useful.*

Giftedness results partially from an early interaction with stimulating environments. Family patterns or persons who provide such stimulating interaction can be found in any culture, at any socioeconomic level, and in spite of many disabling conditions. Such differences, however, may make traditional identification procedures ineffective for discovering such ability. The following guidelines can help search for gifted learners among all populations:

1. Focus on the diversity within the population.
2. Gather data from multiple sources.

3. Use professionals and nonprofessionals who represent various areas of expertise relevant to the program.

4. Plan identification procedures that occur as early as possible and are continuous.

5. Pay special attention to the different ways children from different cultures manifest behavioral indicators of giftedness.[18]

HOW DOES GIFTEDNESS DEVELOP?

Interaction with the environment affects the infant during the prenatal period. Quoting research from many sources, Verny[19] has shown the fetus to be a hearing, sensing, feeling being. An area of concern to many prenatal researchers is the mother's emotional life, which influences the infant's self-esteem and security feelings. Attitudes of the mother seem to be picked up clearly by the infant in utero prior to the sixth or seventh month of pregnancy. Some researchers believe that the mother's attitude toward the child has the greatest effect on its well-being and future welfare.[20,21]

The Importance of Early Learning

The first four years of life are the most critical for human development. Not only is physical survival tenuous, but patterns for both the personality and the actualization of learning ability have begun. The personality established and the type of learning opportunities available can either facilitate or inhibit the development of inherited intellectual capacity. Uzgiris, involved for more than a decade in infant testing, believes that all children be given a chance to develop the full range of their abilities, because the competencies required for the future are unknown. He believes that "intelligence, even as measured by IQ, is a dynamic function, influenced by opportunities and learning, especially during the childhood years."[22] He suggests that the public be educated about the need for support for the education of very young children.

In the process of developing intelligence, young children need a responsive environment. People and objects in the environment can be growth-producing only if they have some meaning or use for the child. The most important focus is not the stages or sequence of development but rather the individual differences that appear with that development. These differences are in the ability to perform and to profit from the experiences provided. Age is an inadequate index of neurological and physical maturation, as both are changed by the child's environment and genetic program. The availability of many resources, including the parent and teacher, can allow children to stretch beyond known areas, to experiment with new materials and ideas, and to develop at their own pace and in their own style.

The curriculum for all preschool children should be rich in variety and stimulating in process, especially for children who are developing faster and show higher levels of intelligence. Their experiences should include more activities allowing self-direction, exposure to more abstract concepts, and more involvement with the tools and skills needed in reading, mathematics, science, research, art, music, and writing, and the world in which they live. A home or classroom that seeks to optimize growth in young children will organize responsive, individualized learning environments. It takes more complex planning and structuring to allow the necessary freedom and independence that develop high levels of interaction for young children and can ultimately produce higher levels of intelligence.

Social-Emotional Development

The social-emotional characteristics of individuals who are gifted are difficult to generalize, as are all other areas. However, we can look at characteristics commonly found, knowing that not all of them apply to any one gifted person. Given the opportunity for healthy development, social-emotional adjustment usually proceeds faster in gifted children than among the rest of the population. We must be concerned with the gifted child's social interaction *with* other people, not just social adjustment *to* others. A compilation of social-emotional characteristics of gifted children results in a positive profile:

- When compared with chronological peers, young gifted children feel more comfortable with themselves and with their interpersonal relationships.
- Bright children tend to be more independent and less conforming to peer opinions, more dominant, more forceful, and more competitive than are typical learners.
- Gifted children prefer their intellectual peers to their chronological age peers, resulting in a social preference for older children and adults.
- Concern for universal problems and the welfare of others begins much earlier than with more typically developing children. Children who are gifted become aware of issues of morality and justice very early.[23]
- Until secondary school the social status of bright children is reported as high and their classmates prefer them as companions. At secondary level this seems to diminish unless they also exibit other factors, such as athletic ability.[24]

For the highly gifted child, social adjustment takes on an added dimension. These children have more problems finding other children to whom they can relate. They become bored with school work and find fewer mental challenges within the school setting. The more highly gifted the child, the more the risk of social maladjustment and unhappiness increases.[25]

High levels of developed cognitive ability do not guarantee high levels of social-emotional development. Perfectionism, adult expectations, intense sensitivity, alienation, inappropriate environments, and/or role conflicts can lead to a lack of confidence and a helpless orientation toward perceived failure. When low levels of social-emotional development interact with their heightened perfectionism, we find ineffective problem solving and increasingly lowered self-concept.

WHY IS GIFTED EDUCATION NEEDED?

Giftedness arises from an interactive process that involves challenges from the environment stimulating and bringing forth innate capabilities and processes. Because the growth of intelligence is dynamic, gifted children require challenges appropriate in complexity, level, and pacing to their development. If they do not progress, they will regress; the human mind/brain cannot be maintained. Such children are often two to eight years beyond the concepts and skills being taught to their chronological-age peers. As long as schools are organized into age-grouped classes, gifted children will often find inappropriate material, pacing, and level of learning in their classrooms. Gifted education provides differentiation of the curriculum to meet the needs of bright children as well as opportunities for these students to interact with their intellectual peer group. To retain their giftedness, and also to further their potential, children who are gifted must participate in programs appropriate to their level of development.

Thomas Jefferson said, "There is nothing more unequal than equal treatment of unequal people." Our political and social systems are based on democratic principles. The public school, as an extension of those principles, purports to provide an equal educational opportunity for all children to develop to their fullest potential. It is then undemocratic to refuse gifted children the right to educational experiences appropriate to their level of development. When human beings are restricted in their development, they often become bored, frustrated, and angry. There is physical and psychological pain in being thwarted, discouraged, and diminished as a person. At present, less than one-half of the possible gifted learners in the United States are reported to be receiving education appropriate to their needs. *Equal opportunity does not mean the same opportunity, but rather an appropriate opportunity.*

When the needs of learners who are gifted are considered and the educational program is designed to meet these needs, these students make significant gains in achievement and their sense of competence and well-being is enhanced.[26] Gifted learners in appropriate programs learn to work more efficiently and they develop good problem-solving skills and see solutions from many viewpoints. They experience concepts and materials in a dynamic relationship and can use their knowledge as a background for unlimited learning.

Society gains from the advancement of all abilities and from the highest development of all its members, whatever their strengths.

HOW CAN THE NEEDS OF GIFTED LEARNERS BE MET?

Programs Designed for Delivery of Services to Gifted Learners

The primary goal of programs for students who are gifted is to provide opportunities for them to meet the needs that cannot be met in a regular classroom program, whether in the areas of content, process, and/or enrichment. What is done for each child depends on assessment data. Programs for the gifted learner do not begin with different curricula or different structures for learning, but with the unique needs of the gifted learners. The program is different only because, and in the same way, that the learner's needs are different. Generally, a gifted program should

- Provide opportunities and experiences particularly suited to and differentiated for the needs of the learners who are gifted and through which they can continue developing their potential.
- Establish an environment that values and enhances intelligence, talent, affective growth, and intuitive ability.
- Be articulated with general education programs—comprehensive, structured, and sequenced across grade levels.
- Allow active and cooperative participation by the gifted students and their parents.
- Be an integral part of the school day and provide resources from the school and the community.
- Provide time, space, and encouragement for gifted students to discover themselves, their powers, and their unique abilities.
- Provide opportunities for gifted students to interact with children and adults of various abilities, including the bright and talented, and to be challenged to know humanity for its uniqueness and connectedness.
- Encourage gifted students to find their place in society by discovering what abilities and in what areas they wish to contribute.

There are many options for organizing programs for gifted learners. The choice of organization will not assure that the needs of the gifted students will be met, only that within the structure those needs could be met. Factors other than structure, such as teacher skill and administrative and community support, can determine the quality of the program. Because no one structure can meet the needs of all learners who are gifted, providing an array of planned services is the best practice.

Level I

Regular classrooms: With modifications, regular classrooms can meet the needs of mildly gifted students. Such modifications include clusters (grouping five to seven gifted students to provide for peer interaction), continuous assessment, flexible grouping, differentiation of the curriculum (including acceleration and enrichment), and individualization of instruction (planning so that each child's needs are met). Team teaching and cross-grading with students from several age levels enhance the possibility that students will be able to work at their own level and pace.

Level II

Adjunct programs: Adjunct programs can be added to the regular classroom to provide for moderately gifted students. Such programs could include mentors, internships, independent study, resource rooms, and special classes after school or during the summer.

Level III

Special classes: Special classes, such as those that group only identified gifted students together, are needed for highly gifted students. These classes could be scheduled for part of the school day, with heterogeneously grouped classes available for electives. Or, special classes could meet for the entire day, providing the accelerated pace and complexity these students need.

Level IV

Special schools: Some students are so far beyond the curriculum and pacing of their age group that they need special schools, such as magnet schools, or acceleration to university settings.

Homogeneous and heterogeneous grouping practices have important contributions to make to teaching and learning. In the 1971 hearings held by the U.S. Department of Health Education and Welfare, gifted students expressed preference for programs in which they are separated for part of the day, but not totally segregated from other students. They asked for flexibility in their programs and curriculum. Homogeneous grouping can provide stimulation by peers (students with like abilities in any area, not just of a similar age), support skill development, and meet specific needs. Heterogeneous grouping can develop social skills, introduce new experiences or information needed by a whole class, and build a community of learners.

Some program models used to provide services for learners who are gifted are discussed here.

The Pyramid Project

This model is an outgrowth of the Richardson Foundation Study.[27] It starts with a broad base of able learners whose individual needs are met by acceleration and enrichment in the regular classroom. The second level serves fewer students who have more specialized needs and who require special classes. The third level contains even fewer exceptionally gifted students who find their needs met in special schools. This model provides an array of services.

The Enrichment Triad/Revolving Door Model

The Enrichment Triad was developed to aid in the differentiation of curriculum for gifted learners and its delivery of services component. The Revolving Door Model is essentially a resource room adjunct program.[28] A wide array of goals, strategies, and procedures provide services for elementary and secondary students. The model assumes that giftedness reflects behavior resulting from an interaction among three basic clusters of human traits—above-average abilities, high task commitment, and high levels of creativity. The model also assumes that gifted behaviors can be developed, that they are not always present, and that service should be provided only when such behaviors are exhibited. It is basic to the operation of the model that a talent pool be identified comprising 15 percent to 20 percent of the school population. These students must be provided with performance-based learning situations in the regular classroom that can help teachers identify which individuals and small groups should revolve into advanced-level experiences based on their interest in particular topics or problem areas. Detailed procedures have been worked out to support the operation of this model.

The Autonomous Learner Model

Developed in the late 1970s to meet both the social-emotional and cognitive needs of gifted high school youngsters, the autonomous learner model[29] is presented in a special class setting, generally using one period at specified times throughout the week. The model is expected to be in place for at least three years and to contain five essential dimensions: orientation, individual development, enrichment activities, seminars, and in-depth study. Although the model is not a total program for learners who are gifted, it meets social-emotional needs and encourages independence in the learning setting.

The Hopkins Acceleration Model

This model has developed educational opportunities in several areas of radical acceleration.[30] These classes differ from most homogeneously grouped programs for the gifted in several ways: students are selected from measures of specific aptitude, the students self-select into increasingly difficult classes with heavy loads, there is a maximum use of learning time, the material is fast-paced and uses a high level of abstraction and complexity, no class time is spent on practice, activities are kept to a minimum, the material is individualized, and the program demands intensive self-study. Programs in math and language arts using this model are found at universities throughout the country. The model best serves students who are highly gifted and excel in a specific academic area, especially mathematics.

To meet the needs of gifted learners requires a planned, coordinated, continuous program. This program must be open and responsive to the changing individual, while providing continuous challenge and an adequate diversity of content and process. As we draw from more traditional gifted education models, the community, parents, students, and staff must make the decisions of structure and intent. Some goals can be generalized; others must be set by the teacher, the student, and the parent in a cooperative effort.

Differentiating the Curriculum and Individualizing Instruction

A differentiated curriculum addresses the characteristics of gifted learners and the needs those characteristics create. Gifted learners can be challenged to continue their development if the content is modified by increasing the levels and complexity of materials available, if the process strategies include flexible pacing, and if the range of acceptable products are increased. An appropriate curriculum for gifted learners should meet their immediate needs and also should allow continuous progress in both skill and content. The curriculum should be increasingly difficult, interdisciplinary, broad-based and thematic, comprehensive, and provide for any needed acceleration. Students who are gifted must be allowed to challenge existing ideas, discover new ideas, focus on open-ended tasks, and integrate the core curriculum with high-level thinking skills.

One way to ensure that such provisions are made is to preplan a scope and sequence that reflects the needs of the district as well as those of the students. A scope and sequence given to students can provide motivation and empowerment as students see what they have already mastered and discover the possibilities ahead. Such informed students can become partners in the learning process.

Once the curriculum has been differentiated and the materials and strategies are available, meeting the needs of each individual student becomes possible. Individualizing instruction is a way of organizing learning so the rate, content, schedule, experiences, and depth of exploration available to all students stem from their assessed achievement and interests. Individualization can be done in steps: (1) assess each student's needs and individualize the level and pace of instruction; (2) involve the student in the selection of goals; (3) incorporate self-directed and independent study and self-selection of learning activities and materials from teacher organized choices; and finally, (4) with the student, cooperatively assess and select goals, learning materials, activities, and instructional techniques. The teacher now becomes a consultant and a resource.

Some strategies for differentiating the curriculum and individualizing the instruction are discussed here.

Curriculum Compacting

The curriculum compacting system[31] was designed to provide evidence through pre- and posttesting procedures about a student's mastery of the skills and concepts required in the regular curriculum. Once a skill or concept has been learned, it is wasteful for the student to keep reviewing the information or skill. More appropriate curricular experiences can be planned when we know what the students already know and what they need to learn.

The Taxonomy of Educational Objectives: Cognitive Domain

Benjamin Bloom[32] and his colleagues present an organized way of developing cognitive ability. Awareness of this structure allows the teacher to plan different activities at many levels, making it easier to meet the needs of a variety of learners. All students need to experience learning at the levels of knowledge, comprehension, application, analysis, synthesis, and evaluation. Students who are gifted must have the opportunity to work increasingly at the higher levels of this taxonomy.

The Inquiry Model

Jerome Bruner[33] believed that any discipline could be taught at any age if the basic structure of the discipline were communicated in ways the child could understand. The Inquiry Model[34] gives students practice in solving problems by establishing the properties of all objects or systems involved in the problem, finding which objects or systems are relevant to the problem, and discovering how they function in the solution. Sessions are designed to help students learn to formulate and test their own theories and to become aware of their own learning processes.

Metacognition

Metacognition is the conscious knowledge of one's cognitive processes and capabilities that allow one to monitor, regulate, and evaluate one's own cognition.[35] By use of the process, students can become more efficient and flexible learners. Carr and Borkowski[36] believe that explicit training in metacognitive skills enhances academic achievement, intelligence, and creative problem solving.

Integrative Education Model

The model was developed by Barbara Clark[37] to synthesize the current findings from brain research, the new physics, general systems theory, and psychology as they relate to education and to show the application of these data to optimal learning and teaching. The model presents a process of learning that is flexible, complex, and individualized. It allows variations in pace, level, and grouping while encouraging student choice, participation, and involvement. It optimizes learning for all students by offering brain-compatible teaching experiences in all subject areas. The model integrates the major areas of brain function in the learning process, including cognitive functions (verbal, rational, analytic, and the visual, spatial, gestalt); physical functions (movement and sensing); affective functions (both intra- and interpersonal); and intuitive functions. By setting the integrative processes in a responsive learning environment, the model takes advantage of the latest data on learning and teaching.

Numerous other strategies can be used to differentiate and individualize the learning experience. Even though many of the strategies can be used with all learners, they are especially important to the education of the gifted students as they allow flexibility, continuous progress, and a focus on individual needs.

HOW CAN THE CULTURALLY DIVERSE GIFTED LEARNER BEST BE SERVED?

It is important to delineate the population we are discussing. The terms *economically disadvantaged, low socioeconomic status* (SES), and *culturally diverse* have often been used interchangeably. This practice is misleading. Some children of low socioeconomic status are also culturally diverse; many are not. Some culturally diverse students are of low socioeconomic status or economically disadvantaged, but many are not. In this discussion, *economically disadvantaged* is called *low SES* and refers to students being reared by poor, low SES parents out of the economic (rather than cultural) mainstream. This population seems characterized by the values and attitudes often found as a result of poverty. In referring to culturally diverse learners, we speak of any student whose rearing is more typical of a culture that differs significantly in values and attitudes from the dominant culture. These students have unique problems even when not reared in conditions of poverty.

Children raised with significantly different values and attitudes from those of the dominant culture often face conditions that promote limited intellectual development, unfavorable socialization experiences, unequal school opportunities, and occupational discrimination. These conditions work to lower motivation and achievement. The students attend school less regularly than do other groups of students and drop out in greater numbers. When these conditions restrict a stimulating interaction with the environment, student talents are often lost due to the dynamic nature of gifts and talents; ability must be nurtured if it is to grow.

How giftedness is expressed or if it is allowed to be expressed depends both on the genetic patterns and anatomical structure of the individual and on the support and opportunities provided by that individual's environment. Stimulating environments significantly change the brain, allowing accelerated, complex, and integrated function, or giftedness.[38]

Intelligence is a dynamic process that depends on a constant and stimulating interaction with the environment. It thus is imperative that appropriate learning experiences be provided by the home and the school. It is the responsibility of the family, cultural group, and school to engage in attitudes and practices known to bring out the highest levels of intelligence and ability unique to each child.

A report for the U.S. Department of Education[39] revealed that even though students from low-income backgrounds comprised 20 percent of the student population, only 4 percent of them perform at the highest levels on standardized tests. Such students were much less likely to be enrolled in academic programs that could open the access to college enrollment. The report recommended identification procedures including the use of a preselection process wherein students are encouraged to develop and display their skills and abilities over an extended period of time. Such a process could increase their possibilities to show advanced abilities appropriate for admission into a gifted program. As in many other studies, the use of multiple criteria for identification was also recommended.

In a study of the family's role in the success of low SES gifted learners, Joyce Van Tassel-Baska[40] reported that families of successful students encourage and monitor progress, communicate high expectations and standards for academic achievement, and view socioeconomic circumstances as motivators to succeed. These families were perceived as a major source of encouragement and influence.

Giftedness at the highest level can be found in every cultural, racial, and ethnic group. However, particular cultural groups encourage some skills and abilities more than others. This difference results from differing values, attitudes, and opportunities. What is valued by the culture is produced by the culture. Where the culture's values and beliefs approximate those of the dominant culture, development of the dominant culture's values is often facilitated. Cultural group support may enable children in that group to reach outstanding achievement in any situation. However, within some cultures, the overlay of the problems of poverty makes it difficult to assess potential achievement and may inhibit development or achievement in any area.

Every culture instills both advantages and limiting attitudes in its children before they enter the schools. The same can be said for every family from every area of the country, regardless of the culture. Families who want to help their children become all they can be need to be aware of any limiting practices in order to reduce them as much as possible. With an awareness of what facilitates and what inhibits growth, families can find a way to strengthen the positive attitudes and abilities without weakening the ties the child has with the culture.

In her discussion of people who are gifted and from culturally diverse populations, Alexenia Baldwin[41] notes that the literature often focuses on the deficits rather than the strengths. She suggests that educators need to hold three basic assumptions as they define the populations, set their educational goals, and determine effective systems of instruction and evaluation. These assumptions are that

1. Giftedness exists in all human groups, and how these abilities are expressed does not represent an innate capacity of the group.
2. Identification of gifted individuals can be made on other than the usual standardized tests.
3. Behaviors unique or special to a cultural group can serve as indicators of high level abilities to conceptualize and organize phenomena.

Baldwin believes that educators should be concerned with their attitudes toward cultural differences; their knowledge of cultural and ethnic history and traditions; the availability of resources (written and human) related to other cultures; the flexibility of the organization in accommodating programs for the culturally diverse gifted child; and their knowledge when they work with children from various cultures.

Children who are gifted have now begun to gain the attention of many organizations and communities of the diverse cultures. More than 177 different tribes and communities of American Indians have begun to search out the gifted among them as they focus on the improvement of educational opportunities for their children. Eskimos and the Aleuts are concerned about the recognition of talent among their children. As the diverse groups within the Asian American population attend to the needs of their gifted learners they have begun to find that the image of their children as model achievers can work against them. Given this great variety of the Asian American community and the large proportion who come from low socioeconomic conditions, traditional measures for identification of the gifted are unlikely to be appropriate for all children.

African American gifted children continue to confound people who attempt to identify them. A number of researchers, such as Shade and New in Chapter 16 of this book, describe the unique cultural characteristics of African American children and how their culture influences their learning styles and behaviors. Social class is a strong variable that influences the academic performance of African American children. About one-third of African American families are prospering, and the number of professionals rose 50 percent in the past decade. However, the vast majority of African Americans are far from realizing their potential, with alarming numbers dropping out of school, becoming teenage parents, involved in the penal system, or dying at an early age. African Americans who are gifted continue to find limited opportunities either within the schools or the professional world, in large part because of the large number concentrated within the lower-class population.

The Hispanic population is increasing rapidly and now makes up a large percentage of the school population in California. Also, like the other cultures, the Hispanic population includes a variety of groupings. The population also shares strong cultural beliefs, a common language, and similar traditions. DeLeon[42] presents a thoughtful rationale for the lack of success Hispanic students have with current identification procedures resulting in their underrepresentation in gifted programs. Hispanic children have consistently been shown to be more field dependent than are Anglo children. That is, they rely on external guidance, accept the prevailing field, and find it more difficult to separate an item from its context. Family socialization practices encourage responsibility to the family unit and obedience to the head of the house. The result is that Hispanic children often have a strong group identity and express themselves differently than do the children of the dominant culture. DeLeon concludes that these children are as proficient as any others in concept attainment but differ in the type of information they process most effectively and in the situation that aids their processing. We must change our narrow linear, analytic, rational definition and identification of giftedness if we are going to find and nurture individuals who are gifted among this population.

The following suggestions can help parents, counselors, and teachers work successfully with culturally diverse gifted learners. According to Frasier[43] and to Colengelo and Zaffrann[44] gifted learners should be helped to

1. Develop questioning, introspective attitudes.
2. Understand and explore the problems they may face as they become upwardly mobile.
3. Align their cultural values with those of the dominant culture.
4. Develop their own individuality and establish their personal cultural identity.
5. Cope with peer pressures not to succeed, when they exist.
6. Remediate any areas of skill that are lacking, especially limited language skills.
7. Explore opportunities in a variety of career options.

I add that we need to help culturally diverse populations to

■ Deal with excessive pressures to succeed as they are perceived to be models for others.
■ Learn to value all persons, regardless of cultural or gender identity.
■ Learn of the strengths of each culture and the unity of all people.

SUMMARY

This chapter explores the concepts of intelligence and giftedness. Neither intelligence nor giftedness can be limited to a rational, linear definition. These dynamic concepts should be defined to reflect the interactive involvement of both the inherited capabilities and the environmental opportunities that allow the actualization of those capabilities. The concept and the definitions must take into account the variety of ways intelligence and giftedness can be expressed and the wide range of characteristics that can give evidence for this high level of development.

Information on how giftedness develops and on the importance of the early learning experience to the growth of the child cognitively, socially, and emotionally was reviewed. Children who are developing in this accelerated and complex way need appropriate educational experiences both before and during their schooling. The curriculum can meet their needs through differentiation and individualization of instruction.

Finally, the unique problems of the culturally diverse gifted student was explored, with attention to some populations that find difficulty being recognized within the system. If instruction is individualized and the curriculum is differentiated, a separate curriculum for these populations would not be necessary. What will be important is that teachers and other people involved in programs for students who are gifted hold positive attitudes toward cultural differences and are aware of cultural and ethnic history and traditions. They should know of the many available resources related to diverse populations. The program should be flexible and responsive to each child's needs. All children have a right to develop to their highest potential. Educators must assure them of that right.

QUESTIONS AND ACTIVITIES

1. In what ways are the definitions of giftedness discussed in this chapter similar? In what ways are they different? Given these definitions, how would you respond to the idea that giftedness is a social construct. (See Chapter 1 for a discussion of social constructs.)

2. List three steps used in finding learners who are gifted. Discuss problems that may occur at each step. How would you resolve those problems?

3. Interview several parents of gifted and regular students and ask them to share their views on the physical, social, and emotional development of their children. In what ways are gifted and regular students similar? Different?

4. Compare and contrast differentiating curriculum and individualizing instruction. Give examples of each approach.

5. What resources and training will you need to teach gifted students?

6. Organize two groups of students to debate the following question: Is gifted education needed?

7. Write a brief paper on strategies you would use to meet the needs of gifted learners in a regular classroom.

8. Identify and critique five models used to provide services for learners who are gifted. Which model would you use? Why?

9. "Educators' have a special responsibility to identify and provide services to gifted students who are bilingual, culturally diverse, minority, and/ or from low-income homes." Do you agree with this statement? Why or why not?

NOTES

1. Lewis Terman, "Mental and Physical Traits of a Thousand Gifted Children," in Lewis Terman, ed., *Genetic Studies of Genius,* Vol. I (Stanford, Calif.: Stanford University Press, 1925).

2. Howard Gardner, *Frames of Mind* (New York: Basic Books, 1983).

3. Paul Witty, *The Gifted Child* (Boston: Heath, 1951).

4. Joseph Renzulli, *The Enrichment Triad Model: A Guide for Developing Defensible Programs for the Gifted and Talented* (Mansfield Center, Conn.: Creative Learning Press, 1977).

5. David Krech, "Psychoneurobiochemeducation," *Phi Delta Kappan* L. (1969): 370–375.

6. M. Rosenzweig, "Environmental Complexity, Cerebral Change and Behavior," *American Psychologist* 21 (1966): 321–332.

7. M. Rosenzweig, "Experience, Memory and the Brain," *American Psychologist* 4 (1984): 365–376.

8. Richard Thompson, Theodore Berger, and Stephen Berry, "An Introduction to the Anatomy, Physiology, and Chemistry of the Brain," in Merlin Wittrock, ed., *The Brain and Psychology* (New York: Academic Press, 1980).

9. Krech, "Psychoneurobiochemeducation."

10. Rosenzweig, "Environmental Complexity, Cerebral Change and Behavior."

11. Krech, "Psychoneurobiochemeducation."

12. Thompson, Berger, and Berry, "An Introduction to the Anatomy, Physiology, and Chemistry of the Brain."

13. Krech, "Psychoneurobiochemeducation."

14. David Feldman and L. Goldsmith, *Nature's Gambit: Child Prodigies and the Development of Human Potential* (New York: Basic Books, 1986).

15. Leta Hollingworth, *Children above 180 IQ* (Yonkers-on-Hudson, N.Y.: World Books, 1942).

16. Linda Silverman, *The Plight of the Highly Gifted.* Paper presented at the California Association for the Gifted Annual Conference, Fresno, n.d.

17. Barbara Clark, *Growing Up Gifted,* 4th ed. (Columbus, Ohio: Merrill-Macmillan, 1992).

18. Mary Frasier, "The Identification of Gifted Black Students: Developing New Perspectives," *Journal for the Education of the Gifted* 3 (1987): 155–180.

19. Thomas Verny, *The Secret Life of the Unborn Child* (New York: Summit Books, 1981).

20. M. Huttunen, and P. Niskanen, "Prenatal Loss of Father and Psychiatric Disorders," *Archives of General Psychiatry* 35 (1978): 429–431.

21. D. Stott, "Follow-Up Study from Birth of the Effects of Prenatal Stresses," *Developmental Medicine and Child Neurology* 15 (1973): 770–787.

22. I. Uzgiris, "Issue: Infant Intelligence Test Arouses Controversy," *ASCD Udate* 5 (1989): 4–5.

23. Ruth Martinson, *Educational Programs for Gifted Pupils* (Sacramento: California State Department of Education, 1961).

24. Abe Tannenbaum, *Gifted Children* (New York: Macmillan, 1983).

25. Silverman, *The Plight of the Highly Gifted.*

26. Clark, *Growing Up Gifted.*

27. June Cox, Neil Daniel, and Bruce Boston, *Educating Able Learners: Programs and Promising Practices,* (Austin: University of Texas Press, 1985).

28. Renzulli, *The Enrichment Triad Model.*

29. George Betts, *The Autonomous Learner Model* (Greeley, Colo.: Autonomous Learning Publications Specialists, 1985).

30. Julian Stanley, "The Case for Extreme Educational Acceleration of Intellectually Brilliant Youths," in John Gowan, Joseph Khatena, and E. Paul Torrance, eds., *Educating the Ablest: A Book of Readings,* 2nd ed. (Itasca, Ill.: F. E. Peacock Publishers, 1979).

31. Renzulli, *The Enrichment Triad Model:*

32. Benjamin Bloom, ed., *Taxonomy of Educational Objectives.* Handbook I, *Cognitive Domain* (New York, David McKay, 1956).

33. Jerome Bruner, *The Process of Education* (Cambridge, Mass.: Harvard University Press, 1960).

34. J. Richard Suchman, *The Elementary School Training Program in Scientific Inquiry* (Urbana: University of Illinois Press, 1962).

35. J. Flavell, "Metacognition and Cognitive Monitoring: A New Area of Cognitive-Developmental Inquiry," *American Psychologist* 34 (1979): 906–911.

36. M. Carr and J. Borkowski, "Metamemory in Gifted Children," *Gifted Child Quarterly* 1 (1987): 40–44.

37. Clark, *Growing Up Gifted.*

38. Rosenzweig, "Environmental Complexity, Cerebral Change and Behavior."

39. J. Alamprese and W. Erlanger, *No Gift Wasted: Effective Strategies for Educating Highly*

Able, Disadvantaged Students in Mathematics and Science. Vol. I: *Findings, Final Report* (Washington, D.C.: Cosmos Corp., 1989).

40. Joyce Van Tassel-Baska, "The Role of the Family in the Success of Disadvantaged Gifted Learners," *Journal for the Education of the Gifted* 1 (1989): 22–36.

41. Alexenia Baldwin, "Programs for the Gifted and Talented: Issues Concerning Minority Populations," in F. Horowitz and M. O'Brien eds., *The Gifted and Talented Developmental Perspectives* (Washington, D.C.: American Psychological Association, 1985).

42. J. DeLeon, "Cognitive Style Difference and the Underrepresentation of Mexican Americans in Programs for the Gifted," *Journal for the Education of the Gifted* 3 (1983): 167–177.

43. Mary Frasier, "Counseling the Culturally Diverse Gifted," in N. Colangelo and R. Zaffrann, eds., *New Voices in Counseling the Gifted* (Dubuque, Iowa: Kendall/Hunt, 1979).

44. Nicholas Colangelo and R. Zaffrann, "Special Issues in Counseling the Gifted," *Counseling and Human Development* 5 (1981): 11–12.

A major goal of school reform is to restructure the curriculum and organization of schools so that students from diverse racial, ethnic, and social-class groups will experience educational success.

School Reform

Reforming schools so that all students have an equal opportunity to succeed requires a new vision of education and social actors who are willing to advocate for and participate in change. The three chapters in Part Six explore three important steps in school reform: implementing the characteristics of effective schools, recognizing how culture influences learning and teaching, and involving parents in schools.

In his chapter on effective schools, Lawrence W. Lezotte argues that school improvement is a process, not an event. Lezotte describes the characteristics of effective schools and gives his readers a set of principles for creating them. Barbara J. Shade and Clara A. New examine culture as a key variable in student learning. They give examples of ways that culture can be used to improve instruction. Cherry A. McGee Banks discusses ways to involve parents in schools. She also argues that parent involvement is an important factor in school reform and student achievement.

In his chapter on effective schools, Lezotte states that education for all means more than everyone must go to school. It means that everyone can and will be educated. Even though there has been some progress in providing all students with an equal opportunity for education, much more is needed. Lezotte's chapter explains why effective school practices are an important tool for increasing educational opportunity.

Lezotte gives his readers a historical overview of the effective schools movement. The overview includes a discussion of *Equality of Educational Opportunity* by James Coleman, a review of research on effective schools, a rationale for implementing effective schools, and a list of the characteristics of effective schools. Readers will be particularly interested in the section that contrasts districtwide versus school-based processes for creating more effective schools.

Shade and New argue that culture is a cogent variable in student learning. Modal cultural characteristics of groups such as African Americans and Anglos are contrasted with school culture. Shade and New state that the ideal student from the perspective of school culture sits quietly in his or her own seat, looks only at the teacher, answers questions when called on, and performs the required work in the manner prescribed. They conclude that the school's cultural norms and expected behaviors often conflict with the cultural norms and behaviors of students.

According to Shade and New, building a classroom climate that acknowledges, accepts, understands, and accommodates various instructional and communication patterns is the teacher's first task. Teachers can make their classrooms more inviting to students by adapting their work, communication, and teaching styles to the behavioral styles of their students. Cooperative groups and peer tutoring are two ways that Shade and New suggest teachers adapt their teaching styles.

The third chapter in Part Six examines parent involvement. Parents can be a cogent force in school reform. Parents, perhaps more than any other group, can mobilize the community to support school reform. Parents have first-hand knowledge about the school's effectiveness and can be vocal advocates for change. As consumers of educational services, parents can raise questions that are difficult for professional educators and administrators to raise, such as: "What is the proportion of males in special education classes?" and "What is the ethnic breakdown of students enrolled in higher-level math and science classes?"

Banks argues that parents are more willing to work for school reform when they are involved in schools. They are more likely to become involved in schools when parent involvement opportunities reflect their varied interests, skills, and motivations. For example, many students come from single-parent homes or from homes with two working parents. The traditional approach to parent involvement with mothers spending time during the day at their children's school will not work for most parents today. Banks suggests ways to expand traditional ideas about parent involvement and to increase the number and kinds of parents involved in schools.

CHAPTER 15

Effective Schools: A Framework for Increasing Student Achievement

■ LAWRENCE W. LEZOTTE

Our democratic society cannot be what our schools are not. Nowhere is our commitment to this belief more apparent than in the following statements. First, a system of free public schooling must be made available to *all* children. Second, at specified ages, all children *must* attend school. In his book *The Conflict in Education in a Democratic Society,* Robert Hutchins suggests that perhaps the greatest idea the United States has given the world is education for all.[1] The world is entitled to know whether this means that everybody can be educated, or simply that everybody must go to school.

As the United States approaches the end of the twentieth century, we have made significant progress toward Hutchins's vision of educating all children. Each state has established a system of free public education for all of its children. Each state has established compulsory schooling laws that require every child to attend those free public schools or their equivalent. Even though the struggle to assure universal access to quality schools is far from settled, it is nevertheless true that all students are required to attend school for at least a minimum number of years, regardless of their race, gender or social class.

The 1954 U.S. Supreme Court decision *Brown* v. *The Board of Education of Topeka, Kansas,* represented a milestone in the struggle to assure equal educational opportunity for all. That general principle is now established, even though court cases involving more subtle legal questions regarding access to public education continue. After the 1950s, the battle line for democratic education shifted. Researchers began to ask whether minority students, especially African Americans, were participating in the schools' programs and services in proportion to their numbers in the population. Here, again, some progress has been realized, but much more is required.

Minority children are still overly represented in special education programs, low track, and other remedial programs. They lag behind their nonminority counterparts in rates of graduation, proportion going to postsecondary education, and participation in more academically rigorous programs, especially mathematics and science. Researchers documenting the problem have begun to identify programs and other strategies that seem to be helpful in assuring more success for more students, especially groups that have profited little from schooling in the past.[2]

One program that has resulted from this research and has become widely used by educators throughout the United States is school improvement based on effective schools research.[3] This program has been described by some people as the "effective schools movement." It represents a program of school reform based on research and descriptions of effective school practices that now span about twenty-five years.[4]

HISTORICAL PERSPECTIVE ON THE EFFECTIVE SCHOOLS MOVEMENT

This overview presents a brief description of the effective schools movement, organized around five relatively distinguishable periods. During the first period the problems of definition and the subsequent search for the "effective school" were discussed. In the following period, a series of case studies designed to capture the organizational culture of the identified effective schools were completed. The third period represented a critical transition—from describing the effective school to creating more effective schools, one school at a time. In the fourth period, the larger organizational context and the local school district came to play an important role in school improvement—demonstrating how the school district could enhance or impede improvement of schools, one school at a time. Finally, there is some discussion of the current federal and state policies and programs that are being implemented to ensure the availability of more effective schools for more children.

Phase I: Search for Effective Schools

The story of the effective schools movement began in July 1966, with the publication of *Equality of Educational Opportunity* by James Coleman et al.[5] The controversial findings that Coleman and his colleagues reported became widely disseminated and debated. This excerpt from the Coleman study summarizes the issue of effective schools:

> *Schools bring little influence to bear on a child's achievement that is independent of his background and general social context. . . . This very lack of an independent effect means that the inequality imposed on children by their home, neighborhood and peer environment are carried along to become the inequalities with which they confront adult life at the end of school. For equality of educational opportunity must imply a strong effect of schools that is independent of the child's immediate social environment, and that strong independence is not present in American schools.[6]*

Coleman and his colleagues clarified the public policy issue by bringing into sharp contrast the question of whether student achievement derives more from the homes from which children have come or the schools to which they are sent. Coleman said that the issue has been, and is likely to continue to be, fundamental to the discourse on student achievement for a long time. It is basic in that it questions the usefulness of increasing public investments in public schools if, in fact, schools do not (and seemingly cannot) make a difference. Unfortunately, public acceptance of the Coleman hypothesis still constitutes a formidable obstacle to the advancement of educational equity and to the general improvement of student achievement through schooling.

Fortunately, several researchers did not accept the Coleman hypothesis. Initially working independently, each began to formulate a research strategy that would, if successful, begin to challenge the hypothesis. Their strategy was to go into the real world of public schools and see if they could identify individual schools that represented clear exceptions to Coleman's theory. The first-generation studies conducted by these researchers became the foundation for the research base of the effective schools movement.[7]

Readers interested in an in-depth synthesis of the early research and public policy debate should read Levine and Lezotte, *Unusually Effective Schools: A Review and Analysis of Research and Practice.*[8] Five additional syntheses of the effective schools research have been published. These papers are easily accessible and, when read in the order of their publication, do a good job of tracking the effective schools research, associated policy issues, and the research criticisms.[9]

Even though there is some risk in depending totally on syntheses conducted by other researchers, these five different summaries do an excellent job of setting forth the research and policy base for what has come to be called the effective schools movement. Beginning with the Coleman Report and reviewing the various summaries, you can observe several important issues and conclusions associated with this research base.

The validity of Coleman's theory remains largely intact if one judges student achievement by means of broad-gauged, standardized, norm-referenced measures designed to find differences among the test population. These measured differences in student performance tend to be more directly associated with home and family background factors. If, on the other hand, one measures student achievement by assessing student mastery of basic school skills taught as a part of the curriculum, then the differences in school-to-school effects become more marked, and a stronger case is made for the school effect. The conclusion is that the issues of measurement have been, and probably always will be, at or near the center of the debate on effective schools.

Because of the centrality of the measurement questions, any discussion of school improvement must begin with this question: What would we be willing to accept as observable, measurable evidence of school effectiveness or school improvement? If there is no consensus on answers to this question, it is doubtful that school improvement would result. Phrased in a more colloquial way: If you don't know where you are going, any road—or perhaps no road—will get you there.

To help schools with the discussion of acceptable evidence of school improvement, the following definition of an effective school is offered. *An effective school is one that can demonstrate the joint presence of quality (acceptably high levels of achievement) and equity (no differences in the distribution of that achievement among the major subsets of the student population).* Achievement of these criteria must be demonstrated in outcome terms reflective of the school's teaching for learning mission.

Effective schools case study research has proven Coleman and his colleagues wrong in one sense. This literature clearly demonstrates, in numerous settings, that some schools are able to attain remarkably high levels of pupil mastery of basic school skills, even though these schools are serving large proportions of economically poor and disadvantaged students, minority and nonminority. The criticisms of the effective schools research have been many and pointed, but the one fact seems to stand up against all the criticisms: Some schools are able to achieve these extraordinary results. As long as such places exist, the effective schools debate is not a discussion of theory, but a discussion of commitment and political will.

Phase II: Descriptions of Effective Schools

During the second major period of the movement, the attention of researchers turned toward the internal operations of effective schools. Ironically, the search for effective schools captured the interest of social scientists and policymakers, but not necessarily of educational practitioners. School leaders, teachers, and local boards of education began to take a more active interest in the effective schools research as the descriptions of the effective schools made their way into the literature and language of the educational community.

During this period, researchers sought to answer the following general question: In what ways do effective schools differ from their less effective counterparts? Their research methodology generally consisted of three steps. First, effective schools, based on measured outcomes, were identified and paired with schools that were similar in all respects except for the more favorable student outcome profile. Next, field researchers were sent into these pairs of schools. They conducted interviews, observations, and surveys designed to develop as rich a description of the life of these schools as possible. Finally, the data were analyzed with the following question in mind: What are the distinctive characteristics of the effective schools that seems to set them apart from their less effective counterparts?

From the field research emerged descriptions of certain characteristics that seemed to indicate how these schools were able to maintain their exceptional status. Edmonds described five factors in his early research:[10]

- The principal's leadership and attention to the quality of instruction
- A pervasive and broadly understood instructional focus
- An orderly, safe climate conducive to teaching and learning
- Teacher behaviors that convey the expectation that all students will obtain at least minimum mastery
- The use of measures of pupil achievement as the basis for program evaluation

Since that original listing, many other studies have cross-validated the original findings. Some of the more recent studies have described additional factors, and others have sought to make the original Edmonds's factors more explicit and more operational.[11] New studies have also looked closely at elementary schools, as did Edmonds in his original research. Other more recent studies have taken the characteristics or factor theory of the effective school to the secondary levels as well.[12] In addition, the researchers have now documented the existence of the correlates in settings other than those characterized as serving primarily economically poor and minority student populations. Finally, the research has been expanded to include studies in other countries, particularly in Great Britain.[13]

What major conclusions seem to emerge from this expanding array of descriptive studies of the organization and operation of effective schools? First, schools in which students master the intended curriculum *do* share a describable list of institutional and organizational variables that seem to coexist with school effectiveness. Second, these core factors seem to be robust in that they have endured across the various studies. Third, the effective school can and generally does stand alone, even among its counterparts in the same local school district. The major implication is that the institutional and organizational mechanisms that coexist with effectiveness can be attained by individual schools, one school at a time. This suggests that effective schooling is within the grasp of the teachers and administrators who make up the teaching community of the single school.

With the publication of these descriptions of the effective school, practitioners and community members began to take a more active interest. It became clear that more schools could organize themselves to achieve these extraordinary results. The important question began to refocus itself: How could the knowledge about these effective schools become the basis for the purposeful transformation through planned change programs for even more schools?

Phase III: Creating More Effective Schools—One School at a Time

When school practitioners began to discover that the effective school could be characterized by a relatively short list of alterable school variables, some educators began to see new possibilities for their schools. Their reasoning seemed to proceed along the following line: If these individual schools had the wherewithal to make their schools effective, as suggested by the original effective schools descriptions, then individual schools ought to accept the responsibility for doing so. The problem was that the original research provided little guidance as to how the effective schools became effective (that is, the processes involved). In the more common language of the 1980s, the effective schools research provided a vision of a more desirable place for schools to be but gave little insight as to how best to make the journey to that place.

As a result, three problems emerged. First, in many cases, central offices and local boards of education, not knowing a better way, tried to mandate that their local schools become effective—and the sooner the better. This led many teachers and building-level administrators to conclude that the effective schools process was just another top-down model of school improvement.

Second, many principals were told that they were responsible for making their schools effective and that it was a matter of administrative responsibility. As a result, principals often erroneously concluded that they were expected to make their schools effective by themselves. This created anxiety and a great deal of resistance, for the principals had not been trained to be agents of change. Their evaluations generally had been based on the efficient management of school processes, rather than on results. Additionally, principals could not understand how their low-achieving students could learn, when many, if not most, of them came from low-income families.

Third, teachers began to see the effective schools process as an administrative mechanism that implied that teachers were not already doing their best, given the existing working conditions. To many teachers, creating a more effective school meant simply working harder. Given these apparently insurmountable problems and the resistance they engendered in the major stakeholders to more effective schools, why was the movement not stopped in its tracks?

The survival of the effective schools movement, even against these significant obstacles, seemed to depend on the implementation strategies used by schools. This overview focuses on the processes used by Edmonds and Lezotte as they responded to the numerous invitations to work with schools. Their experience was repeated by many other facilitators of effective schools research, with some variations in the processes.

When the problems of implementation were first addressed, we believed that if we were going to ask schools to change their practices on the basis of the research findings, we should use research to guide us in the implementation processes as well. We reviewed three interrelated bodies of research grounded in notions of school change to see what lessons they could teach us. Because school change could be regarded as people change, the research on effective staff development was examined. And because school change also could be considered organizational change, the literature on effective organizational development, especially as applied to the school, was reviewed. Whether school change is to be thought of as people change or systems change, it clearly was being approached as planned change. Thus, the literature on planned change was studied. Fortunately, the lessons to be learned from the various research data added up to the same general conclusions. Among the guiding principles, we concluded the following about creating more effective schools:

- Preserve the single school as the strategic unit for the planned change.
- Teachers and other members of the school community must be an integral part of the school improvement process; principals, though essential as leaders of change, cannot do it alone.
- School improvement, like any change, is best approached as a process, not an event. Such a process approach is more likely to create a permanent change in the operating culture of the school that will accommodate this new function called continuous school improvement.
- The research would be useful in facilitating the change process, but it would have to include suggestions of practices, policies, and procedures that could be implemented as a part of the process.
- Finally, like the original effective schools, these improving schools must feel that they have a choice in the matter, and, equally important, they must feel that they have control over the processes of change.

With these guiding principles, the task of creating school plans to take the school from its current level of functioning toward the vision of effectiveness as represented in the research was undertaken. Literally hundreds of schools launched their effective schools processes. Some did it with help from the outside; some chose to proceed on their own. Some followed the guidelines of the lessons we had learned, even without knowing the research per se; and others chose to try to implement change and ignore what the research on successful change has reported. As a result of this diversity in approaches, we can say that effective schools research worked for some and not for others. Fortunately, it has worked for enough schools so that a growing number can proudly claim that they have the results to prove that more of their students are learning, and learning at a higher level. They feel empowered to commit their professional energies to the proposition that even more students can and will learn in their schools in the future.

Two major conclusions can be drawn from the lessons from this period of the effective schools movement. First, even though researchers do not have all of the answers, the literature on successful change clearly establishes that some strategies of planned change do work better than others. Second, the process of school improvement based on the effective schools research takes time, involvement, and commitment. Whenever one tries to gloss over any one of these essential prerequisites, the results are soon diminished. Clearly, when effective schools processes are followed appropriately, school improvement is affected. However, when effective schools processes are not implemented properly, they fail to produce more effective schools for more students.

Phase IV: Districtwide Programs Based on Effective Schools Research

The early efforts to implement programs of school improvement based on the effective schools research clearly supported the individual school as the strategic unit for change. Effective schools research emphasizes that if school improvement is going to occur, it will take place one school at a time.

Experience with the school-by-school model has taught a number of valuable lessons that, taken together, reinforce the districtwide concept associated with this phase of the effective schools movement. Two forces have combined to reinforce the current emphasis on the overall district planning model. First, political necessity associated with the generalized educational reform movement of the 1980s meant that local school districts needed a comprehensive program of school improvement if they were going to satisfy their various constituencies. It would not serve the interests of the local board and superintendents if, when asked about their commitment to school improvement, they could say only that they were doing what they were told by state mandates, although some buildings in their district were engaged in an effective schools process. The effective schools model represented a viable, manageable, and, therefore, attractive district response to the local call for a program of school improvement.

The second force evolved independent of these larger political considerations. Individuals working with the effective schools model at the school level realized that individual schools exist as a part of the larger legal, political, and organizational setting of the local school district. It became clear that one could successfully effect school improvement at the individual school level and still ignore this layered context. It also became clear that this would be difficult to do.

Furthermore, when an individual school's faculty set out on their own to plan and implement their program, they often found themselves being challenged by their colleagues, or at least being impeded by district level policies, patterns, and practices.

These two forces were joined, and a new, stronger formulation of the effective schools process resulted. This formulation still places great emphasis on school-level change, but it now also emphasizes the larger organizational context and its role in supporting and enhancing the individual school's efforts. The formulation builds on the notion of a district plan that supports school change. In this plan, the policies, programs, and procedures generally thought to be beyond the control of a single school are aligned to support the effort. Those who believe in the collaborative approach at the school level strongly advocate that the district plan be written by a collaborative group of teachers, building and district administrators, and even community and parent representatives. This group begins to model the collaborative process at the district level. Once the plan was written, it would go to the local board of education where, one hoped, it would be approved without significant modifications. This action then would establish the plan as a matter of official policy and as the guiding force for school improvement in the district and in each of its individual schools.

Two challenges must be faced in the district planning process. First, the plan must address the necessary changes in district-level policies and programs to ensure that school-level change can occur. Second, the plan must not go so far as to mandate what each school must do in its improvement plan. The first set of challenges, when handled successfully by the district planning group, give guidance, direction, and the human and financial resources to the school-level improvement process. However, if this plan goes too far, the sense of ownership and involvement leading to the essential commitment at the school level gets lost.

The current emphasis on the district model for sustained school improvement serves several valuable functions. It acknowledges that there are no unimportant adults in the system. It also acknowledges the critical role of the superintendent and the members of the board of education in providing leadership and vision for school improvement. As a matter of fact, this phase of the effective schools process makes it clear that without sustained leadership from the superintendent, it is unlikely that the effective schools movement will become all that it could be. This model also recognizes the need to couple more tightly and ensure alignment between the school site and the district office. Finally, it communicates to school-level personnel that they are central to school effectiveness and that all other personnel should stand ready to do whatever they can to help.

Early efforts at implementing effective schools produced an expanded list of individual schools that benefit from these efforts. The increasing emphasis on the district-level programs are also beginning to show encouraging signs that districts can move if their efforts reflect the appropriate degrees of coordination and institutional commitment. More time is needed to further refine the districtwide process. But as each preceding phase builds on and adds to what has gone before, the fundamental belief that all students can and will learn is reinforced.

THE EFFECTIVE SCHOOLS MOVEMENT
AS A VIABLE REFORM STRATEGY

The 1980s will be recorded in United States educational history as a decade of educational reforms; many reforms were attempted and some were successful. Policymakers have taken three approaches to school reform. Each strategy rests on a different set of assumptions on how we can best assure reform of our schools.

Approaches to School Improvement

Reforming Teacher Training

When the call for school improvement first went out across the nation, colleges and universities, especially the teacher training institutions, stepped back, and asked themselves, What is our role in K–12 education? The primary role of higher education has traditionally been that of staffing the enterprise of the public schools. Every teacher and administrator must successfully pass through somebody's gates of higher education to receive teaching credentials.

Trying to restaff schools with new kinds of teachers as openings become available must be viewed as a long-term, developmental approach to school improvement. We believe that the schools and colleges of education should get on as soon as possible with the mission of improving teacher training. However, this approach is too slow to be the primary strategy of school improvement. No matter what they learn in teacher-training courses, new teachers on their first jobs are quickly socialized into the culture of the school. They are not likely to initiate significant changes in that culture.

State-Mandated Reform

The second major approach to school improvement involves top-down mandates. In more than forty states, either the governor, the legislature, the state board of education, or the state superintendent has put a ribbon around a set of educational innovations and has fired those educational innovations into the local schools or districts through a top-down, outside-in, mandate-driven approach to school reform.

The history of school change is replete with failed attempts to try to change the schools in an enduring way through that model. Perhaps the harshest criticism of the state-mandated approach to school reform is in the study by John E. Chubb,[14] a senior policy analyst at Brookings Institution. In 1987, Chubb and his colleagues looked at the probable impact of the state-mandated reform in the forty states and concluded that the probable impact would vary from zero to negative. In almost every case what was put forward as an educational reform was not a reform at all, but rather was an educational add on. Most mandates ask the local schools to do more. Local schools are already overburdened with expectations, given the short time and the limited resources with which they have to work. State-mandated models leave much to be desired. A more promising approach would be to watch what happens in states that provide funds and trained consultants to help establish mandate programs.

Internally Initiated Reform

The third major approach to effective long-term school improvement involves implementation through district commitment and by school-level team building and action. Throughout the United States educators in a large and growing number of schools are asking, What is the possibility for improving schools by going straight to the individual district and the individual school and using an internal renewal model—an organizational development model that involves planning and implementing programs of school improvement from within?

The effective schools model evolved through the 1970s and 1980s. Effective schools research has demonstrated that effective, enduring change occurs when schools plan and implement programs of school improvement one school at a time. School effectiveness occurs one school at a time. The individual school is the strategic unit for planned change and school improvement.

Assumptions of Internally Initiated School Improvement

An important set of basic beliefs, discussed below, undergirds the internal renewal model. These beliefs define an organizational culture that is conducive to sustained school improvement. In many ways these assumptions, when present in a school, prepare the school for a coordinated change effort.

■ *Only two kinds of schools exist in the United States: improving schools and declining schools.* Many educators hold onto the notion that if they do again what they have been doing, they will continue to be successful. Consider one reason why this thinking is off base. Public schools need to respond to a significant, substantial change in the nature of the students in public schools today. Demographics are changing. The number of middle-class children in the schools is declining, and the number of low-income children is increasing. The ethnic diversity of the student population is also increasing. Either we are adapting to meet the needs of these new students, or, relatively speaking, we are declining in our effectiveness. The faculty of the individual school has a choice: It can decide to become more effective or it can decide to continue business as usual and lose effectiveness.

■ *Every school can improve, regardless of current levels of success.* In this whole approach to school improvement, we are pursuing improvement potential. We seek to do this by helping school faculties to see the new possibilities. We work to empower teachers and administrators in a school to put forward programs of curriculum and instruction that will capitalize on that potential for improvement. Targets of school improvement will vary from school to school.

■ *The potential for improvement already resides in every school.* The men and women who work in the school possess the capacity to do better. The school improvement process is organized to draw on that potential. Almost any community in the United States would be satisfied for a long time with the school improvement that would result simply by tapping the full potential of the people who work in their schools. But many schools are not well organized for reform. We have not tried to use an internal renewal model in the past, and this potential represents a new opportunity for internal renewal that we must pursue in the press for school improvement.

■ *In school improvement, no adults in the school are unimportant.* Even though the individual teachers and the teaching/learning process are of vital importance, the adults outside the classroom (the principal, other support people, the custodian, the cooks, the bus drivers) play a significant role in setting the tone or climate in our schools. School improvement efforts should involve all of those people in some way because they contribute to the overall effort.

■ *School improvement is a process, not an event.* It represents an endless succession of incremental adjustments. Many people have the notion that improvement can start today and end at some specified time; they do not realize that improvement is a continual process. What is done today needs to be evaluated and altered to meet the needs of tomorrow. Improvement is never ending. Boards of education and communities need to understand that school improvement is a process and not an event. The good news is that you can start school improvement right away. But the bad news (if you want to think of it as bad news) is that you will never finish, because there will always be a next level to aspire to in our schools.

■ *The people working in the school now—teachers, administrators, support staff, and others—are in the best position to manage the change process.* We are not convinced that there is a significant and enduring role for the outside person or agency. This view is contrary to many innovations we have tried. We used to think that improvement would come by bringing in a new curriculum, a new approach to classroom organization, or some other means outside the school. We have finally come to realize, by looking at both effective schools and other successful organizations in the private sector, that the people inside the organization are in the best position to improve the outcomes of that organization.

■ *Teachers and administrators are already doing the best they know to do, given the conditions under which they find themselves.* What we have to do is to change what people know *and* change the conditions under which they operate. To achieve this goal, the school must become a learning community; this task will take time.

■ *Internal renewal requires that an ongoing discourse on school improvement be established and sustained in each school and in the district as a whole.* One problem we have now is design defect. By that we mean a lack of structure, organization, or functioning that is needed to assure ongoing discourse on school improvement. It is almost as if the architect of the U.S. public school left off the back porch on which this conversation was to occur.

Because ongoing discourse on improvement is not an accepted norm, when you *do* begin to talk about school improvement in most schools, people think you are asking them to participate in a strange or even unfamiliar process. People are likely to say, Why do we have to be involved in school improvement? We are already doing a good job. If it's not broken, don't fix it. What they are really saying is that in most schools, talking about school improvement is not a natural occurrence. This design defect must be corrected to allow for discourse on school improvement. But three essential prerequisites must be in place.

First, school-based discourse on school improvement among the adults who work in a school requires a common language, a language of improvement. To launch a systematic program of school improvement in your school or district, you have to plan a strategy for introducing all staff members to the common language of school improvement.

Second, a structure through which this discourse can—and will—flow must be created. Such a collaborative, school-based, school improvement team should include a cross-section of teaching faculty, the school principal, and other people—both in and outside the school. This discourse on school improvement should not be limited to the team, but that group is in a position to take leadership and provide the language for discussion that will lead to making plans for improvement.

Third, finding time in each school for this group to meet is essential. One major shortcoming in our schools today is the limited time staff members have to meet and talk about school improvement. Local boards of education and the superintendent must convince the community that this time to meet and to talk about school improvement is critical. Creating more time for planning, curriculum review, and staff development is going to be a major challenge to local boards of education for two reasons. Time is a code word for money, more time will cost more money—and that is always a problem. Equally important, some people in the community may believe that a teacher is only at work when he or she is in the presence of students. However, these three prerequisites—a common language, a school improvement team, and time—are essential for creating viable discourse on improvement in our schools.

The assumptions, or basic beliefs, and prerequisites that we have just reviewed hold true for virtually any model of internal renewal for schools.

SUMMARY

This chapter begins with the declaration that U.S. society cannot be what our schools are not. We are at a time in our history when schools can lead this nation closer to the democratic ideal. Bold leadership on the part of all educators, buttressed by broad parental and community support, can truly make a significant difference in our world during our lifetime. This nation needs leaders who dare to dream that all students can learn, leaders who have the courage to say that what students learn depends on what we, as educators, do. And we need leaders who have the wisdom to use all available knowledge to move us toward that dream. Teachers and administrators who have these prerequisites are in charge of our destiny. The effective schools framework can have a positive influence on that destiny if our leaders have the will to use it on behalf of all children.

QUESTIONS AND ACTIVITIES

1. What were some of the social and political factors that led to the search for effective schools?

2. In what ways do effective schools differ from less effective schools?

3. Compare and contrast individual school and districtwide strategies for implementing school improvement programs. Give examples of each approach.

4. What are the advantages and disadvantages of each approach to school improvement discussed in this chapter? Be sure to consider the views of educators, parents, and students.

5. Interview a group of educators in your community to determine to what extent they agree or disagree with the assumptions of school improvement discussed in this chapter.

6. Discuss this statement: Our society cannot be what our schools are not. Do you agree or disagree with the statement? What is your vision of an effective school?

7. Form a group of several of your classmates. Develop a rating scale based on the characteristics of effective schools.

8. Discuss some reasons educators resist implementing effective school research. Why has the effective schools movement continued to survive?

NOTES

1. Robert Hutchins, *The Conflict in Education in a Democratic Society* (New York: Harper, 1953).

2. Robert E. Slavin, Nancy L. Karweit, and Nancy A. Madden, eds., *Effective Programs for Students at Risk* (Boston: Allyn and Bacon, 1989); Michael S. Knapp and Patrick M. Shields, eds., *Better Schooling for the Children of Poverty: Alternatives to Conventional Wisdom* (Berkeley, Calif.: McCutchan Publishing Corporation, n.d.).

3. Ronald Edmonds, "A Discussion of the Literature and Issues Related to Effective Schooling." Paper prepared for the National Conference on Urban Education, St. Louis, Missouri, 1978; Wilbur B. Brookover, Laurence Beamer, Helen Efthim, Douglas Hathaway, Lawrence Lezotte, Stephen Miller, Joseph Passalacqua, and Louis Tornatzky, *Creating Effective Schools: An Inservice Program for Enhancing School Learning Climate and Achievement* (Holmes Beach, Fla.: Learning Publications, 1982); Barbara O. Taylor, ed., *Case Studies in Effective Schools Research* (Dubuque, Iowa: Kendall-Hunt Publishing Company, 1990).

4. Edmonds, "A Discussion of the Literature and Issues."; Daniel U. Levine and Lawrence W. Lezotte, *Unusually Effective Schools: A Review and Analysis of Research and Practice* (Madison: National Center for Effective Schools Research and Development, 1990). (Available from University of Wisconsin, 1025 West Johnson, Suite 685, Madison, Wisc., 53706).

5. James S. Coleman, Ernest Q. Campbell, Carol J. Hobson, James McPartland, Alexander M. Mood, Frederic D. Weinfeld, and Robert L. York, *Equality of Educational Opportunity* (Washington, D.C.: U.S. Government Printing Office, 1966).

6. Ibid., p. 325.

7. Among the studies frequently cited are George Weber, *Inner-City Children Can Be Taught to Read: Four Successful Schools* (Washington, D.C.: Council for Basic Education, 1971); Wilbur E. Brookover et al., "Elementary School Climate and School Achievement," *American Educational Research Journal* 2 (1978): 301–318; Ronald R. Edmonds and John R. Frederiksen, *The Identification and Analysis of City Schools That Are Instructionally Effective for Poor Children.* ERIC Document 170 396, 1979.

8. Levine and Lezotte, *Unusually Effective Schools.*

9. Glen Robinson, *Effective Schools: A Summary of Research.* (Arlington, Va.: Educational Research Service, 1983); Donald MacKenzie, "Research for School Improvement: An Appraisal of Some Recent Trends," *Educational Researcher* 4, (April 1983): 5–17; Stewart C. Purkey and Marshall S. Smith, "School Reform: The District Policy Implications of the Effective Schools Literature," *The Elementary School Journal* 3 (January 1985): 353–389. One summary of research on effective schools was incorporated in Thomas Good and Jere Brophy, "School Effects," in *Third Handbook of Research on Teaching,* Merlin C. Wittrock, ed., (New York: Macmillan Publishing Co., 1986), pp. 570–602 (a project of the American Educational Research Association). The most

recent summary is Levine and Lezotte, *Unusually Effective Schools.*

10. Edmonds, "A Discussion of the Literature and Issues."; Edmonds, "Some Schools Work, More Can," *Social Policy* (March/April 1979): 28–32.

11. Brookover et al., "Elementary School Climate."

12. Michael Rutter, Barbara Maughan, Peter Mortimore, and Janet Ouston, *Fifteen Thousand Hours: Secondary Schools and Their Effects on Children* (Cambridge, Mass.: Harvard University Press, 1979); John E. Chubb and Terry M. Moe, *Politics, Markets, and America's Schools* (Washington, D.C.: The Brookings Institution, 1990); Paut T. Hill, Gail E. Foster, and Tamar Gendler, *High Schools with Character* (Santa Monica, Calif.: The Rand Corporation, 1990).

13. Peter Mortimore, Pamela Sammons, Louise Stoll, David Lewis, and Russell Ecob, *School Matters* (Berkeley: University of California Press, 1988).

14. John E. Chubb, *The Dilemma of Public School Improvement: Major Findings and Conclusions* (Washington, D.C.: The Brookings Institution, 1987).

CHAPTER 16

Cultural Influences on Learning: Teaching Implications

■ BARBARA J. SHADE and CLARA A. NEW

One basic tenet supported by educators in the United States is that teachers should be cognizant of and attend to individual differences. Generally, the elements of student diversity on which teachers focus are variables related to race, gender, ethnicity, exceptionality, and development. Culture also is a dimension on which students vary. However, this variable is often ignored by educators.

WHAT IS CULTURE?

Culture is, in part, an aggregation of beliefs, attitudes, habits, values, and practices that form a view of reality. This systemized pattern of thought serves as a filter through which a group of individuals view and respond to the demands of the environment or, as Nobles[1] suggests, culture is a collective approach to the world that provides a group, and individuals within that group, a design for living. Edward Hall,[2] an influential authority on culture, points out that cultural patterns are generally invisible and are experienced by individuals, and by the people with whom they interact, as normal ways of acting, feeling, and being. Another way of defining culture is to conceptualize it as the modal personality of a unique group of people that provides rules and guidelines for appraising and interpreting interactions with the events, people, or ideas encounted in daily living.

Cultural diversity is probably one major element on which teachers should concentrate because it has a substantial influence on how students approach the learning process. This is particularly important when students from African American, Hispanic, Native American, and Asian groups are members of the class. Although many items discussed here apply to the cultural influence on learning for all groups, this chapter concentrates on the African American student as a way to focus the discussion.

The cultural orientation most prevalent within the African American community was developed as a response to a common perception of oppression through slavery and discrimination and a belief that special skills are needed to exist and function in a color-conscious society. In addition, African Americans are socialized into mainstream U.S. culture, with its emphasis on justice, liberty, freedom, democracy, competition, power, and money. Thus, the perspective of many African Americans is an amalgamation of both African and Anglo-Saxon beliefs, attitudes, customs, and practices designed to facilitate acculturation and adaptation to a racially stratified society.

This cultural orientation differs significantly from that of the middle-class Anglo-Saxon community. This community perceives that society reinforces and acknowledges their existence. Their fate or life chances are not controlled by invisible codes based on skin color and most social institutions (particularly the school) are predicated on their life orientations and values. This is the perspective in which most teachers are socialized.

When these two views of the world meet in the classroom, inharmonious ideas emerge on how each party is to act, how material is to be learned, and what educational outcomes are acceptable. In current educational vernacular, this incongruence of perspectives is identified as differences in style. This incompatibility is most evident in (1) behavioral expectations and social interaction style, (2) communication style, and (3) learning style. The first two stylistic dimensions are related to the classroom environment in which teaching and learning occur; the third dimension is of concern in the development of appropriate instructional strategies.

Behavioral Style

School culture, no matter where the institution is located, has a carefully defined behavioral norm that seems to have emanated from the early religious schools. It requires conformity, passivity, quietness, teacher-focused activities, and individualized, competitive noninteractive participation of students. The ideal student in this culture sits quietly in his or her own seat, looks only at the teacher, answers the questions when called on, and performs the required work in the manner prescribed.

Teachers generally describe African American children as not adhering to these expectations. Data collected at workshops with teachers around the country[3] indicate that many teachers hold these common perceptions of African American children: (1) they have difficulty staying in their seats and are constantly moving around the classroom talking with their neighbors; (2) they appear to lack control because they often fail to raise their hands to give answers—they merely call them out; and (3) they are unable or unwilling to complete their assigned work unless they receive help from the teacher. In general, teachers in public schools perceive African American children, particularly males, as excessively active. DellaValle[4] confirmed this view in a research study in an urban, predominantly African American junior high school. When were rated on activity, almost half of the students could not sit for any length of time, 25 percent could sit when interested in the lesson, and only 25 percent engaged in teacher-preferred passivity. This active approach to learning is often viewed as disruptive behavior within the school culture.

The students express surprise, bewilderment, and anger over the negativism evident in these teacher perceptions. They suggest that teachers do not understand them and are racist, mean, punitive, and unwilling to help them learn. More important, they translate the teachers' response as personal rejection.

The bases for these divergent views are different perceptions about appropriate behavior. Schmeck and Lockhart[5] suggest that the active behavior of African American students is typical of individuals who fit Eyesneck's extroverted personality. Because they need strong sensory stimulation, extroverts seek that excitation. Boykin[6] refers to this activeness as "behavioral verve." He concluded that African American students generally reside in environments that condition them to expect a variety of environmental interactions with constant change of focus and interest. They often perceive the school environment as monotonous and thus interject some variety by ceasing to work and by looking and walking around. In his observation of eighth-grade classes, Morgan[7] found that African Americans were more likely to initiate events or seek peer or teacher assistance on assignments than were Anglo-American students.

Because African American children are often perceived as not performing to behavioral expectations, teachers tend to be overcritical of them. As Irvine[8] notes, African American pupils are more likely to receive more negative academic and behavioral feedback than are Anglo-American pupils. Moreover, in an effort to produce the behavioral responses with which they feel most comfortable, teachers often concentrate on control and classroom management issues. It thus is not surprising to find African American students disproportionately represented in the suspension, expulsion, and discipline statistics of school systems throughout the country. An even more damaging response results when teachers view this behavior as indicative of students with less potential and lower academic ability. The results are mislabeling and mismanagement of the teaching-learning process for these students.

To some extent, this difference in understanding about behavioral expectations is also related to cultural variations in communication.

Communication Style

Communication is the process by which a sender transmits messages to a receiver. Within this process are a verbal code, a nonverbal code, and set of guidelines to help individuals use the codes appropriately. Children come to understand that to function in their families, peer group, classroom, or community and learn as much as they can, they must communicate effectively.

The development of the communication process occurs within the child's culture. Cultural groups teach children an accepted vocabulary with its accompanying grammatical and syntactical structure. The culture also provides an orientation about what information is important to transmit and receive, the appropriate way to listen, methods for getting attention, what represents an acceptable voice level, and how to read nonverbal or kinesic codes. Equally important to the process is the development of the context for assessing and interpreting the information received. As a number of researchers[9] point out, students who enter school from African American, Native American, or linguistically different cultural groups often find that their communication styles and their communication contexts are significantly different from those promoted by the school. The result is mutual misunderstanding.

Bidialectalism and bilingualism are the most obvious indications of cultural diversity. In schools with an English-only and standard-dialect orientation, students work at retaining their community language while trying to understand and use the accepted communication patterns of the school. Hanna[10] and others who observe this code-switching note that this situation often results in major cognitive overload for linguistically different individuals. These students are constantly engaged in translating concepts that may or may not be congruent within the two languages. Thus, these students must make a cognitive switch between the two verbal codes while trying to learn new material at the same time. This is often very frustrating.

The communication pattern least recognized as a cultural variation is encompassed in the expressiveness and affective domain of verbal delivery. Heath[11] points out that the socialization of African American children generally focuses on the development of performers. In both verbal and nonverbal language, they are more theatrical, show greater emotion, and demonstrate faster responses and higher energy. Kochman[12] suggests that African American speakers are more animated, more persuasive, and more active in the communication process. They often are perceived as confrontational because of this style. On the other hand, the school, and most Anglo-American teachers, are more oriented toward a passive style, which gives the impression that the communicator is somewhat detached, literal, and legalistic in use of the language. Most African Americans find this style distancing and dissuasive. Their cultural orientation produces a variety of meanings for a single word or utterance, and they often learn to respond or interpret the meaning of communication from intonation, facial expressions, and body language, as well as from the verbal code. This stylistic confrontation often creates interpretive confusion.

Some teachers also observe that many African American children, when asked questions, give only minimal answers; others give no answers or appear to be caustic or sarcastic in their responses. On the playground, however, the same children give elaborate explanations of rules of a game or descriptions of an event. Many teachers do not understand that in the traditional African American community, children are not usually expected to be information givers and are infrequently asked direct questions. Communication differences in the nonverbal mode are found in the requirements for space between the communicators and how they visually engage during conversation. African Americans are more likely to require less space between the communication and more indirect gaze when listening to another person, whereas the traditional school culture expects more space between the communicants and more direct visual contact when speaking with each other. These stylistic variations may produce further communication barriers.

From the students' perspective, teachers also send inappropriate messages, either intentionally or unintentionally, through their verbal and nonverbal communication styles. Simpson and Erickson,[13] in their study of sixteen teachers in an urban school district, found that Anglo-American teachers paid more attention both verbally and nonverbally to males than to females than did African American teachers. More important, Anglo-American educators gave significantly more verbal and nonverbal criticism to African American students than to other students. Other researchers report that teachers in settings with many students of color often display negative nonverbal behavior when interacting with these students even though their verbal behavior is positive.[14] The overall result, from the students' perspective, is a feeling of rejection, which leads to a sense of alienation.

The communication process is vitally important to the teaching and learning interaction. However, even when these barriers are removed, others are erected if the presentation of new concepts and ideas does not take into consideration how groups learn to learn.

Learning Styles

One of the most talked about concepts in education today is the idea of learning style. How this concept is defined, depends on the thesis of the researcher and the particular dimension being analyzed. In general, the concept of learning style can consist of the examination of individual preferences in social interaction; for this discussion, however, we focus on different orientations to the intricacies of how individuals and groups acquire knowledge.

The three areas most often delineated in the discussing of how individuals learn are information processing (that is, how information is perceived or gathered), the schemata or memory base to which it is attached, and how individuals choose to think about the information in order to arrive at a decision for action. Culture appears to influence each dimension by providing guidelines that help an individual select the strategies to use in each arena. These guidelines translate into individual preferences or style. Witkin and his associates[15] refer to this culturally induced strategy-selection process as cognitive style; J. P. Guilford[16] labels it the executive control of the intellect. Other theorists call it metacognition (thinking about thinking). Regardless of the label, the basic premise is that culture induces different approaches to how individuals use their mind by providing a set of rules that become preferred methods of acquiring knowledge. The two areas most affected by culture are those that influence ways of perceiving and ways of thinking.

Perceptual Style

Through socialization, people develop a preference for certain sensory modalities. They respond positively to material when their preferred mode of reception is used for transmitting information to be learned. Individuals develop these preferences when they find that certain portrayals of ideas help them memorize and comprehend the concepts. In two studies with African American adolescents using various learning style tasks that identify preferred modalities, symbolic representation such as graphs, pictures, and videos ranked at the top of their preferences, followed by linguistic or oral presentations, manipulatives or haptic/kinesthetic materials, and then print.[17]

Perceiving via any modality is not an inherent trait. In the acquisition of knowledge, students are taught what to look for; what lines, graphs, symbols on which to focus; and what to overlook. As Elgin[18] suggests, learning to comprehend pictures or objects within the environment is taught within the context of learning about life. Without this instruction, pictures or objects would become variegated patches of light and shadow or undistinguishable masses. For example, children in U.S. culture are likely to be exposed to images on billboards, in picture books, or in Saturday morning cartoons. Understanding the labels and meanings of these images depends on the explanation as well as on various conventions or referential connections made for them by the adults in their environment.

In the research area most associated with cultural influences on perceptual style, groups are identified as being field independent or field dependent. Using a test in which various geometric shapes are hidden within distracting lines, individuals are asked to find the forms. This requires spatial ability as well as visual literacy, or what some theorists call iconic reasoning or pictorial competence. More important, it assumes previous socialization with manipulation of geometric figures and that the representation of various spatial objects in pictures is perceived in the same manner by everyone. Individuals who are able to ignore the distractions and find the forms correctly are field independent; people who have difficulty finding the forms are field dependent.

Researchers have found that African Americans are more likely to be field dependent; that they do not perceive or identify the forms as readily as other groups.[19] The same results are found for Hmong or Laotian immigrants.[20] On the other hand, some Native American students are more likely to be field independent.[21] This is not surprising; the cultural symbols in the art of some Native American groups are geometric figures intricately developed within woven fabric or baskets.

Many researchers suggest that many Mexican American students are also field dependent. This finding is based on the use of the rod-and-frame type tests, which are primarily kinesthetic measures. Few studies have used the Group Embedded Figure Tests, as have been used with the other populations. Mexican American perceptual style may be situationally and contextually based. As Wober[22] identified several decades ago, changing the modality of the test also changes the results when examining the issue of perceptual differences.

A companion to the perceptual process and an equally important aspect of learning is the ability to conceptualize, define, interpret, evaluate, ponder, or perform once people have determined what they have perceived. This becomes the companion process best described under thinking style.

Thinking Style

The process of thinking can be defined as how people process information. The definition of thinking, however, cannot be limited to the use of one model or conceived as a process involved in only one situation. What cognitive scientists are coming to understand is that thinking is multidimensional—it depends on the context in which thinking must occur, and it depends on the product expected as a result of the thinking process. Thinking may produce opinions; this suggests that individuals have to consider their beliefs, attitudes, and values; thinking may also produce choices selected from options; this requires critical evaluation. It also yields performance of skills based on the consideration of approaches or the requirements. Or thinking can produce a design, object, or idea not yet in existence.[23]

How one thinks seems to involve many different processes, such as reasoning, problem solving, planning, remembering, reading, writing, classifying, criticizing, imagining, appraising, synthesizing, and transforming. The cultural dimension involved in thinking centers on how the task is perceived and interpreted and also on how various cognitive processes are used. The influence of culture on learning in two important content areas—mathematics and writing—is an informative example of the cultural dimension in thinking.

Many people believe that learning mathematics consists of discovering already existing truths of formal logic. Recent studies, however, suggest that mathematics as a discipline cannot be separated from the social realm in which it is used.[24] Children learn to use mathematical knowledge based on the language, tools, and practices through which important concepts are introduced in their culture.

An example of how language affects mathematics is suggested by Stigler and Baranes.[25] They describe studies indicating that Chinese language may facilitate the acquisition of counting skills because it provides a more coherent conceptualization of numbers which help people to think about some important abstract mathematical concepts. Orr,[26] on the other hand, suggests that African American students have difficulty with mathematics because Black English Vernacular (BEV) does not contain some prepositional constructs that are important in understanding some quantitative relationships.

Devices endemic to different societies also influence mathematical thinking. The Japanese abacus, for example, helps students in mental calculation. As with the compass rose, which was used by early navigators, the abacus provides a framework or schemata around which individuals can decipher, conceptualize, and reason about quantitative information. These tools become cognitive devices that foster the use of certain cognitive processes in a certain way. The culture of West Africa, particularly the Yoruba of Nigeria and the Dahomey (which is the cultural heritage of many African Americans) had complex counting systems using cowrie shells that provided the same type of help in mathematical learning.[27] Perhaps the maintenance of various African linguistic structures without these particular cultural dimensions creates a specific mathematical thinking barrier that hampers some African Americans in mathematics. This hypothesis merits testing.

Writing is a complex form of communication that allows individuals to use their language to communicate their perceptions. According to Farr[28] and others, writing also is a reflection of cultural understanding. More important, when writing is taught as the presentation of accepted societal language, it usually specifies certain patterns of reasoning, ways of presenting arguments, and specific organizational structures. The identification of acceptable writing within a school context intimates that it uses language and a method of presentation embedded in the cultural beliefs and conventions of the academic subculture of Anglo-American society. Students from other cultural communities, such as the African American community described by Heath,[29] are forced to perform and respond using cognitive approaches and linguistic patterns and conventions that differ from their own. For example, many observers note that African American children are taught to be flexible and adaptable in their use of language and to use creative verbal play encompassing frequent metaphors and similes.[30] They also are taught to view a physical object holisticly rather than as an accumulation of attributes. These skills are often negated by the methods of writing instruction in schools. Each language is taught as a series of subskills rather than in a holistic and creative manner that uses the students' particular communicative orientation.

The variations in approach to behavior, communication, perceiving, and thinking are not differences that affect students' ability to learn. They represent a diversity of opinions and ideas about how to function. Teachers must realize that the desired outcomes can be the same for all children. There exists, however, variation in how these outcomes can be achieved. This variation is one of style precipitated by differences in socialization and orientation. The teacher's challenge is to provide opportunities for students to function and learn in ways comfortable to them so they can acquire the information necessary and achieve the educational goals. Some teaching suggestions are discussed below.

CREATING A CULTURALLY COMPATIBLE CLASSROOM

Learners do not arrive in a classroom with inherent motivation. They require invitations from the teacher suggesting that they are welcome, that they belong, and that learning is a task at which they can succeed. Invitational barriers for students of culturally diverse communities are often erected because teachers and students do not have the same understanding or perceptions of what is acceptable behavior and do not communicate from the same perspective. In other words, classroom climate is affected by the styles of the teacher and the learner, which are a reflection of the cultural orientation of each participant. Developing a climate that acknowledges, accepts, understands, and accommodates various interactional and communication patterns becomes the teacher's first task.

Classroom Climate

Non-Anglo students relate best to teachers who are flexible, supportive, accepting, creative, tolerant of individual differences, and determined to ensure that learning occurs. These teachers strive to involve students of color in school tasks by developing a classroom that generates warmth and fosters healthy social interactions.

The social dimensions of a classroom are important to motivating many children to engage in learning. A review of patterns of cognition found that African Americans are more likely to be person specialists.[31] This orientation teaches individuals to be be empathetic with people and social dimensions of the environment and to ignore the more impersonal or inanimate cues. Studies indicate that African Americans attend to facial expressions and social situation nuances and frequently use the interpersonal dimensions of a situation rather than rules when making decisions.[32] Teachers who capitalize on this strength use cooperative or social groups, peer tutoring, and curriculum materials with social applications and meaning. These are salient approaches for facilitating teaching and learning.

Work Style

The approach to a task is most often a primary consideration of teachers because the behavioral style of students tends to set the tone for classroom management.

Most African American students work best when they can set the context for work and are allowed frequent cognitive diversions while engaged in the task. To adapt to the active behavioral style of African American children teachers may need to manipulate the physical environment.

The location of furniture, materials, and resources should support student efforts to accomplish the tasks assigned. Strategic arrangement of classroom furniture can help define contexts that complement student movements. Students sitting in classrooms where seats are placed in random positions are discouraged from cooperative learning. For many African American students, this physical arrangement is antithetical to their particular cultural orientation. When the students attempt to make the classroom more compatible by moving, teachers' frustration levels often rise. The teachers then attempt to control student behavior under the guise of preventing them from disturbing others. Placing the teacher's desk close to the students, using small groups that are easily changed depending on the activity, and changing the furniture layout during the year keep students interested and provide motivation for completing the tasks assigned.

Communication Style

Teachers must know each student. One of the best ways to become aware of individual needs is through social conversation. Teachers might begin the first two weeks of class with unstructured oral conversation that permits students to talk freely about themselves. Teachers can make observations about comfort level, preferred conversational style, student expectations and perceptions, and the similarities among and between the learners that can facilitate planning for immediate and future instruction. This approach emphasizes that learning is a personal endeavor, and it permits the teacher to bring students and content together without devaluing either.

Natural, unstructured social conversation also is an effective tool for helping teachers develop keen observation abilities and refine their interpersonal listening skills and for diminishing the tendency to label inaccurately social and learning behaviors exhibited by students from diverse cultures. Even students for whom social conversation is less familiar will have ideas about what is important to them, and they benefit from the camaraderie of nonjudgmental social interaction. Leadership in this kind of activity shifts from the teacher to the students, giving them ownership and control over content and its merit.

On the first day of class, teachers can enhance the climate by establishing the concept of inclusiveness. They can use the language experience concept to extend and enrich students' interpersonal communication in the classroom. Cultural idioms tend to flow freely during unstructured conversational exchange. Many of these expressions have corresponding counterparts in school vernacular, are more accurate descriptively, and are references for teachers whose backgrounds are disparate from those of students of color. To build on this cultural capital, teachers can list words and expressions from their communities on wall charts and in personal dictionaries. The lists should be used for brainstorming as immediate follow-up activities and added to the on-going word bank.

Given the opportunity to speak without restrictions on grammatical and expressive conventions, students reveal information about preferred ways of learning in relaxed social situations that can be transferred to the classroom.

When teachers acknowledge and use students' words and cultural expressions, they provide fertile opportunities for students of color to expand their functional vocabularies and concept categories. Because the words have personal significance, they become part of students' classroom vocabularies. This approach also provides concept maps that can be used to develop writing projects. Teachers must be prepared to relate students' contributions to the outcomes of instruction if students are to feel valued and make consistent effort.

Folk literature is another valuable aid to instruction. It contains the nuances of language, behavior, reasoning, and values to which many students of color can personally relate, because most tales, fables, and proverbs have been primarily transmitted by word of mouth from generation to generation. Folk literature usually explains life's purpose with tenets that are part of today's cultural socialization practices. For many students of color, folk literature satisfies the need to find meaning in the learning process. Teachers can dramatize and become griots, wearing story hats and going from group to group to relate tales that students discuss and evaluate in terms of living in today's world. An entertaining presentation grabs the students' attention. It facilitates socialized ways of learning, perceiving, and doing for students for whom the modeling process is important.

Content presented in game format stimulates and challenges. Teachers should create, as well as purchase, games that promote social interaction and intellectual stimulation. For example, brainstorming word meanings and word problems in math or science or through a television game-show format can meet students' need for cooperative affiliation, varying and exuberant communication styles, the freedom to think out loud, and the opportunity to learn from peers. Teachers should know which channels of learning need strengthening for groups and for individual students before selecting commercial games. The narrower the functions of a game, the more quickly interest ebbs.

To enhance the communication climate in the classroom, teachers must always be alert to student needs. Many students of color need unlimited opportunities to hear and feel themselves think out loud as they interact with each other and the teacher, assess who they are in the class/school setting, examine their relatedness, and determine the degree of control they have over themselves in the immediate environment. What appear to be intentional, disruptive outbursts during rigidly structured communication periods are frequently "Ah-ha" experiences—the student has perceived a relationship.

Having established a common environment, teachers then should teach in ways that accommodate culturally socialized ways of perceiving and thinking—often labeled learning style.

Learning Styles

One stylistic change teachers must make to accommodate cognitive style variations is to move from teacher telling to teaching showing. Observational learning is reinforced in the African American community for many reasons. Through the use of observation, individuals can determine rules, assess people who might create problems for them, and facilitate adaptation and survival. One mother in the Heath study points out "keeping his eyes open," and watching others are the only ways her child can learn about the world around him.[33] A similar approach is used in the Native American community. Children go with adults to various contexts and learn through observation.

Learning styles must also be addressed in the curriculum materials and texts used to present information. Generally, children who are culturally compatible with the school believe that written information has authority. They are also willing to learn and repeat this information. Establishing a cognitive link between the texts and many culturally different learners is often difficult because of the communication bias inherent in the material. Learners must have a framework or a schemata to which new information can be attached if they are to understand the concept and memorize it. As Love[34] points out, knowledge must have a special relationship with the learner if it is to be learned. Gordon, Miller, and Rollack[35] note that African Americans and other students of color are asked to learn and relate to material that

- Often has not been produced in their community or culture
- Is not presented from their perspective
- Tends to ignore their existence and often demeans their personal characteristics
- May distort or misinterpret data
- Makes unwarranted generalizations that differences are deficits.

In addition, the material often depicts experiences alien to the children who must use and memorize it.

Teaching materials that ignore the perspectives and the experiences of children of color make comprehension and conceptualization of the material almost impossible. Like code switching, the student must develop the frame of reference and then attempt to understand the concept. This process of continual translation creates cognitive overload for the learner. Much of this pressure can be relieved by ensuring that the materials used represent the various communities and perspectives of different groups—not just cosmetically, but also intrinsically.

Because it is difficult to find such materials, teachers can help students by letting them preview materials and identify links to their own experiences. Specific artifacts or concepts with visual, tactile, and aural media, as well as resource people and literature, music, and drama also can help students simultaneously perceive the ideas or knowledge by methods that are familiar to them. For example, having students list unfamiliar words and then learn to spell, define, and use them in their own way before they encounter them in reading material helps keep their attention focused on the context and gives them control over what they want to learn. Brown and Palinscar[36] found that allowing students to read passages and suggest what might happen next or how the story might end or defining the characters before reading the material facilitated links that enhanced student comprehension of the text.

Intuition is a thinking style that influences learning. It is prevalent within the African American community but often ignored in school. Arnheim[37] points out that there are two ways of knowing: through the intellect and through intuition. Each of these cognitive acts has a part in learning. Individuals who use the intellect make chains of logical inferences or understand the parts of a problem or situation. Intuition, according to Arnheim, enables people to apprehend the interaction or the gestalt of a situation.[38] In other words, they assess the situation as a unified whole.

Although there is need for more research aimed at assessing how students learn, from various standardized measures and observations of scholars, it appears that many African American children prefer to use a synergetic style of thinking rather than the analytical one often promoted in texts and schools.[39] This style might be conceptualized as processing that moves from the whole to the part rather than from the parts to the whole. Some learning style theorists refer to this as global thinking. Individuals who approach information in this manner prefer to understand the context or the entire situation in which the concepts are occurring and then to develop an understanding of each related part. Ausubel refers to this as needing an advance organizer.[40] Other researchers suggest that these individuals prefer to engage in deductive rather than inductive reasoning and problem solving. To capitalize on this approach, teachers need to provide a context and a definition or conceptualization of the final product before beginning to teach various segments. They may also find that discovery projects help students who approach thinking in this way.

The most important key to developing skills in teaching that are compatible with different thinking styles is to remember that the thinking process varies by subject and content area. How individuals process scientific and mathematical information is not the same process they use in developing writing skills or comprehending stories. To discover how students think in these different situations requires more teacher-student interaction. The Japanese method of teaching mathematics provides an excellent example of how this interaction can work. When a student obtains an incorrect answer on a mathematics problem in a Japanese classroom, the child is asked to put the problem on the board and discuss the thinking process for arriving at the answer with the rest of the class. In U.S. classrooms, the teacher usually tells the student the correct answer and gives reason for the incorrect answer. Clearly, it is more difficult to determine how people process information if you do not listen to their reasons for making choices, forming opinions, or producing an idea.

A FINAL CAVEAT

Many differences discussed in this chapter are often perceived by educators as indications of cultural disadvantagement or deficiency. This perspective is predicated on the unicultural assumption that the current way of functioning is the only approach to teaching and learning. This is not the thesis of this chapter.

A multicultural approach to education is based on the assumption that all groups have strengths that contribute to the fabric of U.S. society. The United States is one of the most unique countries on the globe because of its diversity. As such, we have the opportunity to meld the values, perspectives, practices, and genius of many cultures into a heterogeneous yet compatible environment. This philosophical orientation is predicated on the concept of cultural congruence or cultural compatibility (that is, that the perspectives of all individuals can be incorporated, appreciated, admired, accepted, and used in the search for our desired societal outcomes). This recognition of individual differences is a fundamental thesis of multicultural education.

SUMMARY

This chapter explores culture as a key factor in student learning. Modal cultural characteristics of African Americans are contrasted with school cultural characteristics. Examples of ways that the school's cultural norms and expected behaviors conflict with the cultural norms and behaviors of students are discussed. The incongruencies of school and student culture are evident in the behavioral expectations and social interaction style, communication style, and learning style of students. How teachers can adapt their teaching styles to the behavioral styles of their students are also examined.

QUESTIONS AND ACTIVITIES

1. Interview several teachers in your community and ask them to describe the classroom behavior of African American students. Are their descriptions similar to or different from those included in this chapter?

2. Form a discussion group with other members of your class. Review several of the teaching materials used by students in your community. Do the materials include the perspectives of children of color? How would you use the materials?

3. What is an advance organizer? Why is it important? Give an example of how you would use an advance organizer.

4. Define *learning style* and give examples of different learning styles.

5. Make a chart giving examples of how you can vary your teaching style to meet the needs of students from diverse cultures.

6. Form a small group and use *In the Beginning: Creation Stories from around the World* by Virginia Hamilton (New York: Harcourt Brace, 1988) to discuss the similarities and differences in the values and perspectives of people in different parts of the world.

7. How might knowledge about ethnic cultural difference be misused to stereotype students? How can stereotyping be avoided?

8. What resources and training do you need to teach students from diverse cultural backgrounds? How can you increase your knowledge about different cultural groups?

NOTES

1. Wade W. Nobles, "Infusion of African and African American Culture." Handout at the Third Annual Staff Development Conference, Detroit Public Schools, January 19, 1990.

2. Edward T. Hall, *The Silent Language* (New York: Anchor Books, 1959); see also Edward T. Hall, *The Hidden Dimension* (New York: Doubleday and Company, 1966).

3. Barbara J. Shade, "Cultural Ways of Knowing: An Afrocentric Perspective." Paper presented at

the Summer Institute of the Council of Chief State School Officers, August 1990.

4. Joan C. DellaValle, "An Experimental Investigation of the Relationship between Preference for Mobility and the Word-Pair Recognition Scores of Seventh-Grade Students to Provide Supervisory and Administrative Guidelines for the Organization of Effective Instructional Environments. Doctoral dissertation (St. Johns University, 1984).

5. Ronald R. Schmeck and Dan Lockhart, "Introverts and Extroverts Require Different Learning Environments," *Educational Leadership* 43 (1983): 54–55.

6. A. Wade Boykin, "Task Variability and the Performance of Black and White School Children: Vervistic Explorations," *Journal of Black Studies* 12 (1982): 469–485.

7. Harry Morgan, "Assessment of Students' Behavioral Interactions during On-Task Classroom Activities," *Perceptual and Motor Skills* 70 (1990): 563–569.

8. Jacqueline J. Irvine, "Teacher Communication Patterns as Related to the Race and Sex of the Student," *Journal of Educational Research* 78 (1985): 338–345.

9. Shirley Brice Heath, *Ways with Words* (Cambridge: Cambridge University Press, 1983); Susan U. Philips, *The Invisible Culture: Communication in Classroom and Community on the Warm Springs Indian Reservation (New York: Longman, 1983).*

10. Judith L. Hanna, *Disruptive School Behavior: Class, Race, and Culture* (New York: Homes & Meier, 1988).

11. Heath, *Ways with Words.*

12. Thomas Kochman, *Black and White: Styles in Conflict* (Chicago: University of Chicago Press, 1981).

13. Adelaide W. Simpson and Marilyn T. Erickson, "Teachers' Verbal and Nonverbal Communication Patterns as a Function of Teacher Race, Student Gender, and Student Race," *American Educational Research Journal* 20 (1983): 183–198.

14. Irvine, "Teacher Communication Patterns."

15. Herman A. Witkin, Carol A. Moore, Donald R. Goodenough, and Patricia W. Cox, "Field-Dependent and Field-Independent Cognitive Styles and Their Educational Implications," *Review of Educational Research* 47 (1977): 1–64.

16. J. P. Guilford, "Cognitive Styles: What Are They?" *Educational and Psychological Measurement* 40 (1980): 715–735.

17. Shade, "Cultural Ways of Knowing."

18. Catherine Z. Elgin, "Representation, Comprehension and Competence," in Vernon. A. Howard, ed., *Varieties of Thinking* (New York: Routledge, Chapman and Hall, Inc., 1990).

19. Barbara J. Shade, "Afro-American Cognitive Patterns: A Review of the Research," in Barbara Shade, ed., *Culture, Style, and the Educative Process* (Springfield, Ill.: Charles C Thomas Publishers, 1989).

20. Christine Hvitfeldt, "Traditional Culture, Perceptual Style, and Learning: The Classroom Behavior of Hmong Adults," *Adult Education Quarterly* 36 (1986): 65–77.

21. Cheryl Utley, *A Cross-Cultural Investigation of Field-Independence/Field-Dependence as a Psychological Variable in Menominee Native American and Euro-American Grade School Children* (Madison: Wisconsin Center for Education and Research, 1983).

22. Mallory Wober, "Sensotypes," *Journal of Social Psychology* 70 (1966): 181–189.

23. Vernon. A. Howard, ed., *Varieties of Thinking* (New York: Routledge, Chapman and Hall, Inc., 1990).

24. James W. Stigler and Ruth Baranes, "Culture and Mathematics Learning," in Ernst Z. Rothkopf, ed., *Review of Research in Education,* Vol. 15 (Washington, D.C.: American Educational Research Association, 1988), pp. 253–306.

25. Ibid.

26. Eleanor W. Orr, *Twice as Less* (New York: W. W. Norton & Co., 1987).

27. Beatrice Lumpkin, "African and African-American Contributions to Mathematics." Portland Essays in Multicultural/Multiethnic Curriculum (Portland, Ore.: Portland Public Schools, 1987).

28. Marcia Farr, "Language, Culture, and Writing: Sociolinguistic Foundations of Research on Writing," In Ernst Z. Rothkopf, ed., *Review of Research in Education,* Vol. 13 (Washington, D.C.: American Educational Research Association, 1986) pp. 195–223.

29. Heath, *Ways with Words.*

30. Kochman, *Black and White;* also see Hanna, *Disruptive School Behavior.*

31. Brian R. Little, "Specialization and the Varieties of Experimental Experiences," in Seymore Wapner et al., eds., *Experiencing the Environment* (New York: Plenum Press, 1976).

32. Barbara J. Shade, "The Influence of Perceptual Development on Cognitive Style: Cross-Ethnic Comparisons," *Early Child Development and Care* 51 (1989): 137–155.

33. Heath, *Ways with Words,* 84.

34. James M. Love, "Knowledge Transfer and Utilization in Education, in Edmund W. Gordon, ed., *Review of Research in Education,* Vol. 12, (Washington, D.C.: American Educational Research Association, 1985), pp. 337–386.

35. Edmund Gordon, Fayneese Miller, and David Rollock, "Coping with Communicentric Bias in Knowledge Production in the Social Sciences," *Educational Researcher,* 19 (1990): 14–19.

36. Ann Brown and Annemarie S. Palinscar, "Interactive Teaching to Promote Independent Learning from Text," *The Reading Teacher* 39 (1986): 770–777.

37. Rudolph Arnheim, "The Double-Edged Mind: Intuition and the Intellect," in Elliot Eisner, ed., *Learning and Teaching: The Ways of Knowing,* Eighty-Fourth Yearbook of the National Society for the Study of Education (Chicago: University of Chicago Press, 1985), pp. 77–96.

38. Ibid.

39. Barbara J. Shade, "Is There an Afro-American Cognitive Style?: An Exploratory Study," *The Journal of Black Psychology* 13 (1986): 13–16.

40. David Ausubel, "The Facilitation of Meaningful Verbal Meaning in the Classroom," *Educational Psychologist* 12 (1977): 162–178.

CHAPTER 17

Parents and Teachers: Partners in School Reform

■ CHERRY A. McGEE BANKS

I looked around the room and felt a tremendous sense of pride, knowing I played a small part in bringing this diverse group of parents, educators, and community members together. It wasn't easy. It took a great deal of hard work. In fact, there were days when I felt like giving up.

Two years ago a local newspaper published a report on our public schools. The report stated that students of color were more likely than White students to receive long-term suspensions from school, have below-average grades, and not participate in certain extracurricular activities or academic programs. The newspaper report also stated that even though the schools were desegregated, entire classrooms within schools were almost all White or had mostly students of color. The report concluded that practices within the school district had effectively barred students of color from full participation in the educational process.

The report resulted in a bitter debate that pitted people from different racial, ethnic, and social-class groups against each other. Soon after the publication of the report, rumors began circulating that the school district had set up a private school for middle-class White students within the public school system. Questions were raised about the high financial requirements for participation in certain extracurricular activities, the district's wide use of tracking, and the rationale for certain entrance requirements for advance placement classes and programs for gifted students.

Many people felt that the school district was being unfairly criticized. They believed that the school district was responding to the varied needs of students. They also believed the district had set objective standards for school behavior and participation in academic classes and programs. They did not believe that a school system could be unfair if everyone was judged by the same standard.

Some parents were particularly concerned about the possibility of eliminating certain extracurricular activities. They stated that even though some extracurricular programs such as skiing and horseback riding were expensive, those kinds of activities gave students who could never make the basketball, football, or track team a chance to participate in a sports activity. Moreover, they noted that many students paid for these activities by working during the summer or after school.

In general, there was an underlying feeling among these parents that if all parents took the time to work with their children at home, communicated the importance of education to their children, and made financial sacrifices for them, more low-income students and students of color would be successful in school.

Everyone seemed to have his or her own answer to our school districts' problem with disproportionality. They proposed solutions that ranged from keeping everything the same and doing a better job of communicating why the system was fair to reforming the curriculum, hiring new administrators and teachers, and eliminating tracking.

In the heat of the debate, a group of parents and teachers began meeting to talk about how they could help our district come together and do a better job of educating all of our students. After several meetings we decided to pull together a broad-based group of parents, community members, teachers, and administrators to talk about our concerns. Our first meetings were tense. Parents blamed teachers, teachers blamed administrators, and administrators blamed special interest groups of parents and community members. Even though it wasn't pleasant, our feelings had to be expressed before we could really start talking with each other.

Our first breakthrough came when the superintendent asked each of us to describe a perfect school. We were so caught up in criticizing or supporting the current system that we hadn't given any thought to what we really wanted for our children.

One teacher stated that her perfect school would incorporate technology in ways that would reduce our reliance on textbooks. She noted that information was doubling every 900 days. Many people on the committee were amazed when they learned that the body of information available today would quadruple by the time our kindergarten students graduated from high school.

That teacher's vision of a perfect school led us into discussions about the importance of communicating information that was known within the educational community to the broader community, the role of the economy in influencing the ability of educators to create an effective learning environment, and the changing demographic profile of our community. As we talked about these issues, we had to acknowledge the social-class, racial, and ethnic diversity within our community. We also had to realize that our students would be working in an increasingly interconnected global world society with people from different religions and races and with people who may have different values.

These discussions made us realize the extent to which the world was changing. We learned that during times of change, people tend to seek out the familiar and cling to the past. We acknowledged our fears about change and realized that we shared many concerns. After many months, we began to find common ground. That common ground grew out of candid discussions and an open, fair process characterized by trust and respect.

Even though our visions of a perfect school were different, each of us had such a vision. We began to realize that our diversity was a strength. It gave us the ability to bring different perspectives to the table and raise different questions. We also began to accept the conflict that resulted from our diversity. Our challenge was to make sure that the conflict did not become dysfunctional by allowing it to fall into personal attacks or focusing on the past.

Our process continues, but it has not been without victories. Each small victory is a building block in a school district that is becoming more effective for all students. Our committee will very likely become a standing committee because our goals and means change as we move forward. We've learned that the future is a journey, not a destination. Our actions today alter our tomorrows. As we moved forward into an ever changing landscape, we recognized the importance of taking risks.

INTRODUCTION

This example of parent involvement moves beyond the traditional view of parent involvement where parents work with their students' teachers. It raises important questions about how and when parents should be involved in schools. For example; should parents be full partners with teachers and administrators in school reform? Should parents be involved in identifying and resolving issues related to school reform? If so, what role(s) should they play in that process? How does their role(s) relate to the role(s) that classroom teachers should play? Should parents have a voice in determining curriculum, instruction, and/or staffing? How important is it for parents and educators with different points of view and from diverse backgrounds to work together? This chapter examines these and other questions that teachers must confront as they work to improve educational opportunities for all children.

WHAT IS PARENT-COMMUNITY INVOLVEMENT?

Parent-community involvement is a dynamic process that encourages, supports, and provides opportunities for parents and educators to cooperate in the education of students. An important goal of parent-community involvement is to improve student learning. In a comprehensive review of research on parent involvement, Anne Henderson found that there is compelling evidence that parent involvement improves student achievement.[1] Effective parent involvement can also improve student attendance and social behavior.

To be effective, parent involvement must be conceptualized broadly. It must provide opportunities for parents to be involved in different settings and at different levels of the educational process. Some parents may want to focus their energies on working with their own children at home. Other parents may want to work on committees that make decisions effecting students throughout the school district.

Parent-community involvement is also an important component of school reform. Many tasks involved in restructuring schools, such as setting goals and allocating resources, are best achieved through a collaborative problem-solving structure that includes parents, community members, and educators.

Parents and community groups help form what John Goodlad calls "the necessary coalition of contributing groups."[2] Educational reform needs the support, influence, and activism of parents and community groups. Schools are highly dependent on and vulnerable to citizens who can support or impede change. Parents and community leaders can validate the need for educational reform and can provide an appropriate forum for exploring the importance of education. They can also extend the discussion on school improvement issues beyond formal educational networks and help generate interest in educational reform in the community at large.[3] Parents and community leaders can help provide the rationale, motivation, and social action necessary for educational reform.

WHY IS PARENT-COMMUNITY INVOLVEMENT IMPORTANT?

Parent involvement is important because it acknowledges the importance of parents in the lives of their children, recognizes the diversity of values and perspectives within the school community, provides a vehicle for building a collaborative problem solving structure, and increases the opportunity for all students to learn in schools.

Parents are often children's first and most important teachers. Students come to school with knowledge, values, and beliefs they have learned from their parents and communities. Parents directly or indirectly help shape their children's value system, orientation toward learning, and view of the world in which they live. Parents can help teachers extend their knowledge and understanding of their students. Through that knowledge and understanding, teachers can improve their teaching effectiveness.

Most parents want their children to succeed in school. Schools can capitalize on the high value most parents put on education by working to create a school environment that reflects an understanding of the students' home and community.[4] When schools conflict with their students' home and community, they can alienate students from their families and communities and cause stress and confusion.

For example, many African American and White working-class parents use direct language when they interact with their children.[5] A working-class parent who wants her child to share a cookie may say, "Joyce, give Barbara half of your cookie." Teachers, however, frequently use indirect language when they issue directives. A teacher who wants Joyce to share her cookie may say, "Joyce, wouldn't you like to share your cookie with Barbara?" Lisa Delpit notes that the teacher's veiled command may suggest to Joyce that she has a choice when in fact she does not.[6]

To create a harmonious environment between the school, home, and community, teachers need to know something about their students' community and home life. Teachers need to be knowledgeable about parents' educational expectations for their children, languages spoken at home, family and community values and norms, as well as how children are taught in their homes and communities.[7] Parents also need information about the school. Parents need to know what the school expects their children to learn, how they will be taught, and the required books and materials their children will use in school. Parents also need to know how teachers will evaluate their children and how they can support their children's achievement.

Students, parents, and teachers all benefit from parent involvement in schools. When parents help their students at home, students perform better in school.[8] Although we do not know exactly why students show improvements when their parents are involved in their education, we do know that parental involvement increases the number of people who are supporting the child's learning. Such involvement also increases the amount of time the child is involved in learning activities. Parent involvement allows parents and teachers to reinforce skills and provides an environment that has consistent learning expectations and standards. Parents also become more knowledgeable about their child's school, its policies, and the school staff when they are involved in schools. Perhaps most important, it provides an opportunity for parents and children to spend time together. During that time, parents can communicate a high value for education, the importance of effort in achievement, and a high positive regard for their children.

Teachers and principals who know parents treat them with greater respect and show more positive attitudes toward their children.[9] Teachers generally see involved parents as concerned individuals who are willing to work with them. They often believe that parents who are not involved in school do not value education.

Parent involvement helps both parents and teachers become more aware of their need to support student learning. Student improvements that result from parents and teachers working together can increase each teacher's sense of professionalism and each parent's sense of parenting skills. A cooperative relationship between teachers and parents also increases the good will of parents and promotes positive community relations.

Historical Overview

Parent involvement in education is not new, but its importance and purpose have varied at different times in U.S. history. In the early part of the nation's history, families were often solely responsible for educating children. Children learned values and skills by working with their families in their communities.

When formal systems of education were established, parents continued to influence their children's education. During the colonial period, schools were viewed as an extension of the home. Parental and community values and expectations were reinforced in the school. Teachers generally came from the community and often knew their students' parents personally and shared their values.

At the beginning of the twentieth century, when large numbers of immigrants came to the United States, schools were used to compensate for the perceived failures of parents and communities. Schools became a major vehicle to assimilate immigrant children into U.S. society.[10] In general, parents were not welcomed in schools. Students were taught that their parents' ways of speaking, behaving, and thinking were inferior to what they were taught in school. In his 1932 study of the sociology of teaching, Waller concluded that parents and teachers lived in a state of mutual distrust and even hostility.[11]

As society changed, education became more removed from the direct influence of parents. Responsibility for transmitting knowledge from generation to generation was transferred from the home and community to the school. Education was seen as a job for trained professionals. Schools were autonomous institutions staffed by people who were often strangers in the community. Teachers did not necessarily live in their students' neighborhood, know the students' parents, or share their values.

Over time, schools were given more and more duties that traditionally had been the responsibility of the home and community. For example, parental responsibility for sex education was delegated partly to the schools.[12] Schools operated under the assumption of *in loco parentis,* and educators were often asked to assume the role of both teacher and substitute parent.

In a pluralist society, what the school teaches as well as who and how the school teaches can create tensions between parents and schools. Issues ranging from what the school teaches about the role of women in our society to mainstreaming students with disabilities point to the need for educators, parents, and communities to work together. Today, more and more parents, educators, and community leaders are calling for parent involvement in schools. Parents and educators are concerned about parent involvement, and a majority of both groups feel that it is important and necessary.[13] However, parents and educators are unsure about what forms this involvement should take. Often the views of parents and teachers conflict about meaningful ways to involve parents in the educational process.[14]

Parent and Community Diversity

Student diversity mirrors parent and community diversity. Just as teachers are expected to work with students from both genders and from different ethnic groups and social classes, parent involvement challenges teachers to work with a diverse group of parents. Some parents with whom teachers work are from different racial and ethnic groups, single parents, parents with special needs, low-income parents, parents with disabilities, or parents who do not speak English. Some parents are members of several of these groups.

Diversity in parent and community groups can be a tremendous asset to the school. However, it can also be a source of potential conflicts and frustrations. Some parents are particularly difficult to involve in their children's education. They resist becoming involved for several reasons. Stress is an important reason for their lack of involvement. The pressures to earn a living and take care of a home and children can put a great deal of stress on parents. At the end of the day, some parents just want to rest. Other parents do not believe they have the necessary educational background to be involved in their children's education. They feel intimidated by educators and believe that education should be left to the schools. Others feel alienated from the school because of negative experiences they have had there or because they believe the school does not support their values.[15] In addition, many parents today are products of the "me" generation. These parents are primarily concerned with narcissistic endeavors. They are involved in self-development and career-advancement activities. They have limited time available for school involvement, and it generally is not a priority in their lives.[16]

The increase in the number of grandparents who are providing primary care to their grandchildren is another example of parent diversity. Approximately 3.2 million children under the age of eighteen live with their grandparents.[17] Twelve percent of African American, 5.8 percent of Latino, and 3.6 percent of White children live with grandparents.[18]

Three groups of parents who tend not to be included in school involvement activities are described below. These include parents with special needs, single-parent families, and low-income families. These groups were selected to illustrate particular problem areas for parent involvement. The specific groups of parents discussed should not be interpreted as an indication that only parents from these groups are difficult to involve in schools or that all parents from these groups are difficult to involve in schools. Parents from all groups share many of the concerns discussed here, and there are examples of parents from each group discussed who are actively involved in schools.

Parents with Special Needs

Families with special needs include a wide range of parents. Families with special needs are found in all ethnic, racial, and income groups. Chronically unemployed parents, parents with long-term illness in the family, abusive parents, and parents with substance-abuse problems are examples of parents with special needs. Although parents with special needs have serious problems that cannot be addressed by the school, teachers should not ignore the importance of establishing a relationship with them. Knowing the difficulties students are coping with at home can help teachers create environments that are supportive during the time students are in school. Schools can help compensate for the difficult circumstances students experience at home. The school can be the one place during the day where a student is nurtured.

Abusive parents require special attention from the school. It is important for the school to develop policies on how to treat suspected cases of child neglect or abuse. It is generally helpful for one person to be in charge of receiving reports and other information. All states require schools to report suspected cases of child abuse.

Working with special-needs families generally requires district or building support to develop a list of community outreach agencies for referral. Although some special-needs parents may resist the school's help, they need someone they can trust and turn to for help. Working with these parents can show them that they are not alone. All parents want to feel that they are valued and adequate human beings. They do not want to be embarrassed.[19] Some parents with special needs will be able to be actively involved in schools, but many will be unable to become involved on a regular basis. An important goal for working with parents with special needs is to keep lines of communication open. Try to get to know the parents. Do not accept a stereotypical view of them without ever talking to them. Encourage parents to be involved whenever and however they feel they are able to participate. Be prepared to recommend appropriate community agencies to the family. Try to develop a clear understanding of your student's home environment so that you can provide appropriate intervention at school.

Parents who are involved in school may be willing to serve as intermediaries between the school and uninvolved parents. In an ethnography of an inner-city neighborhood, Shariff found that adults shared goods and services and helped each other in an effort to help the children in a family.[20] Educators can build on the sense of extended family that may exist in some neighborhoods to form community support groups for students whose parents cannot be involved in school. Regardless of the circumstances students confront at home, teachers have a responsibility to help them perform at their highest level at school.

Single-Parent Families

One of the most significant social changes in the United States in the last twenty years is the increase in the percentage of children living with one parent. In 1970,

11.9 percent of children under age eighteen lived with one parent. By 1989, 24.3 percent of children under eighteen lived with one parent.[21] This increase was particularly significant for African American children. The number of African American children under eighteen living with one parent increased from 31.8 percent in 1970 to 45.8 percent in 1980, and to 54.5 percent in 1989.[22] There was a slight decrease in the number of White children under eighteen living with one parent between 1970 and 1980. In 1970, 18.9 percent of White children under eighteen lived with one parent compared to 15.1 percent in 1980. However, by 1989, 18.8 percent of White children under eighteen lived with one parent.[23]

Many children who live with one parent are from divorced homes or are the children of unwed mothers. In 1988, 49.48 percent of all marriages in the United States ended in divorce.[24] Teenage wives had a divorce rate almost twice as high as that of wives ages thirty-five to thirty-nine.[25] The number of premaritally conceived births and births to unmarried women has also continued to increase. In 1988, 40 percent of the first-born children of women ages fifteen to twenty-nine were born to single women.[26]

Single-parent families share many of the hopes, joys, and concerns about their children's education as two-parent families. Because they have limited time and energy to attend school functions, they are sometimes viewed as unsupportive of education. However, when teachers respond sensitively to their needs and limitations, they can be enthusiastic partners with teachers. Some suggestions for working with single parents are listed below. Many of these suggestions apply to other groups of parents as well.

1. Provide flexible times for conferences, such as early mornings, evenings, and weekends.

2. Provide baby-sitting service for activities at the school.

3. Work out procedures for acknowledging and communicating with noncustodial parents. For instance, under what circumstances are noncustodial parents informed about their children's grades, school behavior, or attendance? Problems can occur when information is inappropriately given to or withheld from a noncustodial parent.

4. Use the parents' correct surname. Students will sometimes have different names from their parents.

Low-Income Families

In 1990, a family of four with total money income less than $13,359.00 lived below the poverty level.[27] The poverty level is an official governmental estimate of the income necessary to purchase a minimally acceptable standard of living. In 1990, the Census Bureau noted that the number of people in the United States living below the poverty level was rising. Poverty in the United States increased from 12.8 percent in 1989 to 13.5 percent in 1990.[28] Although the 1990 poverty rate was lower than the 1983 poverty rate of 15 percent, the percentage of people living in poverty in 1990 was higher than at any time during the 1970s.[29] There were 2.1 million more Americans living in poverty in 1990 than in 1989.[30] The median household income of $29,943.00 in 1990 was 1.7 percent below that of 1989.[31]

The trend of rising poverty and declining income hit Whites and Hispanics harder than African Americans. White males experienced the greatest drop in income. In 1990, the incomes of White males fell for the third consecutive year to an average of $27,866.00.[32] This was a 3.6 percent decline from their 1989 average income. The average income of women in 1990 remained unchanged at $19,816.[33]

Although the increase in the poverty rate of African Americans was below that of Whites and Hispanics, in 1990 more Blacks lived in poverty than either Whites or Hispanics. The poverty rate for African Americans in 1990 was 31.9 percent compared to 10.7 percent for Whites and 28.1 percent for Hispanics.[34]

The poverty rate for children is also rising. In 1990, the poverty rate for children rose to 20.6 percent compared to 19.6 percent in 1989 and 16.6 percent in 1967.[35] The number of children living in poverty is related to the number of female-headed households. Married couples had the lowest poverty rate in the nation in 1990—5.7 percent.[36]

Almost 77 percent of homeless families are headed by a single parent.[37] That parent is usually a female who has two or three children. A 1988 study conducted by the U.S. Conference of Mayors found that 25 percent of the homeless were children.[38] These children were members of homeless families, runaways, or children rejected by their parents. Runaways and children who were rejected by their parents accounted for 10 percent of the homeless population in such cities as Denver, Los Angeles, New Orleans, and San Francisco.[40] In 1988, the Department of Education estimated that there were 220,000 homeless school-age children in the United States.[41] Of those children, more than 65,000 do not attend school regularly.[42]

Low-income parents are generally strong supporters of education. They see education as a means to a better life for their children. However, they are often limited in their ability to buy materials and make financial commitments for activities such as field trips. Many of the suggestions listed for single-parent families also apply to low-income families. Schools can provide workbooks and other study materials for use at home as well as transportation for school activities and conferences. This will increase the ability of low-income families to become more involved in their children's education. The school can offer support to low-income families by establishing a community service program. Students can help clean up neighborhoods and distribute information on available social services. The schools can provide a desk space for voter registration and other services. Perhaps the most important way for schools to work with low-income parents is to recognize that low-income parents can contribute a great deal to their children's education. Although those contributions may not be in the form of traditional parent involvement, they can be very beneficial to teachers and students. The values and attitudes parents communicate to their children and their strong desire for their children to have a better chance in life than they had are important forms of support for the school.

TEACHER CONCERNS WITH PARENT-COMMUNITY INVOLVEMENT

Many teachers are ambivalent about parent and community involvement in education. Even though teachers often say they want to involve parents, many are suspicious of parents and are uncertain of what parents expect from them. Some teachers wonder if parents will do more harm than good. They think parents may disrupt their routine, may not have the necessary skills to work with their children, may be inconvenient to have in the classroom, and may show interest only in helping their own child, not the total class. Even teachers who think they would like to involve parents are not sure they have the time to do it or do not know exactly how to involve parents.[43] Many teachers believe that they already have too much to do, and working with parents would make their overburdened jobs impossible.

Many of these concerns result from a limited view of the possibilities for parent involvement. When many parents and teachers think of parent involvement, they think it means doing something for the school generally at the school or having the school teach parents how to become better parents. In today's society, a traditional view of parent involvement inhibits rather than encourages parents and teachers to work together. Traditional ideas about parent involvement have a built-in gender and social class bias and are a barrier to most males and low-income parents.

When parent involvement is viewed as a means of getting support for the school, parents are encouraged to bake cookies, raise money, or work at the school as unpaid classroom, playground, library, or office helpers. This form of parent involvement is generally directed to mothers who do not work outside the home. However, the number of mothers available for this form of involvement is decreasing. The number of married mothers in the work force increased from 39.5 percent in 1970 to 54.8 percent in 1984.

When parent involvement is viewed as a means to help deficient parents, the school provides parents with information on how to become better parents. This view of parent involvement is often directed toward culturally different and low-income parents. This approach often makes parents feel they are the cause of their children's failure in school. Teachers are presented as more skilled than parents. Parents and teachers may become rivals for the child's affection.[44]

Cultural perspectives play an important role in the traditional approach to parent involvement. In Chapter 2, Bullivant points out the importance of understanding a social group's cultural program. To be effective, parent and community involvement strategies should reflect what Bullivant calls the core of the social group's cultural program. He states that the core consists of the knowledge and conceptions embodied in the group's behaviors and artifacts and the values subscribed to by the group.

The parent-as-helper idea is geared toward parents who have the skills, time, and resources to become school helpers. Not all parents want to or feel they can or should do things for the school. Whether parents are willing to come to school is largely dependent on the parents' attitude toward school. This attitude results in part from their own school experiences. The parent in need of parenting skills assumes that there is one appropriate way to parent and that parents want to learn it. Both of these conceptualizations—the parent as helper and the parent in need of parenting skills—are derived from questionable assumptions about the character of contemporary parents and reflect a limited cultural perspective.

STEPS TO INCREASE PARENT-COMMUNITY INVOLVEMENT

Teachers are a key ingredient in parent-community involvement. They play multiple roles, including facilitator, communicator, and resource developer. Their success in implementing an effective parent-community involvement program relates to their skill in communicating and working with parents and community groups. Teacher attitude is also very important. Parents are supportive of the teachers they believe like their children and want them to succeed. Teachers who have a negative attitude toward students will likely have a similar attitude toward the students' parents. Teachers tend to relate to their students as representatives of their parents' perceived status in society. Teachers use such characteristics as class, race, gender, and ethnicity to determine students' prescribed social category.[45]

Below are five steps you can take to increase parent-community involvement in your classroom. These steps involve establishing two-way communication, enlisting support from staff and students, enlisting support from the community, developing resource materials for home use, and broadening the activities included in parent involvement.

Establish Two-Way Communication between the School and Home

Establishing two-way communication between the school and home is an important step in involving parents. Most parents are willing to become involved in their children's education if you let them know what you are trying to accomplish and how parents can help. Teachers should be prepared to do some outreach to parents and not to wait for them to become involved. Actively solicit information from parents on their thoughts about classroom goals and activities. When you talk with parents and community members, be an active listener. Listen for their feelings as well as for specific information. Listed below are seven ways you can establish and maintain two-way communication with parents and community members.

1. If possible, have an open-door policy in your classroom. Let parents know they are welcome. When parents visit, make sure they have something to do.

2. Send written information home about school assignments and goals so that parents are aware of what is going on in the classroom. Encourage parents to send notes to you if they have questions or concerns.

3. Talk to parents by phone. Let parents know when they can reach you by phone. Also, call parents periodically and let them know when things are going well. Have something specific to talk about. Leave some time for the parent to ask questions or make comments.

4. Report problems to parents, such as failing grades, before it is too late for them to take remedial action. Let parents know what improvements you expect from their children and how they can help.

5. Get to know your students' community. Take time to shop in their neighborhoods. Visit community centers and attend religious services. Let parents know when you will be in the community and that you are available to talk to them at their home or at some other location.

6. If you teach in an elementary school, try to have at least two in-person conferences a year with parents. When possible, include the student in the conference. Let the parent know in specific terms how the student is doing in class. Find out how parents feel about their children's level of achievement, and let them know what you think about the students' achievement level. Give parents some suggestions on what the student can do to improve and how they can help.

7. Solicit information from parents on their views on education. Identify their educational goals for their children, ways they would like to support their children's education, and their concerns about the school. There are a number of ways to get information from parents, including sending a questionnaire home and asking parents to complete it and return it to you, conducting a telephone survey, and asking your students to interview their parents.

Enlist the Support of Other Staff Members and Students

Teachers have some flexibility in their classrooms, but they are not able to determine some of the factors that influence their ability to have a strong parent involvement program. For instance, the type and amount of materials available for student use can determine whether a teacher can send home paper, pencils, and other materials for parents to use with their children. If teachers are allowed to modify their schedules, they can find free time to telephone parents, write notes, and hold morning or evening conferences with parents. The school climate also influences parent involvement. However, school climate is not determined by one individual; it is influenced by students, teachers, the principal, and the school secretary. Teachers need support from staff, students, the principal and district level staff to enhance their parent involvement activities.

Your students can help solicit support for parent and community involvement from staff and other students. Take your class on a tour of the school. Ask the class to think about how their parents would feel if they came to the school. Discuss these two questions: Is there a place for visitors to sit? Are there signs asking visitors to go directly to the office? Ask your students to list things they could do to make the school a friendlier place for parents.

Invite your building principal to come to your classroom and discuss the list with your students. Divide the class into small groups and have them discuss how they would like their parents involved in their education. Ask them to talk to their parents and get their views. Have each group write a report on how parents can be involved in their children's education. Each group could make presentations to students in the other classrooms in the building on how they would like to increase parent involvement in their school.

If funds or other support is needed from the district office for your parent involvement activities, have the students draw up a petition and solicit signatures from teachers, students, and parents. When all of the signatures are gathered, they can be delivered to an appropriate district administrator.

Building principals and district administrators can give you the support you need to:

1. Help create and maintain a climate for positive parent-community involvement. This can include supporting flexible hours for teachers who need to be out of the classroom to develop materials or to work with parents. Teachers can be given time out of the classroom without negatively affecting students. Time can be gleaned from the secondary teacher's schedule by combining homerooms one day a week, by team-teaching a class, or by combining different sections of a class for activities such as chapter tests. At the elementary school level, team teaching, released time during periods when students are normally out of the classroom for specialized subjects such as music and art, or having the principal substitute in the classroom are ways to provide flexible hours for teachers.

2. Set up a parent room. The parent room could be used for a number of functions, including serving as a community drop-in center where parents could meet other parents for a cup of coffee, or as a place for parents to work on school activities without infringing on the teachers' lounge. It could also be used as a waiting room for parents who need to see a student or a member of the school staff.

3. Host parent nights during which parents can learn more about the school, the curriculum, and the staff.

4. Send a personal note to students and to their parents when a student makes the honor roll or does something noteworthy.

5. Develop and distribute a handbook that contains student names and phone numbers, PTA or other parent group contact names, and staff names and phone numbers.

6. Ask the school secretary to make sure visitors are welcomed when they come to the school and are given directions as needed.

7. Encourage students to greet visitors and help them find their way around the building.

Enlist Support from the Community

To enlist support from the community, you need to know something about it. The following are some questions you should be able to answer.

1. Are there any drama, musical, dance, or art groups in the community?

2. Is there a senior-citizen group, a public library, or a cooperative extension service in the community?

3. Are employment services such as the state employment security department available in the community?

4. Are civil rights organizations such as the Urban League, Anti-Defamation League, or NAACP active in the community?

5. What is the procedure for referring people to the Salvation Army, Goodwill Industries, or the State Department of Public Assistance for emergency assistance for housing, food, and clothing?

6. Does the community have a mental-health center, family counseling, or crisis clinic?

7. Are programs and activities for youth such as Boys and Girls Clubs, Campfire, Boy Scouts, Girl Scouts, YMCA, and the YWCA available for your students?

As you learn about the community, you can begin developing a list of community resources and contacts that can provide support to families, work with your students, and provide locations for students to perform community service projects. Collecting information about your students' community and developing community contacts should be viewed as a long-term project. You can collect information as your schedule permits and organize it in a notebook. This process can be shortened if several teachers work together. Each teacher could concentrate on a different part of the community and share information and contacts.

Community groups can provide support in several ways. They can develop big sister and big brother programs for students, provide quiet places for students to study after school and on weekends, donate educational supplies, help raise funds for field trips, set up mentor programs, and tutor students.

Community groups can also provide opportunities for students to participate in community-based learning programs. Community-based learning programs provide an opportunity for students to move beyond the textbook and experience real life.[46] Students have an opportunity to see how knowledge is integrated when it is applied to the real world. It puts them in touch with a variety of people and lets them see how people cope with their environment.

Community-based learning also enhances career development. It can help students learn about themselves, gain confidence, and better understand their strengths and weaknesses. Students can learn to plan, make decisions, negotiate, and evaluate their plans. Here are some examples of community work.[47] Students can:

- Paint an apartment for an ill neighbor
- Clean alleys and backyards for the elderly
- Write letters for people who are ill
- Read to people who are unable to read
- Prepare an empty lot as a play area for young children
- Plant a vegetable garden for the needy
- Collect and recycle newspapers

Develop Learning Resources for Parents to Use at Home

Many of the learning materials teachers use with students at school can be used by parents at home to help students improve their skills. The materials should be in a format suitable for students to take home and should provide clear directions for at-home completion. Parents could let the teacher know how they liked the material by writing a note, giving their child a verbal message for the teacher, or by calling the school. Reginald M. Clark has written a series of math home-involvement activities for kindergarten through eighth grade. The activities are included in a booklet and are designed to help students increase their math skills. Parents are able to use the creative activities to reinforce the skills their children learn at school.[48] These kinds of materials are convenient for both parents and teachers to use.

It is important for teachers to have resources available for parents to use. This lets parents know that they can help increase their children's learning and that you want their help. Simply telling parents they should work with their children is not sufficient. Parents generally need specific suggestions. Once parents get an idea of what you want them to do, some will develop their own materials. Other parents will be able to purchase materials. You can suggest specific books, games, and other materials for parents to purchase and where these learning materials are available.

Some parents will not have the financial resources, time, or educational background to develop or purchase learning materials. With your principal's help or help from community groups, you can set up a learning center for parents. The learning center could contain paper, pencils, books, games, a portable typewriter, a portable computer, and other appropriate resources. The learning center could also have audiocassettes on such topics as instructional techniques, classroom rules, educational goals for the year, and oral readings from books. Parents could check materials out of the learning center for use at home.

Broaden the Conception of Parent and Community Involvement

Many barriers to parent-community involvement can be eliminated by broadly conceptualizing parent-community involvement. Parents can play many roles, depending on their interests, skills, and resources. It is important to have a variety of roles for parents so that more parents will have an opportunity to be involved. It is also important to make sure that some roles can be performed at home as well as at school. Below are five ways parents and community members can be involved in schools. Some of the roles can be implemented by the classroom teacher. Others need support and resources from building principals or central office administrators.

Parents Working with Their Own Children

Working with their own children is one of the most important roles parents can play in the educational process. Parents can help their children develop a positive self-concept and a positive attitude toward school as well as a better understanding of how their effort affects achievement. Most parents want their children to do well in school and are willing to do whatever they can to help them succeed. Teachers can increase the support they receive from their students' homes by giving parents a better understanding of what is going on in the classroom, by letting parents know what is expected in the classroom, and by suggesting ways they can support their child's learning.

You can work with parents to support the educational process in these three ways:

1. Involve parents in monitoring homework by asking them to sign homework papers.

2. Ask parents to sign a certificate congratulating students for good attendance.

3. Give students extra points if their parents do things such as sign their report card and attend conferences.

Some parents want a more active partnership with the school. These parents want to work with you in teaching their children. Below are three ways you can help parents work with their children to increase their learning.

1. Encourage parents to share hobbies and games, discuss news and television programs, and talk about school problems and events with their children.

2. Send information home on the importance of reading to children and include a reading list. A one-page sheet could be sent home stating, "One of the best ways to help children become better readers is to read them. Reading aloud is most helpful when you discuss the stories, learn to identify letters and words, and talk about the meaning of the words. Encourage leisure reading. Reading achievement is related to the amount of reading kids do. It increases vocabulary and reading fluency." Then list several books available from the school library for students to check out and take home.

3. You can supply parents with materials they can use to work with their children on skill development. Students can help make math games, crossword puzzles, and other materials that parents can use with them at home.

Professional Support Person for Instruction

Many parent and community members have skills that can be shared with the school. They are willing to work with students as well as teachers. These people are often ignored in parent and community involvement programs. A parent or community member who is a college professor could be asked to talk to teachers about a topic that interests them or to participate in an in-service workshop. A bilingual parent or community member could be asked to help tutor foreign-language students or to share books or magazines written in their language with the class. Parents who enjoy reading or art could be asked to help staff a humanities enrichment course before or after school or to recommend materials for the course. Parents and community members who perform these kinds of duties could also serve as role models for your students and would demonstrate the importance of education in the community. Review the list below and think of how you could involve parents and community members in your classroom. Parents and community members can:

- Serve as instructional assistants
- Correct papers at home or at school
- Use carpentry skills to build things for the school
- Tutor during school hours or after school
- Develop or identify student materials or community resources
- Share their expertise with students or staff
- Expand enrichment programs offered before, after, or during school such as Great Books and art appreciation
- Sew costumes for the school play
- Type and edit a newsletter

General Volunteers

Some parents are willing to volunteer their time but they do not want to do a job that requires specific skills. When thinking of activities for general volunteers, be sure to include activities that can be performed at the school and activities that can be performed at home. Some possible activities include:

- Working on the playground as a helper
- Working in the classroom as a helper
- Working at home preparing cutouts and other materials that will be used in class
- Telephoning other parents to schedule conferences

Decision Makers

Some parents are interested in participating in decision making in the school. They want to help set school policy, select curriculum materials, review budgets, or interview perspective staff members. Roles for these parents and community members include school board member and advisory council member. Serving on a site council is another way for parents to participate in decision making. Site councils are designed to increase parent involvement in schools, empower classroom teachers, and allow the people who implement educational decisions to make them.

The Comer model is an effective way to involve parents, classroom teachers, and other educators in decision making.[49] Comer believes schools can be more effective when they are restructured in ways that encourage and support cooperation among parents and educators.

Comer did much of his pioneering work on parent involvement and restructuring schools in Prince George County, Maryland. There he implemented two committees—the School Planning and Management Team (SPMT) and the Student Staff Services Team (SSST).

The SPMT included the school principal, classroom teachers, parents, and support staff. The SPMT used consensus to reach decisions. In addition, the committee had a no-fault policy, which encouraged parents not to blame the school and educators not to blame parents. The SPMT provided a structure for parents and educators to create a common vision for their school, reduce fragmentation, and develop activities, curriculum, and in-service programs. The SPMT also developed a comprehensive school plan, designed a schoolwide calendar of events, and monitored and evaluated student progress. The SPMT met at least once a month. Subcommittees of the SPMT met more frequently.

The second committee that Comer implemented was the Student Staff Services team (SSST). The SSST was composed of the school principal, guidance counselor, classroom teachers, and support staff, including psychologists, health aides, and other appropriate personnel. Teachers and parents were encouraged to join this group if they had concerns they believed should be addressed. The SSST brought school personnel together to discuss individual student concerns. The SST brought coherence and order to the services that students receive.

SUMMARY

Parent and community involvement is a dynamic process that encourages, supports, and provides opportunities for teachers, parents, and community members to work together to improve student learning. Parent and community involvement is also an important component of school reform and multicultural education. Parents and community groups help provide the rationale, motivation, and social action necessary for educational reform.

Everyone benefits from parent-community involvement. Students tend to perform better in schools and have more people supporting their learning. Parents know more about what is going on at school, have more opportunities to communicate with their children's teacher, and are able to help their children increase their learning. Teachers gain a partner in education. Teachers learn more about their students through their parent and community contacts and are able to use that information to help increase their students' performance.

Even though research has consistently demonstrated that students have an advantage in school when their parents support and encourage educational activities, not all parents know how they can support their child's education or feel they have the time, energy, or other resources to be involved in schools. Some parents have a particularly difficult time supporting their children's education. Three such groups are parents who have low incomes, single parents, and parents with special needs. Parents from these groups are often dismissed as unsupportive of education, but they want their children to do well in school and are willing to work with the school when the school reaches out to them and responds to their needs.

To establish an effective parent-community involvement program you should establish two-way communication with parents and community groups, enlist support from the community, and have resources available for parents to use in working with their children. Expanding how parent-community involvement is conceptualized can increase the number of parents and community members able to participate. Parents can play many roles. Ways to involve parents and community members include parents working with their own children, parents and community members sharing their professional skills with the school, parents and community groups volunteering in the school, and parents and community members working with educators to make decisions about school.

QUESTIONS AND ACTIVITIES

1. Compare the role of parents in schools during the colonial period to that of students today. Identify and discuss changes that have occurred and changes you would like to see occur in parent involvement.

2. Consider this statement: Regardless of the circumstances students experience at home, teachers have a responsibility to help them perform at their highest level at school. Do you agree? Why or why not?

3. Interview a parent of a bilingual, ethnic minority, religious minority, or low-income student to learn more about the parent's views on schools and the educational goals for his or her children. This information cannot be generalized to all members of these groups, but it can be an important departure point for learning more about diverse groups within our society.

4. Consider this statement: All parents want their children to succeed in school. Do you agree with the statement? Why or why not?

5. Interview a classroom teacher and an administrator to determine his or her perceptions of parent-community involvement.

6. Write a brief paper on your personal views of the benefits and drawbacks of parent-community involvement.

7. Form a group with two other members of your class or workshop. One person in the group will be a teacher, the other a parent, and the third an observer. The teacher and the parent will role play a teacher-parent conference. After role playing the conference, discuss how it felt to be a parent and a teacher. What can be done to make the parent and teacher feel more comfortable? Was the information shared at the conference helpful? The observer can share his or her view of how the parent and teacher interacted.

NOTES

1. Anne Henderson, *The Evidence Continues to Grow: Parent Involvement Improves Student Achievement* (Columbia, Md.: National Committee for Citizens in Education, 1987).

2. John I. Goodlad, *A Place Called School: Prospects for the Future* (New York: McGraw-Hill, 1984), p. 293.

3. David S. Seeley, "Educational Partnership and the Dilemmas of School Reform," *Phi Delta Kappan,* 6 (February): 383–388.

4. Stephan Diáz, Luis C. Moll, and Hugh Mehan, "Sociocultural Resources in Instruction: A Context Specific Approach," in *Beyond Language: Social & Cultural Factors in Schooling Language Minority Students* (Los Angeles: California State University, 1986).

5. Lisa D. Delpit, "The Silenced Dialogue: Power and Pedagogy in Educating Other People's Children," *Harvard Educational Review* 3 (August 1988): 280–298.

6. Ibid.

7. Nicholas Hobbs, "Families, Schools and Communities: An Ecosystem for Children," in Hope Jenson Leichter, ed., *Families and Communities as Educators* (New York: Teachers College Press, 1979).

8. Reginald M. Clark, *Family Life and School Achievement: Why Poor Black Children Succeed or Fail* (Chicago: University of Chicago Press, 1983).

9. Ibid.

10. James A. Banks, *Teaching Strategies for Ethnic Studies,* 5th ed. (Boston: Allyn and Bacon, 1989).

11. Willard Waller, *The Sociology of Teaching* (New York: Wiley, 1965).

12. James S. Coleman, "Families and Schools," *Educational Researcher* 16, No. 6 (1987): 32–38.

13. D. L. Williams, Jr., "Highlights from a Survey of Parents and Educators Regarding Parent Involvement in Education," Paper presented at the Seventh National Symposium on Building Family Strengths, Lincoln, Nebr., May 1984.

14. Sara Lawrence Lightfoot, *Worlds Apart: Relationships between Families and Schools* (New York: Basic Books, 1978).

15. Eugenia Hepworth Berger, *Parents as Partners in Education: The School and Home Working Together,* 2nd ed. (Columbus, Ohio: Merrill, 1987).

16. Coleman, "Families and Schools."

17. U.S. Bureau of the Census, *Statistical Abstract of the United States,* 1989, 109th ed. (Washington, D.C.: U.S. Government Printing Office, 1989).

18. Ibid.

19. Berger, *Parents as Partners in Education.*

20. Jagna Wojcicka Shariff, "Free Enterprise and the Ghetto Family," in Jamine S. Wurzel, ed., *Toward Multiculturalism: A Reader in Multicultural Education* (Yarmouth, Me.: Intercultural Press, 1988).

21. U.S. Bureau of the Census, *Statistical Abstract of the United States,* 1989.

22. Ibid.

23. Ibid.

24. Ibid.

25. Ibid.

26. Ibid.

27. Ibid.

28. Jason DeParle, "Poverty Rate Rose Sharply Last Year as Incomes Slipped," *The New York Times,* (Sept. 27, 1991): 1, 11.

29. Ibid.

30. Ibid.

31. Ibid.

32. Ibid.

33. Ibid.

34. Ibid.

35. Ibid.

36. Ibid.

37. U.S. Bureau of the Census, *Statistical Abstract of the United States,* 1989.

38. John W. Wright, *The Universal Almanac, 1991* (New York: Andrews and McMeel, 1990), pp. 201–202.

39. Ibid.

40. Ibid.

41. Ibid.

42. Ibid.

43. David Winkley, "The School's View of Parents," in Cedric Cullingford, ed., *Parents, Teachers and Schools* (London: Robert Royce, 1985).

44. Lightfoot, *World's Apart.*

45. Ibid.

46. Larry McClure, Sue Carol Cook, and Virginia Thompson, *Experience-Based Learning: How to Make the Community Your Classroom* (Portland, Ore.: Northwest Regional Educational Laboratory, 1977).

47. Ibid.

48. Reginald M. Clark, *Home Involvement Activities* (Boston: Houghton Mifflin, 1987).

49. James Comer, "Educating Poor Minority Children," *Scientific American* 259 (1988): 42–48.

Multicultural Resources

Issues and Concepts

Banks, James A., *Multiethnic Education: Theory and Practice,* 2nd ed. (Boston: Allyn and Bacon, 1988).

Bullivant, Brian M., *Pluralism: Cultural Maintenance and Evolution* (Clevedon, Avon, England: Multilingual Matters, 1984).

Davis, Larry E., and Enola K. Proctor. *Race, Gender and Class: Guidelines for Practice with Individuals, Families and Groups* (Englewood Cliffs, N.J.: Prentice-Hall, 1989).

Figueroa, Peter, *Education and the Social Construction of Race* (New York: Routledge, 1991).

Geertz, Clifford, *The Interpretation of Cultures* (New York: Basic Books, 1973).

Gollnick, Donna M., and Philip C. Chinn, *Multicultural Education in a Pluralistic Society,* 3rd ed. (Columbus, Ohio: Merrill, 1990).

Grant, Carl A., and Christine E. Sleeter, *After the School Bell Rings* (Philadelphia: The Falmer Press, 1986).

Hildalgo, Nitza M., Caesar L. McDowell, and Emilie V. Siddle, eds., *Facing Racism in Education* (Cambridge, Mass.: Harvard Educational Review Reprint Series 21, 1990).

Lynch, James, *Prejudice Reduction and the Schools* (New York: Nichols, 1987).

McLeod, Keith, A., ed., *Multicultural Education: A Partnership* (Toronto, Ontario: Canadian Council for Multicultural and Intercultural Education, 1987).

Multicultural Leader, quarterly newsletter published by the Educational Materials and Services Center, P. O. Box 802, Edmonds, Wash., 98020.

Orfield, Gary, and Carole Ashkinaze, *The Closing Door: Conservative Policy and Black Opportunity* (Chicago: The University of Chicago Press, 1991).

Sleeter, Christine E., ed., *Empowerment through Multicultural Education* (Albany: State University of New York Press, 1991).

Sleeter, Christine E., and Carl A. Grant, *Making Choices for Multicultural Education: Five Approaches to Race, Class and Gender* (Columbus, Ohio: Merrill, 1988).

Verma, Gajendra K., ed., *Education for All: A Landmark in Pluralism* (Philadelphia: The Falmer Press, 1989).

Social Class

Cookson, Peter W., Jr., and Caroline Hodges Persell, *Preparing for Power: America's Elite Boarding Schools* (New York: Basic Books, 1985).

Ehrenreich, Barbara, *Fear of Falling: The Inner Life of the Middle Class* (New York: Harper, 1989).

Ellwood, David T., *Poor Support: Poverty in the American Family* (New York: Basic Books, 1988).

Hewlett, Sylvia Ann, *When the Bough Breaks: The Cost of Neglecting Our Children* (New York: Basic Books, 1991).

Jencks, Christopher, and Paul E. Peterson, eds., *The Urban Underclass* (Washington, D.C.: The Brookings Institution, 1991).

Katz, Michael B., *The Undeserving Poor: From the War on Poverty to the War on Welfare* (New York: Pantheon, 1989).

Kotlowitz, Alex, *There Are No Children Here: The Story of Two Boys Growing Up in the Other America* (New York: Doubleday, 1991).

Kozol, Jonathan, *Savage Inequalities: Children in America's Schools* (New York: Crown Publishers, 1991).

Landry, Bart, *The New Black Middle Class* (Berkeley: University of California Press, 1987).

Oakes, Jeannie, *Keeping Track: How Schools Structure Inequality* (New Haven, Conn.: Yale University Press, 1985).

Persell, Caroline Hodges, *Education and Inequality* (New York: The Free Press, 1977).

Schorr, Lisbeth G., with Daniel Schorr, *Within Our Reach: Breaking the Cycle of Poverty* (New York: Doubleday, 1988).

Religion

Bullivant, Brian M., *The Way of Tradition: Life in an Orthodox Jewish School* (Hawthorn, Victoria, Australia: The Australian Council for Educational Research, 1978).

Collie, William E., and Lee H. Smith, eds., "Teaching about Religion in the Schools: The Continuing Challenge," *Social Education* 45 (January 1981): 15–34.

Elaide, Mircea, ed., *The Encyclopedia of Religion,* 6 volumes. New York: Macmillan.

Ellwood, Robert S., Jr., *Introducing Religion from Inside and Outside* (Englewood Cliffs, N.J.: Prentice-Hall, 1978).

Engel, David E., ed., *Religion in Public Education* (New York: Paulist Press, 1974).

Herberg, Will, *Protestant-Catholic-Jew: An Essay in American Religious Sociology* (New York: Anchor Press, 1960).

Lincoln, C. Eric, and Lawrence H. Mamiya. *The Black Church in the African American Experience.* (Durham, N.C.: Duke University Press, 1990).

Rosten, Leo, ed., *Religions of America: Ferment and Faith in an Age of Crisis, A New Guide and Almanac* (New York: Simon & Schuster, 1975).

Smart, Ninian, *The Religious Experience,* 4th ed. (New York: Macmillan, 1991).

Smart, Ninian, and Richard D. Hecht, eds., *Sacred Texts of the World: A Universal Anthology* (New York: Crossroad Publishing Co., 1990).

Smith, Huston, *The Religions of Man* (New York: Harper and Row, 1986).

Turpin, Jonne, *Women in Church History: 20 Stories for 20 Centuries* (Cincinnati: St. Anthony Mesenger Press, 1990).

Gender

Albrecht, Lisa, and Brewer, Rosa M., eds., *Bridges of Power: Women's Multicultural Awareness* (Philadelphia: New Society Publishers, 1990).

Allen, Paula Gunn, *The Sacred Hoop: Recovering the Feminine in American Indian Traditions* (Boston: Beacon Press, 1986).

Amott, Teresa L., and Julie A. Matthaei, *Race, Gender and Work: A Multicultural Economic History of Women in the United States* (Boston: South End Press, 1991).

Andersen, Margaret, and Patricia Hill Collins, eds., *Race, Class, and Gender: An Anthology* (Belmont, Calif.: Wadsworth, 1991).

Asian Women United of California, *Making Waves: An Anthology of Writings by and about Asian American Women* (Boston: Beacon Press, 1989).

Anzaldua, Gloria, *Borderlands/La Frontera* (San Francisco: Spinsters/Aunt Lute Book Company, 1989).

Anzaldua, Gloria, ed., *Making Face, Making Soul: Haciendo Caras, Creative and Critical Perspectives by Women of Color* (San Francisco: Aunt Lute Foundation Books, 1990).

Belenky, Mary Field, Blythe McVicker Clinchy, Nancy Rule Goldberg, and Fill Mattuck Tarrule, *Women's Ways of Knowing: The Development of Self, Voice, and Mind* (New York: Basic Books, 1986).

Bell, Roseann P., Betty J. Parker, and Beverly Guy-Sheftall, *Sturdy Black Bridges: Visions of Black Women in Literature* (New York: Avon Books, 1979).

Bly, Robert, *Iron John: A Book about Men* (Reading, Mass.: Addison-Wesley, 1990).

Butler, Johnella E., and John C. Walter, eds., *Transforming the Curriculum: Ethnic Studies and Women's Studies* (Albany: State University of New York Press, 1991).

Cole, Johnnetta, ed., *All American Women: Lines That Divide, Ties That Bind* (New York: Free Press, 1986).

Collins, Patricia Hill, *Black Feminist Thought: Knowledge, Consciousness, and the Politics of Empowerment* (New York: Routledge, 1990).

Davis, Angela, *Women, Race, and Class* (New York: Vintage Books, 1981).

DuBois, Ellen Carol, and Vicki L. Ruiz, *Unequal Sisters: A Multicultural Reader in U.S. Women's History* (New York: Routledge, 1990).

Franklin, Clyde W., *The Changing Definition of Masculinity* (New York: Plenum Press, 1984).

Gilligan, Carol, *In a Different Voice: Psychological Theory and Women's Development* (Cambridge, Mass.: Harvard University Press, 1982).

Gilligan, Carol, Nona P. Lyons, and Trudy J. Hanmer, eds., *Making Connections: The Relational Worlds of Adolescent Girls at Emma Willard School* (Cambridge, Mass.: Harvard University Press, 1990).

Halpern, Diane F., *Sex Differences in Cognitive Abilities* (Hillsdale, N.J.: Lawrence Erlbaum Associates, 1986).

Humm, Maggie, *The Dictionary of Feminist Theory* (Columbus: Ohio State University Press, 1990).

Jones, Jacqueline, *Labor of Love, Labor of Sorrow. Black Women, Work and the Family from Slavery to the Present* (New York: Vintage Books, 1985).

Klein, Susan, ed., *Handbook for Achieving Sex Equity through Education* (Baltimore: The John Hopkins University Press, 1985).

Melville, Margarita B., ed., *Twice a Minority: Mexican American Women* (St. Louis: The C. V. Mosby Company, 1980).

Mirande, Alfredo, and Evangelina Enriquez, *La Chicana: The Mexican-American Woman* (Chicago: The University of Chicago Press, 1979).

Niethammer, Carolyn, *Daughters of the Earth: The Lives and Legends of American Indian Women* (New York: Collier Books, 1977).

Pleck, Joseph H., *The Myth of Masculinity* (Cambridge, Mass.: The MIT Press, 1981).

Rodgers, Harrell R., Jr., *Poor Women, Poor Families: The Economic Plight of America's Female-Headed Households* (New York: M. E. Sharpe, 1986).

Sadker, Myra P., and David M. Sadker, *Sex Equity Handbook for Schools* (New York: Longman, 1982).

Spelman, Elizabeth, *Inessential Woman: Problems of Exclusion in Feminist Thought* (Boston: Beacon Press, 1988),

Spence, Janet T., Kay Deaux, and Robert L. Helmreich, "Sex Roles in Contemporary American Society," in Gardner Lindzey and Elliot Aronson, eds., *The Handbook of Social Psychology*, Vol. 2, 3rd ed. (New York: Random House, 1985), pp. 149–178.

Tsuchida, Nobuya, ed., *Asian and Pacific American Experiences: Women's Perspectives* (Minneapolis: University of Minnesota, 1982).

Yung, Judy, *Chinese Women of America: A Pictorial History* (Seattle: University of Washington Press, 1986).

Ethnicity and Language

Alba, Richard, *Ethnic Identity: The Transformation of White America* (New Haven, Conn.: Yale University Press, 1990).

Banks, James A., *Teaching Strategies for Ethnic Studies*, 5th ed. (Boston: Allyn and Bacon, 1991).

Banks, James A., and James Lynch, eds., *Multicultural Education in Western Societies* (London: Cassell, 1986).

Berry, Gordon LaVern, and Joy Keiko Asamen, eds., *Black Students: Psychosocial Issues and Academic Achievement.* (Beverly Hills, Calif.: Sage Publications, 1989).

Brandt, Godfrey L., *The Realization of Anti-Racist Teaching* (Philadelphia: The Falmer Press, 1986).

Bullivant, Brian, *The Ethnic Encounter in the Secondary School: Ethnocultural Reproduction and Resistance; Theory and Case Studies* (Philadelphia: The Falmer Press, 1987).

Crawford, James, *Bilingual Education: History, Politics, and Practice* (Trenton, N.J.: Crane Publishing Co., 1989).

Cross, William E., Jr., *Shades of Black: Diversity in African-American Identity* (Philadelphia: Temple University Press, 1991).

Garcia, Ricardo L., *Teaching in a Pluralistic Society: Concepts, Models, Strategies*, 2nd ed. (New York: Harper/Collins, 1991).

Gay, Geneva, and Willie L. Baber, eds., *Expressively Black: The Cultural Basis of Ethnic Identity* (New York: Praeger, 1988).

Gibbs, Jewelle Taylor, and Larke Nahme Huang and associates, *Children of Color: Psychological Interventions with Minority Youth* (San Francisco: Jossey-Bass Publishers, 1990).

Hale-Benson, Janice E., *Black Children: Their Roots, Culture, and Learning Styles*, rev. ed. (Baltimore: The John Hopkins University Press, 1986).

Heath, Shirley Brice, *Ways with Words: Language, Life, and Work in Communities and Classrooms* (New York: Cambridge University Press, 1983).

Imhoff, Gary, ed., *Learning in Two Languages: From Conflict to Consensus in the Reorganization of Schools* (New Brunswick, N.J.: Transaction Books, 1990).

Lomotey, Kofi, ed., *Going to School: The African-American Experience* (Albany: State University of New York Press, 1990).

McAdoo, Harriette P., and John L. McAdoo, eds., *Black Children: Social, Educational, and Parental Environments* (Beverly Hills, Calif.: Sage Publications, 1985).

Neisser, Ulric, ed., *The School Achievement of Minority Children: New Perspectives* (Hillsdale, N.J.: Lawrence Erlbaum Associates, 1986).

Olivas, Michael A., *Latino College Students* (New York: Teachers College Press, 1986).

Ovando, Carlos J., and Virginia P. Collier, *Bilingual and ESL Classrooms: Teaching in Multicultural Contexts* (New York: McGraw-Hill, 1985).

Phinney, Jean S., and Mary J. Rotheram, *Children's Ethnic Socialization* (Beverly Hills, Calif.: Sage Publications, 1987).

Prager, Jeffrey, Douglas Longshore, and Melvin Seeman, eds., *School Desegregation Research* (New York: Plenum Press, 1986).

Shade, Barbara J., ed., *Culture, Style and the Educative Process* (Springfield, Ill.: Charles C Thomas, Publisher, 1989).

Thernstrom, Stephan, Ann Orlov, and Oscar Handlin, *Harvard Encyclopedia of American Ethnic Groups* (Cambridge, Mass.: Harvard University Press, 1980).

Wilson, William Julius, *The Truly Disadvantaged: The Inner City, the Underclass, and Public Policy* (Chicago: The University of Chicago Press, 1987).

Exceptionality

Bloom, Benjamin, *Developing Talent in Young People* (New York: Ballantine Books, 1985).

Clark, Barbara. *Growing Up Gifted*. 4th ed. (Columbus, Ohio: Merrill-Macmillan, 1992).

Colangelo, Nicholas, and Gary A. Davis, *Handbook of Gifted Education* (Boston: Allyn and Bacon, 1991).

Davis, Gary A., and Sylvia B. Rimm, *Education of the Gifted and Talented,* 2nd ed. (Boston: Allyn and Bacon, 1989).

Dorris, Michael. *The Broken Cord* (New York: Harper/Collins, 1989).

Gallagher, James J. *Teaching the Gifted Child,* 3rd ed. (Boston: Allyn and Bacon, 1985).

Goffman, Erving, *Stigma: Notes on the Management of Spoiled Identity* (Englewood Cliffs, N.J.: Prentice-Hall, 1963).

Harring, Norris G., and Linda McCormick, *Exceptional Children and Youth,* 5th ed. (Columbus, Ohio: Merrill, 1990).

Heward, William L., and Michael D. Orlansky, *Exceptional Children: An Introductory Survey of Special Education,* 4th ed. (Columbus, Ohio: Merrill, 1992).

Kerr, B. A., *Smart Girls, Gifted Women* (Columbus: Ohio Psychology Publishing, 1985).

Mehan, Hugh, Alma Herlweck, and J. Lee Meihls, *Handicapping the Handicapped: Decision Making in Students' Educational Careers* (Stanford, Calif.: Stanford University Press, 1986).

Mercer, Jane R., *Labeling the Mentally Retarded* (Berkeley: University of California Press, 1973).

Morsink, Catherine Voelker, *Teaching Special Needs Students in Regular Classrooms* (Boston: Little, Brown, 1984).

Peterson, Nancy C., *Early Intervention for Handicapped and At-Risk Children: An Introduction to Early Childhood-Special Education* (Denver: Love Publishing Co., 1987).

Schulz, Jane B., *Parents and Professionals in Special Education* (Boston: Allyn and Bacon, 1987).

Schulz, Jane B., and Ann P. Turnbull, *Mainstreaming Handicapped Students: A Guide for Classroom Teachers,* 2nd ed. (Boston: Allyn and Bacon, 1984).

School Reform

Apple, Michael W., and Linda K. Christian-Smith, eds., *The Politics of the Textbook* (New York: Routledge, 1991).

Berger, Eugenia Hepworth, *Parents as Partners in Education: The School and the Home Working Together* (Columbus, Ohio: Merrill, 1987).

Bliss, James R., William A. Firestone, and Craig E. Richards, *Rethinking Effective Schools Research and Practice* (Englewood Cliffs, N.J.: Prentice-Hall, 1991).

Brookover, Wilbur, Charles Beady, Patricia Flood, John Schweitzer, and John Wisenbaker, *School Social Systems and Student Achievement: Schools Can Make a Difference* (New York: Praeger, 1979).

Clark, Reginald M., *Family Life and School Achievement: Why Poor Black Children Succeed or Fail* (Chicago: The University of Chicago Press, 1983).

Comer, James P., *School Power: Implications of an Intervention Project* (New York: The Free Press, 1980).

Cremin, Lawrence A., *Popular Education and Its Discontents* (New York: Harper and Row, 1989).

Freedman, Samuel G., *Small Victories: The Real World of a Teacher, Her Students and Their High School* (New York: Harper and Row, 1990).

Gardner, Howard, *Frames of Mind: The Theory of Multiple Intelligences* (New York: Basic Books, 1983).

Goodlad, John I., ed., *The Ecology of School Renewal* (Chicago: The University of Chicago Press, 1987).

Goodlad, John I., and Pamela Keating, eds., *Access to Knowledge: An Agenda for Our Nation's Schools* (New York: The College Board, 1990).

Graham, Patricia Albjerg, *SOS: Save our Schools* (New York: Hill and Wang, 1992).

Johnson, Susan Moore, *Teachers at Work: Achieving Success in Our Schools* (New York: Basic Books, 1990).

Kennedy, Mary M., ed., *Teaching Academic Subjects to Diverse Learners* (New York: Teachers College Press, 1991).

Lightfoot, Sara Lawrence, *The Good School: Portraits of Character and Culture* (New York: Basic Books, 1983).

Presseisen, Barbara Z., *Unlearned Lessons: Current and Past Reforms for School Improvement* (Philadelphia: The Falmer Press, 1985).

Glossary

African Americans United States citizens who have an African biological and cultural heritage and identity. This term is used synonymously and interchangeably with *Black* and *Black American*. These terms are used to describe both a racial and a cultural group. There were about 31 million African Americans in the United States in 1990. They are the nation's largest ethnic group of color.

Afrocentric curriculum A curriculum approach in which concepts, issues, problems, and phenomena are viewed from the perspectives of Africans and African Americans. It is based on the assumption that students learn best when they view situations and events from their own cultural perspectives. (*References:* Molefi Kete Asante, "The Afrocentric Idea in Education," *The Journal of Negro Education,* Vol. 60, No. 2 (Spring 1991): 170–180; Molefi Kete Asante, *The Afrocentric Idea.* Philadelphia: Temple University Press, 1987).

American Indian See *Native American.*

Anglo-Americans Americans whose biological and cultural heritage originated in England, or Americans with other biological and cultural heritages who have assimilated into the dominant or mainstream culture in the United States. This term is often used to describe the mainstream United States culture or to describe most White Americans.

Antiracist education A term used frequently in the United Kingdom and Canada to describe a process used by teachers and other educators to eliminate institutionalized racism from the school and society and to help individuals to develop nonracist attitudes. When antiracist educational reform is implemented, curriculum materials, grouping practices, hiring policies, teacher attitudes and expectations, and school policy and practices are examined and steps are taken to eliminate racism from these school variables. A related educational reform movement in the United States that focuses more on individuals than on institutions is known as *prejudice reduction.*

Asian Americans Americans who have a biological and cultural heritage that originated on the continent of Asia. The largest groups of Asian Americans in the United States in 1990 were Chinese, Filipinos, Japanese, Asian Indians, Koreans, and Vietnamese. Other groups include Laotians, Thai, Cambodians, Pakistanis, and Indonesians. Asians are the fastest growing ethnic group in the United States. They increased 141 percent between 1970 and 1980. There were about 6 million Asian Americans in the United States in 1990.

Cultural assimilation Takes place when one ethnic or cultural group acquires the behavior, values, perspectives, ethos, and characteristics of another ethnic group and sheds its own cultural characteristics.

Culture The ideations, symbols, behaviors, values, and beliefs that are shared by a human group. *Culture* can also be defined as a group's program for survival and adaptation to its environment. Pluralistic nation-states such as the United States, Canada, and Australia are made up of an overarching culture, called a macroculture, that all individuals and groups within the nation share. These nation-states also have many smaller cultures, called microcultures, that differ in many ways from the macroculture or that contain cultural components manifested differently than in the macroculture. (See Chapters 1 and 2 for further discussions of culture.)

Disability The physical or mental characteristics of an individual that prevent or limit him or her from performing specific tasks.

Discrimination The differential treatment of individuals or groups based on categories such as race, ethnicity, gender, sexual orientation, social class, or exceptionality.

Ethnic group A microcultural group or collectivity that shares a common history and culture, common values, behaviors, and other characteristics that cause members of the group to have a shared identity. A sense of peoplehood is one of the most important characteristics of an ethnic group. An ethnic group also shares economic and political interests. Cultural characteristics, rather than biological traits, are the essential attributes of an ethnic group. An ethnic group is not the same as a racial group. Some ethnic groups, such as Puerto Ricans in the United States, are made up of individuals who belong to several different racial groups. White Anglo-Saxon Protestants, Italian Americans, and Irish Americans are examples of ethnic groups. Individual members of an ethnic group vary considerably in the extent to which they identify with the group. Some individuals have a very strong identity with their particular ethnic group, whereas other members of the group have a very weak identification with it.

Ethnic minority group An ethnic group with several distinguishing characteristics. An ethnic minority group has distinguishing cultural characteristics, racial characteristics, or both, which enable members of other groups to identify its members easily. Some ethnic minority groups, such as Jewish Americans, have unique cultural characteristics. African Americans have unique cultural and physical characteristics. The unique attributes of ethnic minority groups make them convenient targets of racism and discrimination. Ethnic minority groups are usually a numerical minority within their societies. However, the Blacks in South Africa, who are a numerical majority in their nation-state, are often considered a sociological minority group by social scientists because they have little political and economic power.

Ethnic studies The scientific and humanistic analysis of behavior influenced by variables related to ethnicity and ethnic-group membership. This term is often used to refer to special school, university, and college courses and programs that focus on specific racial and ethnic groups. However, any aspects of a course or program that includes a study of variables related to ethnicity can accurately be referred to as ethnic studies. In other words, ethnic studies can be integrated within the boundaries of mainstream courses and curricula.

Eurocentric curriculum A curriculum in which concepts, events, and situations are viewed primarily from the perspectives of European nations and cultures and in which Western civilization is emphasized. This approach is based on the assumption that Europeans have made the most important contributions to the development of the United States and the world. Curriculum theorists who endorse this approach are referred to as Eurocentrists or Western traditionalists.

Exceptional Used to describe students who have learning or behavioral characteristics that differ substantially from most other students and that require special attention in instruction. Students who are intellectually gifted or talented as well as those who have learning disabilities are considered exceptional.

Gender Consists of behaviors that result from the social, cultural, and psychological factors associated with masculinity and femininity within a society. Appropriate male and female roles result from the socialization of the individual within a group.

Gender identity An individual's view of the gender to which he or she belongs and his or her shared sense of group attachment with other males or females.

Global education Concerned with issues and problems related to the survival of human beings in a world community. International studies is a part of global education, but the focus of global education is the interdependence of human beings and their common fate, regardless of the national boundaries within which they live. Many teachers confuse global education and international studies with ethnic studies, which deal with ethnic groups within a national boundary, such as the United States.

Handicapism The unequal treatment of people who are disabled, and related attitudes and beliefs that reinforce and justify discrimination against people with disabilities. The term *handicapped* is considered negative by some people. They prefer the term *disabled*. *People with disabilities* is considered more sensitive than *disabled people* because the word *people* is used first and given emphasis.

Hispanic Americans Americans who share a culture, heritage, and language that originated in Spain. The word *Latinos* is sometimes used to refer to Hispanic Americans in certain regions of the nation. Most Hispanics in the United States speak Spanish and are *mestizos*. A mestizo is a person of mixed biological heritage. Most Hispanics in the United States have an Indian as well as a Spanish heritage. Many of them also have an African biological and cultural heritage. The largest groups of Hispanics in the United States are Mexican Americans (Chicanos), Puerto Ricans, and Cubans. In 1990, there were about 22 million documented Hispanics in the United States. In 1988, Mexicans made up 62 percent of Hispanics in the United States; Puerto Ricans, 13 percent; Cubans, 5 percent; and Central and South Americans, 12 percent. Persons who identified themselves only as Hispanics made up 8 percent. Hispanics are one of the nation's fastest-growing ethnic groups of color. They increased 49 percent between 1980 and 1990, from 14.6 to 21.8 million. The nation's non-Hispanic population increased 6 percent during this period. It is misleading to view Hispanics as one ethnic group. Some Hispanics believe that the word *Hispanics* can help to unify the various Latino groups and thus increase their political power. The primary identity of most Hispanics in the United States, however, is with their particular group, such as Mexican American, Puerto Rican, or Cuban.

Mainstream American A United States citizen who shares most of the characteristics of the dominant ethnic and cultural group in the nation. Such an individual is usually White Anglo-Saxon Protestant and belongs to the middle class or a higher social-class status.

Mainstream-centric curriculum A curriculum that presents events, concepts, issues, and problems primarily or exclusively from the points of view and perspectives of the mainstream society and the dominant ethnic and cultural group in the United States, White Anglo-Saxon Protestants. The mainstream-centric curriculum is also usually presented from the perspectives of Anglo males.

Mainstreaming   The process that involves placing students with disabilities into the regular classroom for instruction. They might be integrated into the regular classroom for part or all of the school day. This practice was initiated in response to Public Law 94-142 (passed by Congress in 1975), which requires that students with disabilities be educated in the least restricted environment.

Multicultural education   A reform movement designed to change the total educational environment so that students from diverse racial and ethnic groups, both gender groups, exceptional students, and students from each social-class group will experience equal educational opportunities in schools, colleges, and universities. A major assumption of multicultural education is that some students, because of their particular racial, ethnic, gender, and cultural characteristics, have a better chance to succeed in educational institutions as they are currently structured than do students who belong to other groups or who have different cultural and gender characteristics.

Multiculturalism   A philosophical position and movement that assumes that the gender, ethnic, racial, and cultural diversity of a pluralistic society should be reflected in all of the institutionalized structures of educational institutions, including the staff, the norms and values, the curriculum, and the student body.

Multiethnic education   A reform movement designed to change the total educational environment so that students from diverse racial and ethnic groups will experience equal educational opportunities. Multiethnic education is an important component of multicultural education.

Native American   United States citizens who trace their biological and cultural heritage to the original inhabitants in the land that now makes up the United States. *Native American* is used synonymously with *American Indian.*

People of color   Groups in the United States and other nations who have experienced discrimination historically because of their unique biological characteristics that enabled potential discriminators to identify them easily. African Americans, Asian Americans, and Hispanics in the United States are among the groups referred to as *people of color.* Most members of these groups still experience forms of discrimination today.

Positionality   An idea that emerged out of feminist scholarship stating that variables such as an individual's gender, class, and race are markers of her or his relational position within a social and economic context and influence the knowledge that she or he produces. Consequently, valid knowledge requires an acknowledgement of the knower's position within a specific context. (See Chapter 7 in this book.)

Prejudice   A set of rigid and unfavorable attitudes toward a particular individual or group that is formed without consideration of facts. Prejudice is a set of attitudes that often leads to discrimination, the differential treatment of particular individuals and groups.

Race   Refers to the attempt by physical anthropologists to divide human groups according to their physical traits and characteristics. This has proven to be very difficult because human groups in modern societies are highly mixed physically. Consequently, different and often conflicting race typologies exist.

Racism   A belief that human groups can be validly grouped according to their biological traits and that these identifiable groups inherit certain mental, personality, and cultural characteristics that determine their behavior. Racism, however, is not merely a set of beliefs but is practiced when a group has the power to enforce laws, institutions, and norms, based on its beliefs, that oppress and dehumanize another group.

Religion   A set of beliefs and values, especially about explanations that concern the cause and nature of the universe, to which an individual or group has a strong loyalty and attachment. A religion usually has a moral code, rituals, and institutions that reinforce and propagate its beliefs.

Sex   The biological factors that distinguish males and females, such as chromosomal, hormonal, anatomical, and physiological characteristics.

Sexism   Social, political, and economic structures that advantage one sex group over the other. Stereotypes and misconceptions about the biological characteristics of each sex group reinforce and support sex discrimination. In most societies, women have been the major victims of sexism. However, males are also victimized by sexist beliefs and practices.

Social class   A collectivity of people who have a similar socioeconomic status based on such criteria as income, occupation, education, values, behaviors, and life chances. *Lower class, working class, middle class,* and *upper class* are common designations of social class in the United States.

Contributors

CHERRY A. McGEE BANKS is assistant professor of education at the Universityof Washington, Bothell. She is also president of Educational Materials and Services Center (Edmonds, Washington), an educational initiative that focuses on improving education for special population groups, such as ethnic minorities, women, and exceptional students. She is also editor and publisher of *Multicultural Leader,* a quarterly newsletter. A former teacher in Michigan and specialist in the Seattle Public Schools, she is co-author of *March toward Freedom: A History of Black Americans* and a contributing author of *Education in the 80's: Multiethnic Education.* She is active in efforts to increase parent participation in education and currently serves on the Board of Directors of the Shoreline (Washington) Community College.

JAMES A. BANKS is professor of education and director of the Center for Multicultural Education at the University of Washington, Seattle. He is former chairman of Curriculum and Instruction and a past president of the National Council for the Social Studies. He is a specialist in social studies education and multicultural education and has contributed more than 100 articles and reviews to journals in these fields, including *School Review, Elementary School Journal, Phi Delta Kappan, Social Education,* and *Educational Leadership.* Professor Banks is the author or editor of fourteen books, including *Teaching Strategies for Ethnic Studies,* 5th ed.; *Multiethnic Education: Theory and Practice,* 2nd ed.; and *We Americans: Our History and People.* He is a former teacher in the Joliet, Illinois, Public Schools and at the Francis W. Parker School in Chicago.

BRIAN M. BULLIVANT is reader in education, School of Graduate Studies, Faculty of Education, Monash University (Australia). An anthropologist interested in the influence of culture on education, Dr. Bullivant's books include *The Way of Tradition: Life in an Orthodox Jewish School; The Pluralist Dilemma in Education: Six Case Studies; Race, Ethnicity, and Curriculum; Pluralism: Cultural Maintenance and Evolution;* and *The Ethnic Encounter in the Secondary School.*

JOHNNELLA E. BUTLER is associate professor and chair of the Department of Ethnic Studies at the University of Washington, Seattle. She was formerly on the faculty of Smith College, where she served as chairperson of the Afro-American Studies Department and developed the program in Afro-American Studies. Professor Butler is a specialist in African American literature and women's studies and is particularly interested in how ethnic studies and women's studies can be interrelated. She is the author of *Black Studies: Pedagogy and Revolution* and has contributed to several books, including *Women's Place in the Academy: Transforming the Liberal Arts Curriculum; Feminist Pedagogy;* and *Toward a Balanced Curriculum.* She is co-editor (with John C. Walter) of *Transforming the Curriculum: Ethnic Studies and Women's Studies.*

RODNEY A. CAVANAUGH is a doctoral candidate studying applied behavior analysis and special education in the Department of Educational Studies at The Ohio State University. Prior to beginning graduate study at Ohio State, he taught high school students with learning disabilities throughout most of his fifteen-year teaching career. Mr. Cavanaugh's current research interests and publications involve the use of self-management and generalization strategies to improve the academic performance and productivity of high school students and the independent work skills of preschoolers.

BARBARA CLARK is professor of special education at the California State University, Los Angeles. The vice-president of the National Association for Gifted Children, she is the author of *Growing Up Gifted* and *Optimizing Learning.* A specialist in the education of gifted children, Professor Clark has contributed articles to such publications as *American Middle School Education, The Gifted Children Newsletter,* and *Gifted International.* She is a former teacher of gifted elementary school children.

GENEVA GAY is professor of education at the University of Washington, Seattle. A specialist in curriculum and multicultural education, Professor Gay has contributed to numerous journals and books in these fields. Among the books to which she has contributed are *Teaching Ethnic Studies: Concepts and Strategies; Language and Cultural Diversity in American Education; Teaching American History: The Quest for Relevance; Curriculum Guidelines for Multiethnic Education; Pluralism and the American Teacher: Issues and Case Studies;* and *Considered Action for Curriculum Improvement.* She is the co-editor of *Expressively Black: The Cultural Basis of Ethnic Identity.*

360

CARL A. GRANT is a professor in the Department of Curriculum and Instruction and the Department of Afro-American Studies at the University of Wisconsin-Madison. He has written or edited thirteen books or monographs in multicultural education and/or teacher education. He has also written more than eighty articles, chapters in books and reviews. Several of his writings have received awards. He is a former classroom teacher and administrator. Professor Grant was a Fulbright Scholar in England in 1982–1983 studying multicultural education.

WILLIAM L. HEWARD is professor, Department of Human Services Education, at The Ohio State University. A specialist in the education of learners with disabilities, Professor Heward's research has appeared in numerous journals, including *Exceptional Children, Learning Disability Quarterly, Teacher Education and Special Education, The Elementary School Journal,* and *The Journal of Applied Behavior Analysis.* He has co-authored a number of books, including *Exceptional Children: An Introductory Survey of Special Education,* 4th ed.; *Voices: Interviews with Handicapped People; Working with Parents of Handicapped Children;* and *Applied Behavior Analysis.*

LARRY W. LEZOTTE is senior vice-president of Effective Schools Products, Ltd., in Okemos, Michigan, an organization that provides consultation and publications for school districts that are engaged in reform. A former professor of educational administration and director of the Center for Effective Schools Research at Michigan State University, Dr. Lezotte is one of the pioneers in effective schools research. He is a co-author, with Wilbur B. Brookover and others, of *Creating Effective Schools: An Inservice Program for Enhancing School Learning Climate and Achievement.* His articles have appeared in such journals as *Educational Leadership, The American School Board Journal,* and *The Journal of Negro Education.*

LYNETTE LONG is a psychologist in private practice in Bethesda, Maryland. A former high school teacher and university professor, she has contributed articles to numerous journals and has written or co-authored six books, including *Unparented: American Teens on Their Own; The Handbook for Latchkey Children and Their Parents;* and *Questioning: Skills for the Helping Process.* Dr. Long has done research and training in several areas, including human relations, sex equity, and latchkey children.

CLARA A. NEW is assistant professor of education at the University of Wisconsin-Parkside, where she teaches general methods and methods in early childhood through primary and language arts and children's literature. Her specific interest and research focus is the study of teacher expectations and perceptions for the achievement of African American males. Professor New is a former teacher in the Milwaukee Public Schools and the Dallas Independent School District. She also taught at the University of Wisconsin-Milwaukee.

CARLOS J. OVANDO is professor of education at Indiana University at Bloomington. He previously taught at Oregon State University, the University of Alaska, Anchorage, and the University of Southern California. Professor Ovando is a specialist in bilingual and multicultural education and has contributed to numerous publications in these fields. He has served as guest editor of two special issues of *Educational Research Quarterly* and contributed to the *Phi Delta Kappan* and the *Harvard Educational Review.* He is the co-author of *Bilingual and ESL Classrooms: Teaching in Multicultural Contexts.*

CAROLINE HODGES PERSELL is professor and chair of the Department of Sociology at New York University. Professor Persell is interested in social stratification in education and has examined this issue in two of her books, *Education and Inequality* and *Preparing for Power: America's Elite Boarding Schools,* co-authored with Peter W. Cookson, Jr. Her other books include *Understanding Society: An Introduction to Sociology,* 3rd ed.; *Encountering Society* (with others); and *Quality, Careers and Training in Educational and Social Research.*

DAVID A. SADKER is professor of education at The American University in Washington, D.C., and director of the Master of Arts in Elementary Education. He formerly served as director of the Mid-Atlantic Center for Sex Equity, Teacher Education Programs, and Undergraduate Studies at The American University. A former social studies teacher, Professor Sadker is a frequent lecturer on sex equity and sexual harassment to schools, colleges, and private corporations. He has contributed to numerous publications, including the 1991 edition of *Review of Research in Education,* and is the co-author (with Myra Sadker) of *Teachers, Schools, and Society; Sex Equity Handbook for Schools;* and *Now Upon a Time: A Contemporary View of Children's Literature.*

MYRA SADKER is professor of education at The American University in Washington, D.C., and director of the Master of Arts in Teaching. She was formerly dean of the School of Education and director of the Teacher Preparation Programs. A former language arts teacher, Professor Sadker has contributed to numerous journals and books and offered workshops on sex equity in more than forty states. She is the co-author (with David Sadker) of *Teachers, Schools, and Society; Sex Equity Handbook for Schools;* and *Now Upon a Time: A Contemporary View of Children's Literature.* She is also the co-author of *Sexism in School and Society.*

JANE B. SCHULZ is professor emerita of special education at Western Carolina University. A former special education teacher and reading clinician, Professor Schulz has contributed to a number of professional journals, including *Teaching Exceptional Children* and *Teacher Education and Special Education.* She is the author of *Parents and Professionals in Special Education* and co-author of *Mainstreaming Exceptional Students: A Guide for the Classroom Teacher.* In 1981, she received the Paul A. Reid Distinguished Service Award at Western Carolina University.

BARBARA J. SHADE is professor of education and dean of the School of Education at the University of Wisconsin-Parkside. A licensed school psychologist, Professor Shade has authored many publications for journals and books on the effect of various environmental factors on the personality of African Americans and on the achievement of African-American students. She is the author of an important and influential research review, "Afro-American Cognitive Style: A Variable in School Success?" published in the *Review of Educational Research* 52 (1982): 219–244. She is the editor and contributing author of *Culture, Style, and the Educative Process.*

CHRISTINE E. SLEETER is professor of education at the University of Wisconsin-Parkside. A former special-education teacher, her research focuses on multicultural education and the ways in which race, class, gender, and exceptionality influence how schools operate. She has contributed to many journals, including the *Review of Educational Research, Educational Policy,* and *Harvard Educational Review.* Professor Sleeter is the editor of *Empowerment through Multicultural Education.* She has co-authored a number of publications with Carl A. Grant, including *After the School Bell Rings, Making Choices for Multicultural Education,* and *Turning on Learning.* She also is the author of *Keepers of the Dream: A Study of Staff Development and Multicultural Education.*

MARY KAY THOMPSON TETREAULT is dean and professor of the School of Human Development and Community Service, California State University at Fullerton. A specialist in social studies education and women's studies, Professor Tetreault is particularly interested in how feminist pedagogy can enrich the curriculum for all students and in feminist phase theory. She served as guest editor of a section of *Social Education,* "Getting Women and Gender into the Curriculum Mainstream" (March 1987). She is the author of numerous articles and of the book *Women in America: Half of History.*

JAMES K. UPHOFF is professor of education and human services and Malone Faculty Fellow in Arab-Islamic Studies at Wright State University, Dayton, Ohio. Professor Uphoff is a specialist in social studies education and has done extensive work on religion and education. He has contributed to journals such as *Educational Leadership* and *Social Education.* He is the co-author of *Public Education Religion Studies: Questions and Answers; Religion Studies in the Curriculum: Retrospect and Prospect;* and *Summer Children: Ready or Not Ready for School?*

INDEX